Prisoners of Isolation

Michael Jackson

Prisoners of Isolation:
Solitary Confinement in Canada

UNIVERSITY OF TORONTO PRESS
Toronto Buffalo London

Toronto London Buffalo

Reprinted in paperback 2017

ISBN 978-0-8020-5620-7 (cloth)
ISBN 978-0-8020-6514-8 (paper)

Canadian Cataloguing in Publication Data

Jackson, Michael, 1943–
Prisoners of isolation
Includes index.
ISBN 978-0-8020-5620-7 (bound). - ISBN 978-0-8020-6514-8 (pbk.)
1. Prison discipline - Canada. 2. Prisoners - Legal status, laws, etc. - Canada. I. Title.
HV8728J32 365′.644 C83-098546-8

Cover illustration by B.Z. Hilyer, Vancouver

To Ralph and Hilda Jackson

I believe that very few men are capable of estimating the immense amount of torture and agony which this dreadful punishment, prolonged for years, inflicts upon the sufferers; and in guessing at it myself, and from reasoning from what I have seen written upon their faces, from what to my certain knowledge they feel within, I am only the more convinced that there is a depth of terrible endurance in it which none but the sufferers themselves can fathom, and which no man has a right to inflict upon his fellow creatures.

Charles Dickens, 1842

I cannot tell to those in hell,
The dreams I send above,
Nor how the shrill of whistles kill,
Each passing thought of love.

Within these walls that never fall,
The damned all come to know
The rows of cells - the special hell,
Called Solitary Row.
Jack McCann, 1972

Contents

Preface

This book as originally conceived was aimed at the legal community - lawyers, law students, and judges. As various people read the early drafts, I was encouraged to be more ambitious in my intended audience. Writing for both the legal and larger communities poses certain difficulties. In writing about the law for a legal audience one feels constrained to engage in a form of analysis which generations of law students have had instilled in them as 'the way lawyers think,' in contrast to the way the rest of the world thinks. This sounds élitist, and by and large it is. The fact remains that lawyers do engage in a highly distinctive form of analysis. The parts of this book that describe legal arguments and court decisions relating to 'cruel and unusual punishment,' 'due process of law,' and 'principles of fundamental justice' conform to this distinctive analytic model in order to enable lawyers who read this book to follow and assess the arguments and decisions within the contours of legal scholarship. However, I have sought to provide enough background to the legal arguments to allow other readers to understand and assess the nature, development, and adequacy of principles and processes that have been designed, primarily by lawyers, to protect the individual against the abuse of state power.

Not all of the book is written in the way lawyers typically write about the law. Much of it is about life beyond the law, life in the deepest reaches of maximum-security penitentiaries. In these sections, lawyers will find little to make them comfortable, least of all the impersonal quality that characterizes most legal writing. I make no apologies for this. One of the central themes of the prisoners' experiences described in this book - through their own evidence in the courtroom and their letters from prison - is that carceral practices surrounding solitary confinement reduce prisoners to something less than human beings. This book is intended to provide those concerned about human rights an opportunity to confront the reality of prisoners' lives and to reflect on their own role and responsibility in the face of that reality. Such reflection is not an impersonal process. Neither are the description and analysis that inform it.

Acknowledgments

I would like to thank the many prisoners who shared their experiences with me. Although it is invidious to select from the many who provided me with important insights, I acknowledge particularly the help of Jack McCann, Andy Bruce, Ralph Cochrane, and Edgar Roussel. I would also like to thank the Canadian Corrections Service for their co-operation in enabling me to carry out the research for this book, especially for providing access to institutions and allowing me to interview correctional administrators, staff, and prisoners. In particular I would like to thank J.U.M. Sauvé and Howard Mansfield of National Headquarters in Ottawa; John Dowsett and John Stonowski, the former and present wardens of Kent Institution; J.J. Hayes, a psychologist at the special handling unit in Millhaven; and Malcolm Johnson, a psychologist at the special handling unit in the Correctional Development Centre.

Nicole Daignault and Michael Ignatieff read earlier drafts of the book, and I thank them for their thoughtful suggestions. Fergus O'Connor reviewed the Segregation Code and made helpful proposals for its improvement. To the students in the Administration of Criminal Justice seminar at the University of British Columbia Law School, who were the book's first critical audience, I express my appreciation for their reviews.

I was buoyed up by the continuing enthusiasm provided by Virgil Duff of the University of Toronto Press, and I have benefited from his editorial direction. Kathy Johnson's meticulous editing has undoubtedly refined the text. This book has been published with the help of a grant from the Social Science Federation of Canada, using funds provided by the Social Sciences and Humanities Research Council of Canada, and a grant from the Publications Fund of University of Toronto Press.

To Audrey Fiene who, in typing and retyping the manuscript and commenting on it as it took shape, showed more dedication than any author could reasonably expect, I express my deep gratitude.

Finally, to Marcy, who shared with me many of the experiences that gave rise to this book, and to Shane and Melissa, whose questions about justice, informed by the eyes of childhood, have provoked many of my own, I hope this book in some way makes up for all the times I have not been home.

Prisoners of Isolation

Introduction

For people who are concerned with the law, the prison raises a cluster of disturbing paradoxes. We have become accustomed to seeing the prison as the vindicator of society's collective morality as expressed through the prohibitions of the Criminal Code. For those who dare to attack the security of our person and property, we see the prison as the vehicle for our collective vengeance. Yet, because the prison is the most forceful expression of society's condemnation, it raises the issue of the morality of state power in its starkest form. The prison, seen as the most powerful weapon in our armoury against those who would hurt us, is the part of the criminal-justice system that is the least accessible to our gaze and the least amenable to public accountability. What the prison system does, by and large, it does behind closed doors – indeed, doors not just closed but barred, barbed, or encircled by forbidding walls. The prison has been described by one commentator as 'the darkest region in the apparatus of justice';[1] and by another as the 'outlaw'[2] of the criminal-justice system. This latter characterization implies that the prison, as the agent for defending our collective morality as defined by law, in carrying out its task itself offends against the law.

This book has as its focus the practice of solitary confinement in Canada's maximum-security penitentiaries, a practice that is regarded by those who have experienced it as the ultimate exercise of the prison's power over the lives of the imprisoned. The focus on solitary confinement is not a random choice. As the ultimate exercise of state authority over a prisoner, it can be seen as a litmus test of the morality and legitimacy of the state's dealings with prisoners in lesser exercises of authority. Indeed, that is how many prisoners see the matter.

> People commit a grave error when they disregard what happens in Canada's prisons. They are not separated from society. They are part of it. We live on the same soil, are subject to the same laws, and governed by the same government.

Because of our unique position in society, those facts are often ignored ... prisoners are on the bottom of the social ladder, but nevertheless are on that ladder. One weak rung should make any thinking person very skeptical of trusting the people controlling that ladder. It might well be that the rung they are on would prove itself the next weak one.[3]

This statement, made by a prisoner in 1981, echoes the sentiments expressed by William Allen over 150 years ago.

In prisons a part of the population ... is taken by the ruling powers and placed forcibly in a situation in which they cannot help themselves, from which they are necessarily defenceless and exposed to the last of evils, as well from neglect as from active cruelty. If a part of the population placed in a situation, so immediately under the eye of the ruling powers ... are not taken care of as they ought to be, is it not a matter of moral certainty that the other parts of the population are equally or still more neglected? The behaviour of government, therefore, in this department is a sample of its behaviour in all the rest.[4]

The striking continuity of these statements spanning 150 years is intimately related to the focus of this book; the analysis of solitary confinement, more than any other carceral practice, requires us to look to the social and political origins of the penitentiary system itself.

It was not merely an academic interest in the lessons of history that provided the impetus for this book. That came from prisoners who had been detained for long periods in solitary confinement in the British Columbia Penitentiary and who in 1974 asked me to help them challenge in the courts of Canada the conditions of their confinement. The facts and legal issues surrounding that challenge to solitary confinement in the case of *McCann* v. *Her Majesty The Queen and Dragan Cernetic*[5] form the centre-piece of this book. In reviewing the evidence and legal arguments in this case, which has been described as 'the most ambitious prisoners' rights case ever brought in Canada,'[6] and the penitentiary authorities' response to it, I intend to hold up for analysis the legality of carceral power in the 'Age of Corrections.'

However, the full significance of *McCann* v. *The Queen* can only be understood by considering not only the events that took place in the 1970s but also those that occurred in the 1770s, the years that saw the beginning of the modern penitentiary and the introduction of solitary confinement in the name of reform. My purposes in reviewing this history are to lend insight into the present practice of solitary confinement in the Canadian penitentiary and to aid in understanding the paradoxes with which the prison presents us. It is because of my conviction that those concerned with the law must confront the serious questions involved in the legitimacy of the state's carceral power that I have used the *McCann* case not only to examine the ideological assumptions that gave rise to the penitentiary system, but also to consider the crucial question of the roles of the law, the courts, and lawyers within the prison walls.

1 Solitary Confinement and the Rise of the Penitentiary

Although I will be criticizing the modern practice of solitary confinement in terms of its injustice and cruelty, its historical origins, like those of the penitentiary itself, lie not in the practice of torture and the abuse of state power, but rather in a reform-spirited reaction against such practices. The period between 1775 and 1850 saw dramatic changes in Europe and North America in the state's conception of its right to punish offenders, and the legacy of that period still infuses much of our thinking about punishment and penal institutions. It is not possible to understand the evolution of disciplinary practices in the Canadian penitentiary and the role of solitary confinement without tracing the rise of the penitentiary itself as a distinctive penal institution in England and the United States. Developments in these countries in the eighteenth and early nineteenth centuries provided not only the institutional framework for the establishment of the first Canadian penitentiary, but also a correctional strategy designed to ensure the legitimacy of state authority. It is a paradox of history that a central feature of that correctional strategy - solitary confinement - has come to epitomize the most disturbing abuse of power that exists in the Canadian penitentiary today.

Before 1775, imprisonment was rarely used in England as a punishment for felony. Major crimes were punished with hanging, banishment, transportation, whipping, or the pillory. At the Old Bailey, London's major criminal court, imprisonment accounted for no more than 2.3 per cent of the judges' sentences in the years between 1770 and 1777. Where a prison term was imposed for a felony, the range of offenders was narrow - those convicted of manslaughter, perjury, combining against employers, or rioting - and the sentences were short by modern standards, never longer than three years and typically a year or less.[1] Although few felons were sentenced to imprisonment, most experienced the pains of confinement awaiting trial and, when convicted, awaiting transportation to the colonies or execution. Imprisonment was also used by local justices of the peace to punish summary offences, such as vagrancy, desertion of family, bastardy, offences against the authority of employers, embezzlement of raw materials supplied to cottage workers by employers, theft of farm produce, the taking of firewood from privately owned woods, and minor game offences.[2] But criminal conviction, whether for a felony or a summary offence, was not the predominant basis for imprisonment in the eighteenth century. At the time of John Howard's prison census of 1776, almost 60 per cent of all individuals confined in England and Wales were debtors who were imprisoned until they could give satisfaction to their creditors or until they were discharged as insolvents by an act of Parliament.[3]

There were three major institutions of confinement in eighteenth-century England: the debtors' prisons, the county and borough jails, and the houses of correction. The debtors' prisons were distinctive because of the special position debtors occupied in the hierarchy of prisoners. They could not be made to work, they were permitted to live with their wives and children, and they had full access to visitors from the outside. In the larger debtors' prisons in London, immunity from discipline meant that the debtors were left to police their own community. 'As a result, the social life of the debtors' prison ran unchecked. The Fleet was reputed to be the biggest brothel in London. Howard discovered a beer and wine club in operation in the King's Bench and a committee of inquiry in 1813 discovered a music society there.'[4]

The second type of institution, the county and borough jail, ranged from being located in the dungeon of a medieval castle to little more than a strong-room above an inn. The diversity of the jail's architecture was mirrored in the distinctive status of the various categories of prisoners confined in them: debtors, those awaiting trial, those few felons sentenced to imprisonment, and those convicted and sentenced to transportation or death. Although in theory the different classes of prisoners were supposed to be kept separate from each other, actual practice resulted in the confusion of prisoner categories and the de facto sharing of privileges among prisoners to whom they were legally denied. In the eyes of the prison reformers of the 1780s this confusion was regarded as a major impediment to a rational system of discipline.[5]

The third institution of confinement was the house of correction, or bridewell, which had been in existence since the sixteenth century. The bridewell was developed to enforce the law against vagrancy, and its avowed purposes were to put the vagrant poor to work and to teach them the lessons of industry. The organization of penal labour around economic imperatives had been introduced at about the same time in Europe with the opening of the Rasphuis in Amsterdam.[6]

The theory behind the bridewell was that prisoners would earn their bread and upkeep by hard labour, and the county would recoup its expenses from the sale of prison goods made under the supervision of outside contractors. Like much of the correctional theory in the eighteenth century (and, as we will see, in the twentieth century), this bore little relation to what actually happened. Because many counties were unable to find contractors to put prisoners to work, the local magistrates were obliged to make some minimum dietary provision for the prisoners. Yet there were some bridewells in which no food was provided. It was not uncommon for vagrants brought in from the streets of London to die in prison of hunger. John Fielding, the London magistrate, remarked to an inquiry in 1770 that 'when the magistrate commits a man to [the Gate House in London] for assault he does not know that he commits him there to starve.'[7]

The efforts of the local authorities to limit their financial liability for bridewells, like the keepers' efforts to limit their overhead in running the debtors' prisons and local jails, resulted in a prison regime that relied upon easy access to the outside world. In some jails prisoners were allowed to beg for food and money through 'begging grates.' Visitors' privileges were liberal, since in many cases prisoners depended on aid from their relatives and friends to supplement the little provided by the state. According to Ignatieff, it was common for wives to appear daily at the prison gates with meals for their jailed husbands. They were permitted to remain in the prison from dawn until lock-up, and a bribe to the keeper ensured their continuing companionship by night.[8]

However, if the physical distance between the inside and the outside was not great, the administrative distance was. 'The authority of the Keeper was exercised largely without supervision or scrutiny from the outside. Although the worlds were bound together in symbiotic dependence over matters such as diet and sexual commerce, the prison, in matters of power and finance, was a state within a state.'[9]

In the eighteenth century, because of the decentralization of responsibility for prisons, there were no statutory provisions governing the duties of the keeper of a prison, and the local magistrates rarely placed any limitations on his power. Such basic matters as the program of work and the methods of discipline were left to the untramelled discretion of the keepers. Authority in the prison, 'unbounded by formal rule, was by definition arbitrary, personal and capricious.'[10] In the minds of the prison reformers of the 1770s, the abuses of the prison system – cruelty, unsanitary conditions, inadequate dietary provisions, sexual promiscuity, and corrupt administrative practices – were explained by the absence of rules and the lack of supervision by outside authority.

But while the keepers' discretion was unfettered by formal rule, it was not unlimited. They had to share power, or at least reach an accommodation, with various prisoner communities. The informal sharing of power between the guards and powerful prisoners is well documented in the twentieth century sociology of the prison;[11] prisoner communities appear to have been even more powerful in the eighteenth century. This was particularly the case in the debtors' prisons because of the unlimited access to the outside world and the customary privileges of debtors. In large measure this power-sharing came about because of the small number of custodial staff in the institutions. Since such staff had to be paid by the keeper, it was in his interest to employ as few people as possible and to permit prisoners to police themselves. Rules were laid down, including the levying of a fee on incoming prisoners, and these rules were enforced by a wardsman, chosen by the keeper or by the prisoners themselves. Sometimes the wardsman presided at mock trials to settle disputes or infringements of the rules of the prison.[12] Boxing matches were also used to settle disputes between prisoners.[13] As disturbing as the idea of the cruelty and unregulated discretion of the keepers was to the reformers, more disturbing still was this 'image of an entrenched inmate netherworld, ruling an institution of the state with its own officers, its own customs and its own rituals.'[14]

The English prison system began to show signs of strain during the crime wave that followed demobilization after the War of the Austrian Succession. The London prisons became overwhelmed with the crush of destitute poor awaiting trial for petty property crimes. In April 1750, in the 'Black Assize,' two diseased prisoners from Newgate were standing trial at the Old Bailey; of the people who were infected by them, at least fifty died, including the judge, the jury, the lawyers, and many spectators.[15] The prison crisis of the 1750s reinforced the growing awareness of the need for intermediate penalties between transportation to the penal colonies and hanging. The prosecution of many minor offences was abandoned because the death penalty seemed to be disproportionate to the crime. Henry Fielding, the famous English novelist and a magistrate, wrote of the necessity to find an intermediate penalty combining 'correction of the body' with 'correction of the mind.' He suggested solitary confinement. As he put it, 'there can be no more effective means of bringing a most abandoned profligate to reason and order than those of solitude and fasting.'[16]

It was in the context of a continuing crisis caused by burgeoning prison populations and a growing scepticism about the efficacy of existing forms of criminal punishment that the seminal work of John Howard, *The State of the Prisons in England and Wales*, appeared in 1777.[17] Howard first became concerned with the crisis in the prison system after his appointment as a county sheriff. Unlike most sheriffs, however, Howard took seriously his obligation to inspect the prisons, and visited every prison in England and Wales. *The State of the Prisons* contains both the record of his observations and his blueprint for radical change. Deeply etched into that blueprint was the disciplinary regime of solitary confinement. Howard's work was unique in its exhaustive treatment of English penal institutions, and it drew strength from the comparative perspective with which he imbued his proposals for reform of the system. Howard also visited a number of the more famous European penal institutions, and they provided him with much of the program of discipline that was eventually set out in the Penitentiary Act in 1779.

By the time of Howard's visits to Europe in the 1770s, the concept of solitary confinement had already been introduced in a number of these European institutions. In 1703 Pope Clement XI commissioned the building of a cellular prison for delinquent and criminal youths. The San Michele House of Correction, opened in 1704, has the distinction of being the first penal institution organized along the principles of isolation, work, silence, and prayer. In the work-hall was inscribed in gold *Parum est coercera impropos poena nisi probos efficias disciplina* ('It is of little use to restrain the bad by punishment unless you render them good by discipline'). These words were to become the motto for Howard's own work. The concept behind the prison at San Michele, which harnessed the Catholic tradition of monastic discipline to the purposes of punishment, was further developed by a Flemish politician and magistrate, Jean Philippe Vilain, in the'Octagon,' a prison built under his aegis at Ghent. The institutional regime of the 'Octagon' provided Howard with a model for a reformed English system, and the architecture of the prison, designed to maximize surveillance and minimize the potential for escape, became a model for the early penitentiaries in England, the United States, and Canada.[18]

While John Howard and the other prison reformers of the 1770s drew support from European institutional models, they also owed much of their conceptual framework for a penitentiary regime to other reform movements in England. The broad common thrust of these movements was the need to institutionalize fundamental changes in the morality and behaviour of the poor. Thus, progressive doctors involved with the hygienic reform of hospitals saw their cause as a moral no less than a medical crusade. The sickness of the poor was interpreted as the outward sign of their inward want of discipline and morality. 'Since disease had moral as well as physical causes, hygienic rituals were designed to fulfil disciplinary functions. To teach the poor to be clean, it was necessary to teach them to be godly, tractable, and self-disciplined.'[19] The clear association between the conceptual framework of the hospital and prison reformers is well described by Ignatieff.

> Jonas Hanway [one of Howard's close associates] was arguing within [the doctors'] categories when he described crime as a disease 'which spreads disruption like pestilence and immorality as an epidemical disorder which diffuses its morbid qualities'. Like the doctors, he saw crime arising from the same source as disease, from the squalid, riotous and undisciplined quarters of the poor. Prisons, too, were breeding grounds of pestilence and crime alike. In the fetid and riotous wards of Newgate, the 'contagion' of criminal values was passed from hardened offender to novice, just as typhus spread from the 'old lags' to the recent arrivals. Like the hospital, the penitentiary was created to enforce a quarantine, both moral and medical. Behind its walls, the contagion of criminality would be isolated from the healthy, moral population outside. Within the prison itself the separate confinement of each offender in a cell would prevent the bacillus of vice from spreading from the hardened to the uninitiate.[20]

In his proposals for reform of the prisons, Howard was insistent that punishment, in order to be effective, must maintain its moral legitimacy in the eyes of both the public and the offender. For Howard the most painful punishments and those that aroused the greatest guilt were those that observed the strictest standards of justice and morality.

> From such punishment there could be no psychological escape into contempt for the punisher, assertions of innocence, or protests against its cruelty. Nothing in the penalties' infliction would divert offenders from contemplating their own guilt. Once convinced of the justice of their sentence and the benevolent intentions of their captors, they could only surrender to the horrors of remorse.[21]

It is important to realize that Howard's concern to re-establish the legitimacy of punishment was not simply directed to the law-abiding public; it was equally applicable to the criminals who were subjected to that punishment. This is how Howard himself put it:

> The notion that convicts are ungovernable is certainly erroneous. There is a mode of managing some of the most desperate with ease to yourself and advantage to them. Show them that you have humanity, and that you aim to make them useful members of society; and let them see and hear the rules and orders of the prison that they may be convinced that they are not defrauded in their provisions or clothes by contractors or gaolers. Such conduct would prevent

mutiny in prisons and attempts to escape; which I am fully persuaded are often owing to prisoners being made desperate by profainness, inhumanity and ill-usage of their Keepers. [22]

Howard and the other leading reformers rejected the idea of punishment as an act of vengeance. In the words of Jeremy Bentham, the principal theoretician of utilitarianism, punishment was to be 'an act of calculation, disciplined by considerations of the social good and the offender's needs.'[23] John Howard proposed that the 'gothic mode of correction' be replaced by 'the more rational plan of softening the mind in order to aid its amendment.'[24] As another contemporary commentator put it, 'There are cords of love as well as fetters of iron.'[25]

The paramount question for the prison reformers was how to establish a rational and legitimated system of authority within the prison. The first part of the answer proposed by them was an authority of rules. These rules were to be applied to the staff no less than to prisoners. In place of the keeper's unlimited discretion, Howard laid out a sequence of custodial tasks, inspection tours, roll calls, and night patrols. Other rules were directed against trafficking, verbal abuse, fee-taking, and acts of physical cruelty. The rules were designed to win back the prisons from their keepers by circumscribing the keepers' discretion; they were also designed to win them back from the prisoner subculture. The lives of the prisoners were to be routinized by institutional order. 'In place of the unwritten, customary, and corrupt division of power between criminals and custodians, the reformers proposed to subject both to the disciplines of a formal code enforced from the outside.'[26]

The second part of the reformers' answer to abuse of power was to ensure that the authority of rules was enforced by inspection through the superintendency of magistrates and by the democratic overview of the general public. In Bentham's model of the 'Panopticon,' the plan for a penitentiary published in 1791, both prisoners and guards were under the surveillance of inspectors. The model further envisaged free admission of the public to the inspection towers to keep the inspectors themselves under surveillance.[27] It will be necessary to return to the central features of John Howard's strategy to control the abuse of power in the prison – the delineation of rules governing life inside the walls enforced by a system of inspection from outside – when considering the continuing role that rules and outside inspection play in controlling the abuses of power that have arisen in the Canadian penitentiary of the 1980s.

It is vital to realize that the authority of rules proposed by the eighteenth-century reformers had a dual purpose. 'They were enumeration of the inmates' deprivation, but also a charter of their rights. They bound both sides of the institutional encounter in obedience to an impartial code enforced from outside. As such they reconciled the interests of the state, the custodians and the prisoners alike.'[28] The regime of solitary confinement, which was the centre-piece of the new model of the prison, also had a dual purpose. It was designed to provide a rational punishment that was both the 'most terrible penalty' short of death that a society could inflict and 'the most humane.'[29] That solitary confinement was conceived as a rational and humane form of suffering can be seen in this account written in 1792:

To be extracted from a world where he has endeavoured to confound the order of society, to be buried in a solitude where he had no companion but reflection, no counsellor but thought, the offender will find the severest punishment he can receive. The sudden change of scene that he experiences, the window which admits but a few rays of light, the midnight silence which surrounds him, all inspire him with a degree of horror which he never felt before. The impression is greatly heightened by his being obliged to think. No intoxicating cup benumbs his senses, no tumultuous revel dissipates his mind. Left alone and feelingly alive to the strings of remorse, he resolves on his present situation and connects it with that train of events which has banished him from society and placed him there.[30]

Such was the theory of the penitentiary – 'in the silence of their cells, superintended by authority too systematic to be evaded, too rational to be resisted, prisoners would surrender to the lash of remorse.'[31]

It was this theory of the penitentiary that was embodied in the Penitentiary Act of 1779.[32] Offenders convicted of crimes that otherwise would have rendered them liable for transportation were to be imprisoned for a maximum of two years. During the night they were to be confined in solitary cells, and were to labour in association by day. The labour was to be of the hardest and most servile kind. In place of the intermittent and inadequate diets provided by the county jails, there was to be a regular diet, prescribed by the act as 'bread and any coarse meat or other inferior food, and water or small beer.' William Blackstone, co-drafter of the act, elaborated on the idea of penitentiary confinement in the last edition of his *Commentaries* published before his death.

In framing the plan of these penitentiary houses, the principal objects were sobriety, cleanliness and medical assistance, by a regular series of labour, by solitary confinement during the intervals of work, by some religious instruction to preserve and amend the health of the unhappy offenders, to inure them to habits of industry, to guard them from pernicious company, to accustom them to serious reflection, to teach them both the principles and practice of every Christian and moral duty.[33]

Although the Penitentiary Act authorized the building of two new national prisons, actual construction never took place. However, the Penitentiary Act was to have a profound influence as a model for discipline in the wave of institutional renewal in the years following.

Howard's ideas as embodied in the Penitentiary Act came at a critical time in English penal history. The outbreak of the American War of Independence in 1775 resulted in a sudden halt in transportation to the thirteen colonies. Almost overnight imprisonment was transformed from an occasional punishment for a felony to a sentence of first resort for all minor property crimes. Although the government sought to provide the necessary institutional facilities by refitting retired warships and mooring these 'hulks' on the Thames, it was not able to cope with the crime wave that swept England in the 1780s, caused by demobilization and accompanied by a trade depression following the loss of the colonial market. Prison reformers interpreted the situation in apocalyptic terms as evidence of a breakdown in the moral discipline among the poor. To men who conceived crime as a part of a wider pattern of insubordination among the poor, there was a compelling fascination in the idea of an institution that would give them total control over the bodies, labour, and minds of the poor. 'The penitentiary, in other words, was more than a functional response to a civic institutional crisis. It exerted a hold on men's imagination because it represented, in microcosm, the hierarchical, obedient and godly social order which they felt was coming apart around them.'[34]

Of the new institutions built following the suspension of transportation to the American colonies, the prisons of Gloucestershire represented the embodiment of the penitentiary ideal. These prisons were the work of Sir George Paul who, next to Howard, was the most influential reformer of his generation. After a decade of rising crime rates and institutional overcrowding, Paul had to demonstrate to the Gloucestershire magistrates that reformed institutions could effectively reconcile 'terror' with 'humanity'; and that it was possible to increase the severity of the punishment without compromising its legitimacy in the eyes of the offender and the public.

In the old institutions, where inmates depended on their families and friends for food, the county had been obliged to allow free access to the prisons. At Gloucester the provision by the county of a set diet permitted the authorities to isolate the prisoner from the outside world. That isolation was enhanced by the construction of an eighteen-foot fence. This separation of the deviant from the law-abiding was part of the grand design of the penitentiary ideal, as was the regime of solitary confinement.

This quarantine was seen as the first precondition for moral re-education. It severed prisoners from the peer group support of the criminal milieu outside the walls. The other precondition for reform was solitude. Solitary confinement was designed to wrest the governance of prisons out of the hands of the inmate subculture. It restored the state's control over the criminal's conscience. It divided convicts so that they would be more efficiently subjugated, so that they would lose the capacity to resist both in thought and action.[35]

Penitentiary prisoners in Gloucester not only slept in solitary cells, but also worked in solitary day cells adjacent to their night quarters. They were allowed out for exercise once a day. Howard himself had never advocated the regime of solitary confinement as it was implemented at Gloucester and some of the other county penitentiaries. He believed that solitude should be broken by labour in association and by communal exercise. He feared that unbroken solitude would break the spirit of prisoners and lead them to 'insensibility or despair.'[36]

In fact, the full regime of solitude at Gloucester could not be maintained against the pressure of overcrowding. The prisoners were required to share cells, and labour in association was introduced in place of solitary work in the cells. Even while it was in force, the solitary regime, although presented as humane and reformative, was not readily acceded to by the prisoners. At Gloucester there were frequent disturbances in which prisoners refused to work, and in 1815 there was a full-scale riot.[37]

The most sustained and vocal resistance came from political prisoners for whom, in the 1790s, the penitentiary came to be a symbol of political repression. While political radicals were confined in prisons of all types, particular use was made in the late eighteenth century of the new penitentiaries. They had the facilities for isolating political prisoners from ordinary prisoners, and their better perimeter security could more effectively deter the 'jail delivery riots' to free political prisoners which had become an integral part of the eighteenth-century British political tradition.[38] Moreover, the privileges that had been accorded the gentlemen dissenters of the likes of John Wilkes and Lord George Gordon were not extended in the penitentiaries to the radical artisans of the 1790s. This impairment of political tradition was often accomplished by detaining the radicals under the Habeas Corpus Suspension Acts, which suspended the writ of habeas corpus in certain offences (including treason) for up to a year, permitting arrest and detention without trial, merely on authority of writs issued by the king's secretaries. For the political radicals, therefore, the road to solitary confinement in the penitentiary was characterized by the denial of due process of law. The Jacobin prisoners argued that solitary confinement was a violation of the rights of ordinary prisoners awaiting trial on criminal charges and, presaging a challenge that was to be made in Canada some two hundred years later, that it was a cruel and unconstitutional punishment for those under sentence.

The resistance of political prisoners to the penitentiary took many forms. Ignatieff describes the protest of Kyd Wake, a printer who was sentenced to five years' hard labour in 1796 for hissing and booing the king as he drove in his carriage to the opening of Parliament. This protest took the form of an engraving made by Kyd Wake's wife to raise money to provide extra food for her husband who was imprisoned in Gloucester Penitentiary. This was Kyd Wake's plea against solitary confinement:

> Five years' confinement, even in common gaols must surely be a very severe punishment; but if Judges or Jurors would only reflect seriously on the horrors of solitary imprisonment under penitentiary discipline!! If they would allow their minds to dwell a little on what it is to be locked up, winter after winter, for 16 hours out of the 24, in a small brick cell – without fire – without light – without employment and scarcely to see a face but those of criminals or turnkeys. No friend to converse with when well; or to consult with or to complain to when indisposed. Above all – to be subjected to a thousand insults and vexations, almost impossible to be described, and therefore scarcely to be remedied; but by which continual torment may be, and often is, inflicted. If they would but consider what an irreparable misfortune it is to have a considerable portion of life so wearisomely wasted; they would surely be more tender of dooming any man, for a long time, to such wretchedness. It is a calamity beyond description, more easily to be conceived than explained.[39]

Gilbert Wakefield, a classical scholar and lecturer at Hackney Dissenting Academy, was sentenced to two years in Dorchester Penitentiary for seditious utterance. He wrote of his experience, 'I wonder that men can endure solitary confinement without distraction, melancholy and despair ... Surely such annihilation from active life is highly cruel.'[40]

Coldbath Fields, modelled after Gloucester, opened in 1794. In 1798, the radical artisans of the London Corresponding Society (a working-man's political organization) were imprisoned there, and they mounted a steady attack on the regime of solitary. An article in the society's magazine described the regime as 'an ingenious mode of intellectual torture.' It asserted that 'remorse is to the intellect what the rack is to the body.'[41]

In a debate in the House of Commons in 1800 following the establishment of a commission of inquiry into the treatment of prisoners at Coldbath Fields, one member of the Opposition said of the new penitentiary discipline, 'The late Mr Howard was certainly one of the worthiest men who had ever existed ... [but] if he had been one of the worst he could not have suggested a punishment of a more cruel and mischievious description ... inconsistent with the Constitution of the country.'[42]

The sustained attack against solitary confinement in England in the years after the Napoleonic Wars led members of the new generation of prison reformers, such as Elizabeth Fry, to advocate a regime of 'separate confinement' in which group labour was combined with cellular confinement. In advocating this important modification to the new discipline, the reformers were strongly influenced not only by the reaction against the original regime in England but also by events that had taken place in the United States. It is to those events that I now wish to turn, because, as we shall see, they were not only influential in the further refinement of the penitentiary in England but were to be important in the development of the penitentiary in Canada.

In the United States the dramatic shift from the old-style prison, with its relatively free association with the outside world and its established prisoner counter-culture, to the strict discipline of the penitentiary closely paralleled developments in Europe. In 1776 the Quakers had established a Prisoners' Aid Society in Philadelphia which was subsequently revived in 1787 under the name of the Philadelphia Society for Alleviating the Miseries of Public Prisons. In 1788 the society issued a memorial which, based on its members' study of the practice and theory of the treatment of prisoners, endorsed the regime of solitary confinement and hard labour as the most effective method of reforming criminals.[43]

That endorsement was legislated in an act of 1790 which authorized that a special block of cells should be constructed 'for the purpose of confining therein the most hardened and atrocious offenders ... sentenced to hard labour for a ... term of years.'[44] Following this enactment, a new addition was made to the city jail on Walnut Street in Philadelphia, which has become known in the literature as the cradle of the American penitentiary system. The most hardened offenders were confined in single cells and were kept strictly isolated from each other at hard labour for a period fixed by the court. Their only contacts with the outside were visits by prison officials and members of the Philadelphia Society.

When overcrowding of the old prison at Auburn, New York, required additional carceral capacity, the choice of the cellular system was based on the experience in Pennsylvania. A committee appointed to draw plans for the prison system in the new facility recommended that the prisoners be classified in three groups. The most hardened criminals would be held in solitary confinement; another group would be kept in solitary for three days a week, and a third (the youngest) would be permitted to work in association in the workshops. Torsten Eriksson has described the implementation of these plans.

On December 25, 1821, 80 men, the worst criminals they had, were put into the new cell block. They were given no work, and they were not allowed to meet or speak with anyone other than the prison chaplain (not even the guards) – unless they were ill. Prisoners were forbidden to leave their cells to relieve themselves, even though there were no toilet facilities in the cells. The air was fetid. The French criminologists, Gustav de Beaumont and Alexis de Tocqueville, who provided this information, described the results:

'This experiment, of which such favourable results had been anticipated, proved fatal for the majority of prisoners. It devours the victim incessantly and unmercifully; it does not reform, it kills. The unfortunate creatures submitted to this experiment wasted away so obviously that their guards were appalled. Their lives appeared to be in danger if they remained in prison under the same treatment; five of them had already died in one year; their spiritual condition was no less disturbing; one of them went out of his mind; another took advantage of a moment when a guard had brought him something to hurl himself out of his cell, running the almost certain risk of a fatal fall.'

This was the death sentence of the system of solitary confinement without labour.[45]

As we shall see, that death sentence still awaits execution in the Canadian penitentiary of today.

Shortly after the demise of this experiment with the full rigours of solitary confinement, the regime at Auburn was modified into what has subsequently become known as the 'Auburn system.' The prisoners were put to work in small, strictly supervised groups in workshops and out of doors during the day and were locked up in individual cells at night. Complete silence was to be observed. Breach of this rule was punished by flogging. Discipline was extremely strict in all respects; prisoners were required to walk in lock-step and to keep their eyes downcast.[46] The Auburn system of separate confinement at night and work in association by day, girded by a strictly enforced rule of silence, was to become one of the two dominant models that influenced refinement of the penitentiary ideal in North America and Europe.

The other model, which in North America has become known as the 'Pennsylvania system,' closely parallels the model of discipline initially introduced at Gloucester penitentiary in which prisoners were kept in twenty-four-hour solitary confinement and were assigned work to be performed within their own cells. This was the system that the Pennsylvania Legislative Assembly enacted to govern confinement in the Cherry Hill Penitentiary in 1829. Prisoners worked in their individual cells and exercise was taken in an adjoining yard in isolation from other prisoners. Prisoners were permitted no communication whatever with their families or friends, and they were seldom allowed to receive letters. Only the prison inspectors, ministers and priests, the warden, the doctor, prison staff, and official visitors were permitted to meet with the prisoners.[47] The separation of prisoners from each other was strict and complete.

The warden of Cherry Hill told Demetz and Blouet, two Frenchmen who visited the prison in 1837, of the prisoner who had been sentenced the same day as his accomplice; the prisoner had inquired two years later how things had turned out for the accomplice, even though the two men had occupied neighbouring cells the whole time. The Frenchmen were favourably impressed with the system of separate confinement as practised at Cherry Hill. The following passage from their report, in which they describe the advantages of the system over the Auburn silent regime, summarizes the theoretical underpinnings of solitary confinement in nineteenth-century America:

> In the separate system the prisoners cannot become more depraved. They are not under the influence of their fellow prisoners. The false pride in being even worse than one's fellows, the conceit that prevents a prisoner from submitting to his fate, all these feelings that need approval in order to flourish, evaporate in solitude. Regardless of his nature, the convict is compelled to look at himself. He is alone with his conscience. It does not take him long to grasp that his punishment is a consequence of his errors and that he has been deprived of his freedom because he has made bad use of it. During the first few days he may only hear the voice of his anger, but what purpose does that serve in the deathly silence of his surroundings. He is defeated. That is the point at which work is given to him. This becomes a distraction for his gloomy thoughts, solace, and he applies himself eagerly to the task offered him, which is thus not an augmentation of his punishment.
>
> The possibility of changing the attitudes of criminals through this system has been doubted. But the purpose of the punishment is not so much to chastise as to set an example to society that is beneficial and moral. If in this process, the criminal can be given the possibility of reforming, no effort should be spared to achieve this twofold result. If the criminal is not completely reformed in solitary, he is at least taught calm and regular habits. He is held in order and discipline; he learns to work and to respect the law.[48]

The Cherry Hill Penitentiary was subject to inspection by members of the Philadelphia public who were appointed for two years by the Supreme Court. In 1821, the board of inspectors of the Walnut Street Jail had recognized the severity of solitary confinement without labour and had proposed that a year so spent should be regarded as the equivalent of three years of solitary confinement with labour. Demetz and Blouet had been laudatory of the regime of solitary confinement at Cherry Hill. Other distinguished visitors had the gravest reservations about what they saw happening within its austere walls. Charles Dickens visited the prison in 1842. In his *American Notes* he reflected on what he saw there.

> In its intention I am well convinced that it is kind, humane and meant for reformation; but I am persuaded that those who devise the system and those benevolent gentlemen who carry it into execution, do not know what it is they are doing. I believe that very few men are capable of estimating the immense amount of torture and agony which this dreadful punishment, prolonged for years, inflicts upon the sufferers; and in guessing at it myself, and from reasoning from what I have seen written upon their faces, from what to my certain knowledge they feel within, I am only the more convinced that there is a depth of terrible endurance in it which none but the sufferers themselves can fathom, and which no man has a right to inflict upon his fellow creatures.
>
> I hold this slow and daily tampering with the mysteries of the brain to be immeasurably worse than any torture of the body; and because its ghastly signs and tokens are not so palpable to the eye and sense of touch as scars upon the flesh, because its wounds are not on the surface and it extorts few cries that human ears can hear; therefore I denounce it as a secret punishment which slumbering humanity is not roused to stay.[49]

Charles Dickens's denunciation was read in 1975 to the federal court judge who was asked to declare the continuing use of solitary confinement in the British Columbia Penitentiary cruel and unusual punishment.

Dickens was not the only European commentator to be concerned about the effects of solitary confinement on prisoners' sanity. The Swiss prison system had been much influenced by American developments, and during the 1830s the regimes in Swiss prisons came to resemble more and more closely the Pennsylvania system of solitary. In 1838 two Swiss doctors published critiques of the Swiss prisons on the basis of their effects on the prisoners' mental health. In particular, they stated that in the prisons in Geneva and Lausanne the number of deaths and mental disturbances increased in direct relation to the shift in the Swiss institutions from the Auburn to the Pennsylvania system.[50] However, in a report by an investigating committee in Philadelphia in 1837 it was maintained that comparison of the records in the North American correctional institutions revealed that there were fewer rather than more cases of mental illness in Cherry Hill than in other prisons. The committee was of the view that however greatly one might fear for the prisoners' sanity under the pressure of absolute and continuous solitude without labour, without books, without instruction, and without daily association with prison employees and visitors, the regime at Cherry Hill was such that no one was in danger of losing his mind because of isolation.[51]

Although the debates in the United States and in Europe pivoted around the respective advantages of the two models of penitentiary discipline, it is important to realize that, notwithstanding their diversity, the separate and silent systems had a common basis. In a report made to the New York legislature in 1867, E.C. Wines and Theodore Dwight described that common basis in this way:

> Isolation and labour lie at the foundation of both. They are fundamental principles of both, according to the ideal on which they were formed. The difference is one of application; of mode, and not of principle. In one the isolation is effected by an absolute bodily separation by day as well as by night, and labour is performed in the cell of each individual convict. In the other, labour is performed in common workshops and the isolation at night is secured by the confinement of the prisoners in separate cells, but during the day is of a moral species, being effected by the enforcement, so far as such a thing is possible, of an absolute silence. The bodies of the prisoners are together, but their souls are apart; and, while there is a material society, there is a mental solitude.[52]

Michel Foucault, while agreeing that isolation and labour were the common principles around which both the Auburn and Pennsylvania systems were organized, expressed the differences in more graphic terms: 'Auburn was society itself reduced to its bare essentials. Cherry Hill was life annihilated and begun again.'[53]

The debate that took place on both sides of the Atlantic about the relative advantages of the two systems was not an empty one, however. As Foucault states, 'a whole series of different conflicts stemmed from the opposition between these two models: religious (must conversion be the principal element of correction?), medical (does total isolation drive convicts insane?), economic (which method costs less?), architectural and administrative (which form guarantees the best surveillance?). This, no doubt, was why the argument lasted so long.'[54]

While the influence of the American experience with the two models of penitentiary disciplines was to be felt throughout Europe, it was particularly influential in England. It is important to consider the way in which the American experience was evaluated and implemented in England, because in turn that system came to influence events in Canada. The overcrowding in the English prisons brought about by an increase in the crime rate in the wake of demobilization after the Napoleonic Wars led to the abandonment of the regime of solitary confinement in the institutions that had sought to introduce it. In its place and under the influence of the American experience in Auburn and Sing Sing the rule of silence was extended, and in the 1820s and 1830s the silent system, along with the introduction of the bread-and-water diet and the treadwheel, ushered in an era characterized by an escalation in repressive measures directed against prisoners.[55]

But the debate in England on the silent and solitary systems was far from over. In 1834 the home secretary sent William Crawford, a member of the Prison Discipline Society (established in 1818 by the English Quakers and modelled on the Philadelphia Prisoners' Aid Society), to the United States to investigate the Auburn and Pennsylvania systems and to report on their respective merits. Crawford clearly favoured the Philadelphia system as the more effective and humane method of discipline.

> In judging of the comparative merits of the two systems, it will be seen that the discipline of Auburn is of a physical, that of Philadelphia of a moral character. The whip inflicts immediate pain, but solitude inspires permanent terror. The former degrades while it humiliates; the latter subdues but does not debase. At Auburn the convict is uniformly treated with harshness, at Philadelphia with civility. The one contributes to harden, the other to soften the affections. Auburn stimulates vindictive feelings: Philadelphia induces habitual submission.[56]

Crawford, in advocating the Philadelphia model as the basis for the new Pentonville Penitentiary, cited the English pedigree of its system of discipline, the Penitentiary Act of 1779, and the institution established at Gloucester under Paul's directing hand to emphasize that the American model was in fact 'British in its origin, British in its actual application, British in its legislative sanction.'[57] Crawford recommended, however, that because of the rigours of solitary confinement eighteen months should be the maximum time spent under such a regime.[58]

Crawford's counsel was influential, and work began on the planning and construction of a model prison. Pentonville Penitentiary was opened in 1842 and represented 'the culmination of the history of efforts to devise a perfectly rational and reformative mode of imprisonment, a history that stretches back to John Howard's first formulation of the ideal of penitentiary discipline in 1779.'[59]

Michael Ignatieff's account of Pentonville, more than any other description, provides us with clear images of the nature of solitary confinement in the penitentiary in the nineteenth century.

Standing on a huge 6-acre site, behind 25-foot high walls, it loomed over the workers' quarters around it, a massive, three-pronged fortress of the law.

[The prisoner's cell] was 13½ feet from barred window to bolted door, 7½ feet from wall to wall, and 9 feet from floor to ceiling. The contents were spare: a table, a chair, a cobbler's bench, a hammer, broom, bucket and a corner shelf. On the shelf stood a pewter mug, and a dish, a bar of soap, a towel, and a Bible. Except for exercises and chapel, every minute of his day was spent in this space among these objects ...

In the 1840s a convict's day at Pentonville began at 5:45 A.M. At 6:00 A.M. the convict heard footsteps pausing outside his cell door, and, without looking up, he knew that the warder's eyes were sweeping over him from the inspection hole, checking the order of his cell, making sure that he was at work at his cobbler's bench ... The labour was long and incessant, an hour and a half before breakfast, three hours before lunch, four hours in the afternoon ... After dinner, the prisoner had two hours to himself to pace the cell, to write a letter, to think, or to read from the Bible. At 9:00 P.M. the gas guttered and dropped, levers were pulled, and the double bolts crashed down across the cell door. Lights out. Lying on his hammock, in the blackness of his cell, the convict could hear the muffled tread of the wardens, the clink of their sabres against their leggings, and the clang as they punched in at the clocks posted along the galleries. Sometimes, beneath all the other sounds, he could hear the patter of the prison telegraph through the walls and drainpipes. All night the men struggled through the stone to reach each other with laborious messages as faint as heartbeats ...

The night was the hardest time of all. Sleep was likely to be fitful and restless. A convict worked out the night watching the stars or the clouds scudding across the moon through the cell window, and listening to the catacomb silence ... the wardens came for the ones who cried out and took them down to the infirmary ... Every year at Pentonville between five and fifteen men were taken away to the asylums. If they remained insane, they were confined in the asylum for the rest of their lives; if they recovered, they were brought back to finish their time ...

If the solitude and the silence drove some to madness, it drove a few others to suicide ... Some prisoners were broken by Pentonville, but others were not. A few fought its discipline openly ... the birch and the cat were used on prisoners who assaulted or swore at wardens. For lesser breaches of discipline the usual punishment was a term in the dark cells, black holes in the basement of the building ... Most convicts gave up trying to fight Pentonville. They settled into the routine, kept out of trouble, and waited out their time. Some showed no apparent signs of being damaged by the silence and the solitude, but most prisoners bore its mark.

Upon release, convicts were set off by the visible signs of their confinement – the liberty clothing, the shaven head, and the pallor of their skin.

Then there were the marks inside. Those who observed prisoners upon their release noticed that many suffered from bouts of hysteria or crying. Others found the sounds of the street deafening and asked for cotton wool to stop up their ears ... Even those who thought they had got used to solitude found themselves dreaming about the prison long after. They would hear the bolts crashing shut in their sleep – and the screams.[60]

As I will seek to show, these images continue to have a terrible relevance in the Canadian penitentiary today.

2
The Evolution of Penitentiary Discipline in Canada

CANADA'S FIRST PENITENTIARY: CRUEL AND UNUSUAL PUNISHMENT IN THE NINETEENTH CENTURY

For most of the first half of the nineteenth century serious crime was not the major problem in Canada that it was in England. Very few men and women were convicted of murder, rape, robbery, or burglary. The most common criminal offence was simple larceny.[1] But although the criminal calendars at the assizes in Upper Canada were not taken up with serious offences, it should not be thought that crime was not viewed as a serious problem. J.M. Beattie, in his incisive analysis of contemporary newspaper reports of the judges' charges to grand juries, reports of trials, and editorials, has shown that there was a great deal of public discussion about crime, its causes and the appropriate response of the state. In terms reminiscent of the debate in England, those in Canada who held property and power saw crime not simply as an individual's fall from grace but as a social disease characteristic of the poor, the origins of which lay in a lack of moral sense and indolence. Mr Justice Sullivan, in his charge to the grand jury in 1849, stated:

> I find by the calendar that several prisoners are confined on the charge of burglary, an offence within my recollection almost unknown in the province, but from which its exemption cannot be hoped as population increases, and vice and poverty become consequently more abundant. Burglaries and robberies are usually the crimes of a class utterly vicious and abandoned; and when persons of this description are permitted to swarm, it is in vain to expect that the crime that usually accompanies their presence shall not be also found.
>
> Most people who live in the suburbs of this city [Toronto] or who have extended their walks into the fields in rear of it, must have observed, as I have, the wretched and squalid women, apparently living without home or shelter, scantily clothed, and hovering even in our inclement weather around fires

plundered from the neighbouring woods and fences. These have their attendant ruffians, and no means of prolonging existence but the practice of vice of the most revolting nature. With such beings and their associates incitements to crime are almost invincible. They have little fear from the severity of the law, and no religious or moral sensibility to keep them from evil.[2]

Given that the social dimensions of crime were seen in much the same terms in Canada as in England, it is not surprising that penitentiary discipline was also seen as one of the primary ways to effect the necessary changes in the morality and habits of the poor.

Since crime was thought to be the product of a criminal class that lived in destitution and ignorance, that lived without the restraints of morality and religion, or the restraints that are concerned for their good character imposed on the respectable members of the society, crime could only be prevented and society protected if the habits and behaviour of the lower orders of the population were changed. Industrial schools; houses of industry; prison discipline; these were to be the instruments of reform. Internal discipline and good work habits would succeed in protecting property from the envy of the lower orders where the horrors of the gallows had failed.[3]

The momentum for prison reform as part of a moral crusade against the vagrant poor was accelerated in Canada as it had been in England by the increasing criticisms of the 'Bloody Code,' the harsh criminal code introduced into Quebec and later into Upper Canada from England, which sought to deter crime under the 'great umbrella of terror,'[4] the gallows. But the campaign to abolish the death penalty presumed a new architecture and a technology of discipline, both of which had already evolved in England under the guiding vision of Howard and Paul. In Upper Canada in 1830 the prisons were still subject to most of the vices Howard had spoken of as characteristic of the English prisons of 1770. The local jails were places of detention in which debtors and prisoners awaiting trial or execution were kept with little separation between them. A report of a select committee of the House of Assembly investigating the desirability of building a penitentiary endorsed the following description of the state of the prisons in Upper Canada in 1831:

Imprisonment in the common gaols of the province is inexpedient and pernicious in the extreme, as there is not a sufficient classification or separation of the prisoners, so that a lad who is confined for a simple assault (or crime in which, as there is but little moral turpitude, argues no depravity in the offender) or even on suspicion of crimes of that description and degree, may be kept for twelve months in company with murderers, thieves, robbers and burglars, and the most depraved characters in the province, and a man must know but little of human nature indeed who can for a moment suppose that such evil communications will not corrupt good manners ... Gaols managed as most of ours are, as Lord Brougham well remarks, are seminaries kept at the public expense for the purpose of instructing His Majesty's subjects in vice and immorality, and for the propagation and increase of crime.[5]

The select committee recommended that a penitentiary be built and that it be located in Kingston. The committee's report led to the appointment of commissioners who were to collect information on penitentiaries outside Canada and make recommendations to the House of Assembly as to the system best suited to the needs of Canada. These commissioners visited penitentiaries at Auburn, Sing Sing, and Philadelphia. They reviewed the comparative advantages of the silent and separate systems and recommended that the Canadian penitentiary follow the Auburn model. Their favouring of the Auburn system - work during the day in association with other prisoners under the strict rule of silence, solitary confinement at night - was based on a number of considerations, principally its demonstrated success in several states. The commissioners viewed the Philadelphia system of solitary confinement as experimental and untested.[6]

The commissioners' report resulted in the passage of Canada's first Penitentiary Act, passed in 1834,[7] and the opening of its first penitentiary at Kingston in 1835. The act, borrowing from the preamble of the first English Penitentiary Act of 1779, set out the intentions behind Kingston: 'If many offenders convicted of crimes were ordered to solitary imprisonment, accompanied by well regulated labour and religious instruction, it might be the means under providence, not only of deterring others from the commission of like crimes, but also of reforming the individuals, and inuring them to habits of industry.'[8]

The draftsmen of the act also sought to invest the new penitentiary discipline with legitimacy by adopting John Howard's authority of rules. The rules and regulations established for the penitentiary marked out in precise detail the nature of prison discipline. Section VIII of the regulations dealt with the duty of convicts:

Convicts are to yield perfect obedience and submission to their keepers. They are to labour diligently and preserve unbroken silence. They must not exchange a word with one another under any pretext whatever, nor communicate with one another, nor with anyone else, by writing.

They must not exchange looks, wink, laugh, nod or gesticulate to each other, nor shall they make use of any signs, except such as are necessary to explain

> their wants to the waiters. They must approach their keepers in a most respectful manner, and be brief in their communications. They are not to speak to, or address, their keepers on any subject but as relates to their work, duty or wants ...
>
> They are not to stop work nor suffer their attention to be torn from it. They are not to gaze at visitors when passing through the prison, nor sing, dance, whistle, run, jump, nor do anything which may have the slightest tendency to disturb the harmony or to contravene the rules and regulations of the prison.[9]

As Beattie has aptly stated, 'the point clearly was to impose regularity of labour and good work habits on men who were assumed to have been lazy and idle, while at the same time isolating each man, breaking his spirit, taming his passions and preventing the kind of corruption that indiscriminate intercourse among the prisoners was thought to encourage. So passionately was it held that separation and isolation would work its miracles that the prisoners were not even allowed to look at each other as they marched to and from their cells and at mealtimes.'[10]

It was hoped that the opening of the Kingston Penitentiary would usher in a new era in the treatment of prisoners, with reformation and moral re-education replacing the spectacle of terror. Actual experience during the prison's first decade of operation, however, told a different story. The attempts of Kingston's first warden, Henry Smith, to enforce the silent system were characterized by the royal commission that investigated the penitentiary in 1848 (the Brown Commission) as 'barbarous and inhumane.' This commission had been appointed in response to the litany of charges that had been made against the conduct of the warden. At the centre of these charges was the allegation that he had pursued a cruel, indiscriminate, and ineffective system of punishment in the management of prison discipline. The commissioners, after hearing extensive evidence from prisoners and guards, documented in their report ample proof of this charge against the warden.[11]

For the first seven years of the penitentiary's operation the warden had relied exclusively upon flogging as the sole punishment for offences of all types. The commissioners reported that many of these floggings were inflicted on children: during his first committal in Kingston, an eleven-year-old whose offences were talking, laughing, and idling was flogged, over a three-year period, thirty-eight times with the rawhide and six times with the cats;[12] another boy whose 'offences were of the most trifling description – such as were to be expected from a child of 10 or 11 ... was stripped to the shirt, and publicly lashed thirty-seven times in eight and a half months.'[13] The commission referred to these and similar cases as examples of 'barbarity, disgraceful to humanity.'[14] The commission further documented cases of men and women who had been flogged into a state of insanity. One prisoner was subjected to 'seven floggings with the cats in a fortnight, and fourteen floggings in four weeks with the cats or rawhides. It is very clear that if the man was deranged when he arrived, had any tendency towards it, that the treatment he received was calculated to drive him into hopeless insanity.'[15]

Although Kingston had been conceived as a humane substitute for the regime of terror of the Bloody Code, Warden Smith, in enforcing the silent system, had instituted in the name of reform another system of terror. But whereas the practice of jurors, augmented by the prerogative of mercy, had reduced the incidence of the death penalty, the terror of Warden Smith's penitentiary discipline at Kingston was characterized by rampant escalation. As the commission documented 'the simple facts, that the number of punishments rose from 770 in 1843 to 2,102 in 1845, and from 3,445 in 1846 to 6,063 in the year following, the same number of men being subject to discipline in the latter years ... [show] beyond cavil that the system pursued has been one of the most frightful oppression.'[16]

The clear implication of this catalogue of horror was that the warden had frustrated the fundamental purpose of the penitentiary: to establish a climate in which men and women could be improved and reformed. As the commission reported,

> The exasperation which such a system could only produce must have bid defiance to all hope of reform. To see crowds of full-grown men, day after day, year after year, stripped and lashed in the presence of four or five hundred persons, because they whispered to their neighbour, or lifted their eyes to the face of a passerby, or laughed at some passing occurrence, must have obliterated from the minds of the unhappy men all perception of moral guilt, and thoroughly brutalized their feelings.[17]

Warden Smith's failure was not to be condemned simply in terms of individual sadism; in the minds of the commissioners it bespoke an institutional failure to respond to the underlying causes of crime.[18] The Brown Commission, in its recommendations for the future management of Kingston Penitentiary, affirmed the principles upon which the penitentiary had been established almost twenty years earlier, principles which themselves dated back to the origins of the penitentiary in England. 'To seclude the prisoners from their former associates: to separate those of whom hopes might be entertained from those who are desperate, to teach them useful trades; and to provide them with a recommendation to the world in the means of obtaining an honest livelihood, after the expiration of their term of punishment.'[19]

The commission reviewed the experience at Kingston, analysed comparative experience elsewhere, including the United States and England, and recommended that prison discipline in Kingston should be based on a merger of the silent and the separate systems. The commission recommended that the newly admitted prisoner be detained under a regime of solitary confinement for a period to be left to the discretion of the warden but not to exceed six months. Thereafter he would work and eat in association with other prisoners but would be subject to the rule of silence.

The decision to incorporate an initial period of solitary confinement was based on the commissioners' view that such a regime 'is highly humanizing, calls forth warmly the confidence and affection of the prisoner and gives the officers much influence over his mind, and generally affords a good opportunity for effecting the moral reform of the criminal.'[20] However, the commission was also of the view that 'the human mind cannot endure protracted imprisonment under this system; and that with all the care of the authorities, insanity, to a fearful extent, is to be found within the walls.'[21] The commission's recommended compromise - limiting a solitary regime to a six-month period - mirrored the practice at Pentonville, where by 1847 the initial period of solitary confinement had been reduced from eighteen months to nine months.[22]

The commission was of the view that 'with proper management ... the punishments in a penitentiary may be few in number and moral in character.'[23] However, for persistent infractions of the rules, they recommended placing the prisoner in the solitary confinement cells 'to enable the warden to deal with him individually and endeavour to produce a change.'[24] Only as a last resort was the cat to be used, and then it was to be administered in private. The commission also addressed the principle by which prison discipline was to be administered.

> All convicts should as far as possible be placed on a footing of perfect equality; each should know what he has to expect, and his rights and obligations should be strictly defined. If he breaks the prison rules he should also have the quantum of punishment to which he becomes subject. He should not witness the spectacle of offences similar in enormity treated with different degrees of severity, unless in cases of frequent repetition. One of the most important lessons to be impressed on the convicts' mind is the justice of his sentence, and the impartiality with which it is carried into execution.[25]

The Brown Commission also commented on the principle of outside inspection. The Penitentiary Act of 1835 had established a local board of inspectors with a general jurisdiction to superintend the administration of Kingston. The commission found that this board had proved inadequate to the task of controlling the abuses and excesses of the warden. The commission, having 'pointed out how likely the unrestricted and continued exercise of arbitrary power is to degenerate into apathy or tyranny,'[26] recommended that in place of the local board of inspectors there be appointed national inspectors directly responsible to the executive of the government with an expanded authority to make rules and regulations, and with clearly defined duties to visit and inquire into the management of the penitentiary.

The recommendations of the Brown Commission were clearly within the tradition of John Howard and the prison reform movement. What was to be sought in the carrying out of discipline within the prison walls, if it was to operate as a catalyst for moral transformation, was the re-establishment of the moral legitimacy of punishment. To Howard and the Brown Commission this meant that the jailer, with his virtually unfettered discretion, had to be rendered accountable to the authority of rules and to outside supervision and that the punishment must meet the strictest standards of justice. To their European counterparts such as Decazes, commenting on French penal discipline, it meant that 'the law must follow the convicted man into the prison where it has sent him.'[27]

SOLITARY CONFINEMENT AFTER 1850: THE PRISON OF ISOLATION, CANADA'S 'RADICAL' REFORM

The preference for the separate system of solitary confinement quickly became penal orthodoxy in England: within six years of Pentonville's construction, fifty-four new prisons modelled after it were built.[28] In 1865 the English Prison Act prescribed the system of separate confinement for all prisons in England.[29] In this and in other respects the act embodied recommendation of the Carnarvon Committee Report of 1863, which had concluded:

> In all questions of prison discipline, it appears to the Committee that the principle of separation ... stands first for consideration ... the system generally known as the separate system must now be accepted as a foundation of prison discipline and ... its rigid maintenance is a vital principle to the efficiency of county and borough jails ... The Committee are of the opinion that the principle of separation should be made to pervade the entire system of the prison and no adequate reason has been assigned for the relaxation of the rule in school, chapel or in exercise.[30]

In the words of a modern commentator, the recommendations of the Carnarvon Committee 'mark the eve of an era in which prisoners were to suffer conditions even more rigorous than before, and in which separate confinement was acknowledged to be, not a curative and cleansing process, but a grim and sustained punishment.'[31]

By the second half of the nineteenth century, solitary confinement predominated as the preferred disciplinary regime in Europe, particularly in France, Germany, and Belgium. Albert Krebs, commenting on the influence of John Howard on the prison systems of Europe, writes:

> Development of solitary confinement on the Philadelphia model continued in France as in the rest of Europe. A German judge, Noellner, maintained in 1841 that of the European Commissioners sent out to North America to look at the prison system, not a single one, on his return, did not prefer the Philadelphia system. The First International Prison Reform Conference in Frankfurt am Main in 1846 also commended solitary confinement with only a few dissenting votes. Specialists in the civilized countries had already reached a large measure of agreement on the subject.[32]

In Canada, the principal recommendation of the Brown Commission for the unification of the two disciplinary models with the initial period of imprisonment to be served under the separate system was not implemented. Although the Penitentiary Act of 1851 authorized the construction of up to 'fifty solitary cells with a workshop attached to each cell adapted to carry out the "separate" or "solitary" system of discipline,' this authorization was not acted upon.[33] In 1851, as in 1834, the separate system remained a more expensive system to operate, both because of the higher construction costs associated with the larger cells and the fact that individual cell-work was less remunerative than congregate labour with its possibilities of prisoner work contracts with outside employers.

The proposal for a period of solitary confinement was to resurface in the 1860s, not as a belated attempt to blend the American systems of penal discipline or to respond to the movement in favour of the separate system that Pentonville had heralded in England; rather, it marked the first phase of the 'Crofton' system of prison discipline developed in Ireland. This system of 'reformatory prison discipline' was strongly favoured by the Board of Inspectors of Asylums, Prisons and Public Charities which, from 1859 to 1868, was charged with 'the direction and control of everything relating to the administration of public charity and with the punishments inflicted by justice.'[34]

The Crofton system was based on a phased prison experience in which money incentives, a progressive easing of punitive conditions, and the prospect of conditional release before the expiry of the full term of imprisonment were used to achieve reformatory purposes. For the first eight or nine months of his sentence the Irish prisoner lived under a strict regime of solitary confinement at Mountjoy Prison, labouring in his cell at work intentionally made hard and monotonous. As one commentator put it, 'Mountjoy aimed at the infliction of just punishment and the subduing of the spirits at war with society.'[35]

After his punitive initiation, the prisoner was transferred to one of two other congregate prisons to begin the second or reformatory phase of his imprisonment. Here he was required to work his way through four classifications, his progress determined by a system of marks awarded in the categories of discipline, school and industry. The third phase, 'designed to test the work previously done, as the crucible tests gold,'[36] saw the prisoner transferred to an intermediate or open prison with more privileges and a far less restrictive regime. Thereafter he became eligible for release on a ticket of leave in the fourth and final phase in the system.[37]

The Canadian inspectors, perceiving the existing provincial penitentiary regime as 'one of rigid repression, of uncompromising coercion, one which admits no change or improvement in the condition of the convict as a consequence of good conduct,'[38] advocated a modified Crofton scheme for Canada. In 1861 they recommended that the classification of prisoners be expressed by distinctive badges and money gratuities, and that a scheme of remission of a portion of a sentence be introduced as an inducement to good behaviour.[39] In 1862 they endorsed the idea that an undefined initial portion of the prison term be spent in solitary confinement so that 'every convict who enters the penitentiary may learn those salutary lessons which this portion of prison discipline is so well calculated to teach.'[40]

Although the period of initial solitary imprisonment proposed by the board was to be shorter than the terms in England and Ireland, it was to be 'equal to them in moral and religious appliances, and in strictness of discipline.'[41] The inspectors' recommendations also embraced a third phase modelled after the Crofton system in which additional privileges could be earned for exemplary conduct, but they refrained from endorsing the ticket-of-leave concept.[42] Moreover, in contradistinction to the Irish system, the modified phase system suggested by the inspectors was to be carried out within the confines of a single institution rather than in separate institutions.[43]

The first Penitentiary Act passed after Confederation was drafted by the chairman of the board of inspectors, E.A. Meredith, and sought to provide the legislative framework for the introduction into Canada of the modified Crofton scheme. The act of 1868, stating that 'no system of discipline in Penitentiary can be effective for punishment or true reformation of the criminal unless it be combined with strict separate confinement during some period of the time for which the Court has sentenced him,' authorized the construction of penal cells and the separate confinement of each convict within these cells for a portion of his sentence.[44] The act also introduced a remission system whereby a prisoner could earn up to five days a month off his sentence for good behaviour[45] and enabled prisoners 'of exemplary conduct' to work overtime for money that would be paid to the prisoner's family or to the prisoner on his release.[46]

Following the passage of the new Penitentiary Act, the Justice Department requested plans and estimates for a penal prison. In November 1869, the federal cabinet approved an inquiry into the workings of the solitary system at Philadelphia and elsewhere in the United States, and in 1870 official government approval was given for the construction near Kingston Penitentiary of the new penal prison designed for the purposes of solitary confinement.[47] Work was begun on the prison in 1870, but was discontinued the following year when prisoner labour was required for more pressing projects elsewhere.[48]

The 1868 Penitentiary Act transferred control of the penitentiary from the five-member board of inspectors to a three-member board of directors.[49] In 1875 the superintendency was again transferred to a single inspector of penitentiaries.[50] For the next twenty years the office of inspector was held by one individual, J.G. Moylan. In his annual reports, Inspector Moylan set forth those principles of prison discipline, first enunciated by John Howard, directed to the need to control abuse of power and ensure fairness and justice within the prison walls. They merit reciting:

> It is of paramount necessity that prisoners should realize the fact that the rules are carried out fairly and justly, in order that strict and stern discipline be maintained without exciting constant resistance. They must feel, too, that the officers are simply administering the law, and that in any case of abuse of power on the part of an officer, he will be held to a strict accountability.[51]

> Experience shows that there is no greater mistake in the whole compass of prison discipline than the studied imposition of personal degradation as part and parcel of the punishment.[52]

> No one will deny that society has the right to protect itself, yet not by the exercise of undue severity. The offender is sentenced by due course of law to imprisonment, either for a limited number of years or for life; imprison him, then, but do not put him to death, do not drive him mad or destroy his health ... the law does not sanction this severity; reason, humanity, common justice cry out against it. The vilest criminal, who is sentenced only to confinement and hard labour, has as good a right to require that society should not expose his health, sanity or life to danger, as the most virtuous member of the

community. His safety in these respects, indeed, is to be watched over with even greater care than if he were a free man unspotted by crime. The reason is obvious; those who are at liberty are bound to take care of themselves; if they fall into peril it is their own fault or misfortune; society is not accountable for what it seeks not to control. But with the convict it is far different; the iron grasp of the law is upon him, and he is as helpless for himself as an infant. Thick walls and iron grates surround him; his food is selected and weighed out to him; his allowance of light, air and water is determined, his hours for sleep, labour and relaxation are fixed; his dress, his exercise, his habits in every respect are under the constant and irresistible control of his keepers. He is like clay in the hands of the potter ... Convicts are capital subjects for experiment, for they are not allowed to have any will of their own. Everything is done for them upon a system; they are fed, lodged, dressed, taught, punished and rewarded upon theory. The interior of a prison is a grand theatre for the trial of all new plans in hygiene, education, physical and moral reform; the convict is surrendered body and soul to be experimented upon.[53]

We will have cause to reflect further on Inspector Moylan's graphic description of the prison as a 'grand theatre' and on the prisoners' place behind its enveloping curtain when we consider the modern sequel to solitary confinement.

To Inspector Moylan the experimentation in prison discipline that had gone on in the nineteenth century in Europe and North America had narrowed the field of controversy. 'Here is absolutely the whole question: social or solitary labour by day, which is better? Facts and experience prove the congregated system the more preferable, provided the means exist for isolating the bad and incorrigible from well-disposed convicts.'[54] Inspector Moylan proved to be a consistent advocate of the introduction of a scheme of solitary or separate confinement for the 'incorrigible' prisoners and as part of the initial incarceration of all prisoners along the lines of the Crofton model. On the issue of the 'incorrigibles' he wrote in 1878 that 'the pernicious influence of such characters cannot be exaggerated. Habituated themselves to a life of infamy, callous to every sentiment of morality and rectitude, they delight in relating their evil deeds and experience to others who may be mere tyros in the ways of wickedness and sin. It is not difficult to forecast the effect of such intercourse.'[55]

He explained the rationale behind the separate confinement of the newly received prisoners in terms resonant with the sentiments of Howard and Paul. 'This solitude will afford these persons time and opportunities to enter into themselves, to examine their past lives, their weaknesses, the causes of their fall and misfortunes, in view of amendment and of making firm resolutions against relapse. They will, moreover, become well acquainted with and habituated to the rules and regulations which they are to follow and allow them to share in associated labour or trades.'[56]

The inspector suggested that in order to introduce the solitary system without incurring the expense of building new prisons, the construction plans for the extensions of the new penitentiaries opened between 1870 and 1880[57] should provide for one wing 'having roomy and lightsome cells wherein those bad characters can be placed in separate confinement and then perform their allotted daily labour.'[58]

By 1888, Inspector Moylan's advocacy had made itself felt, for a decision was taken to construct at Kingston Penitentiary a block of cells suitable for the solitary confinement of both incorrigible and habitual offenders and the newly received prisoners. In his 1888 annual report, Inspector Moylan reviewed some of the European experiences with the solitary system, particularly in England and Belgium, to demonstrate that the system, if properly administered, was consistent with his views of the purposes of prison discipline. He cited some of the glowing (albeit self-serving) testimonials from a number of the European delegates to the 1872 London Prison Congress. The Belgian delegate claimed that the recidivism rate of those leaving solitary confinement in Belgian prisons was only 4.46 per cent, whereas it was 68 per cent for those liberated from congregate prisons. The director of the prison at Bruchsal, in Baden, was of the view that separate imprisonment in Germany 'produced excellent results'; that he had seen prisoners live thirteen years in separate confinement 'without any inconvenience' and that in his view 'all prisoners, except 1%, could endure cellular confinement for life without injury ...'[59] Based upon his review, Inspector Moylan confidently asserted that 'the isolation of newly received convicts, for eight to nine months, for the object mentioned by Sir Walter Crofton [for reflection, repentance and religious instruction] and of incorrigibles for at least 18 months, to reform and prevent them from corrupting those who are well inclined, can be tried with all safety. The experiment is certainly well worth a trial; it is the first effectual step towards real and radical reform.'[60]

As the 'Prison of Isolation' (the chilling but compellingly appropriate name given to the new cell block at Kingston) neared completion, Inspector Moylan addressed the nature of the regime under which prisoners would live. The prisoners were to work in their cells, and 'light industries, which would not injure health by being carried on in the cells, by vitiating the air, such as map making, willow and rattan work, broom and cane and chair making, would be suitable, and a very limited output of each kind of such handiwork would not interfere, to any appreciable extent, with outside manufacturers.'[61] The guiding principle for the selection of work in the Prison of Isolation, as elsewhere, was that it be 'calculated to elevate and reform, instead of lowering and degrading' the prisoners.[62] The inspector strongly urged that as a necessary step in devising a system of management and framing suitable rules and regulations for the new Prison of Isolation, a commission be appointed to examine the prison system in Europe where the separate plan was in vogue, particularly in Belgium and Ireland. In urging that the Irish Crofton system be examined, Inspector Moylan cited the characterization of that system by the eminent American penologist Dr Wines: 'an adult reformatory, in which the will of the prison inmate is brought into accord with the will of the prison keeper, and held there so long as that virtue becomes a habit.'[63] There was no doubt in the mind of Inspector Moylan what the Prison of Isolation was designed to accomplish. In 1891, the breaking of a man's corrupted spirit in aid of reformation was a desirable and legitimate purpose of imprisonment.

No commission was appointed, and in 1892 Inspector Moylan, lamenting the lack of precedents and the absence of any existing institution in North America still following the separate or solitary system, drafted a code of rules for governance of the new prison.[64]

The Prison of Isolation was completed and received its first prisoners in 1894, the same year in which Inspector Moylan retired from his twenty-year inspectorate. However, during the time that had elapsed between the decision to begin construction of the Prison of Isolation and its completion, Inspector Moylan's original dual conception of its function had undergone revision. In the new inspector's first report in 1895, it is stated that the prison 'is [to be] used for third term men, incorrigibles and prisoners who have been sentenced for unnatural offences.'[65]

This limitation of function is reflected in the 'Rules and Regulations respecting Prisons of Isolation' which were promulgated in 1893. Section 1 set out the criteria for admission to Canada's first super-maximum institution:

> Any male convict whose conduct is found to be vicious, or who persists in disobedience to the Rules and Regulations of the Prison, or who is found to exercise a pernicious influence on his fellow convicts may be imprisoned in the Prison of Isolation for an indefinite period not to exceed the unexpired term of the convict's sentence.[66]

Before a prisoner could be sent to the Prison of Isolation, the warden was required to transmit to the inspector, for the minister of justice's consideration, his report of the facts, and the reasons justifying such imprisonment. The rules also laid down the regime under which prisoners were to be confined. These included confinement in the special cells; strict silence; separate exercise for about an hour a day in the presence of an officer; employment at such labour as may be ordered; restriction to a special diet for at least three months, subject to the approval of the surgeon; and no visits or letters for the same period. At the end of the three months, subject to their good conduct, prisoners could receive the ordinary prison diet; at the end of three additional months, again subject to good conduct, they were eligible to return to the ordinary cells.[67] The regulations also provided that 'any convict who had been ordered more than once during the same term of imprisonment to undergo confinement in the Prison of Isolation shall be kept there to the expiration of his sentence unless otherwise ordered by the Minister upon the recommendation of the warden, on account of good conduct and well assured amendment.'[68] Furthermore, after confinement in the Prison of Isolation, prisoners were not to return immediately to work in the general population of Kingston; 'as a measure of prevention, but not punishment' they were to be kept on probation in separate working gangs for such time as the warden deemed necessary.'[69] Finally, 'penal class convicts,' as prisoners confined in the Prison of Isolation were known, did not receive any remission time.[70]

The 108 cells in the Prison of Isolation were markedly larger than those in the rest of Kingston Penitentiary. The cells measured some thirteen feet long, nine feet wide, and ten feet high, in contrast to the original cell block in which the cells were ten feet by two feet eight inches by six feet, a size that on more than one occasion had drawn the condemnation of visitors to Kingston.[71] The larger cell size was attributable to the fact that prisoners were required not only to live but also to work in their cells. Although the Prison of Isolation had been viewed as a place to which other penitentiaries could send their incorrigibles, it remained, with a few exceptions, a prison within a prison only for Kingston Penitentiary because of the high cost of transfer from the other penitentiaries.[72]

The inspector's annual reports from 1896 to 1903 contain separate tables listing the names of all prisoners received into the Prison of Isolation and the length of their stay. Between 8 November 1894, the day the Prison of Isolation received its first prisoners, and 30 June 1896, sixty-seven prisoners were received and thirty-eight were discharged, leaving a population of twenty-nine.[73] The length of stay ranged from three to sixteen months. A review of the tables of admission and discharge in subsequent years indicates that although a few prisoners spent up to two years in solitary confinement, the average length of stay was about six months.[74]

The Prison of Isolation was viewed by the authorities as a successful disciplinary strategy. In 1897 the inspector confidently asserted that 'the Prison of Isolation, which is the only institution of the kind in Canada, has fully demonstrated the superiority of the Belgium system as regards to treatment of incorrigibles and criminal cranks ... It is evidence that the extension of the system to the other penitentiaries will enable the authorities to dispense with the "triangle" and other relics of semi-civilization.'[75] In 1901, he reported that 'the direct individual treatment which it affords rarely fails to have the desired effect.'[76] Dr Daniel Phelan, the surgeon at Kingston, was equally complimentary in his views:

> Popular ignorance has confounded the solitary system with the 'separate' or 'isolation' system as carried on here. The 'solitary' system consisted in shutting up unfortunate offenders in subterranean cells without light, books, exercise or employment, and as a consequence mental and physical disease was the result. The fictitious stories regarding the production of insanity by the separate or isolation system are not founded on facts and originated from the experiences of the solitary system. The Prison of Isolation is the best place as a safeguard to mental equipoise. No case of insanity could so far be attributed to it.[77]

A year later he commented, 'I am more than ever convinced of the calming effect of this system on the nervous hierarchy of the inmates ... The cells and corridors are well lighted and ventilated and the sun shines in every cell during some portion of the day in summer, the importance and influence of which in the development and maintenance of a general healthful condition is beyond doubt.'[78]

The Prison of Isolation was never used to its full capacity, and in the years after the turn of the century the number of prisoners sent there declined. In 1903, the last year in which a schedule of prisoners was published in the annual report, only nine prisoners were confined at the end of the year. The small number was attributed by the inspector to the efficacy of the disciplinary regime. In 1908 the Prison of Isolation was closed, only to be reopened in 1911; the surgeon at Kingston enthusiastically heralded the reopening as marking 'a new era in prison management.'[79]

While the Prison of Isolation remained in sporadic use in subsequent years, in 1921, owing to a lack of accommodation for the general population, the cells were divided by wooden partitions and were referred to as the 'east cell block.' While the east cell block continued to be used during the 1920s and 1930s for the segregation of incorrigible prisoners, the concept of separate confinement was abandoned and the prisoners worked in association during the day.[80]

This historical excursus has shown that in Canada the Prison of Isolation was the only institution in which solitary confinement became the centre-piece of a regime of penitentiary discipline. But this is not to say that solitary confinement was otherwise never used. It is quite clear that a term in the dark isolation cells was included in the repertoire of punishment for violation of prison rules from the very first days of the Canadian penitentiary. The Penitentiary Act of 1834 authorized the solitary confinement of prisoners for misconduct in the penitentiary,[81] and this sanction has remained part of the penalty for breach of prison rules. The 1870 rules drawn up pursuant to the 1868 Penitentiary Act authorized 'confinement in the penal or separate cells with such diet as the Surgeon shall pronounce sufficient, respect being had to the constitution of the convict and the length of the period during which he is to be confined.'[82] The rules did not limit the period in which the prisoner could be so confined.[83] This provision for punishment by confinement in the isolated cells was retained in both the 1889 and 1898 regulations.[84]

Although the annual reports of the inspector during the last half of the nineteenth century included summaries of punishments imposed in the penitentiaries, those summaries do not indicate the length of time prisoners spent in the punishment cells. However, some information on this can be gleaned from the punishment books wardens were required to keep. In the 1892 annual report, Inspector Moylan commented on the question of the length of the prisoners' incarceration in the punishment cells:

> The Report and Punishment Book show that in some of the penitentiaries convicts have been kept in the dungeon one and two months and even for a longer period. I have discouraged this practice in my minutes. No doubt such punishment, or rather its equivalent, is as a rule deserved. But in view of the convicts' labour being lost to the penitentiary for so long a time, some mode of punishment other than the dungeon, after a short trial of that, should be adopted. If a week in the dungeon do [sic] not produce the desired effect, longer confinement there generally results in a greater degree of callousness, stubbornness, and resistance to authority.[85]

In 1933, the penitentiary regulations were subjected to a major revision, the first since 1898; while confinement in an isolated cell remained a permissible punishment for violation of prison rules, the period of confinement was restricted to not more than three days.[86] In the same year that the new penitentiary rules were introduced, the superintendent of penitentiaries confidently asserted that 'no convict is kept in solitary confinement in any penitentiary in Canada. Such confinement, either in the ordinary way or as a punishment, has been abolished for many years.'[87]

While this may be an accurate reflection of the fact that by the 1930s the Prison of Isolation had ceased to operate, it is not a proper statement of the continuity of the practice of confinement in isolated cells as punishment for prison offences. No doubt the superintendent perceived the administration of such punishment in the Canadian penitentiary as a qualitatively different form of discipline from that which was practised in the nineteenth century and which had drawn the condemnation of Charles Dickens and other critics of the solitary system. However, judging by the continuity of these practices into the 1970s and 1980s, the superintendent's disavowal of anything akin to nineteenth-century penitentiary discipline existing in 1933 should be viewed as official hyperbole rather than prison reality.

3
Solitary Confinement in the Age of Corrections: Cruel and Unusual Punishment in the Twentieth Century

In the 130 years since the Brown Commission rendered its report on the brutality of the first penitentiary regime at Kingston, there have been many changes in the Canadian penitentiary system, changes that most observers would view as evidence of the progressive liberalizing and humanizing of carceral power. The rule of silence has been abandoned; the cat-o'-nine-tails and other forms of corporal punishment have been prohibited; access to the outside world through visits and correspondence has been expanded; maximum security is now only one of a series of custodial alternatives; in accordance with the 'rehabilitative ideal' (which, to accommodate prevailing theories of criminality, has been redefined to emphasize social and psychological rather than moral growth), there has been an 'enrichment' of the penitentiary regime through various types of programs and the addition to the staff of persons skilled in counselling; and the prisoner's return to society from the penitentiary has been modulated with the introduction of the parole system.[1]

I have said that these changes are seen by most observers of the penal system as part of a pattern of liberalization. Others take a more cynical view, and see a process not of liberalization but rather of the extension and elaboration of control over the lives of prisoners in the name of rehabilitation.[2] (I have written elsewhere on the reality of rehabilitation in the penitentiary, particularly the prisoners' reality,[3] and I shall return to this theme later.)

While there have been changes in the system, there exist certain continuities that link our time with the preceding century. Prisoners are still serving time in Kingston Penitentiary and in other maximum-security institutions built in the nineteenth century on the architectural model of Kingston.[4] Within their austere and forbidding walls, men no longer cry out from the lash as it falls on their bared backs; but the screams that were heard in Cherry Hill and in Pentonville 150 years ago are still heard in Canada's maximum-security penitentiaries today. These screams are not those of the ghosts of the past; they are the screams of the living, of men who still endure the experience of solitary confinement.

As my review of the evolution of the penitentiary in the nineteenth century has shown, solitary confinement was inseparably linked to the disciplinary regime, both in principle and in the language of the penitentiary. Today, one would search in vain to find any reference to it in the statutes, the regulations, or the myriad directives that together form the legislative and administrative structure for penitentiary discipline. If we seek continuity in language in tracing what has become of solitary confinement we will conclude that it, like the cat-o'-nine-tails, has been cast aside as an agent of discipline. But to trust in language would be to err.[5]

In the modern language of the penitentiary, prisoners are not placed in solitary confinement; rather, they are put in 'dissociation.' Within the prison walls dissociation is also referred to as 'segregation,' and is known to prisoners everywhere in North America as 'the hole.'

A prisoner in a Canadian penitentiary may be dissociated under three broad categories. Under section 2.29 of the Penitentiary Service Regulations (which were introduced in 1962 to replace the 1933 regulations)[6] a prisoner who has been found guilty of a serious disciplinary offence may be sentenced to up to thirty days in dissociation. This is referred to in the regulations as 'punitive' dissociation. The other two categories of dissociation, which are referred to as 'non-punitive,' are provided for in section 2.30 of the regulations.[7] Because section 2.30 will be referred to a great deal, it is set out here in full:

(1) Where the institutional head is satisfied that

(a) for the maintenance of good order and discipline in the institution, or

(b) in the best interests of an inmate

it is necessary or desirable that the inmate should be kept from associating with other inmates, he may order the inmate to be dissociated accordingly, but the case of every inmate so dissociated shall be considered, not less than once each month, by the Classification Board for the purpose of recommending to the institutional head whether or not the inmate should be returned to association with other inmates.
(2) An inmate who has been dissociated is not considered under punishment unless he has been sentenced as such and he shall not be deprived of any of his privileges and amenities by reason thereof, except those privileges and amenities that

(a) can only be enjoyed in association with other inmates, or

(b) cannot reasonably be granted, having regard to the limitations of the dissociation area and the necessity for the effective operation thereof.

The two categories of non-punitive dissociation carried out under the authorization of this section are known as 'administrative segregation' and 'protective custody.' The latter category, as its name implies, is designed to protect the safety of the prisoner, and can be (and often is) applied for by the prisoner himself. Protective custody encompasses many sex offenders, informers, or other prisoners who run into trouble while in the general prison population and whose presence in the population is a threat to their own safety.

The number of prisoners in protective custody has escalated in the last ten years. The problems faced by men in protective custody are very real. However, in 90 per cent of the cases it is the prisoner himself who requests his dissociation from the general population. Moreover, those in protective custody are regarded by the penitentiary authorities as a distinct subpopulation and, generally speaking, are permitted to associate with each other in a separate part of the prison and, more recently, in special institutions designated for protective-custody cases. For these reasons I will not be focusing on the problems faced by these men.[8]

My focus is on the other category of dissociation authorized by section 2.30(1)(a), administrative segregation. The section authorizes the institutional head to dissociate a prisoner 'for the maintenance of good order and discipline in the institution,' and confers on the warden of a penitentiary a virtually untrammelled discretion over the lives of prisoners. For those prisoners who become the objects of its exercise it has given rise to a disciplinary regime which, while euphemistically termed 'administrative segregation,' represents a no less tyrannous regime than that which was so clearly condemned by the Brown Commission in 1850. It is a regime which in its continuation of solitary confinement harks back to the origins of the penitentiary and yet which, as it is practised, falsifies and adulterates every one of the principles John Howard espoused.

THE ORIGINS OF A PRISONERS' RIGHTS CASE: *McCANN* v. *THE QUEEN*

Jack Emmett McCann was kept in solitary confinement in the special correctional unit of the British Columbia Penitentiary under the authority of section 2.30(1)(a) from 23 July 1970 until 14 August 1972, a total of 754 days. In May 1973 Jack McCann escaped from the penitentiary. During his brief period of freedom he contacted a reporter for the *Vancouver Sun* and asked him to publicize the conditions under which men were kept in the special correctional unit for months and years at a time. After his recapture and return to the penitentiary on 1 June 1973 he was again placed in solitary confinement, where he remained until 9 May 1974. Shortly after his return to the penitentiary Jack McCann filed a handwritten statement of claim in the Trial Division of the Federal Court of Canada in which he claimed that he was 'being held arbitrarily in solitary confinement and [was] being subjected to cruel and unusual treatment and punishment.'[9] In the fall of 1973 I received a letter from Jack McCann and visited with him in the British Columbia Penitentiary, at which time he showed me a copy of the papers he had filed and told me of the conditions in which he was confined. What was remarkable about the interview was that he spent much of his time explaining the effect that these conditions of confinement had on other prisoners. He asked me if I would interview them and try to do something for them. In particular he asked me to interview Donald Oag, who was in the next cell. When I interviewed Oag I found a man who, after some nine months of continuous solitary confinement in which time he had received only a single visit, appeared almost as a disembodied spirit. His face was ashen, his voice not much above a whisper. I saw on him the marks of his isolation: terrible scars across his neck and on his wrists and arms – the frightful evidence of his suicide attempts.

It was clear to me that issues of great importance were raised by Jack McCann's statement of claim. It was also clear to me that the documents he had filed would receive short shrift in the courts. I undertook to research the issues he had raised and to approach the Legal Aid Society of British Columbia to have senior counsel appointed to litigate these issues. On the basis of that undertaking Jack McCann's statement of claim and the subsequent statement of claim filed on behalf of Donald Oag were adjourned. During the next six months, with the assistance of some very able law students, I researched the relevant law, paying particular attention to the development of prisoners' rights issues in the United States. After the completion of my research I met with the then director of the Legal Aid Society of British Columbia, Frank Maczko, who, in light of the important issues involved, agreed to issue a legal aid certificate to litigate the matter. On the understanding that I would continue to be involved in the interviewing of prisoners and in the preparation of the legal argument, Vancouver lawyers Bryan Williams and Don Sorochan agreed to act as counsel in the case.[10]

Arrangements were then made with the director of the British Columbia penitentiary to interview every prisoner confined in the special correctional unit. A decision was made to file a statement of claim on behalf of a selected group of prisoners whose cases collectively raised the full spectrum of issues to be brought before the court. The plaintiffs whose names appear on the statement of claim filed in the case of *McCann et al.* v. *The Queen and Dragan Cernetic*[11] include men who were regarded as the most dangerous prisoners in the Canadian penitentiary system.[12] Between 1970 and 1974 the seven plaintiffs named in the statement of claim had spent a staggering total of 11½ years in solitary confinement. Jack McCann spent

1,471 days in solitary; the longest continuous periods were 754 and 342 days. Walter Dudoward spent 106 days in solitary; the longest continuous period was 95 days. Ralph Cochrane was in solitary for 552 days; the longest continuous periods were 247 and 107 days. Jake Quiring spent one continuous period in solitary of 231 days. Donald Oag was in solitary for 682 days; the longest continuous period was 573 days. Andrew Bruce was in solitary for 793 days; the longest continuous periods were 338 and 258 days. Melvin Miller was in solitary confinement for 343 days; the longest continuous periods were 145 and 128 days.[13]

In their statement of claim the plaintiffs alleged that their confinement in the special correctional unit (hereafter referred to as SCU) under the purported authority of section 2.30(1) of the Penitentiary Service Regulations abrogated and infringed upon their right to freedom from cruel and unusual treatment or punishment under section 2(b) of the Canadian Bill of Rights;[14] that their confinement in SCU without notice of any charges laid against them and without a hearing before an impartial decision-maker deprived them of their right to a fair hearing in accordance with the principles of fundamental justice and in accordance with the rights guaranteed to them under sections 1(a) and 2(e) of the Canadian Bill of Rights; and that section 2.30(1) of the regulations, in purporting to authorize the director of the British Columbia Penitentiary to impose, at his absolute discretion, confinement of the plaintiffs in SCU, constituted an arbitrary detention and imprisonment and abrogated their rights under sections 1(a) and 2(a) of the Canadian Bill of Rights.

The statement of claim alleged breaches of the Penitentiary Service Regulations in relation to the denial of the monthly review of the plaintiffs' cases required by section 2.30(1); the denial of amenities and privileges protected by section 2.30(2); the denial of adequate facilities for personal health and hygiene protected by section 2.07;[15] and the denial of essential medical and dental care protected by section 2.06 of the regulations.[16] The plaintiffs further alleged that contrary to the provisions of the Criminal Code, tear gas had been used on them in situations where the use of such force was excessive and that high-powered rifles had been pointed at them in circumstances where there was no lawful justification for doing so. The plaintiffs also alleged that during their confinement in SCU, mentally ill prisoners had been confined in the unit with them and had not been provided with the necessary psychiatric treatment required by section 3.05 of the regulations.[17]

The principal relief sought by the plaintiffs was declaratory. They asked the federal court to declare that their confinement in SCU at the British Columbia Penitentiary subjected them to cruel and unusual treatment or punishment, and violated their rights to a fair hearing in accordance with the principles of fundamental justice.

The case came to trial in the Trial Division of the Federal Court of Canada on 19 February 1975. By this time all of the plaintiffs had been released from segregation and Donald Oag had been transferred to an institution in eastern Canada. The day before the trial started Oag was returned to Vancouver, but escaped when he arrived at Vancouver Airport. He was still at large when the court convened the next day. Counsel for the Department of Justice, representing the director of the British Columbia Penitentiary, advised the judge, Mr Justice Heald, that the penitentiary authorities were of the view that the presence of the plaintiffs as a group in open court posed a substantial security risk and that the plaintiffs should be admitted to the court one at a time for the purpose of giving their evidence. Counsel for the plaintiffs urged that such a procedure in effect denied the prisoners their right to participate fully in the trial, and argued that the court had no jurisdiction to bar prisoners in their capacity as plaintiffs from the court except upon the clearest demonstrated evidence that they were disturbing the proceedings and decorum of the court. In the course of argument, the director of the penitentiary and the sheriff appeared satisfied on the issue of security, provided that the plaintiffs remained in leg irons and manacles while they were in the courtroom. Mr Justice Heald ruled nevertheless that he was not satisfied; that as prisoners the plaintiffs had no common-law right to be present during the trial except for the purpose of giving their own evidence; and that under the Federal Court Rules the only power he had was to order them to appear as witnesses.[18] Counsel for the plaintiffs immediately indicated their intention to appeal this ruling to the Federal Court of Appeal.

The Federal Court of Appeal affirmed in somewhat modified form the trial judge's ruling.[19] Meanwhile negotiations commenced between counsel and the solicitor-general. An agreement was reached whereby the plaintiffs were issued temporary absence passes under section 26 of the Penitentiary Act[20] which permitted them to leave the penitentiary under escort for the purpose of appearing at the trial. In this, the first case in which a Canadian court heard extensive evidence from prisoners about conditions of solitary confinement, the presence of those prisoners in the courtroom was by sufferance of the penitentiary authorities, not by any admitted legal right.[21]

SOLITARY CONFINEMENT IN THE BRITISH COLUMBIA PENITENTIARY

The Conditions of Solitary Confinement

The description of the conditions of solitary confinement that follows is taken primarily from the plaintiffs' evidence given at trial, evidence that was accepted as credible by the trial judge.[22] It has been supplemented by my extensive interviews and correspondence with the plaintiffs.

Prisoners confined in administrative segregation in the British Columbia Penitentiary were held in a special unit which at the time of the McCann Trial was officially called the special correctional unit. Subsequently the unit became the 'super-maximum-security unit.' Because of its location atop one of the cell blocks it was known as 'the penthouse.' The unit was built in 1963 following a riot in the previous year, and consisted of four ranges of cells radiating in an H pattern from a small enclosed central courtyard. There were eleven cells in each range. One of the ranges was usually reserved for prisoners sentenced to punitive dissociation following a conviction in Warden's Court for a disciplinary offence. Another tier was designated as the psychiatric tier, and a third was reserved for protective-custody cases. While the protective cases were always kept separate, the lines of demarcation between the other three tiers were not strictly observed.[23]

The cells measured 11 feet by 6½ feet and consisted of three solid concrete walls and a solid steel door with a five-inch-square window which could only be opened from outside the cell. Inside the cell there was no proper bed. The prisoner slept on a cement slab four inches off the floor; the slab was covered by a sheet of plywood upon which was laid a four-inch-thick foam pad. Prisoners were provided with blankets, sheets, and a foam-rubber pillow. About two feet from the end of the sleeping platform against the back wall was a combination toilet and wash-basin. An institutional rule required that the prisoner sleep with his head away from the door and next to the toilet bowl to facilitate inspection of the prisoners by the guards. Failure to comply with this rule would result in guards throwing water on the bedding or kicking the cell door. There were no other furnishings in the cell. One of the expert witnesses described the physical space as 'one step above a strip cell ... a concrete vault in which people are buried.'[24]

The cell was illuminated by a light that burned twenty-four hours a day. The hundred-watt bulb was dimmed to twenty-five watts at night. Andy Bruce described it as being somewhat like the high and low beams of a car. The light was too bright to permit comfortable sleep and too dim to provide adequate illumination. Bruce told the court, 'You never get used to the light.'[25] Walter Dudoward testified that because of the continuous light, 'time didn't exist up there.'[26] The ventilation to the cells was provided by a vent placed high in the back wall. The prisoners testified that it was inadequate; in winter the cells were cold and in summer they were hot and humid. The space under the steel door admitted draughts, which caused the prisoners discomfort since they slept within six inches of the floor. Prisoners were denied all but the most limited personal effects; they were permitted to keep only those letters, books, and magazines that could be contained in one cardboard box. Canteen items were also restricted; prisoners were not allowed to have any items in metal or glass containers. Prisoners could not go to the library. Their privileges were limited to choosing from a sparse collection of paperbacks that were brought into the unit. Prisoners only had cold water in their cells. Twice a week they were given a cup of what was supposed to be hot water for shaving, but which, they testified, was usually lukewarm. They were not permitted to have their own razors, and one razor was shared among all the prisoners on the tier. This, they testified, resulted in the creation or aggravation of skin problems and allergic reactions.

Prisoners were confined in their concrete vaults for 23½ hours a day. They were allowed out of their cells briefly to pick up their meals from the tray at the entrance to the tier and for exercise. That exercise was not in the open air. It was limited to walking up and down the seventy-five-foot corridor in front of their cells. Exercise was taken under the continual supervision of an armed guard who patrolled on the elevated catwalk which ran the whole length of the tier and which was screened from the corridor by a wire-mesh fence. For the rest of the day prisoners were locked up in their cells. They had no opportunity to work; no hobby activities were deemed suitable by security for the special correctional unit; no television programs, no movies, no sports, and no calisthenics were permitted. Prisoners did have a radio panel, although its reception was restricted to two channels. Andy Bruce gave evidence that when he was in one of the observation cells of the unit (reserved for psychiatric cases) the radio was manipulated by the guards in the central control area and was left on for hours with nothing but static; or it was turned to the international band so that the only programs received were in languages foreign to the prisoners.

Prisoners in the unit were subject to a more restrictive visiting regime than the rest of the population. Prisoners spoke to visitors through a screen and conversations were monitored by the staff. No open visits were allowed, and prisoners never had an opportunity for personal contact with their families or for uncensored conversation with their visitors. Standard procedure governing the movement of prisoners from the unit to the visiting area decreed that they be handcuffed to a restraining belt around the waist and that leg-irons be placed on them. Upon returning from the visit, prisoners were subjected to skin-frisks, even though they may never have left the sight of the escorting officer or had any physical contact with their visitors.

The plaintiffs testified that they had great difficulty in obtaining professional medical attention. In Donald Oag's case, his detention in solitary confinement in Kingston Penitentiary had been a major contributing cause of his medical problem. The problem was aggravated by the inadequate treatment Oag received in solitary when he was transferred to the British Columbia Penitentiary. Oag testified that after the riot at Kingston Penitentiary in 1971 during which two prisoners were killed, he and other prisoners were convicted of manslaughter.[27] Immediately following the riot Oag and the other prisoners were taken to Millhaven. On arrival there, 'we were made to run a gauntlet of prison guards armed with baseball bats who beat on us as we passed through them. All of us were chained hand and feet and could do little to protect ourselves.'[28] Oag was placed in dissociation in Millhaven under section 2.30(1)(a) and remained there almost continuously until July 1972.

During this time I suffered severe mental and physical abuse. To give you one example, I was once placed in what is called a Chinese cell. At the time I was placed in this cell there was nothing in it but the bare walls and a hole in the floor for a toilet. I was confined in this cell for 30 days with no clothes, no shower or washing, no exercise and a restricted diet. I was also subjected to being sprayed with a chemical - mace - and given a physical beating. The reasons for this, I was told, was that the guards were not satisfied with the time I was given and were getting even. This was easy for them to do as I was in the hole and isolated. As a result of this I attempted suicide on numerous occasions. Finally I slashed myself so bad I passed out from loss of blood and had to be taken to an outside hospital for a blood transfusion. While I was receiving the transfusion I regained consciousness to see the hospital room full of prison guards. I was in a state of shock, thinking the prison guards were going to beat on me again. I jumped from my bed in fear and dove through a window. As a result of this I fell four floors, breaking my back in three places.[29]

On his transfer to the British Columbia Penitentiary Oag was placed in SCU. He testified that he had extreme difficulty in obtaining proper medication and treatment for his broken back, that prescribed medication was not received for weeks at a time, and that on one occasion when he was put on sleeping medication by the psychiatrist for fourteen days, he received it only on the last four days, having been refused it on the first ten days by the nurse, who was the main agent of communication and treatment in the unit. A back brace and an exerciser had also been prescribed for him. The original brace was made in the institution and was inadequate for its purpose. Months later a proper brace was supplied. The exerciser was never supplied because the staff felt that it constituted a security risk. Other prisoners testified that it would take days before their requests to see a doctor were granted. Jack McCann also testified that on occasions when prisoners slashed themselves the only treatment they received was in the form of bandages applied to the wounds. They were then returned to their cells.

The prisoners gave evidence that they had been confined in SCU with men who were clearly mentally ill but who were not segregated in separate facilities as required by section 3.05 of the regulations.[30] They further testified that these men were not given psychiatric treatment appropriate to their condition. Every one of the plaintiffs spoke of the cases of Tommy McCaulley and Jacques Bellemaire, neither of whom was included as a plaintiff in the court action. I had interviewed Tom McCaulley in the spring of 1974 in order to obtain a statement from him regarding his treatment in SCU. I was told by security officers that McCaulley was so dangerous and unpredictable they did not want to bring him down to the room I had been using for interviewing prisoners confined in the unit. Instead, arrangements were made for me to interview him in the unit itself. That interview took place in the tiny office located on one side of the main control area. I sat in the back of the office at a table, and McCaulley's seat was placed on the side of the table close to the door. The officer in charge told me that if McCaulley tried anything they would be able to get to him quickly, at least quickly enough so that he would not be able to hit me more than once or twice. McCaulley was escorted from his cell to the central control area by no fewer than six officers, all of whom kept their distance from him. He was shown to his seat in the office, and I told him who I was and why I was there. Although Jack McCann had told me that he had explained the lawsuit to McCaulley while they were out on exercise, McCaulley did not seem to understand what I was talking about. He responded to my questions about his treatment with assertions that the prison did not exist, that 'there was nobody down there.' I was unable to make much sense of his remarks. I concluded that Tommy McCaulley was so out of touch with reality that he could not properly instruct counsel with regard to his participation in the lawsuit.

The plaintiffs testified that McCaulley was quite normal when he had been in the population, but that after long periods in SCU he had gone over the edge of sanity, making it virtually impossible for the other prisoners to talk with him. They gave evidence that he would smash his fists on the steel door of his cell and scream at the guards for hours on end. On occasions when I was in the unit I heard McCaulley screaming; when I walked back to the main gate of the penitentiary five storeys below I could still hear his screams and his banging. Guards in SCU told me that McCaulley would lose control completely and would smear himself and his cell with faeces. The psychiatrist at the penitentiary, Dr Muthana, gave evidence at the trial that McCaulley was psychotic and that he exhibited symptoms of schizophrenia and autistic behaviour with disturbance of affect and thought disorder. Dr Muthana agreed that McCaulley was in great need of psychiatric help and that the facilities in the SCU for people in his state were 'atrocious.' He conceded that he could not think of anything less adequate for McCaulley than solitary confinement in SCU.[31]

The plaintiffs also all referred to Jacques Bellemaire. They testified that while in SCU Bellemaire developed a delusion that there was a 'machine' in his cell which was trying to get him. Andy Bruce recounted an incident in which Bellemaire, while out of his tier on exercise, came to Bruce's window and told him that a 'machine' had held him while Bruce was slashing his arms with razor blades. Bruce asked him to show him the cuts and Bellemaire pointed to various places on his arms. As Bruce put it, 'I guess they were there to him but there was nothing there that I could see'[32] The terror of Bellemaire's delusions became so overwhelming that he set fire to his cell in order to rid himself of the 'machine.' Mel Miller gave evidence that he had written to the solicitor-general stating that Bellemaire was not fit to be in solitary confinement. He testified that he had shown his letter and the solicitor-general's reply to the director, and that he had told the psychiatrist that unless Bellemaire was released he would die in solitary.

I interviewed Jacques Bellemaire in May 1974. Bellemaire spoke little English and I arranged to interview him again with a French interpreter. He told me of the machine in his cell that was trying to destroy him. On the occasions that I saw Bellemaire he appeared to be a man utterly without hope. Whereas the lawsuit was seen by other prisoners in SCU as a prospect for change, its initiation seemed to offer no comfort to Jacques Bellemaire. Five days after my last interview with him, Bellemaire hanged himself in solitary confinement. Andy Bruce was in the cell next to Bellemaire when he died.

> He didn't actually hang himself. He just tied that thing around his neck and just laid down and died and that was it, and then after he died [the nurse] came up there, just the way they hauled him out, it got me really hot. They just threw him on a blanket and dragged him off the tier, and left the guy's legs and arms dragging along the floor. I was screaming at them about that.[33]

Jack McCann testified that just before Bellemaire hanged himself he told McCann, 'the machine says I am dying today.'

It should have become apparent that the conditions of solitary confinement in SCU extended beyond the physical dimensions of imprisonment, harsh as they were. Dr Stephen Fox, one of the expert witnesses called by the plaintiffs, told the court, 'it takes more than just a concrete vault to make it what it is ... It is not the case that the physical facility alone constitutes the pain and suffering ... To understand the extent of the cruelty [we must consider] the administrative environment and the security environment.'[34]

The special correctional unit is different from the rest of the penitentiary in ways that go beyond the physical differences in the cells, the denial of access to work and hobbies, and the restrictions on exercise. The separation from the ordinary prison world is marked by more than the presence of another set of locked doors. In SCU the worst things about prisons – the humiliation and degradation of the prisoners, the frustration, the despair, the loneliness, and the deep sense of antagonism between the prisoners and the guards – are intensified. The distinctiveness of SCU is palpable. At the trial, the prisoners tried to describe to the court some of the manifestations of the distinctive atmosphere of SCU. Typically, their descriptions related to the nature of their interaction with the guards because it is in that relationship that much of the desperation and hostility of the place is concentrated.

The plaintiffs described the procedure that took place when they left their cells for their exercise period or to pick up their meals. In addition to the two guards posted outside the row of cells, a third guard armed with a rifle was stationed on the catwalk. As the prisoners walked the tier, certain guards would always follow them with their rifles pointed in the direction of the prisoners, sometimes at their heads. The guards would 'click the hammers' of the guns, even though the prisoners were totally confined within their tier and separated from the guards by a locked door at the end of the corridor and by the wire mesh on the catwalk. Several of the plaintiffs testified that the constant presence of an armed guard conveyed to them that they were perceived as always dangerous, and the prisoners then responded in ways that amounted to a self-fulfilling prophecy. Ralph Cochrane told the court, 'they use psychology on you. They try to mold individuals to react their way because it justifies their concept. They play this brain-washing game.'[35]

Jake Quiring, in speaking of the 'game' he perceived the guards to be playing, voiced a sentiment that could well have emanated from one of Inspector Moylan's annual reports: 'You've got to have justice but all that anybody understands here is violence.'[36]

There is a perverse symbiotic relationship between guards and prisoners in SCU.[37] The guards, by perceiving the prisoners as the most dangerous and violent of men, can justify to themselves the intensity of the surveillance and the rigours of detention. Prisoners, by responding to that perception of dangerousness with acts of defiance, have at least one avenue of asserting their individuality and their autonomy, of making manifest their refusal to submit.[38] The treadwheels of the nineteenth-century penitentiaries are no longer with us, but in SCU we have created a psychological treadmill put into motion and maintained by ever-increasing hostility and recrimination.[39]

The plaintiffs gave evidence of acts of harassment and humiliation practised on them by the guards which bespeak the extent to which the normal and admittedly hostile relationship between guards and prisoners was magnified to the level of gratuitous cruelty. Jack McCann described how, on returning from visits, he would be skin-frisked in the central control area of the SCU in front of as many as eight guards. He was made to strip, open his mouth, lift up his testicles, and spread his buttocks while officers made degrading and humiliating remarks. He told the court of an officer who came down to his cell after another prisoner had slashed himself and asked McCann if he would like a razor-blade so that he could 'slash up' and join his friend. McCann and other prisoners described provocative acts directed at Tommy McCaulley, such as throwing hot water on him or goading him on the rare occasions when he was sitting quietly in his cell. They gave evidence of guards waking them up in the middle of the night by kicking on the steel doors.[40]

The plaintiffs related incidents in which they were subjected to the unwarranted and unauthorized use of tear gas.[41] Both Bruce and McCann gave evidence of an incident that occurred in September 1970 when they and other prisoners were banging on the bars of the cells because a prisoner who was an epileptic was not answering calls. The prisoners tried to attract the attention of the officer on duty to ask him to go down to the man's cell. The officer came, opened Bruce's window, and sprayed him in the face with gas. Bruce testified that he immediately hit the floor and then staggered over to the sink, trying to splash water on his face to get rid of the gas. Subsequently he developed a severe rash, his skin peeled, and he suffered itching and swelling of his face for a considerable time thereafter. His blankets, which were impregnated with the gas, were not changed, nor were his clothes. Miller gave evidence of a gassing incident that took place in 1973. Miller was on a regime in which he was sleeping during the day so as to minimize his contact with the guards. As he was sleeping, he felt he was being smothered. He woke up to find that his eyes were running and that his cell was full of tear gas. He called out and a guard came down. Miller was told by other guards that an officer had accidentally discharged the gas. Miller testified that only his cell was affected and that the gas lingered on for four or five days. Even though it was admitted to be an accidental gassing, he was kept in the same cell and his bedding was not changed. Evidence was also given at trial of several incidents of gassing which the director of the institution acknowledged were not justified by the commissioner's directives. One of these incidents, recorded in the 'unusual incidents diary,'[42] reads, 'Inmate 5232 Augustine refused oral medication from hospital officer, refused needle, gas used and inmate given needle.' A former guard called by the plaintiffs testified that while he was working in SCU another guard sprayed gas in a prisoner's face 'as a lesson for the future.' It would be an idle question to ask whether that 'lesson for the future' has anything to do with John Howard's vision of the pedagogy of penitentiary discipline.[43]

The Criteria and Process of Confinement

I have suggested that in order to understand the conditions of solitary confinement it is necessary to consider more than just the physical dimensions of confinement. Of particular importance are the process by which prisoners are placed in solitary and the process by which they are released. I have described how those who designed the original model of penitentiary discipline perceived the necessity for the regime to be governed by rules that would render accountable the hitherto unregulated discretion of the keeper and would also demonstrate to the prisoner the justice of his sentence and punishment. To ask how fair and free from arbitrariness is the process whereby prisoners are placed in and released from solitary throws us back to the original ideals of the penitentiary; yet, since fairness and freedom from arbitrariness are touchstones of legality enshrined in the Canadian Bill of Rights (and now in the Canadian Charter of Rights and Freedoms), the question provides us with a framework of inquiry relevant and essential to the continuing legitimacy of penitentiary discipline.

In the *McCann* case the plaintiffs gave evidence of being placed in solitary confinement without any notice of the grounds for dissociation and without any hearing at which evidence was presented against them or opportunity given for them to challenge the case against them or to make representations on their own behalf. They also testified that they had no knowledge of any monthly review such as that required by section 2.30. Jack McCann and Ralph Cochrane both testified as to the manner of their confinement in SCU in December 1972. McCann described the process in a letter written while he was still in solitary:

> On December 18, 1972, we [McCann and five other prisoners] were taken from our cells and put in the Special Correction Unit. We were not told as to why this action was taken. On December 19 there were certain statements made on [a] radio station where five of our names were mentioned and some derogatory remarks and allegations were made. The following three days, various news journals ... contained statements given to them by the Director of the BC

Penitentiary ... pertaining to the fact that an inmate had been found to have acertain amount of weapons in his possession and that a certain number of inmates had been put in segregation, as it was thought there was an alleged conspiracy by these inmates ... These articles were our only indication as to why we may have been segregated. On Friday afternoon, December 22, two senior staff members spoke to us individually and the only thing they said was that they were holding an investigation and asked us if we had anything to say. We were not told what the investigation was about or if any of us were supposed to be involved in any way. Later on that same day an inmate ... was put in the same tier as the rest of us. It was at this time through him that we learned that it was he who was caught with the weapons and that the rest of us were all suspected of somehow being involved with him ... By this time, although we still had not been told anything by officials, we had no choice but to assume that it is we six to whom the articles in the news journals refer. By the manner in which these articles appeared in the newspapers, the Director was already under the assumption that the six of us had conspired to escape. This was before there was even an investigation. We adamantly deny the assumed allegation. We have now been held in segregation since December 18 without the benefit of a hearing, the laying of any charges or the production of any kind of evidence. This type of action is a denial of natural justice and to my belief, against the Canadian Bill of Rights. We are under severe mental stress not knowing what is going on and this unusual and unjust treatment amounts to conviction without trial. On Tuesday January 9, 1973, a senior staff member told [the other inmate] that the rcmp would be out to see him and that he was to be charged in outside court.[44]

Jack McCann and Ralph Cochrane were kept in SCU until 21 February 1973. At no time were they given a hearing or confronted with the reasons for their confinement. The sense of injustice they felt at this process can be seen not only from McCann's letter but also from the seventeen-day hunger strike which they went on over the Christmas holidays to assert their innocence and protest their detention without a hearing.

Dr Richard Korn compared the process by which a prisoner enters the general prison society with that involved in entering SCU: 'He enters the general prison society as a result of a hearing in a court of law. The charges are specific, he has an opportunity to present his own case, to cross-examine witnesses, all of the rights and amenities that are provided under the presumption of innocence ... In general if a prisoner has had a fair trial, he will accept the process of getting to prison.'[45] The process of entering administrative dissociation is bereft of these features of due process. In recounting their experiences with entering dissociation under section 2.30, all of the plaintiffs expressed their sense of injustice and of the illegitimacy of the process.

Section 2.30(1)(a) authorizes dissociation on the vaguest of criteria – 'the maintenance of good order and discipline in the institution.' Since these words are no more than a restatement of the overall responsibility of the head of the institution, they really provide no guidelines or criteria for the drastic restraint placed on a prisoner's liberty by confining him in SCU. Not only are there no articulated criteria within section 2.30 against which to measure the detention or release of an SCU prisoner, but the evidence given by the director and the head of security concerning the reasons for detention and release for the plaintiffs did not reveal any consistent standards. Rather, the evidence suggested that the decision to place a man in solitary is made on the basis of rumours, hunches, and intangible feelings based on the prisoner's past reputation or his present attitude. Dr Korn described the process of admission to and release from SCU as 'highly capricious, arbitrary and in its design and effect ... [it] is mystifying and to me fails to satisfy any human criterion of predictable process.'[46]

The following case studies are designed to elaborate on the nature of the process leading to and from administrative dissociation. They will provide the data against which to measure how far we have progressed in achieving the penitentiary's original goals of circumscribing the unbridled discretion of the keeper and demonstrating to prisoners the justice of carceral power.

The Case of Donald Oag

On his transfer to the British Columbia Penitentiary in January 1973 from Millhaven, Donald Oag was placed in the special correctional unit. At that time a notation was made in the unusual-incidents diary that on his way to British Columbia he had tried to stab one of the airline stewardesses with a fork. Oag gave evidence that he was told sometime after his transfer to the penitentiary that he was being held in SCU because of this alleged attempted stabbing. When I interviewed Donald Oag in the fall of 1973 he adamantly denied that this incident had ever taken place. He told me that prior to boarding the plane he had been given a sedative and remained under sedation for the entire journey. I pursued the matter and was told by a member of the classification staff that the stabbing incident was the reason for Oag's confinement in SCU. I wrote to the penitentiary authorities requesting that proper inquiry be made into this allegation. That inquiry substantiated Donald Oag's assertions; the alleged stabbing had never taken place. The allegation was removed from Oag's file, but he was not released from SCU. At the trial, the assistant director of security said that Oag was not released because of a 'value judgment that his attitude towards incarceration was not satisfactory.'[47]

Further evidence of the unprincipled and arbitrary nature of the decision to place a man in dissociation can be seen from the evidence relating to Oag's reviews in 1974. The assistant director of security testified that, prior to 1974, he received a weekly report from the officer in charge of SCU which he forwarded to the inmate-training board. That board, which met weekly, would review the report, and any comments made about a particular prisoner would be entered in the prisoner's file to constitute what was termed at the trial 'the running score.' However, there was no formal monthly review of each prisoner by the board, and it was left to the initiative of the chairman of the board, classification officers, or other staff to suggest such a review. When Mr Dragan Cernetic became director of the penitentiary in January 1974 he set up a new procedure whereby a subcommittee consisting of classification and security staff reviewed each case on a monthly basis and presented its report to the inmate-training board for consideration.

Early in 1974 Oag had been charged in outside court with stabbing another prisoner while in SCU. In February, the inmate-training board stated that Oag was required to remain confined under section 2.30(1)(a) pending the disposition of his criminal trial. In March, the review committee recommended that Oag remain in SCU pending the outcome of the criminal trial. In April and May the committee reported that Oag did not present a behaviour problem and that he accepted that he must remain in SCU until his trial. After the May review Oag was acquitted of the stabbing, but was not released from SCU. Subsequent entries in Oag's running score show that he had protested his continued detention, been 'disrespectful' to the guards, and developed 'behaviour problems.' These entries provided new reasons for keeping him in SCU. Using a prisoner's justifiable protest at not being released as the reason for further dissociation constitutes a Catch-22 for the prisoner in SCU.

The Case of Jack McCann

Jack McCann was confined in SCU from July 1970 until August 1972. For long periods during this time his running score indicated that he was 'quiet and co-operative.' The July, August, September, October, November, December, and January reports all used that terminology. However, McCann was not released. In fact, his 'quiet and co-operative' behaviour was not even perceived in a positive way; a January 1971 entry describes him as 'quiet and co-operative but this attitude might belie the mental activity which could take a devious route.'[48]

It is clear that neither Jack McCann's behaviour nor his attitude in SCU was the determining factor in his release. Rather, his generally perceived 'dangerousness' was seen as inconsistent with release to the population.

Indeed, in one of my first interviews with the assistant director of security I was told that McCann would never leave dissociation as long as the assistant director was in charge.

The Case of Ralph Cochrane

Ralph Cochrane was transferred from the British Columbia Penitentiary to Dorchester Penitentiary shortly after a prison disturbance in October 1973.[49] Just prior to his transfer Cochrane had spoken to two members of parliament who had come to the prison at the request of the inmate committee. The assistant director of security, Mr Leech, gave evidence at the trial that he suspected Cochrane had some influence in the institution and that it was in the interest of good order for him to be removed at a time of disturbance and unrest. He was transferred back to the British Columbia Penitentiary in January 1974 and was immediately placed in SCU under section 2.30(1)(a). Under cross-examination, Mr Leech conceded that Cochrane was placed in SCU at that time because Mr Leech 'could not prove beyond a reasonable doubt that Cochrane was not involved in the original disturbance.'[50] Cochrane remained in dissociation for three months. He was put into dissociation again in July 1974 following his escape from the penitentiary in a refrigerated truck. The director, Mr Cernetic, gave evidence that although he had told Cochrane that he would remain in SCU pending the outcome of his charges of escape, the real reason he had placed Cochrane in solitary confinement was to protect him from penitentiary staff who had been acutely embarrassed by the manner of his escape. Mr Cernetic stated that he felt that after Cochrane's trial and conviction there would be no reason for the staff to be angry with Cochrane. However, if we accept the protection of Cochrane as a legitimate purpose, placing him in SCU seems the least likely way to assure that protection, given that in SCU the guards would be able to vent their resentment free from the scrutiny of the rest of the population and with relative immunity from censure. This rationale for detention would also lead to the logical conclusion that, had Cochrane been acquitted of the escape, Mr Cernetic would have been forced to keep him in SCU, because Cochrane would certainly have been exposed to harassment on his return to the population by guards who would have felt that he had not received his just deserts.

The Cases of Andy Bruce and Jake Quiring

Andy Bruce was confined in SCU on his transfer from Prince Albert pending the resolution of criminal charges arising from his taking of hostages in Prince Albert.[51] Mr Cernetic stated that Bruce was placed in dissociation because he was very frustrated, and it was felt that if he was released into the population while the court case was pending, he might try to escape. However, as was brought out in Mr Cernetic's cross-examination, there is a dubious logic to this reasoning. Keeping Bruce in SCU undoubtedly made it more difficult for him to communicate with his lawyers, a fact which Bruce testified increased rather than alleviated his frustration.

It would seem to follow, however, from Mr Cernetic's stated reasons for keeping Bruce in dissociation that it was not the nature of the charges outstanding against a prisoner that kept him in dissociation but rather his attitude toward those charges. We can test the consistency of that rationale. At the same time that Bruce was detained in SCU, Jake Quiring, who had also been involved in the Prince Albert hostage-taking, was also kept in dissociation. Yet Mr Cernetic conceded that there was no evidence of frustration on the part of Quiring, and Mr Leech testified that Quiring, while in SCU, was 'above average' in his behaviour. It would seem to follow that the reasons Mr Cernetic gave for keeping Bruce in SCU would have required Quiring's release. Quiring was not released. The unprincipled nature of Quiring's detention was compounded by the fact that even after the disposition of his charges he was still not released. More than one month after that disposition, he was finally permitted to come back into the population.

Although the prison officials had cited pending charges as the reason for retaining Oag, Bruce, Quiring, Cochrane, and at times McCann in SCU, the plaintiffs gave evidence and it was admitted by Mr Leech that other prisoners with charges of the most serious nature pending against them had been released from SCU into the population before the final disposition of their cases. During the period the plaintiffs were in SCU, two prisoners who were facing charges of escape from lawful custody, possession of dangerous weapons, and attempted murder arising from a shoot-out with sheriff's officers were dissociated for only part of the time prior to their trial. These men were facing charges far more serious than those against Cochrane, Oag, or McCann and as serious as those against Quiring and Bruce, yet they were not subjected to the same treatment as the plaintiffs. No satisfactory explanation was given by Mr Cernetic or Mr Leech of the inconsistency in the application of the rationale of 'dissociation pending outstanding charges.'[52]

Like the process and rationale of placement in and release from solitary confinement, the security regime under which prisoners live while in solitary is unprincipled and inconsistent. Jack McCann gave evidence that while Officer Mangleson was in charge of SCU he had allowed prisoners extended exercise periods. The officer's practice was to permit prisoners to exercise both in the morning and in the afternoon if they so desired. Some prisoners chose to sleep in the morning and exercise in the afternoon. When Officers Carrier and Berrie took command, they reduced the exercise period to half an hour without any prior notice or explanation. On the first morning of the unannounced new regime several of the prisoners chose to sleep in and wait for the afternoon exercise. However, Officers Carrier and Berrie refused to let anyone exercise in the afternoon, saying that everyone had been given the half-hour opportunity in the morning. When the prisoners protested by shouting and banging on their cell doors, several of them were gassed.

George Brown, a witness called by the plaintiffs, gave evidence that while he was in SCU he asked for a special razor to shave, since he had a skin condition and had received a special permit from the prison doctor to use a Trak II razor rather than the normal razor issued in SCU. Because he had not been provided with the special razor he had not shaved and had grown a beard. The officer in charge of SCU, citing a rule that prisoners were not allowed to have beards, ordered Brown to shave with a normal razor. When he refused, Brown was handcuffed, dragged out of his cell, and laid on a table in the central control area where, with six officers holding him, he was forcibly shaved. In the process he suffered severe cuts on his throat, causing profuse bleeding. Charges of assault were laid against the officers concerned, and they were convicted of those charges in provincial court.[53]

At the very time when George Brown was being ordered to shave, at the very time when he was strapped to the table and a razor taken to his face, SCU prisoners McCann, Miller, and McCaulley were wearing full beards.[54] McCann gave evidence that he had never been given an order to shave prior to the Brown incident, and Miller was still wearing a beard when he gave his evidence.[55]

Administrative Dissociation - Punishment or Treatment?

Section 2.30(2) of the penitentiary service regulations states:

> An inmate who has been dissociated is not considered under punishment unless he has been sentenced to such, and he shall not be deprived of any of his privileges and amenities by reason thereof, except those privileges and amenities that,
> (a) can only be enjoyed in association with other inmates, or
> (b) cannot reasonably be granted having regard to the limitations of the dissociation area and the necessity for the effective operation thereof.

Because of the very restrictive interpretation given by the security staff at the British Columbia Penitentiary to subparagraph (b), prisoners in SCU were deprived of all the privileges and amenities enjoyed by other prisoners in relation to matters such as hobbies work, exercise, and other programs. With few exceptions, the regime under which they lived was identical to that imposed on prisoners who had been sentenced to punitive dissociation under section 2.29 of the regulations for a serious disciplinary offence. Prisoners in punitive dissociation were additionally deprived in that they had no radios, were not allowed tobacco or reading materials, did not receive desserts with their meals, and had their bedding removed from the cell during the day.

While there is little difference between the physical conditions of punitive and non-punitive dissociation, there are substantial differences between the process by which prisoners enter the two regimes and the duration of their stay. Under section 2.29 and relevant commissioners' directives,[56] the prisoner can only be placed in punitive dissociation when he has been sentenced at a disciplinary hearing. The prisoner must be given written notice of the disciplinary charge; he has the right to cross-examine and present evidence at the hearing; and the decision is required to be based on evidence that establishes guilt beyond a reasonable doubt. As I have shown in another study,[57] in its actual operation this model of procedural due process is subject to serious flaws, but there is at least an opportunity for the prisoner to know what he is accused of and on what basis he is to be judged guilty. There is no such similar procedural opportunity available to a prisoner prior to being placed in administrative dissociation.

These procedural differences in the way prisoners enter administrative and punitive dissociation are important, but even more fundamental is the difference in the extent of confinement. Under section 2.29 a prisoner cannot be sentenced to more than thirty days in punitive dissociation; it is therefore a finite punishment. Administrative dissociation under section 2.30 is subject to no such limitation. It is potentially infinite in its duration up to the expiry of the prisoner's sentence. As we shall see when analysing the effects of administrative dissociation on the prisoners, this infinite duration occupies a conspicuous place in the catalogue of terror.

All of the plaintiffs gave evidence that they viewed dissociation under section 2.30(1)(a) as a punishment; indeed, because of its indefinite duration, it was seen as a much more severe punishment than punitive dissociation. This is how Andy Bruce put it:

> [Punitive dissociation]'s easier, it's a hell of a lot easier when you know when you're getting out, you got a date in your mind and you know that's when you're going to be released and you're going to go back to the population. When you're doing indefinite seg. it just hangs over your head. You don't know what you're

supposed to do to get out of there because there is nothing you can do. It's entirely up to them. They say it depends on your behaviour but there's nothing you can do. You can't do nothing except get worse, and when you do get worse, they say that's why you're up there.[58]

It is not only the prisoners who perceive administrative dissociation as a punitive measure. Evidence was given at trial of two practices that strongly suggest that the authorities, despite section 2.30(2), also see it as a punishment. First, prisoners suspected of having committed some disciplinary offence were placed in SCU under section 2.30 instead of being charged with an offence and tried in a disciplinary hearing in accordance with section 2.29. This practice in effect enables the institution to punish alleged disciplinary offences without giving the prisoner the benefit of a trial or hearing and permits the imposition of a sentence of dissociation far in excess of that permitted under section 2.29.

The second practice was the extension of a punishment of dissociation that has been duly imposed by a disciplinary court for an offence under section 2.29 by keeping the prisoner in dissociation under section 2.30(1)(a) on the expiry of his section 2.29 sentence. In practical terms this meant that the prisoner, on the expiry of his definite sentence under section 2.29, was taken out of F tier and placed in H tier for a further indefinite sentence, which was not preceded by any formal charge or hearing.

The evidence of Walter Dudoward showed that he was the victim of the tyranny of both these practices in 1973. Dudoward testified that he was on the inmate committee seeking to negotiate with the institutional authorities for better conditions in the British Columbia Penitentiary (including the conditions in SCU). When these negotiations broke down, a serious disturbance occurred in the penitentiary and Dudoward, along with all other members of the inmate committee, was placed in dissociation under section 2.30(1)(a). At no time was he charged with an institutional offence or given any hearing. He was in dissociation from 3 October until 29 November 1973. On that date Dudoward received a sentence of thirty days' punitive dissociation following a hearing on a disciplinary charge resulting from an incident involving himself and a guard. At the end of that sentence of dissociation, he was moved from F tier to H tier and maintained in dissociation under section 2.30(1)(a), where he remained until the end of March 1974. The assistant director of security, Mr Leech, said that Dudoward was kept in SCU because, while Dudoward was serving his sentence of thirty days punitive dissociation, information came to Mr Leech that a hand-gun was going to be brought into the institution by one of the staff; Dudoward was to receive the gun for the purpose of assassinating two of the guards should the opportunity arise. Mr Leech testified that the RCMP were contacted and that they conducted an investigation. However, no criminal charges were ever brought against Dudoward for conspiracy to escape or to possess weapons, and no internal disciplinary charges were filed. He was simply kept in SCU for a further four months under section 2.30. The director, Mr Cernetic, stated in his evidence that before he came to the penitentiary as director he had known Walter Dudoward and that there was nothing in his record or in his institutional behaviour to suggest that he was the type of prisoner who would be involved in such a desperate plot. Mr Cernetic, in fact, ordered Dudoward's release from dissociation at the first available opportunity after he became director.[59]

The Effects of Solitary Confinement

The full effects of placing prisoners in solitary confinement for long periods of time are not easily understood. Indeed, in this area many of our normal methodologies for assessing effects on behaviour fall to the ground. Since very few of us have ever been placed in a situation remotely analogous to that in which prisoners in solitary confinement find themselves, we cannot use the valuable lessons of our own experience. If we turn to science we find - and I will elaborate on this later - that 'there are few reports in the scientific literature on sensory deprivation among prisoners. Most of the studies that are available have used volunteer subjects and have been of relatively short duration. Few adverse effects have been reported in these studies and there are no reports on the effects of long term confinement.'[60]

The task of understanding the effects of dissociation is also complicated by a tendency to focus on the physical conditions of confinement. This tendency is part of our general perception of imprisonment as above all else a physical punishment. The tendency is compounded among those who gravitate to the study and practice of criminal law because the law is concerned primarily with physical harms to the person, to property, or to public order. In the world of lawyers, therefore, the points of reference for crime and punishment are primarily physical. However, in the world of letters there is a rich literature which conceives of crime and punishment in ways that focus on the psychological dimensions of suffering. As I will endeavour to show, Dostoevsky is a surer guide than Glanville Williams in understanding what it is that we do, in the name of the criminal law, when we send men to the solitary-confinement cells.

The importance of understanding the effects of solitary confinement in terms beyond the physical was recognized by the study group on dissociation appointed in 1975 by the federal solicitor-general to consider 'the usefulness of dissociation as a method of punishment, the effectiveness of dissociation as a means of protecting inmates, and the living conditions that exist in both types of dissociation from the point of view of humane treatment and the negative effects of prolonged isolation.'[61] The study group found that 'most segregated inmates complained more about the manner in which they were treated than the physical conditions in which they lived,' and that 'the physical milieu is not as crucial to the inmate as the psychological.'[62] Having noted the lack of adequate scientific studies on long-term dissociation, the study group set out the factors they felt were likely to affect the degree to which segregation was detrimental to a prisoner: the reason for being segregated; the process by which the prisoner is segregated; the physical facilities and routine; the lack of contact with staff and other prisoners; the length of the period of segregation; the uncertainty as to when a prisoner will be released; and the process by which the prisoner is returned to the population. The study group devoted just three pages of its report to an elaboration of these factors.[63] During the *McCann* case some four weeks of evidence was given, much of it relating to the effects of solitary confinement. In fact, the evidence of the plaintiffs and their expert witnesses constitutes the largest body of data so far assembled for the purpose of documenting the effects of long-term segregation. Dr Richard Korn, in his evidence, said that in light of the hiatus in the scientific literature, 'there are no experts other than the prisoners ... This is the only evidence available to science.'[64]

Before turning to the evidence of the prisoners, however, something should be said about that evidence. Mr Justice Heald stated in his judgment that he accepted the plaintiffs' account of the effects on them of the conditions in SCU. Despite this finding, it may occur to some readers that perhaps it was in the plaintiffs' interests to paint the bleakest possible picture of life in solitary confinement. It is important to understand the price paid by the plaintiffs in giving evidence at this trial. The plaintiffs, in seeking to make the court understand the full horror of their confinement, had to relive their experiences in solitary. Jack McCann and Mel Miller broke down in the court under the strain of that remembrance. It was not an easy thing for prisoners to admit in front of the guards with whom they would go back to the prison that the solitary confinement experience broke them down. Such an admission is easily interpreted as a sign of weakness, and for many prisoners in the super-macho society of maximum security, weakness must never be shown in front of penitentiary staff. Such is the nature of the relationship between the keeper and the kept. But some of these plaintiffs, in an effort to avoid the continuation of what they believed to be a barbarous system, were prepared to admit in front of their guards that they could be brought to tears when they recalled and relived what had been done to them and to their friends in solitary.

The plaintiffs faced another great difficulty in presenting their evidence. They were talking about events quite beyond the experience of the man who was being asked to pass judgment on those events. Hermann Hesse has eloquently captured their dilemma:

> To express in words something that refuses to be put into words ... what gives these experiences their weight and persuasiveness is not their truth ... but their reality. They are tremendously real, somewhat the way a violent physical pain or a surprising natural event, a storm or earthquake, seem to us charged with an entirely different sort of reality, presence, inexorability, from ordinary times and conditions.[65]

With these matters firmly in mind we can now consider how the plaintiffs explained the effects of solitary confinement.

Andy Bruce described the hallucinations he suffered during the two-year period in which he was in solitary: 'You see things and people you know aren't there. You try to tell yourself it isn't happening.'[66] He spoke of a recurring dream in which he picked up a book and read several hundred pages, of going to sleep and waking to find himself reading the pages again and wondering whether he had ever read them in the first place. After a while the distortion of reality 'gets a hold of you,' and it became clear to him that he was going 'stir-bugs.' When he was in solitary he found it impossible to concentrate. People's speech made no sense to him. Words would come at him, but they were separate, they did not hang together. When reading, he said he would 'read half a sentence and then chase the rest of the sentence around the page.'[67] He gave evidence that when Tommy McCaulley 'went to pieces, I went a little crazy too, because I saw what it was doing to my friends.'[68] He said that he saw himself starting to slide and that he slashed himself on several occasions.

When Andy Bruce was asked how he coped with being in solitary, his answer had a chilling ring to it: 'It was strictly a hate score. You get twisted about it, your frustration turns to hate towards the guards and all the people who keep you there.'[69] For Andy Bruce this sustaining force of hatred was something he took with him during his brief return to the population.

> You start hating a lot, that's the only way I kept it away from me, you know, going buggy. That was really the big reason why I couldn't function when I got down [in the population] because after being up there for so long, and like I say, you got to hate, you got to hate them all the time, and you come down to the population and you know it's just a completely different scene, you just can't get along, it seems you can't get along unless you're hating somebody, unless you're

really bitter, like I couldn't get along, conversations and stuff like that, I couldn't fit into them and people talk to you and that, and I just couldn't handle it. So used to just being bitter.[70]

Ralph Cochrane and Walter Dudoward also described the build-up of hatred and bitterness while in SCU. Even after his release, Cochrane told the court, 'my feelings of hostility will never leave, but I fight it because I realize my own bed of bitterness can destroy me.'[71] Cochrane described for the court how in SCU his 'sense of time deteriorated, action became slowed down, awkward, mumbling, everything became dull, nothing alive happened up there.'[72] Dudoward said he became very paranoid and found himself 'spinning.' He coped with solitary 'by just negative feeling, by hating.'[73] Dudoward talked of the continuing torment he endured after coming down from solitary. The noise of Tommy McCaulley banging on the cell door was a constant reminder of what was happening up in SCU. He said that the hatred and the bitterness still remained with him and had given rise to a deep resentment of authority which, notwithstanding his criminal record, had never been there prior to his experience in SCU.[74]

Jake Quiring told the court that after months in solitary he became very 'emotional' and felt that he was out of control.[75] Melvin Miller told the court that after a time in solitary he would see holes in the cement wall start to move around the cell; that in solitary, 'except when you have visits, you never get to see the grass or the sun. The only way you know it's raining is by the sound of the rain on the roof.' Unlike their predecessors in history – the men in solitary in Pentonville Penitentiary – prisoners in SCU are denied the privilege of seeing the clouds scud across the sky in front of the moon. Miller described the effect solitary had on him.

If I put myself back to the circumstances I'm afraid I'm going to offend you. I'm afraid you won't understand. How in hell do you cope with loneliness in a god-damned cell 23½ hours a day with the light burning on you. You get severe headaches. You feel hate, frustration. I can't say just how fucking bad this is and the effects it has on other prisoners. You see people slash themselves and the guards say he's just looking for attention. Beat me, break my arms, I can handle that. But how do you cope with insanity? You have no idea in the world the effects it has on you. I've known of men who beat their heads against the wall. You don't have anything. You don't know how long you'll be there. You have no reasons ... I've been down [from scu] for 20 days and I can still see that goddamn light.[76]

Melvin Miller's plea against solitary confinement, uttered in 1975, echoes Kyd Wake's plea from Gloucester Penitentiary in 1796.

Melvin Miller was visibly shaken after giving his evidence. Dr Stephen Fox, in his testimony, commented on the continuing effect of Miller's experience in solitary.

Miller cannot be subjected any further ... There is no question that he is ready to die rather than do any more of that ... I think that what we saw here when Miller consented, much maybe against his will, to try to convey to this Court some of what he felt from that experience, he did so at incredible cost to himself, because to go back there has shaken him and uprooted him and distressed him beyond what he had anticipated. He didn't want to go back there in his mind, and he went back for this court ... to demonstrate what the nature of this thing is and for the benefit of the court to understand the nature of it, but only at great cost to himself at this time.[77]

At the time of the trial Jack McCann had probably spent more time in solitary than any other prisoner in the Canadian penitentiary system. This is how he described his feelings about his years in solitary confinement.

I think treatment in scu is terrible. I am reminded every day I wake up and when I go to sleep. Men put up there with no concrete reason, no way of knowing how long they'll be up there, no decent answers to questions. No good communication to classification officers – the lies, the deceit, the stringing along, no one would ever be straight with me. The harm it had on others was most affecting on me. It hurt me, I was close to that point myself many times. I had no physical outlet for emotions. I used to break down and cry. Persons mutilating would not even get stitched up by a doctor, just bandaged by nurses and then brought back. I've never slashed up, maybe I am a moral coward, but I want to die my way, not their way ...

All you live on in scu is bitterness and hatred. For some guys that's not enough. Their hatred reaches the point when they have to see blood, even if it is their own ...

Up there I have fears of losing my sanity, fears of losing my friends, fears of myself. There is no physical fear, I can put up with that.[78]

Jack McCann gave evidence that in 1967, while he was in SCU, on three successive days other prisoners slashed themselves. He was given the job of cleaning up the blood in their cells. McCann 'begged and pleaded to be let out of solitary.' Yet another prisoner slashed himself. McCann could take no more and he set himself on fire in his cell. He described to the court what he saw as the flames engulfed him: 'I remember watching the space beneath the door get bigger. I thought I could crawl beneath it and be free ... I wanted to get out - I don't care if I die, I never want to go back to that position again.'[79] In a letter to a friend written in July 1972, McCann explained his feelings:

What am I anyway? a moral coward because I can't end it ... Do they really think I'm a mental case that can't associate with other people. If this is their thinking, why keep me here when they can send me to the bughouse. I'll tell you why, because they don't know what I am and they reject the words of the people who know me. You know something, I don't think they believe I'm human. They can't! To them I'm some sort of object, yet undefined, that they must fool around with once in a while to amuse themselves. Dear, I'm not only frustrated, I'm bitter. I think I'm a real first-class cynic. I question their motives on anything or everything and don't believe a word they say any more. I am ... envious. Not envious of your freedom on the street as much as your freedom to the right to fresh air and freedom to the sunshine.[80]

McCann gave evidence that when he was returned to the population after five years of solitary confinement he felt 'lost in the fresh air.' When McCann escaped in 1973, he got in touch with a member of the press and asked him to publicize the condition of men in solitary confinement. He also stated that his escape was precipitated by rumours that he was going back into solitary.

Dr Stephen Fox, in commenting on the effects of solitary on McCann, said, 'self-immolation, setting yourself on fire ... is as far into it as I can imagine anyone can go, into total insanity, of reduction to nothing, the hopelessness, the meaninglessness, the violence, the cycle of destruction.'[81] On the cumulative effect of McCann's long years in solitary, Dr Fox states that 'there is a scepticism and a doubt about the nature of himself and his own ability to deal in any positive way with another human being. There is a serious undermining of the capacity to feel and to communicate. There is a substantial anger which endangers everyone, endangers himself and those around him, not physically, but endangers his relationship to them.'[82]

Jack McCann wrote a series of poems while in solitary. One of these, entitled 'My Home is Hell,' was read to the court. Here are some of the stanzas:

My home is hell in one small cell
That no man wants to own,
For here I spend my life condemned
A man the world disowns.

So I, the damned, within walls crammed
Lie in my man-made grave
A man all men condemned for sin
But no man strives to save.

Each lonely dawn that night spawns
I stand and face the wall
In bitterness and loneliness
I await the whistle's call.

Men scream and yell within my hell
But I'm a man alone,
My tears of pain, like bitter rain,
Spill down on naked stone.

Here every gate is one of hate,
Love has no place to hide
For each lost fool who breaks a rule
The way to hell is wide.

The things men hate and mutilate,
Are those that all men value.
The mind of man, the will within,
The spirit that God gives you.

The right to sin, but rise again,
A free man, not a slave,
To find a friend and at the end,
Escape a pauper's grave.

I cannot tell to those in hell,
The dreams I send above,
Nor how the shrill of whistles kill,
Each passing thought of love.

Within these walls that never fall,
The damned all come to know,
The row of cells – the special hell,
Called Solitary Row.

Where seconds cheat and hunger eats
The belly of each slave,

Where gas is shot and each man rots
In his lonely grave.

To sleepless nights, to glaring lights,
To guns and bars and chains,
To walls of stone and men alone,
In years I can't regain.

To those who take my dreams and make
Me live in hell forever,
To those who lash - and try to smash,
The human spirit forever.

To those who steal the things I feel
And sow my heart with sorrow,
Each farewell I bid in hell,
Is lost in each tomorrow.[83]

While the evidence of the plaintiffs in the *McCann* case represents the most detailed elaboration so far available of the conditions and effects of solitary confinement in a Canadian maximum-security penitentiary, an extensive interpretation of and commentary on that evidence was given by expert witnesses in the fields of penology, psychology, and psychiatry. The plaintiffs called Dr Richard Korn, Dr Stephen Fox and Dr Tony Marcus. Dr Korn, who at the time of the trial was the executive director of the Center for the Study of Criminal Justice at Berkeley, California, is an eminent penologist who brought to bear in his evidence not only the benefit of many years of study and analysis of the correctional system but also actual experience in running a penitentiary and having responsibility for the establishment of a special segregation unit. Dr Stephen Fox, professor of psychology at the University of Iowa, has done extensive research in the area of sensory deprivation and has studied the effects of solitary confinement on prisoners. Both Dr Korn and Dr Fox have testified before congressional committees in the United States on prison conditions and have given expert evidence before the U.S. courts on the effects of solitary confinement. They interviewed all the plaintiffs, visited SCU and spoke to the director and other members of the staff at the penitentiary. Dr Marcus, acting head of the department of psychiatry at the University of British Columbia, has had extensive experience with prisoners in the British Columbia Penitentiary and had been the senior investigator in a study of dangerous sexual offenders being held in protective custody at the penitentiary under section 2.30(1)(b).[84]

Both Dr Korn and Dr Fox were asked to explain what they understood to be the purpose of placing a prisoner in solitary confinement under the kind of regime that existed at the British Columbia Penitentiary. Dr Korn, drawing on his own experience as assistant warden in the New Jersey State Penitentiary, testified that it was to 'break their morale, to break down their capacity to resist, to get them into a submissive state, that is the objective ... I thought it was either them or us, and unless we could break them down psychologically and make them submissive they were unsafe to us and to the community.'[85]

Dr Fox, in defining what he understood to be the purposes behind the regime in SCU, stated that 'it is designed, I believe, not so much for security purposes but to reduce the individual to that condition where there is no conceivable human resistance, where they represent essentially nothing ... The purpose is ultimately to show that on instant demand you will comply, that you will not move a muscle that is not demanded, that is not requested, in the belief, of course, that compliance will move into the street.'[86]

Dr Fox testified that the effect of this was to reduce the prisoner to a state where he had no self-respect, no identity, no dignity. However, 'to relinquish, to admit to the psychological suicide of non-identity, is essentially to violate all conceivable meaning in the evolution of mankind ... To come to have no meaning, to come to be nothing, is essentially the greatest human suffering, that is to say, it ultimately leads to insanity and suicide.'[87]

The expert witnesses described the process by which solitary confinement reduces prisoners to the position of being non-persons by reference to the sociology of the prison. The prison forms a separate society in which a prisoner has his role, his job, and his friends, all of which are related to his sense of dignity and autonomy. Dr Korn explained the effect of taking the prisoner out of that society and placing him in the prison-within-a-prison that is SCU.

When he leaves that society, when he is, in his mind, capriciously removed from the only society that he has, for reasons he knows not, for a duration he knows not ... he passes into a nightmare, he becomes a non-person. There is nobody that relates to him as a person; he is an object, and this is a catastrophe from which he can only preserve himself in a variety of ways which are in themselves sick. He is condemned to survive by techniques which would unfit him for that open society and it was very obvious in several of the witnesses ... they pointed out the ways they had found to survive in isolation interfered with them when they went out into the open prison.[88]

Dr Korn, in assessing the process which he had helped initiate in New Jersey and which, based on the evidence, he saw being continued at the British Columbia Penitentiary, told the court,

> This process is fool-proof. If you keep it up long enough, it will break anybody, the more heroic they are, and the more they resist, the more determined you get ... We kept them there for years and when they were finally broken down, we let them out ... Then I began to see what I was doing ... and said, 'We must stop this, the ends do not justify the means, this is a form of murder, it has to stop.'[89]

Dr Fox explained in equally graphic language the implications of the process of breaking prisoners down psychologically:

> The demand for ultimate and total compliance is to create a creature who has no respect for their life, and to make a creature that has no respect for their own life, they already long ago have no respect for your life. They write your life off long before they write their own life off. Do you follow what I am trying to say? I am trying to say, when a person comes to have no dignity, and no self-respect, no identity, you are faced with the most violent, the most dangerous possible human being. You can't reduce men to that, you risk your life to reduce them to that ... This desire, the good intentioned desire to create compliance ... forgets that there is a place beyond which you don't want to go, there is an area you do not want to enter, and that is to move to the place where you have eliminated all possible dignity.[90]

In describing the nature of the struggle that ensues where the institution, through solitary confinement, tries to stamp out all resistance to its demand for total compliance, Dr Fox explained how such a struggle could end. He referred to the case of Jacques Bellemaire: 'Bellemaire would not go out willingly, but ultimately lost all being, lost touch with the total world. Life had no meaning for him at all. He was nobody. He was nothing. He complied, he became nothing, but in his mind the price for being nothing is death.'[91]

Dr Fox spoke of Tommy McCaulley in the context of bringing prisoners to the very margins of sanity.

> When McCaulley becomes insane to your face, they are McCaulley, that is all there is to it. There is not one of them who will tell you anything different. This is a fact. Each one of them is a part of McCaulley, and it was a part of them that had gone to that place where McCaulley is, exactly to that place where McCaulley is, where all rationality has left them and they have come back from

that place only by some freak accident of their own prior upbringing. But there is not one of them that does not hear their own voices screaming when McCaulley screams. They are McCaulley. They are McCaulley's insanity and in them is McCaulley's insanity. When he becomes insane and moves towards death, like Bellemaire did, when they see insanity approaching self-extinction, they know that part of them is moving to that place and they have to live with their own insanity and it is in front of them. There is no way to escape that part of yourself. When you sit with a madman, the part of you that is insane becomes explicit. You live with the part of you that has become more and more insane, so it is even more intense. You cannot tolerate it. When the blood runs in front of their cells, it is their blood ... When they see death approach, it is their death that approaches.[92]

In explaining the anger, the violence, the insanity that solitary confinement induces, the expert witnesses referred both to the philosophical concept of undermining the very humanity and dignity of the individual and to a body of scientific data which shows that inescapable punishment causes violent and psychotic behaviour. Dr Fox explained the concept of punishment-induced aggression: 'It happens in every animal from goldfish to humans. It happens predictably, scientifically, and reliably. Sustained punishment without escape, without any instrumental response to terminate it ... where there is nothing to learn will result in violence in every animal we have ever studied.'[93]

Relying upon the evidence presented by the plaintiffs, Dr Fox described how the situation in the SCU at the British Columbia Penitentiary amounted to inescapable punishment. He gave the example of Jack McCann's running score; month after month, he showed 'quiet and co-operative' behaviour, and yet was not released from SCU. In Dr Fox's view the reason McCann was not released was because he had been placed in SCU not for any particular violation but rather because of 'a malaise, it is a fear, a paranoia, the uncertainty of his behaviour.'[94] Because there was nothing McCann could do to allay this, because even his quietness and co-operation were taken to be suspicious, his confinement in SCU was inescapable punishment without a goal.

There is no goal. It is almost as though he has come to understand that the keeper does not have anything that he wants ... in a concrete way, except the total compliance, the total disappearing. There is nothing to learn, there is nothing to do, there is only to be there in a state that finally will reduce the fear of the keeper, the irrational fear of the keeper, not based on a particular act but the feeling of discomfort in your presence because your reputation and your background, or something, your attitude, your arrogance ... [95]

Addressing himself to the review process, Dr Fox concluded that it was meaningless because there was nothing specific to review. There was no measure against which to test progress except in some kind of vague, unarticulated way. Given this fact, simply having something called a 'review' was even more frustrating for the prisoner because it was a sham, a hollow mockery. Dr Fox states that the effect of this kind of process was 'to undermine, to generate anger, violence, uncertainty, resentment; there is nothing else that can emerge in that situation.'[96]

Dr Korn explained to the court the effects of particular aspects of the solitary confinement experience. He described the way prisoners experience time in solitary.

> Free men spend time. Prisoners do time. Doing time is a specific activity, a calling, an art. Time itself is a force, it has its own action. Offenders are hit with their time and the word for a prison sentence is a jolt. Prison time is almost palpable. It not only has force, it has mass and weight. Too heavy a sentence can suffocate ...
>
> [In scu] time stops and begins to crush and you have that suffocation, you have the tiny space, the relative inaction, and that crushing experience and then the mind begins to play its tricks to save itself. You begin by fantasies ... and then after a while you lose control of that process of fantasy, and the internal TV takes over, and it is usually nightmares.
>
> One of the ways they keep alive is by fantasies of retaliation which is a very human thing to do. You see yourself as a victim of overwhelming forces. You are deprived of autonomy ... These men, deprived of self-determination and feeling abused, can keep themselves alive only by fantasies and feelings of fury which, in a way, sets them up for going back and among other things severely endangers the staff. So in process and experience and in consequence, it is a catastrophe and an unnecessary one.[97]

Sometimes the fantasies become hallucinations.

> [A hallucination] is a waking dream. It is a dream you are having with your eyes open and that is very frightening. That is what madness is ... You have to make sense of it, how do you make sense of something that is crazy. So you create a rational explanation. There is a machine. That puts you out of touch with everybody. You see, you can't talk to anyone about it so some of the frustrations that the plaintiffs talk about, I try to help this man, I tried to reach him, I couldn't reach him. The terrible effect that has on other prisoners, because the unspoken thing is 'that could be me.' Keep men long enough there and that is the destination for everybody.[98]

Hallucinations are detrimental to the good order of the institution. 'An individual who has hallucinated extensively will carry back with him the potentiality to lose touch and to be destructive or violent again. There will be flashback hallucinations just as there are with drugs. Impulsive, erratic and dangerous, unpredictable behaviour will carry back.'[99]

Dr Fox expanded on the implications when prisoners are returned to the population from solitary: 'What can they bring to the population? They bring the paranoia, the insanity, the fear, the violence into the population and the incidence increases and increases. It is not serviceable to the population. It is not serviceable to the public. It is not serviceable to the prisoner.'[100]

Both Dr Fox and Dr Korn were asked to give their opinions on the permanence of the detrimental effects of solitary confinement such as had been experienced by the plaintiffs. Dr Korn responded, 'I would say that the effects are lifelong. They can be overcome with a great deal of support. They are not necessarily fatal to sanity but they are, they represent, a permanent possibility. Things like a heart attack you recover from.'[101]

In Dr Fox's opinion,

> There is a loss of something in these people produced by these conditions which is never recoverable, and I say that with total conviction, and what is lost is the ability to love. That may sound non-scientific in the court, and that may sound beyond the area of expertise; but I think the Court can understand exactly what it means to lose the ability to love anything, including yourself, and the dilemma that society is faced with when you are presented with a person who loves nothing, who has lost the ability to love, because without that there can be no compassion, no understanding, there can only be – what remains can only be violence.
>
> Their minds have been torn away in a manner which is not reversible ... and I mean that by their own statements each of these people has said to me 'Yes, yes, there is a part of me that will never return because I cannot feel about human beings the way I used to feel about them, because I know that they are capable of acts so incredible to me that my faith in them is so severely undermined. I am sceptical and dubious, I am cynical about the nature of human beings who induce this pain and will tear away from me the things that I most want to recover – my ability to love anything or anyone, which I had enough trouble with before I came into this place.'[102]

Dr Tony Marcus characterized the treatment of men in SCU as 'an attempt to crush the human spirit.' His opinion of the plaintiffs' treatment was that 'it had undermined, burnt into them a sense of hate, mistrust, tension that they carry with them as part of their personality. It has only added to their negative character. In no way has it helped. It has served no positive penal purpose in the prison structure. It has denied them the capacity to function as people who can tolerate human situations. It has put so much hate and paranoia into them that I fear it is permanent. It is a destructive impairment of their emotional lives.'[103]

Both Dr Fox and Dr Korn were asked to compare the psychological suffering caused by solitary confinement with physical punishment.

> It is worse, there is no physical punishment which can approach this ... There is no fear for these people of physical death, it is easier than the time. It is simply termination of your life. That is not painful, it is over, it is done, but to cling to your life in this morass of continuous torture is a much, much heavier thing to do than physical death ... It is easier to die than to undergo the pain ... Most of them prefer to die, they hang themselves rather than sustain it. That's what the suicides are about.[104]

> The evidence simply is that if you keep people long enough, they will engage in self-torture, simply to focus the pain. So obviously if the inmates choose the infliction of punishment, physical punishment, they have indicated the answer to that question. Physical pain which is definite, which they can control ... is much more bearable than the torment they can neither understand nor control.[105]

The primary witness called by the defendants in the *McCann* case was Dr Peter Suedfeld, who is acknowledged to be the leading Canadian researcher in the area of sensory deprivation. Dr Suedfeld did not interview any of the plaintiffs nor, except for part of McCann's testimony, was he present in court when they gave their evidence. In his review of the scientific literature on sensory deprivation Dr Suedfeld testified that controlled experimental data with human subjects were limited to the results of three weeks of sensory deprivation on volunteers; these studies had been done in conditions where the subjects could terminate the experiment at any time. They were therefore not comparable to the situation in SCU. Dr Suedfeld indicated that no controlled study of long-term solitary confinement had been done.

The few studies that have looked at the effect of solitary confinement on prisoners have been concerned with prisoners who spent short periods in solitary. In the early 1970s Paul Gendreau conducted a controlled experiment designed to test the effect of solitary confinement on prisoners' self-identity and stress levels. The study investigated the effect on the prisoners of ten days of solitary confinement, '*this being the longest time inmates usually remained in solitary*' [emphasis added].[106] The experiment consisted of randomly assigning sixteen volunteer prisoners to two groups: one group was placed for ten days in solitary-confinement cells, and the other group followed the regular institutional routine. The confined group and the control group were both given a series of tests to assess the effect of isolation on prisoners' self-identity as defined in terms of a set of core constructs. The two groups were also examined to determine their plasma cortisone values, heart rate, respiration, and body temperatures. These tests were designed to demonstrate the existence of altered stress levels. The researchers concluded that 'the plasma cortisone results in the study failed to confirm the clinical expectation that solitary confinement would be more stressful than routine prison life.'[107] They also found that 'the personal constructs of the confined prisoners became more consistent during confinement,'[108] implying that solitary confinement did not induce any change in the prisoner's self-identity. The differences between the circumstances of this study and the situation faced by prisoners in SCU are self-evident. Prisoners in SCU are not volunteers; they cannot terminate their confinement at will (four prisoners withdrew from the experiment); unlike the prisoners who took part in the experiment, they are not perceived by the guards in a positive way as contributing to the increase in scientific knowledge; their confinement is of indefinite duration and is usually for a much longer period than ten days.[109]

A second study on prisoners was carried out at the Regional Psychiatric Centre in British Columbia by Dr Suedfeld and Dr Chunilal Roy, the medical director of the centre. This was not a controlled experiment. Four prisoners had been sentenced to thirty days' punitive dissociation by a disciplinary board for causing a disturbance. The experimental manipulation consisted of modifying the normal institutional response while the prisoners were in solitary cells. The staff were instructed to maintain the normal procedures until a significant change occurred in the behaviour of the prisoners. When such a change was observed, social and physical reinforcement was applied. Reinforcers included making conversation, taking the prisoner out of the cell for a shower, or giving him a cigarette or a cup of coffee. Two of the prisoners were released after serving ten days in solitary. The other two served the full thirty days. The researchers concluded, based upon limited follow-up, that there appeared to have been good short-term effects in these cases in that the men were better adjusted and posed fewer behavioural problems after being returned to their normal routine.[110]

Although the Suedfeld and Roy study seeks to demonstrate that there may be positive advantages to the use of dissociation under certain circumstances, the description contained in the report of the prisoners' behaviour while in dissociation corroborates certain aspects of the plaintiffs' evidence in the *McCann* case. One of the prisoners 'in the second week of his admission to the isolation unit was found to be hallucinating sporadically. He became calm but incoherent and slept heavily. He was unsteady on his feet.'[111] Another prisoner, 'on the fourth day, began to show inappropriate behaviour such as giggling and staring into space for long periods. He reported that he had no appetite and slept for long stretches of time.'[112]

Dr Suedfeld, in response to questions concerning the permanent psychological effects of long-term confinement, stated:

> They vary tremendously, depending upon the individual ... I would say that people who have problems adapting in the first place to any environment or to normal environments would have problems adapting to that environment [solitary confinement] ... I would expect that for many people after some prolonged period of time, especially if there is no hope of being released from that environment, things would tend to become inadequate and an individual would then take on another form of reaction to the environment. That may take place in the form of apathy, fantasizing, general withdrawal from the external environment, some kind of inner life, and in some cases, I expect it would lead to psychosis.[113]

In his written summary of evidence, Dr Suedfeld remarked that 'isolation as a punitive technique sometimes serves only to exacerbate problems of aggression and resentment. In such cases, it is obviously counterproductive and should be abandoned.'[114] In his oral testimony Dr Suedfeld stated that the effectiveness of isolation 'is doubtful enough to warrant its rejection in this context. Furthermore its use in punishment probably detracts from its potential utility in therapy. For these reasons I would be happy, for one, to see it removed from the repertoire of punitive techniques.'[115]

The defendants also called Dr George Scott, the senior psychiatrist in the Canadian Penitentiary Service. For the purposes of giving his evidence, Dr Scott prepared statistics for the British Columbia Penitentiary that were designed to compare the effects of living in SCU with living in the general prison population. These statistics showed that in 1974 11 per cent of the population in SCU were involved in slashing incidents, compared to 1 per cent in the general population; 6.4 per cent of the prisoners in SCU committed suicide, compared to 0.9 per cent in the general population; 8.3 per cent of the prisoners in SCU were involved in acts of violence, compared to 7.5 per cent in the general population.[117]

Dr Scott explained that while slashing was most unusual in the non-prison society, it did occur more frequently in prison, and his statistics showed that the incidence increased dramatically with men placed in solitary confinement. According to Dr Scott, the reasons for the slashings usually involved 'frustration, aggravation, resentment and hostility. Usually there are very frustrating circumstances that individuals can't handle. In other words, he has got no solution. He can't act out so he acts in.'[117]

Dr Scott's statistics and his explanations are fully congruent with Dr Fox's evidence on the concept of punishment-induced aggression.

4
McCann v. *The Queen*: The Structure of the Legal Argument

In describing the process, the conditions, and the effect of solitary confinement in SCU it has been necessary to elaborate considerably on the statement of facts contained in the judgment of Mr Justice Heald in the *McCann* case. Mr Justice Heald, displaying the economy characteristic of the judiciary, reviewed the facts only in so far as they were necessary to reach his conclusions in law. My purpose in elaborating on the facts has been to locate them in their historical and psychological contexts and to convey the nature of carceral power as it has come to be exercised in our maximum-security penitentiaries. In this chapter, in which I analyse the law pertaining to solitary confinement, because the legal arguments presented to the court encompassed a theory for judicial intervention in prison decision-making and an analytical framework for bringing the rule of law to bear within the prison, I will elaborate on the nature of those legal arguments well beyond the explication found in the judgment of the court. Furthermore, because my analysis seeks to inform future decision-making rather than simply review the historical record, in setting out the arguments presented in *McCann* I will consider not only how those arguments were received by the court but also how they have flourished or foundered in the subsequent development of the law, including the effect of the enactment of the Canadian Charter of Rights and Freedoms.

In order to achieve this dual purpose of describing the legal arguments presented in 1975 and tracing subsequent developments in the law without interrupting the chronology of the *McCann* case, I have adopted a specific method of organization in this chapter. The main text contains the arguments presented to the court in *McCann*; the notes form a subtext which traces subsequent developments. This subtext will be of particular interest to lawyers.

THE ROLE OF THE COURTS IN THE PRISON: THE RATIONALE FOR INTERVENTION

At common law, the person convicted of felony and sentenced to imprisonment was regarded as being devoid of rights. A Virginia court declared just over a century ago that a prisoner 'has, as a consequence of his crime, not only forfeited his liberty, but all his personal rights except those which the law in its humanity accords to him. He is for the time being the slave of the State.'[1] This view flowed historically from the old English practices of outlawry and attaint, the consequences of which were that the convicted felon lost all civil and proprietary rights and was regarded in law as dead. The warden of Kingston Penitentiary was properly reflecting the traditional status of the felon when in 1867 he wrote, 'so long as a convict is confined here I regard him as dead to all transactions of the outer world.'[2]

Although the concept of civil death was abolished in most common-law jurisdictions by the end of the nineteenth century, the prisoner continued to be viewed in law as a person without rights.[3] It was this view that provided the original rationale for courts in Canada, the United States, and England to refuse to review the internal decision-making of prison officials. That rationale was later supplemented by the view that 'judicial review of such administrative decisions [would] subvert the authority of prison officials, the discipline of prisoners, and the efforts of prison administrators to accomplish the objectives of the system which is entrusted to their care and management.'[4] The effect of this hands-off approach was to immunize the prison from public scrutiny through the judicial process and to place prison officials in a position of virtual invulnerability and absolute power over the persons committed to their institutions.[5]

Since the 1960s, Canadian courts, like their American and English counterparts, have begun to develop some understanding of the need for and the legitimacy of judicial intervention behind the prison walls. It has been increasingly recognized that a prisoner, far from being the slave of the state, should retain 'all the rights of an ordinary citizen, except those that are expressly taken away from him by statute or that he loses as a necessary consequence of incarceration.'[6] In *R.* v. *Miller and Cockriell*,[7] McIntyre J cited with approval the words of Brennan J in *Furman* v. *Georgia*,[8] a decision of the Supreme Court of the United States:

> An individual in prison does not lose 'the right to have rights.' The prisoner retains the constitutional rights ... to be free of cruel and unusual punishments and to treatment as a 'person' for purposes of due process of law ... A prisoner remains a member of the human family ... His punishment is not irrevocable.[9]

This recognition of 'prisoners' rights' is part of a larger development which, while more pronounced in the United States, is clearly evident in Canada, where we have seen the extension of legal rights to racial minorities, mental patients, the disabled, welfare recipients, children, and the largest of all 'minorities,' women. This development has been explained by sociologists as relating to the evolution of 'mass society,' the social movement that seeks to integrate every group into the political, economic, and legal systems of society.[10] In the context of prisoners' rights, Jacobs has argued persuasively that the rising expectations and demands of prisoners should be seen as the consequence of the progressive realization of this mass society.[11]

The case for judicial intervention in the prison to ensure that the rule of law prevails has not, however, been argued with reference to sociological theses. In *Palmigiano* v. *Baxter*,[12] a decision of the United States Federal Court of Appeal for the First Circuit, the court articulated the modern legal argument for judicial intervention behind prison walls.

Prison officials, facing complicated and combustible situations each day, must be free to make a wide range of decisions. Much must be left to their good faith and discretion ... Time has proved, however, that blind deference to correctional officials does no real service to them. Judicial concern with procedural regularity has a direct bearing upon the maintenance of institutional order; the orderly care with which decisions are made by the prison authority is intimately related to the level of respect with which prisoners regard that authority. There is nothing more corrosive to the fabric of a public institution such as a prison than a feeling amongst those whom it contains that they are being treated unfairly. The control of official discretion within prison walls is vital for other reasons as well. Most decision making of correctional personnel is less visible to the public than is the decision making of other public officials, and therefore less likely to benefit from the inherent constraints of public discussion and scrutiny. Prisoners themselves have no opportunity to participate in a political process which might otherwise provide some guidance for official discretion. Moreover, because prisoners are under the constant care and supervision of correctional personnel within 'total institutions' which regulate every aspect of their lives, there exist awesome possibilities for misuse of discretion to the extent that decisions which affect prisoners in important ways may be made arbitrarily or based upon mistakes of fact. Finally, it is coming to be realized that almost all of the ... indiyiduals who are at any one time subject to correctional authority will eventually rejoin the rest of our citizens outside the prison walls; if they are to learn to respect public authority and to participate in the democratic control of that authority as normal citizens, they need to be able to challenge what appears to be arbitrary assertions of power by correctional officials during the course of their confinement.[13]

It was this thesis which the plaintiffs in *McCann* urged the Federal Court of Canada to adopt. To the extent that it seeks to prevent the abuse of discretion by prison officials and to ensure the legitimacy of carceral authority, judicial intervention is directly linked with John Howard's principle of outside inspection. It adds to that principle the assertion that an independent judiciary has an important role to play in guaranteeing the vigilance of that inspection.

CRUEL AND UNUSUAL PUNISHMENT OR TREATMENT

The first of the plaintiffs' two primary claims was that their confinement in SCU at the British Columbia Penitentiary amounted to the imposition of cruel and unusual punishment contrary to section 2(b) of the Canadian Bill of Rights, which reads:

> 2. Every law of Canada shall, unless it is expressly declared by an Act of the Parliament of Canada that it shall operate notwithstanding the Canadian Bill of Rights, be so construed and applied as not to abrogate, abridge or authorize the abrogation, abridgment or infringement of any of the rights or freedoms herein recognized and declared, and in particular no law of Canada shall be construed or applied so as to ... (b) impose or authorize the imposition of cruel and unusual treatment or punishment.[14]

In their argument to the court the plaintiffs traced the historical origins of section 2(b) to the English Bill of Rights of 1689. They submitted that since the similar, albeit narrower, prohibition on cruel and unusual punishment contained in the Eighth Amendment to the United States Constitution also has its historical roots in the same English source, American judicial decisions on the Eighth Amendment were particularly relevant in any enquiry into the proper meaning to be given section 2(b) of the Canadian Bill of Rights.

This was not the first time that this argument had been raised. In *R.* v. *Miller and Cockriell*, a case dealing with the relationship between the death penalty and section 2(b), Mr Justice Robertson, in a majority judgment of the British Columbia Court of Appeal, suggested that the Canadian courts should not rely upon American decisions on the Eighth Amendment because of the differences between the U.S. Constitution and the Canadian Bill of Rights and the different approaches used by American and Canadian courts in statutory interpretation based on different conceptions of judicial review.[15] The plaintiffs submitted that such a wholesale rejection of the relevance of U.S. decisions was far too sweeping. Mr Justice McIntyre, in his dissent in *Miller and Cockriell*, dealt with the argument that the American cases on cruel and unusual punishment were not relevant to judicial determination of the meaning of section 2(b):

> The differences between the American constitutional system and our own are many and obvious. They need no precise definition here. It does not follow, however, that all judicial attitudes and expressions emanating from the United States are inapplicable in Canada. Furthermore, it is not true, that in dealing with the concept of cruel and unusual punishment we are borrowing from the United States. The rejection of cruel and unusual punishment was declared in English law in the 17th century ... and is said to find its roots in Magna Carta. The English Bill of Rights of 1688 declared in s. 10: that excessive bail ought not to be required nor excessive fines imposed; nor cruel and unusual punishment inflicted.
>
> In doing so the Bill recited that the Lords and Commons were making the declaration 'for the vindicating and asserting [of] their ancient rights and liberties.' This principle as part of the law of England became the law of what is now a part of Canada after the British conquest of the French colonies in North America and was thus known in Canadian jurisprudence even before the revolution which led to the creation of the United States of America. Framers of the United States Constitution in the Eighth Amendment provided 'excessive bail shall not be required nor excessive fines imposed nor cruel and unusual punishment inflicted ...' They were then adopting English law which had become or was to become Canadian law and consideration of this question and its mention in the Canadian Bill of Rights involves the introduction of no foreign concept into our Canadian system.[16]

Mr Justice McIntyre also doubted the continuing validity of the argument that American cases were irrelevant because of the differences in judicial review in the two countries. Reciting the majority decisions of Ritchie J in *R.* v. *Drybones*[17] and Laskin J (as he then was) in *Curr* v. *The Queen*,[18] which make it clear that the Bill of Rights may have a sterilizing effect upon federal legislation if that legislation cannot be sensibly construed and applied so as not to abrogate one of the rights or freedoms recognized by the bill, he stated, 'This argument would have had compelling force prior to the passage of the Canadian Bill of Rights in 1960. That enactment, however, has changed the situation and some element of judicial review of legislation has been imported into our system'[19] He concluded his review of the relevance of the U.S. decisions by saying, 'I am fully aware that American authority does not bind me ... but I have found it helpful in seeking principles upon which this matter should be considered in a civilized society.'[20]

The United States Supreme Court, in its decisions on the Eighth Amendment, has enquired into the English antecedents of the prohibition against cruel and unusual punishment. The decision of Mr Justice Marshall in *Furman* v. *Georgia* contains a scholarly discussion of that history.

The Eighth Amendment's ban against cruel and unusual punishments derives from English law. In 1583, John Whitgift, Archbishop of Canterbury, turned the High Commission into a permanent ecclesiastical court, and the Commission began to use torture to extract confessions from persons suspected of various offences. Sir Robert Beale protested that cruel and barbarous torture violated Magna Carta, but his protests were made in vain.

Cruel punishments were not confined to those accused of crimes, but were notoriously applied with even greater relish to those who were convicted. Blackstone described in ghastly detail the myriad of inhumane forms of punishment imposed on persons found guilty of any of a large number of offences. Death, of course, was the usual result.

The treason trials of 1685 – the 'Bloody Assizes' – which followed an abortive rebellion by the Duke of Monmouth, marked the culmination of the array of horrors, and most historians believe that it was this event that finally spurred the adoption of the English Bill of Rights containing the progenitor of our prohibition against cruel and unusual punishments. The conduct of Lord Chief Justice Jeffreys at these trials has been described as an 'insane lust for cruelty' which was 'stimulated by orders from the King' (James ii). The Assizes received wide publicity from Puritan pamphleteers and doubtless had some influence on the adoption of a cruel and unusual punishment clause. But, the legislative history of the English Bill of Rights of 1689, indicates that the Assizes may not have been as critical to the adoption of the clause as it is widely thought. After William and Mary of Orange crossed the Channel to invade England, James ii fled, Parliament was summoned into session, and a Committee was appointed to draft general statements containing 'such things as are absolutely necessary to be considered for the better securing of our religion, and liberties.' An initial draft of the Bill of Rights prohibited 'illegal' punishments, but a later draft referred to the infliction by James ii of 'illegal and cruel' punishments and declared 'cruel and unusual' punishments to be prohibited. The use of the word 'unusual' in the final draft appears to be inadvertent.

This legislative history has led at least one legal historian to conclude 'that the cruel and unusual punishments clause of the Bill of Rights of 1689 was, first, an objection to the imposition of punishments that were unauthorized by statute and outside the jurisdiction of the sentencing court, and second, a reiteration of the English policy against disproportionate penalties,' and not primarily a reaction to the torture of the High Commission, harsh sentences or the Assizes.

Whether the English Bill of Rights prohibition against cruel and unusual punishments is properly read as a response to excessive or illegal punishment, as a reaction to barbaric and objectionable modes of punishment, or both, there is no doubt whatever that in borrowing the language and including it in the Eighth Amendment, our Founding Fathers intended to outlaw torture and other cruel punishments.[21]

The United States Supreme Court has indicated in the clearest terms that whatever the original meaning of the English Bill of Rights' prohibition against cruel and unusual punishment, the court was not to be imprisoned within those historical origins in approaching the Eighth Amendment. The amendment has not been regarded as a static concept; as Chief Justice Warren said in an often-quoted phrase, 'The Amendment must draw its meaning from the evolving standards of decency that mark the progress of a maturing society.'[22] Similarly, it was submitted in the *McCann* case that Parliament, in passing the Canadian Bill of Rights in 1960, did not intend to give a restricted meaning to section 2(b). The section's very wording embraces treatment as well as punishment, and indicates that the clause was intended to operate in the context of modern Canadian society, and was not to be bound by the narrow historicism of England in 1688. Further, to read 'cruel and unusual' as a prohibition simply against illegal punishment or treatment would be to assign the clause to the status of mere rhetoric. Clearly, it would not have been necessary for Parliament to pass a special enactment protecting Canadian citizens against punishment and treatment for which there was no lawful authorization.

In one of the earlier Canadian decisions, *R.* v. *Buckler*,[23] His Honour Judge Carlson, in seeking guidance in the proper interpretation of section 2(b), looked to the Universal Declaration of Human Rights (1948), article 5, which reads, 'no-one shall be subjected to torture or to cruel, inhuman or degrading treatment or punishment.'[24] He also quoted the views expressed by two respected criminal law scholars on this clause:

Underlying this proposition are the two ideas that punishment may offend against human rights because (a) it imposes unnecessary suffering, that is, suffering not justified by some purpose other than the infliction of suffering, and (b) even if it does not inflict unnecessary suffering, it may constitute an affront to human dignity and decency.

Little more need be said about these two ideas than that they must be related to the social circumstances standards of living, and attitudes to the individual citizen in each country.[25]

As Morris and Howard point out, the concern here is not with the narrow matter of illegal and disproportionate penalties: it encompasses a much wider issue. The plaintiffs in *McCann* suggested that in drafting section 2(b) in 1960, it was improbable that the Canadian Parliament intended to depart from the provisions of international customary law embodied in the Universal Declaration, given that Canada was one of the signatories to the declaration.[26]

The plaintiffs submitted that in interpreting the meaning of section 2(b) it was relevant to look to the developing law in the United States under the Eighth Amendment; not only does it trace a common heritage to the English Bill of Rights but also, as with the Universal Declaration, the American courts have held that the underlying concern of the Eighth Amendment is the protection of human dignity. In other words, in dealing with a concept grounded in history they have not permitted themselves to be imprisoned by that history; rather, they have interpreted the concept so that it reflects an underlying human value similar to that expressed in the Universal Declaration of Human Rights. The plaintiffs submitted that the same underlying value of the protection of human dignity is recited in the preamble to the Bill of Rights and ought to be protected by section 2(b).[27]

At the time of the *McCann* case, the leading American case on the Eighth Amendment was *Furman* v. *Georgia*,[28] which dealt with the constitutionality of the death penalty. Although all nine justices wrote separate opinions, the plaintiffs in *McCann* argued that the opinion of Brennan J, one of the majority striking down the death penalty, was particularly relevant because it contained a careful review of previous decisions of the Supreme Court and sought to draw from them the principles that had been developed by the court in interpreting the Eighth Amendment. It was the Brennan judgment that commended itself to Mr Justice McIntyre and heavily influenced his reasoning in *Miller and Cockriell*.

Mr Justice Brennan, drawing upon the decision of the Supreme Court in *Trop* v. *Dulles*,[29] saw the unifying principle of the Eighth Amendment in this way:

> The basic concept underlying the [clause] is nothing less than the dignity of man. While the State has the power to punish, the [clause] stands to assure that this power be exercised within the limits of civilized standards.
>
> At bottom, then, the cruel and unusual punishments clause prohibits the infliction of uncivilized and inhuman punishments. The State, even as it punishes, must treat its members with respect for their intrinsic worth as human beings. A punishment is 'cruel and unusual' therefore if it does not comport with human dignity.[30]

Mr Justice Brennan derived from the jurisprudence of the Supreme Court a set of principles to test whether a challenged punishment comports with human dignity.

The primary principle is that a punishment must not be so severe as to be degrading to the dignity of human beings. Pain, certainly, may be a factor in the judgment. The infliction of an extremely severe punishment will often entail physical suffering ... Even though 'there may be involved no physical mistreatment, or primitive torture' (*Trop* v. *Dulles*), severe mental pain may be inherent in the infliction of a particular punishment.[31]

In *Trop* v. *Dulles*, where the court held that punishment by expatriation violated the Eighth Amendment, the holding was based in part on the conclusion that the punishment inflicted severe mental pain. But, as Mr Justice Brennan pointed out, it is not just the presence of severe pain that has led American courts to strike down certain punishments.

The barbaric punishments condemned by history, punishments which inflict torture such as the rack, the thumb-screw, the iron boot, the stretching of limbs, and the like are of course attended with acute pain and suffering. But when we consider why they have been condemned, however, we realize that the pain involved is not the only reason. The true significance of these punishments is that they treat members of the human race as non-humans, as objects to be toyed with and discarded. They are thus inconsistent with the fundamental premise of the clause that even the vilest criminal remains a human being possessed of common human dignity.[32]

A second principle which Mr Justice Brennan felt to be inherent in the Eighth Amendment is that the state must not arbitrarily inflict a severe punishment: 'This principle derives from the notion that the State does not respect human dignity when, without reason, it inflicts upon some people a severe punishment that it does not inflict upon others.'[33]

Mr Justice McIntyre in *Miller and Cockriell* enlarged upon this principle. 'In a civilized community the arbitrary imposition of a severe punishment is abhorrent. Modern concepts of law, morality and decency require that permissible punishment be imposed according to law, according to ascertained or ascertainable standards, and equally upon those who qualify for its infliction.'[34]

Mr Justice Brennan identified a third principle: 'a severe punishment must not be unacceptable to a contemporary society ...'[35] The question is whether there are objective indicators from which a court can conclude that contemporary society considers a severe punishment unacceptable. Accordingly, the court's task is to review the history of a challenged punishment and to examine society's present practices in respect to its use.[36]

The final principle identified in Mr Justice Brennan's judgment is that a severe punishment must not be excessive:

Punishment is excessive under this principle, if it is unnecessary. The infliction of a severe punishment by the State cannot comport with human dignity when it is nothing more than the pointless infliction of suffering. If there is a significantly less severe punishment adequate to achieve the purposes for which the punishment is inflicted, the punishment inflicted is unnecessary and therefore excessive ... Although the determination that a severe punishment is excessive may be grounded in the judgment that it is disproportionate to the crime, the more significant basis is that the punishment serves no penal purpose more effectively than a less severe punishment.[37]

Having identified the four principles, Mr Justice Brennan went on to explain their interrelationship.

There are, then, four principles by which we may determine whether a particular punishment is 'cruel and unusual.' The primary principle, which I believe supplies the essential predicate for the application of the others, is that a punishment must not by its severity be degrading to human dignity. The paradigm violation of this principle would be the infliction of a torturous punishment of the type that the clause has always prohibited. Yet it is unlikely that any State at this moment in history would pass a law providing for the infliction of such a punishment. Indeed, no such punishment has ever been before this Court. The same may be said of the other principles. It is unlikely that this Court will confront a severe punishment that is obviously inflicted in wholly arbitrary fashion; no State would engage in a reign of blind terror. Nor is it likely that this Court will be called upon to review a severe punishment that is clearly and totally rejected throughout society; no legislature would be able even to authorize the infliction of such punishment. Nor finally, is it likely that this Court would have to consider a severe punishment that is patently unnecessary. No State today would inflict a severe punishment knowing that there was no reason whatsoever for doing so. In short, we are unlikely to have occasion to determine that a punishment is fatally offensive under any one principle.[38]

After reviewing the punishments that the court had held to be within the prohibition of the clause (twelve years in chains at hard and painful labour, *Weems* v. *United States*;[39] expatriation, *Trop* v. *Dulles*; and imprisonment for being addicted to narcotics, *Robinson* v. *California*[10]), Mr Justice Brennan continued:

Each punishment, of course, was degrading to human dignity, but of none could it be said conclusively that it was fatally offensive under one or the other of the principles. Rather, these 'cruel and unusual punishments' seriously implicated several of the principles, and it was the application of the principles in combination that supported the judgment. That, indeed, is not surprising. The function of these principles, after all, is simply to provide means by which a Court can determine whether a challenged punishment comports with human dignity. They are, therefore, interrelated, and in most cases it will be their convergence that will justify the conclusion that a punishment is 'cruel and unusual.' The test, then, will ordinarily be a cumulative one. If a punishment is unusually severe, if there is a strong probability that it is inflicted arbitrarily, if it is substantially rejected by contemporary society, and if there is no reason to believe that it serves any penal purpose more effectively than some less severe punishment, then the continued infliction of that punishment violates the command of the clause that the State may not inflict inhuman or uncivilized punishments upon those convicted of crimes.[41]

In the *Miller* and *Cockriell* case, Mr Justice McIntyre, in his review of the standards which he felt were appropriate to the application of section 2(b) of the Bill of Rights, formulated this restatement of the Brennan tests.

It would not be permissible to impose a punishment which has no value in the sense that it does not protect society by deterring criminal behaviour or serve some other social purpose. A punishment failing to have these attributes would surely be cruel and unusual if it is not in accord with public standards of decency and propriety, if it is unnecessary because of the existence of adequate alternatives, if it cannot be applied upon a rational basis in accordance with ascertained or ascertainable standards, and if it is excessive and out of proportion to the crimes it seeks to restrain.[42]

In the American cases on the Eighth Amendment the cruelty of the punishment rather than its unusualness is the principal criterion by which its propriety is judged. The courts have declined to give the word 'unusual' a restricted meaning. In *Furman* v. *Georgia*, Mr Justice Marshall noted that the original draft of the English Bill of Rights referred to 'illegal' and 'cruel' punishments. Adopting the reasoning of Anthony Granucci,[43] he suggested that the use of the word 'unusual' in the final version must be attributed simply to chance and sloppy draftsmanship. Chief Justice Burger, who dissented on the issue of whether the death penalty came within the prohibition of the Eighth Amendment, agreed that 'the term "unusual" cannot be read as limiting the ban on cruel punishments or somehow expanding the meaning of the word "cruel."'[44] In *Trop* v. *Dulles*, Chief Justice Warren clearly indicated that the approach of the Supreme Court was to examine 'the particular punishment involved in light of the basic prohibition against inhuman treatment, without regard to any subtleties of meaning that might be latent in the word "unusual."'[45]

In *Miller and Cockriell*, Mr Justice McIntyre, after referring to the scholarly literature and the American case law, concluded:

> It is permissible and preferable to read the words 'cruel' and 'unusual' in section 2(b) of the Bill of Rights disjunctively so that cruel punishments, however usual in the ordinary sense of the term, could come within the proscription. The term 'unusual' refers in my view not simply to infrequency of imposition ... but to punishments unusual in the sense that they are not clearly authorized by law, not known in penal practice or not acceptable by community standards.[46]

The majority of the Court of Appeal in *Miller and Cockriell* preferred a conjunctive interpretation, wherein a punishment must be both cruel *and* unusual, and, 'assuming for the sake of the argument that hanging is cruel punishment,' concluded that it was not unusual. The court gave several reasons for its conclusion. First, death as a punishment for murder is not unusual in the ordinary and natural meaning of the word; in England from time immemorial murder was punishable by death, and had been so in Canada before and since Confederation, despite the fact that as a result of executive clemency no death sentences had been carried out in recent years. Second, Parliament must have thought in 1973 (when the capital-murder provisions being challenged were introduced) that the death penalty for murder was not an unusual punishment and that there was therefore no need to use the words 'shall operate notwithstanding the Canadian Bill of Rights.'[47] A further line of reasoning adopted by the majority was that even if Parliament thought that the punishment was an unusual one, it nevertheless wished it to be the punishment for murder by enacting the provisions of the Criminal Code in 1973; therefore these provisions impliedly repealed section 2(b) or excluded it from applying to the death penalty.[48]

At the time of the *McCann* trial only the decision of the Court of Appeal in *Miller and Cockriell* had been rendered, and the plaintiffs contended that the judgment of Mr Justice McIntyre was a more principled guide to the tests to be applied in determining whether the conditions in SCU violated section 2(b) of the Bill of Rights. The plaintiffs sought to distinguish the majority decision in *Miller and Cockriell* on the basis that the court there had been heavily influenced by the fact that what had been challenged was an amendment to the Criminal Code passed by Parliament after the adoption of the Bill of Rights and after extensive public debate. In the *McCann* case, what was being challenged was not a legislative provision, but rather the application of a regulation. As a piece of delegated legislation on which no parliamentary scrutiny had been brought to bear it could not be said that there was any legislative intent that section 2(b) not apply.[49]

Courts in the United States have applied the 'cruel and unusual punishment' clause of the Eighth Amendment primarily in relation to the conditions of prison life. These cases, the *McCann* plaintiffs contended, were of particular interest in suggesting avenues of inquiry to be undertaken by the federal court. The plaintiffs, in citing the American cases, were not seeking mirror images of the conditions in SCU, but rather hoped to give substance to the nature of the prohibition contained both in the Eighth Amendment and in section 2(b) of the Bill of Rights.[50]

In *Jordan* v. *Fitzharris*[51] prisoners challenged the conditions of solitary confinement in Soledad Prison in California. Chief Judge Harris of the United States Federal District Court identified three general approaches to the 'cruel and unusual punishment' clause.

> The first approach is to ask whether, under all the circumstances, the punishment in question is of such character as to shock general conscience or to be intolerable to fundamental fairness ... Secondly, a punishment may be cruel and unusual if greatly disproportionate to the offence for which it is imposed ... Finally, a punishment may be cruel and unusual when, although applied in pursuit of a legitimate penal aim, it goes beyond what is necessary to achieve that aim.[52]

The conditions under review in that case - the use of a 'strip' cell in which prisoners were kept naked - were, in physical and sanitary terms, worse than those in SCU; but, to the extent that the period of time spent in the cell was only twelve days and the relevant regulations limited it to sixty consecutive days, they were less severe. In finding that the conditions violated the Eighth Amendment, Chief Judge Harris described the effects that this type of solitary confinement had on prisoners.

> [It] results in a slow burning fire of resentment on the part of the inmates until it finally explodes into open revolt, coupled with violent and bizarre conduct. Requiring man or beast to live, eat and sleep under the degrading conditions pointed out in the testimony creates a condition that inevitably does violence to elemental concepts of decency.[53]

Novak v. *Veto*[54] challenged the conditions in a Texas prison which, like those in Soledad, were physically more debilitating than those in the British Columbia Penitentiary, although they were imposed for a much more limited time. Circuit Judge Tuttle, in applying the general tests indicated in *Jordan* v. *Fitzharris*, stated that implicit in the decisions of the Supreme Court on the Eighth Amendment is the notion that embedded in this society are certain standards of human decency:

> [These standards] put a limit on the kind of punishment we will inflict on anyone regardless of his offence. Though we may be dealing here with some of the most incorrigible members of our society (although not solely), how we treat these individuals determines, to a large extent, the moral fibre of our society as a whole and if we trespass beyond the bounds of decency, such excesses become an affront to the sensibility of each of us.[55]

While many of the American cases have focused on the physical and sanitary conditions in solitary-confinement units, increasing attention has been paid to the psychological effects of the solitary regime. In *Sostre* v. *McGuinnis,*[56] Judge Feinberg, addressing the issue of long-term solitary confinement, stated:

> In this Orwellian age, punishment that endangers sanity, no less than physical injury by the strap, is prohibited by the Constitution. Indeed, we have learned to our sorrow in the last few decades that true inhumanity seeks to destroy the psyche rather than merely the body.[57]

Wright v. *McCann*[58] dealt with the practice in the New York State prison system that permitted indefinite detention in conditions of solitary confinement. The court concluded that this allowed

> the Sword of Damocles to hang for considerable periods of time and unquestionably must cause mental aggravation and unrest in a prisoner's mind, solely because of indefiniteness ... Deputy Warden Delong, who has apparently peremptorily imposed a great number of segregation confinement sentences, mostly indefinite, testified in his deposition ... if the prisoner in segregation did not come around to the unwritten criteria he wanted, such criteria being subjective and derived from custom, he had the discretion under certain circumstances to keep a prisoner in segregation during his whole term.[59]

Although *Spain* v. *Procunier*[60] was decided after judgment was rendered in the *McCann* case, the decision of District Judge Zirpoli is of special interest because the prisoners in that case had criminal and penitentiary records similar to those of some of the *McCann* plaintiffs; in addition, they were confined under a similar regime and for reasons that corresponded with the rationales for confinement of several of the *McCann* plaintiffs.[61] The prisoners in *Spain* v. *Procunier* had been jointly indicted on three counts of murder of correctional officers and two counts of murder of other prisoners. They had been also indicted on several separate counts of aggravated assault on three other officers. The prisoners had been confined in maximum-security segregation on the first and most restricted tier of San Quentin's Adjustment Center since August 1971.[62] At the time of trial, they had spent in excess of four years in segregation. The prison authorities cited the prisoners' pending trial on murder and assault indictments as the primary justification for their continuous confinement in segregation.

Like SCU, the Adjustment Center 'is the newest ... of San Quentin's antiquated housing facilities'; but according to Judge Zirpoli, 'it nevertheless has become a "hole" for isolated segregation because of the prolonged and restrictive housing conditions and dehumanizing restraints placed upon those who are housed there.'[63] The court described cell conditions in the Adjustment Center at San Quentin. Like those in SCU, the concrete cells contained no furnishings other than a sleeping platform, a sink, and a toilet. Unlike the SCU cell, the San Quentin cell had a barred rather than a solid door, was equipped with a light that could be controlled by the prisoner and with a sink that provided both hot and cold water. The regimes in both institutions were similar. Prisoners were not permitted to work or to engage in recreational activities, and all visits took place behind screens. During visits, prisoners were at all times required to wear special white coveralls and were restrained by hand manacles, waist belts, leg-irons, and neck chains. They were strip-searched before and after such visits. With the exception of the neck chains, these were the prevailing practices for visits in SCU. Prisoners in the Adjustment Center were confined to their cells twenty-four hours a day, except for periods of tier exercise (in the corridor), one prisoner at a time, one hour per day, five days a week. However, the court found that in practice the exercise time actually worked out to less than five days a week and often to less than one hour per period. Prisoners were never permitted yard or outdoor privileges or exercise. In addition to the regular cells, the Adjustment Center had a series of 'management cells,' each of which had a small anteroom with a solid steel door. These cells were used for disciplinary purposes.[64]

Judge Zirpoli, on the basis of the extensive evidence heard from the prisoners, former guards, and expert witnesses, held:

> The continued segregated confinement of plaintiffs to the first tier of the Adjustment Center not only militates against reform and rehabilitation of plaintiffs, but is so counterproductive that it instills in them a deeper hatred for

and alienation from the society that initially justly put them there. Plaintiffs live in an atmosphere of fear and apprehension and are confined under degrading conditions without affirmative programs of training or rehabilitation and without possible rewards or incentives from the State which will give them a semblance of hope for their transfer out of the Adjustment Center. The Court comes to the conclusion that the continuous segregation of plaintiffs 24 hours a day, except for meager out-of-cell movements and tier exercise; the denial to plaintiffs of fresh air and regular outdoor exercise and recreation; the unwarranted and cruel use of tear gas to remove plaintiffs from their cells with its consequent dangers of injuries to plaintiffs or occupants of nearby cells; and the abhorrent and shocking use of excessive restraints, the combined form of hand manacles, waist belt, leg chains and neck chains for all of plaintiffs' out-of-prison movements, constitutes cruel and unusual punishment.[65]

Judge Zirpoli also found that the prison authorities' 'vague assertions that plaintiffs are revolutionary, disruptive, destructive, militant, aggressive or violent and their specifically asserted primary claim that plaintiffs must be held in the Adjustment Center until the termination of the ... trial (on charges as to which they are presumed to be innocent) fail to constitute a rational security related justification for the continued confinement of the plaintiffs in the Adjustment Center.'[66]

'CRUEL AND UNUSUAL' PUNISHMENT: THE PRINCIPLES APPLIED TO SOLITARY CONFINEMENT

As the final step in their legal argument on the application of section 2(b) to their confinement in SCU, the plaintiffs in the *McCann* case sought to apply the principles developed by Mr Justice Brennan in *Furman* v. *Georgia* (as they had come to be applied in the American prison cases on solitary), and those articulated by Mr Justice McIntyre in *Miller and Cockriell*.

Mr Justice Brennan's first principle was that 'the punishment (or treatment) must not be so severe as to be degrading to the dignity of human beings.' The plaintiffs cited the evidence of their expert witnesses that solitary confinement in SCU was 'an attempt to crush the human spirit,' was designed 'to reduce the individual to that condition where there is no conceivable human resistance, where they represent essentially nothing' and 'to break their morale ... to break them down psychologically and make them submissive.' They cited their own evidence that they were reduced to self-mutilation and self-immolation, that they were forced to live with the imminent threat of their own insanity and death made manifest by the presence among them of men who were driven insane, of men who did indeed kill themselves on solitary row. They submitted that all this evidence amply demonstrated that their treatment was, in design and effect, degrading to the dignity of human beings.

Mr Justice Brennan's second principle held that 'a severe punishment must not be unacceptable to a contemporary society' and must 'accord with public standards of decency and propriety.' He suggested that the task of the court is to review the history of the challenged punishment. There is support for this approach in the judgment of Chief Justice Laskin in *Miller and Cockriell* where, in addressing the question of the relevant tests for the application of section 2(b), he stated that

> ... there are social and moral considerations that enter into the scope and application of Section 2(b). Harshness of punishment and its severity in consequences are relative to the offence involved but, that being said, there still may be a question (to which history, too, may be called in aid of its resolution) whether the punishment prescribed is so excessive as to outrage standards of decency.[67]

The plaintiffs' argument reviewed the historical origins of solitary confinement and its eventual abandonment as a general penal practice. The plaintiffs pointed specifically to the 1892 codification of criminal law which provided that 'the punishment of solitary confinement or of the pillory shall not be awarded by any court.'[68] They argued that Parliament had specifically outlawed the punishment of solitary confinement as being inconsistent with evolving standards of decency as they had developed to that point. How could it be said that these standards now permitted penitentiary officials, under the guise of an ambiguous regulation, to impose that which was so clearly rejected nearly one hundred years ago?

The historical research carried out for the purpose of this book shows that this argument, to the extent that it was based on the provision of the 1892 code, was not well founded. Within two years of the promulgation of the new code, the Prison of Isolation - specifically designed for solitary confinement - was opened at Kingston Penitentiary. However, the same research that shows that solitary confinement was not thought to be offensive to evolving standards in 1892 also reveals a useful framework for pouring historical content into the test of evolving standards in the context of prison conditions. In 1889, the inspector of penitentiaries, in his annual report to the minister of justice, refers to the changes made in the 'convict uniform' which had so distinctively identified prisoners as outcasts of society.

> If there be one thing more than another in any system of prison administration that is calculated to demoralize and stamp out every vestige of manhood and

self-respect, it is the zebra and piebald raiment which forms such a cruelly distinctive and prominent feature of some penal institutions. This barbarous relic of a period when no consideration was extended to the convict, when no interest was felt in his amelioration or well being, should, with the 'goose step' be incontinently done away with everywhere as *out of keeping with our progress and enlightenment* and unworthy of a Christian people [emphasis added].[69]

Practices calculated to stamp out a person's self-respect and dignity were seen in 1889 to be the essence of barbarous penal techniques. When the evidence given in *McCann* is applied to the framework of evolving standards suggested by Inspector Moylan, it becomes clear that solitary confinement in the 1980s, like the zebra and piebald uniform of the 1880s, is 'a barbarous relic ... out of keeping with our progress and enlightenment.'

The third principle identified by the American cases was that the punishment must not be arbitrarily inflicted. According to Mr Justice McIntyre's restatement of the test, a punishment will conflict with section 2(b) 'if it cannot be applied on a rational basis in accordance with ascertained or ascertainable standards.' The plaintiffs in *McCann* submitted that they had described a system of decision-making in which men were confined in SCU, not necessarily because of what they had done, but because of what their reputations and attitudes were perceived to be by prison officials who could and did rely upon intuition rather than on any reasoned judgment based on proved facts. The only consistent theme which could be derived from that evidence, reinforced by the evidence of their treatment in SCU, was the tyrannical theme of arbitrariness.

The fourth principle was that the punishment or treatment must not be excessive. In Mr Justice Brennan's formulation, solitary confinement would be excessive if it served no legitimate penal purpose or if it went beyond what was necessary to achieve a legitimate penal purpose. Mr Justice McIntyre's restatement separated the discrete elements of Mr Justice Brennan's principle: solitary confinement would violate section 2(b) of the Bill of Rights if it served no legitimate penal purpose, if it was unnecessary because of the existence of adequate alternatives, or if it was excessive and out of proportion to the evils it sought to restrain. Professor Berger has referred to these refinements of Mr Justice Brennan's excessiveness test as the 'social purpose test,' the 'necessity test,' and the 'disproportionality test.'[70]

The evidence in the *McCann* case from both the plaintiffs' and the defendants' witnesses demonstrated that solitary confinement in the British Columbia Penitentiary under the conditions prevalent in the SCU served no legitimate penal purpose. Dr Korn defined the regime as cruel:

'Cruelty is the infliction of pain either gratuitously or by intent without ... effective regard to the welfare of the person on whom it is being inflicted ... it is suffering to no useful end to either party.'[71] When asked whether solitary confinement as practised at the British Columbia Penitentiary served a penal purpose, he replied that it served no reasonable or rational penal purpose in terms of deterrence, long-range control, treatment, or reformation.[72]

The director of the penitentiary, Mr Cernetic, did not disagree with Dr Korn's assessment. During the course of his cross-examination the following exchange took place:

q And you agree with me, do you not, that solitary confinement as it has been practised under Section 2.30A at the bc Penitentiary does not serve any positive penal purpose?
a In view of the facilities we are utilizing.
q And the program that you have to design because of those facilities.
a That's correct.[73]

Mr Cernetic admitted that he had stated that he would like to see the solitary-confinement unit at the British Columbia Penitentiary closed.[74]

The plaintiffs, in the course of their argument, conceded that for the stated purpose of section 2.30(1)(a), the 'maintenance of good order and discipline in the institution,' it was legitimate in certain situations to dissociate prisoners from the general population. I will deal later with what those situations might be. However, the evidence in the *McCann* case showed clearly that the effects of solitary confinement in SCU engendered such feelings of hatred and rage in those subjected to it that it undermined and threatened the very objective it was supposed to further.[75] The plaintiffs argued that the legitimate purpose of dissociating prisoners could be accomplished through an alternative regime that did not have the debilitating features of solitary confinement. The plaintiffs' experts were asked to inform the court of what the 'adequate alternatives' might be, specifically for the purpose of laying an evidentiary foundation for this part of the 'cruel and unusual' test. The regime put forward by Dr Korn included several important components. Within a physically secure perimeter, prisoners would retain all their rights and privileges. Dissociated prisoners would be entitled to have visits from other prisoners within the secure perimeter, subject to the visitors being carefully frisked; they would also be allowed to receive visits from people in the 'free world.' They would have access to therapists of their choice in order to develop the trust that was totally lacking in their relationships with the prison psychiatrist in SCU. The cells would be larger. Prisoners would be permitted more personal effects, because prisoners subjected to this extreme form of confinement need more rather than less reinforcement of their sense of identity. There would be no constant illumination in the cells, and prisoners would not be required to arrange their bodies in any particular way during sleep.[76]

Dr Korn commented on his proposed regime as compared to that of SCU: 'What I couldn't understand in the BC Penitentiary is the gratuitous cruelty, the unnecessary cruelty. I can understand rigour when it is necessary but what I can't put together is the unnecessary aspect of it ... the tininess of the cell, the threadbare character of the articles.'[77]

Dr Korn found the twenty-four-hour illumination primitive; the requirement that the prisoners sleep with their heads by the toilet so that their heads were visible to the guards he characterized as 'gratuitous and shocking.' In Dr Korn's regime, prisoners would exercise under the sky. As he put it, even 'condemned men walk in the yard.'[78]

In addressing the question of alternatives, Dr Fox described the process of negotiating solutions to the inherent dilemmas involved in confining prisoners beyond the already restrictive regime of maximum-security imprisonment. Citing some proposals developed by me for dealing with the more general problem of prison discipline,[79] he suggested that there had to be an acceptance on the part of the prison administration, the guards, and the prisoners that they were all part of a community and that the only alternative to the constant escalation of force and counterforce was 'a program of equal dialogue, and self-determination inside of the institution.'[80] That dialogue must be a three-way affair between the prisoners, guards, and administration, with all parties accepting their reciprocal relationship to one another and their joint responsibility for ensuring that prison life, which to varying degrees they all shared, respected each other's common humanity and dignity. The guards' participation was essential to this process: 'they are not robots to be assigned that nightmare up there and say 'deal with it' ... they need full voice in that dialogue. It is a three-way dialogue because they are all members of that family.'[81]

Under the present conception of SCU, prisoners confined there are not perceived to be members of any prison community or family. As Dr Fox put it: 'SCU is casting out. They are no longer members of the community. There is nothing to deal with, there is no way of solving the problem because they are not in your purview, they are cast-outs; they are not part of your life any more. Once you are cast out there is nothing but violence and anger. You become outlawed.'[82]

Mr Cernetic and the assistant deputy of security, Mr Leech, conceded that, given their purposes for dissociating prisoners, many of the restrictive features of the SCU which Dr Korn had described as 'gratuitous cruelty' were dictated by the way the SCU was constructed and by the lack of adequate staff. They admitted, in other words, that the present repressive regime was not related to any legitimate penal purposes, but resulted from budgetary limitations. The plaintiffs suggested to the court that 'human considerations and constitutional requirements are not to be measured or limited by dollar considerations.'[83]

THE JUDGMENT OF THE COURT ON 'CRUEL AND UNUSUAL' PUNISHMENT

Mr Justice Heald ruled that confinement of the plaintiffs in SCU did constitute cruel and unusual punishment or treatment within the meaning of section 2(b) of the Bill of Rights. In so finding he applied the tests set out in Mr Justice McIntyre's judgment in *Miller and Cockriell*, preferring it to that of the majority of the Court of Appeal. However, the way in which the McIntyre tests are applied in the *McCann* judgment is somewhat elliptical, and some elaboration is necessary in order to assess the contribution the judgment makes to the interpretation of the 'cruel and unusual punishment' clause.

Mr Justice Heald, having adopted Mr Justice McIntyre's view that the terms 'cruel' and 'unusual' are to be viewed disjunctively, proceeded to deal with the terms conjunctively, characterizing the treatment of prisoners in SCU first as 'cruel' and then as 'unusual.' In finding that the treatment was cruel, Mr Justice Heald cited the fact that the plaintiffs' experts, Dr Korn, Dr Fox, and Dr Marcus, 'had no hesitation in describing it as cruel treatment.' He added that 'when the expert evidence is considered along with the evidence of the plaintiffs themselves, I have no hesitation in concluding that the treatment afforded them in solitary at the BC Penitentiary has been cruel.'[84]

One way of reading Mr Justice Heald's conclusion would be to see it as a referential incorporation of the experts' personal views of what constitutes cruelty. Indeed, this is just how Mr Justice Toy in the later case of *R.* v. *Bruce, Lucas and Wilson*[85] so interpreted it. That case involved criminal charges of forcible confinement brought against three prisoners, including Andy Bruce, who had taken hostages inside the penitentiary when they were in the general population. Their defence was that of 'necessity'; they stated that they honestly believed that they were about to be returned to SCU and took the hostages as the lesser evil to avoid the greater evil of being placed in confinement that amounted to the imposition of cruel and unusual punishment or treatment. Dr Korn and Dr Fox testified before Mr Justice Toy as witnesses for the defendants. In refusing to follow Mr Justice Heald's conclusion that the conditions in SCU were cruel and unusual (the conditions in *Bruce et al.* were in all material respects identical to those which were the subject of the *McCann* case) Mr Justice Toy viewed Mr Justice Heald's conclusion that the conditions amounted to cruel treatment as being based upon the definitions of cruelty proferred by the expert witnesses. Mr Justice Toy was of the opinion that in giving their definitions, Dr Fox and Dr Korn 'were, quite naturally for them, carrying on their dialogue in the witness box in the language of their discipline, namely Psychology ... In the context of construing and/or applying the laws of this country, however, such terminology overstates or exaggerates the effects and consequences on the accused in the context of section 2(b) of the Bill of Rights.'[86]

It can be argued, however, that Mr Justice Heald was not simply adopting the experts' definitions of cruelty expressed in the technical language of psychology. Dr Korn's definition of cruelty was directly related to Mr Justice McIntyre's test of the punishment's unnecessary and gratuitous nature. Similarly, the conclusions of Dr Marcus and Dr Fox that the regime in SCU was cruel were related to the test of whether the punishment degraded the dignity of the prisoners as human beings. The evidence of these witnesses was extensively reviewed by Mr Justice Heald, and his reference to their characterization of treatment in SCU as 'cruel' is to be seen against the backdrop of that review.

In dealing with the concept of 'unusual' Mr Justice Heald applied the tests of Mr Justice McIntyre. He concluded, based on the evidence of the expert witnesses and the admission of the director of the penitentiary, that the treatment served no positive penal purpose.[87] However, the penal-purpose test was identified by Mr Justice McIntyre not as a separate one for 'unusual' but rather for the compendious phrase 'cruel and unusual.' Indeed, Mr Justice Heald seemed to acknowledge this in his application of the other McIntyre tests: 'Furthermore, even if it served some positive penal purpose, I still think the treatment would be cruel *and* unusual because it is not in accord with public standards of decency and propriety, since it is unnecessary because of the existence of adequate alternatives [emphasis added]'.[88]

In concluding that the regime in SCU did not accord with public standards of decency and propriety, Mr Justice Heald did not rely upon the historical analysis submitted by the plaintiffs. He found that this non-accordance arose because he was 'satisfied that adequate alternatives do exist which would remove the 'cruel and unusual' aspects of solitary while at the same time retaining the necessary security aspects of dissociation.'[89] Mr Justice Heald appears here to be making the 'public decency' test conditional upon the 'necessity' test. However, Mr Justice McIntyre clearly saw the tests of public decency and necessity as discrete, and not as so interrelated that the violation of the latter was a prerequisite to the violation of the former. In addition to giving no independent meaning to the public decency test, Mr Justice Heald did not make any reference to the 'arbitrariness' test in reaching his conclusion on 'cruel and unusual.'

Mr Justice Heald sought to buttress his finding that the treatment in SCU was 'unusual' by finding that even given the restricted meaning ascribed to that phrase by the majority of the British Columbia Court of Appeal in the *Miller and Cockriell* case – that is, its ordinary and natural meaning as defined by the dictionary – certain aspects of the regime came within that definition.In support of this conclusion he cited the evidence of Andy Bruce and Jake Quiring that in light of their experience in other solitary-confinement units in Canadian penitentiaries the conditions in the SCU at the British Columbia Penitentiary were the worst they had experienced; the evidence of Mr Cernetic that at least in two other Canadian maximum-security institutions there were superior facilities for fresh-air exercise; the evidence of guns being pointed at the prisoners (which put the SCU 'in a class by itself'); the evidence of Dr Korn that 'it was unique in his experience to see rifles in a segregation unit'; and the lack of evidence that the twenty-four-hour light was 'usual' in other Canadian penitentiaries or that the mandatory sleeping position was employed elsewhere. Moreover, the length of time spent in solitary by the plaintiffs was 'of itself sufficient to categorize the treatment of them as unusual.'[90]

The task of formulating and applying the relevant principles underlying section 2(b) to conditions in the penitentiary arose a second time one year after the *McCann* judgment. As I have already indicated, Mr Justice Toy, in *R.* v. *Bruce, Lucas and Wilson*, having before him evidence and legal argument substantially similar to that presented in *McCann* regarding the conditions in SCU, refused to follow Mr Justice Heald's finding that those conditions constituted cruel and unusual punishment. Mr Justice Toy based that refusal on three grounds. First, in his opinion the disjunctive interpretation of the phrase 'cruel and unusual' was 'in error in view of the non-acceptance of the alternative or disjunctive interpretation by any of the members of the Court who wrote judgments in the Supreme Court of Canada in *Miller and Cockriell*.'[91] With great respect to Mr Justice Toy, there is a double flaw in his argument. First, Chief Justice Laskin, writing for himself and two other members of the court, in viewing the 'cruel and unusual' clause as 'a compendious expression of a norm,' adopted a broad approach to the clause which is much closer to the disjunctive approach than the conjunctive. Second, as I have already described, Mr Justice Heald, having stated his preference for the disjunctive approach, went on in the course of his judgment to consider separately both the cruelty and the unusualness of the treatment in SCU, and in effect applied the conjunctive approach favoured by the majority of the Supreme Court of Canada.

The second reason given by Mr Justice Toy for not following Mr Justice Heald involves the meaning ascribed to the term 'cruel.' I have previously dealt with this point and have shown that Mr Justice Toy's inference that Mr Justice Heald simply adopted the meaning given that term by expert witnesses is not a proper reading of the Heald judgment.

The third reason given by Mr Justice Toy is that in his approach to the term 'unusual' Mr Justice Heald diverges from the approach taken by Mr Justice McIntyre, whom he purported to follow.[92] I have already commented on the extent to which Mr Justice Heald confused the McIntyre tests, although, since Mr Justice McIntyre was not prepared to accord the term 'unusual' any limiting role on the proper meaning to be given section 2(b), Mr Justice Toy's point is hardly a weighty one.

Mr Justice Toy proceeded to apply his own interpretation of the proper tests to be used in construing section 2(b). Referring to the dictionary definition of 'cruel' as 'disposed to inflict suffering, indifferent to or taking pleasure in others' pain; merciless, pitiless, hardhearted,' he reviewed the evidence. While he was persuaded that 'if one gives effect to the concept of indifference in the dictionary definition of cruel, many events in the paths of [the defendants'] lives have been cruel,'[93] he concluded that at least some of the damage done to the prisoners had been inflicted outside of the solitary-confinement experience and was to some extent of their own making. Mr Justice Toy stated that there were many undesirable aspects of the SCU; in particular, the continued confinement of McCaulley in the unit and the lack of outside exercise. He remarked that 'if I were looking at the concept of administrative segregation in the light of the meaning of the word cruel alone, [these are] aspects of the programme that I would like to see legislatively changed.'[94] Citing the dictionary definition of 'unusual' as 'not often occurring or observed, different from what is usual, out of the common, remarkable, exceptional,' the judge held that in light of the evidence (which was less complete on this issue than in the *McCann* case), he remained 'unconvinced that the administrative segregation practised at the BC Penitentiary should, by itself, be considered unusual, even according to the common meaning of the word.'[95]

Mr Justice Toy then proceeded to apply to the overall conditions in SCU the formula for construing section 2(b) that was adopted by Chief Justice Laskin in *Miller and Cockriell* 'in the absence of any other guide from the majority judgment.'[96] That formula he understood to be directed to a consideration of whether 'the punishment prescribed [is] so excessive as to outrage standards of decency.' Applying that formula, Mr Justice Toy, after noting that 'Canadian society has not had to concern itself with what goes on behind the prison walls, and, unlike the subject of capital punishment, there have not been made apparent any discernible guidelines which would indicate to me what the current standard of public decency is,'[97] concluded that the people who are admitted to the SCU under administrative segregation are not 'subjected to a harshness so severe that public decency dictates that the Court should decide that it be stopped.'[98]

Mr Justice Toy referred to the evidence placed before him concerning the existence of alternative regimes but dismissed that evidence as irrelevant since in his view this test had not found favour in any of the Supreme Court judgments in *Miller and Cockriell.* This part of Mr Justice Toy's judgment is perplexing. Chiding Mr Justice Heald for adopting the broad disjunctive approach to 'cruel and unusual,' and citing that as a reason for not following the federal court judge, he then adopts Chief Justice Laskin's compendious approach to the term, which clearly favours a broad interpretation. Furthermore, in seeking to discern in the one passage cited a formula for the interpretation of section 2(b), Mr Justice Toy, in applying the chief justice's statement of what in effect are the public-decency and excessive-punishment principles, failed to consider the rest of the chief justice's analysis. After the passage cited by Mr Justice Toy, Chief Justice Laskin proceeded to review the arguments addressed to the court by those who challenged the death penalty. Those arguments embraced the four principles developed by Mr Justice Brennan in *Furman* v. *Georgia* as reformulated by Mr Justice McIntyre - the principles of degradation of human dignity, arbitrariness, unacceptability in terms of public decency, and excessiveness in light of the existence of less severe alternatives. The chief justice, far from suggesting that these tests were not appropriate criteria for the application of section 2(b), proceeded to deal with each in turn. Although he concluded that the death penalty did not conflict with any of them, it is inconceivable that the chief justice would have devoted over half of his judgment to detailing carefully why the death penalty as administered in Canada did not conflict with a set of principles if those principles were not relevant to the analysis in the first place. The chief justice gave particular attention to the principle of excessive punishment, which, as we have seen, was heavily relied upon by Mr Justice Heald and so readily dismissed as irrelevant by Mr Justice Toy.

In *Miller and Cockriell*, the appellants contended that the purposes of punishment in relation to the murder of policemen or prison guards could be equally well served by providing for a lesser punishment such as life imprisonment. They presented evidence to show that there was no convincing proof that the imposition of capital punishment had any deterrent effect as far as murder was concerned. The chief justice rejected their argument on two grounds. First, he was of the view that the burden of proof was not, as the appellants had argued, on Parliament to show that capital punishment was an effective deterrent. Second, in assessing the issue of the purposes of punishment, it was not proper to limit that inquiry to one of general deterrence. Parliament could legitimately have regard to retribution or to the social outrage that may reasonably find expression in a penal policy of a mandatory death penalty for what the community regards as the most outrageous types of murder. Furthermore, there was a legitimate social purpose in protecting police officers and prison guards in relation to prisoners already serving life sentences, for whom the death penalty would operate as a deterrent.[99]

As I have attempted to show, the plaintiffs in *McCann* clearly demonstrated both that the regime in SCU served no legitimate penal purpose and that the legitimate penal purpose of dissociation could be achieved by alternative means. The plaintiffs assumed the burden of proof and, in Mr Justice Heald's view, met that burden. The defendants in *Bruce, Lucas and Wilson* presented the same evidence on the lack of penal purpose of the regime at SCU and the existence of adequate alternatives. A careful reading of the chief justice's judgment in *Miller and Cockriell* suggests that Mr Justice Toy was in error in rejecting this evidence and in rejecting the relevance of the underlying test of excessiveness.

For quite different reasons, therefore, neither the *McCann* nor the *Bruce, Lucas and Wilson* judgment provides an adequate analytical framework for the proper interpretation of the right not to be subjected to cruel and unusual punishment or treatment, now entrenched in section 12 of the Canadian Charter of Rights and Freedoms. It is suggested that in any future prison litigation focusing upon this right the arguments presented by the *McCann* plaintiffs will provide a surer guide to a principled approach to the limits of carceral authority.[100]

PROCEDURAL FAIRNESS AND SOLITARY CONFINEMENT

The second of the plaintiffs' primary claims was that confinement in SCU without notice of charges, without a hearing before an impartial decision-maker, without a right to make full answer and defence, and without a right to present and cross-examine witnesses deprived the plaintiffs of the right to a fair hearing in accordance with the principles of fundamental justice and contrary to the provisions of section 2(e) of the Canadian Bill of Rights, and of the right not to be deprived of the security of the person except by due process of law, as guaranteed by section 1(a) of the Bill of Rights.

The conceptual thread which linked this part of the plaintiffs' case was procedural fairness. Whereas the 'cruel and unusual punishment or treatment' argument sought to place substantive limits on the conditions under which the state could confine those prisoners who, for legitimate penal purposes, were required to be segregated from the main prison population, the procedural-fairness argument sought to gird the legitimate exercise of state authority with sufficient procedural protection to ensure that power was exercised in a fair and just manner to prevent its abuse. The concern underlying both these arguments is the need to place limits on carceral power at the point of its most draconian exercise.[101]

The plaintiffs' claims to procedural fairness were conceived within the tradition of Howard's and Moylan's insistence on public and visible superintendency of the prisons and of an amply developed administrative-law framework which has at its centre 'the assumption by the courts of supervisory powers over certain tribunals in order to assure the proper functioning of the machinery of government.'[102] Yet at the time of the *McCann* trial there was a remarkable dearth of Canadian judicial authority dealing with the rights of prisoners to procedural fairness in disciplinary decisions within the prison walls. In contrast with the well-developed jurisprudence on prisoners' rights in the United States, the Canadian courts had followed the traditional hands-off approach to prison cases. Only in the case of *R.* v. *Institutional Head of Beaver Creek Correctional Camp, ex parte McCaud*[103] had an appellate court countenanced the possibility of judicial review of a prison decision on the basis of lack of procedural fairness. In that case a prisoner in a federal penitentiary applied by way of a writ of certiorari to review a disciplinary decision made by the superintendent of the institution. The sole issue before the court was whether an institutional head acting in his disciplinary capacity was amenable to a writ of certiorari if he acted without jurisdiction. The applicant alleged that he was denied a hearing, was denied the right to give evidence, and was not told the charges against him, and that the punishment imposed was not authorized by law. Although the court did not have before it sufficient particulars of the acts of the superintendent that were objected to, the Ontario Court of Appeal felt it desirable to consider generally 'the implications of an institutional head acting with respect to discipline imposing sanctions for infractions of discipline.'[104]

The court held that although the major commitment of an institutional head is to make administrative decisions not amenable to judicial review, there were circumstances where the scope of his office required him to act in a judicial manner because his decision may affect the civil rights of the prisoner.[105] In such cases his decisions were reviewable. The court, in distinguishing between decisions that were purely administrative in character (and hence non-reviewable) and those that were required to be exercised judicially (and hence reviewable), stated that the proper test to apply was 'whether the proceedings sought to be reviewed have deprived the inmate wholly or in part of his civil rights in that they affect his status as a person as distinguished from his status as an inmate.'[106]

The court enumerated the civil rights to which a prisoner is entitled that may be affected by the acts of the institutional head. The court stated that since the prisoner's right to liberty was nonexistent during the period of his lawful confinement, all decisions of the officers of the penitentiary service with respect to the place and manner of confinement were exercises of authority which were purely administrative. Also, the withdrawal of or restrictive interference with privileges, the normal punishment for minor disciplinary offences, and the crediting or abstaining from crediting of earned remission were not regarded by the court as acts affecting any civil rights of the prisoner as a person, and hence were administrative and non-reviewable. The court held that forfeiture of statutory remission, since it extended the length of imprisonment, affected a prisoner's right to liberty, and hence the decision to forfeit must be exercised judicially. The court also held that the ordering of corporal punishment was a punishment that affected the civil rights of a prisoner to personal security and was therefore the exercise of a power that was by its nature judicial.

The *Beaver Creek* court went on to find that a prisoner became entitled to certain statutory rights that were contained in the Penitentiary Act and the regulations made thereunder. Non-observance of provisions in the act or its regulations would have a debilitating effect on the institutional head's jurisdiction and would be reviewable. However, commissioner's directives made pursuant to the act and regulations (and which contain the substance of the procedural code governing the conduct of disciplinary hearings in the penitentiary) did not confer any rights on prisoners, being in the realm of administrative policy. Non-observance of these directives would not give rise to a denial of prisoners' rights sufficient to support judicial review.

Where an institutional head is required to act judicially he must observe the principles of fundamental justice. The court held these principles to mean

> that the inmate affected must be fully informed of the disciplinary offence he is alleged to have committed, that he be given a fair opportunity to present his case and the evidence relevant to matters he is called upon to face, and that the decision of the institutional head be arrived at judicially upon material properly before him and not capriciously or in reliance upon some consideration not relevant to the charge.[107]

In *Beaver Creek* the prisoner's lawyer had argued that the superintendent's action infringed the provisions of section 2(e) of the Bill of Rights which requires a fair hearing in accordance with the principles of fundamental justice for the determination of a prisoner's rights and obligations. In response to this argument the Ontario Court of Appeal held that, on its interpretation of the Penitentiary Act, where the civil rights of a prisoner may be affected by the decision of an institutional head, there must be a fair hearing in accordance with the principles of fundamental justice, and thus there was no conflict with the Bill of Rights. In other words, the interpretation placed on the Penitentiary Act by the court in relation to decisions affecting the civil rights of a prisoner was as restrictive on the actions of an institutional head as the provisions of the Canadian Bill of Rights. By necessary implication the court held that section 2(e) of the Bill of Rights was inapplicable to administrative decisions not affecting a prisoner's civil rights.

On its face, the *Beaver Creek* case seemed to create substantial impediments to the plaintiff's arguments in *McCann* that confinement in SCU must be preceded by a hearing in accordance with the principles of fundamental justice. Was not such a decision an administrative one affecting merely the 'place and manner of confinement' and hence non-reviewable? The plaintiffs in *McCann* demurred to this implication of *Beaver Creek* by pointing out to Mr Justice Heald that in defining which prison decisions affected a prisoner's civil rights (thus requiring a fair hearing) and which did not, the Ontario Court of Appeal did not have before it any detailed evidence of the nature of those prison decisions and their impact on prisoners' lives. Mr Justice Heald had had the benefit of over three weeks of extensive evidence on these matters and, the plaintiffs submitted, was in a better position than the Ontario Court of Appeal to draw conclusions as to whether, in light of the prison reality, a particular decision affected the civil rights of a prisoner.

Given this premise, the plaintiffs in *McCann* went on to point out several problematic features of the Ontario Court of Appeal's classification of prison decisions in light of the reality of the federal penitentiary system. In *Beaver Creek*, the court was quite prepared to consider a decision involving corporal punishment as judicial because of its impact on the prisoner's right to personal security. The court saw it as punishment *upon* the person as compared to punishment *of* the person such as, in its view, would be involved in the alteration of locale or nature of confinement. However, the plaintiffs submitted that the evidence of the effects of solitary confinement which had been presented to Mr Justice Heald left no doubt that dissociation of the kind the plaintiffs had endured had a massive impact on a prisoner's right to personal security. The difference between a strapping and confinement in SCU is the difference between a physical impact and a psychological impact on personal security. The plaintiffs contended that in terms of its enduring quality, confinement in SCU left a far more indelible imprint on them than the purely physical imprint of the strap. The plaintiffs reminded Mr Justice Heald of the evidence of Dr Korn and Dr Fox: 'The evidence simply is that if you keep people long enough, they will engage in self-torture, simply to focus the pain ... Physical pain which is definite, which they can control, is much more bearable than the torment they can neither understand nor control.'[108]

A second functional limitation of the *Beaver Creek* classification concerned the approach of the Ontario Court of Appeal to the concept of liberty. That approach was that upon the passing of sentence, the prisoner, for the period of his lawful confinement, loses all his rights to liberty. Liberty was seen here as an all-or-nothing proposition; one is either 'free' by being out of prison or 'unfree' by being in prison. The plaintiffs submitted that this is not in accord with the realities of prison life. That reality is that even after the fact of imprisonment, a prisoner retains a certain freedom of mobility and communication while in the general population of the prison. As one commentator put it, 'there is a significant quantum of institutional and traditional liberty to which every inmate remains entitled while incarcerated.'[109] The plaintiffs called Mr Justice Heald's attention to the qualitative change from confinement in the general population to confinement in the SCU and to Dr Korn's evidence that the prisoner's placement in administrative segregation 'is the most fateful decision in his prison life.'[110] The plaintiffs contended that the decision to place a man in SCU so dramatically affected the nature of his imprisonment, so dramatically curtailed his institutional freedom, that it is required to be made on a judicial basis.

In the absence of any other Canadian decision on the issue of when procedural fairness must be accorded in prison decision-making, the plaintiffs submitted that it was relevant to look at the case law that had been developing in the United States. A comparative inquiry, they argued, was particularly valid because many of the cases had been preceded by extensive trials in which the details of prison life and prison decision-making had been laid before the court, and because the legal issue before the American courts had been essentially the same as the one urged on Mr Justice Heald: which prison decisions have such an important impact on a prisoner's life that they must be preceded by a fair hearing?

The American prison cases in this area have centred on the applicability of the Fourteenth Amendment to the U.S. Constitution, which guarantees that the states shall not deprive any person of life, liberty, or property without due process of law. The courts, in approaching the questions of when and to what extent due process has to be afforded in the prison context, have looked at the realities of prison life and have accepted the concept of institutional liberty as being within the protection of the Fourteenth Amendment. The prevailing approach of the American cases has been to ask whether the decision under review caused the prisoner 'grievous loss' so as to outweigh the governmental interest in summary adjudication.[111]

In *Landman* v. *Royster*,[112] inmates of the Virginia prison system brought a class action, maintaining that they had been placed in solitary confinement and/or had had statutory remission taken from them without due process of law. The court heard extensive evidence on the practices of the disciplinary system of the Virginia state prisons and the procedures whereby men were placed in solitary confinement. In his judgment, Merhige J described the conditions and procedures for transfer to 'C-cell,' the segregation unit at the Virginia State Farm, in this way:

> C-cell inmates ... enjoy substantially fewer privileges than men among the general population. Prisoners in C-cell cannot be employed in a work program; thus they are denied the opportunity to earn money ... Religious services and educational classwork are unavailable, although men may be visited by a chaplain. There is no access to a library, although the men can receive magazines ... The likelihood of release on parole is almost nonexistent to men placed in C-cell and in practice there is no chance that lost good time will be restored. In addition, showers are permitted only at weekly intervals instead of daily and men in some segregation units are unable to exercise outdoors.
>
> The question whether a man should be placed in C-cell in the first instance ... is not always determined by disciplinary committee hearings. This decision may be made by the Superintendent alone ... It was [the Superintendent's] practice ... to interview all prisoners in C-cell every six months to determine whether return to general population was indicated. Criteria determining the decision to place a man in C-cell or remove him were extremely hazy. A man's attitude, his disruptiveness, tendency to challenge authority, or non-conforming behaviour, as reflected in written or oral guard's reports, may condemn him to maximum security for many years.[113]

In his legal analysis Merhige J rejected the argument that the right to be free of substantial restraints of solitary confinement or to earn statutory remission were matters of mere legislative or administrative grace. He held that both the decision to take away remission and to place a man in solitary had substantial effects on a man's life amounting to 'grievous loss': 'A man in solitary confinement is denied all human intercourse and any means of diversion ... Loss of good time credit may in effect amount to an additional prison sentence.'[114]

The judge also stated that once it was decided that a deprivation had such a substantial effect on a prisoner's life that it must be preceded by due process, it was not relevant whether the institution chose to present that deprivation in terms of a 'punishment' or as a technique for maintenance of 'control' or 'security.' The real issue was the actual effect of the decision, given the realities of the prison, and not the labels that the prison administrators chose to use.

In his ruling, Merhige J held that before imposition of solitary confinement or loss of statutory remission, due process required that a prisoner be given a hearing before an impartial tribunal, notice of charges, the right to cross-examine adverse witnesses, a decision based on the evidence and, in certain circumstances, the right to counsel or counsel substitute.

It is also important to note that Merhige J, in coming to his conclusions, made a careful analysis of the legitimate interests of prison administration in the allocation of scarce resources for rehabilitative purposes and in the speedy determination of disciplinary infractions. He concluded that the rules of procedural fairness he deemed necessary would not impede these legitimate interests.

In *Clutchette* v. *Procunier*,[115] inmates in San Quentin sought declaratory relief on the ground that the procedures relating to solitary confinement did not meet minimal standards of due process. In San Quentin, as in British Columbia Penitentiary, a distinction existed between a sentence of punitive dissociation limited to thirty days and confinement in the segregation tier or adjustment tier for an indefinite time. In its judgment, the Court of Appeals for the Ninth Circuit described the conditions in this way:

> There is very little difference between 'isolation' and the Adjustment Center. Adjustment Center inmates are compelled to spend their days in idleness, confined to their cells 23 hours a day, seven days a week. None of the ameliorative programs provided for the general prison population are available to them. Because they are not permitted to work, they lose even the meager wages with which they could make minor purchases at the canteen. They cannot enroll in vocational training programs or attend school. They are barred from church services, movies, television, and all other forms of recreation and entertainment which might help to relieve the monotony of prison life.[116]

The court, applying the test of grievous loss, stated:

> Measured against this reasoning, the argument that a state prisoner is committed to the custody of the Department of Corrections and as such may be confined in any manner chosen by the Director, subject only to statutory

guidelines and the proscriptions of the 'cruel and unusual punishment' clause of the viiith Amendment, is unpersuasive. It is based on the theory that 'custody is custody' regardless of how it is carried out, and that a prisoner suffers no real loss or gain when the nature of his custody is changed. This court has already implicitly rejected this theory ... While prisoners may have no vested right to a certain type of confinement or certain privileges, it is unrealistic to argue that the withdrawal of those privileges they do have or the substitution of more burdensome conditions of confinement would not, under their 'set of circumstances' constitute a 'grievous loss.'[117]

The court ruled that the decision to place a prisoner in solitary confinement was required to be made in conformity with due process, and laid down rules similar to those set out in *Landman* designed to ensure that such decisions were made fairly.

In *U.S. ex rel. Miller* v. *Twomey*,[118] a case concerning solitary confinement in Illinois's Stateville, the Court of Appeals for the Seventh Circuit clearly accepted the concept of institutional liberty as being within the protection of the due process clause. The court stated:

Liberty protected by the due process clause may – indeed, must to some extent, co-exist with legal custody pursuant to conviction. The deprivation of liberty following an adjudication of guilt is partial, not total. A residual of constitutionally protected rights remains ... The view once held that an inmate is a mere slave is now totally rejected. The restraints and the punishment which a criminal conviction entails do not place the citizen beyond the ethical tradition that the courts respect the dignity of intrinsic worth of every individual. 'Liberty' and 'custody' are not mutually exclusive concepts.[119]

The court, applying the test of grievous loss, stated:

Quite obviously, what impairs his residuum of liberty, is sufficiently 'grievous' to amount to a constitutional deprivation. The consequences of conviction of crime involve not merely the loss of liberty enjoyable in a free society, but additionally, the subsequent relatively minor impairments which are inevitably associated with membership in a closely supervised prison society. On the other hand, we are also convinced that additional punishment inflicted upon an inmate may be sufficiently severe, and may represent a sufficiently drastic change from the custodial status theretofore enjoyed, that it must be classified as 'grievous loss.'[120]

The court, after carefully analysing the effects of solitary confinement, held that at a bare minimum due process required written notice, a dignified hearing at which the accused may be heard, an opportunity to request that other witnesses be called or interviewed, and an impartial decision-maker. It should be noted that also at issue in the case was the due process applicable to disciplinary proceedings resulting in the loss of statutory remission. The court held that the minimum degree of due process applicable in that case was the same as for a decision resulting in solitary confinement.

In *Sands* v. *Wainwright*,[121] the plaintiff Sands, as a result of a disciplinary-committee hearing, was placed in punitive segregation in the Florida State Prison for an indefinite time, on a special diet. After serving twenty-seven days in punitive segregation, he was transferred to administrative segregation. There was no hearing before the disciplinary committee. Sands contended that his placement in administrative segregation deprived him of the due process of law. In the judgment of the court, the conditions of administrative segregation were set out:

> Each cell in administrative segregation is equipped with a bed and bedding, a toilet and a wash basin with hot and cold running water, both of which are controlled by the inmate. Each cell has a radio speaker; and, if the radio system is turned on by the responsible custodial officers, the inmate can select either of two channels which have in turn been selected by the responsible custodial officers. Alternatively, the inmate can turn it off. Lighting is provided by a single bulb which is controlled by the Correctional Officers. In administrative segregation, the inmate is provided with coveralls and shower slides (shoes) as his clothing. These are changed two times a week. Inmates are not restricted with regard to diet and receive the same rations as those in general population. Each and every meal is served and consumed in the cell. A member of the medical department sees the inmates confined in the administrative segregation cells each 48 hours. While in the cell, the inmate may converse with those others close to him.
>
> While confined in administrative segregation, the inmate never gets out of the cell for exercise; he never gets out of the cell for sunshine; he never gets out of the cell to go to work; he never gets out of the cell to go to church; he never gets out of the cell to go to school; he never gets out of the cell to go to the tv room; and he never gets out of the cell to go to the prison law library.
>
> Each week an inmate confined to administrative segregation is taken out of his cell three times to take a shower. The time interval allowed is between three and ten minutes, and during this time the inmate must go to the shower room, take a shower and come back. While confined in administrative segregation, an inmate cannot see the other inmates on the wing.[122]

The court, in its analysis of due process within the prison, stated:

Because of the prison structure, inmates have generally been thought to be without a portfolio of rights. Most benefits and advantages have been considered to be matters of privilege, not right, which the prison authority may in its full discretion, distribute to deserving inmates. This Court has no quarrel with the prison authorities' right to grant, as matters within its discretion, whatever privileges it deems appropriate to those within its custody; however once a privilege is granted, it becomes, to some extent at least, vested. Once the privilege is granted, the inmate is entitled to it. Thus, in terms of constitutionally permissible distinctions, there is no distinction between 'rights' and 'privileges.'[123]

The court went on to hold that confinement in punitive or administrative segregation and loss of statutory remission collectively and severally constituted grievous losses and required adherence to due process. In the case of administrative dissociation, this was held to mean that a prisoner must be afforded a fair and impartial hearing at which he must be informed of the reason for his confinement in administrative segregation and allowed the opportunity to be heard.

In *Crafton* v. *Luttrell*,[124] a case involving challenges to both administrative and punitive dissociation in the Tennessee State Penitentiary, the court analysed the differences between the two kinds of confinement. Of punitive dissociation, the court stated that 'the essential purpose ... is discipline. To this end, rule violators are isolated in solitary confinement from the general prison population, and are made to sacrifice certain privileges and opportunities available to other inmates.'[125] Of administrative dissociation, the court stated: 'The purpose of administrative segregation is to provide a place of temporary maximum custody to protect an individual, others, and to promote and maintain order. Administrative segregation is recommended for those men with serious problems of maladjustment, mental illness, or sexual abnormality, to the degree that their safety or the safety of others is threatened in the normal day to day status.'[126]

The court found that 'as a practical matter ... administrative segregation is utilized in many instances as a disciplinary measure for an inmate's violation of a specific prison rule.'[127] The court also stated that it did not matter whether a measure is characterized as 'punishment' or 'for the welfare of the institution'; rather, the relevant inquiry was 'what effect the measure has on the liberty of the prisoner involved. Regardless of how labelled, if commitment to administrative segregation constitutes a grievous loss, the minimum procedural safeguards are called into play.[128]

After setting out an extensive analysis of the conditions and regimes in punitive and administrative dissociation, the court held that 'commitment to administrative segregation constitutes a substantial loss of prisoner liberty, and that this loss may, in some instances, exceed the grievous loss resulting from punitive segregation confinement.'[129]

The court, in considering the minimum requirements of due process, looked not only at the need for a hearing prior to placing a man in solitary, but also at the nature of the review process. It concluded that 'an inmate facing administrative segregation should know not only the reasons for his segregation, but also that his situation and adjustment will be reviewed regularly with the goal being his return to the general prison population.'[130]

The issue of the application of due process protection in the prison came before the Supreme Court of the United States for the first time in 1974 in the case of *Wolff* v. *McDonnell*.[131] In that case it was alleged that disciplinary proceedings in the Nebraska State Prison System violated the due process guarantee of the Fourteenth Amendment. The disciplinary procedures under review were similar to those in operation in the Canadian federal penitentiary system in 1975. The Nebraska legislation classified disciplinary offences and provided that, except in flagrant or serious cases, misconduct was to be punished by withdrawal of privileges. For flagrant or serious misconduct the legislation authorized the loss of statutory remission and confinement in a disciplinary cell. The legislation also authorized the use of segregation for administrative purposes not associated with punishment. The court, in reviewing the legislation, noted that forfeiture of statutory remission affected the term of confinement; placement in a disciplinary cell involved alteration of the conditions of confinement. Dealing with the matter of statutory remission (which was the specific matter before the court) Mr Justice White, in the majority opinion, held that the prisoner's interest in remission 'has real substance and is sufficiently embraced within the Fourteenth Amendment liberty to entitle him to those minimum procedures appropriate under the circumstances and required by the due process clause to ensure that the state created right is not arbitrarily abrogated. This is the thrust of recent cases in the prison disciplinary context.'[132]

The court held that in the circumstances due process required written notice of charges, a hearing, the right to call witnesses and present documentary evidence in defence when this would not be unduly hazardous to institutional safety or correctional goals, and a written statement of fact-finding as to the evidence relied upon and the reasons for the disciplinary action taken.[133] The Supreme Court rejected the idea that confrontation and cross-examination of witnesses were constitutionally required under the due process clause for prison disciplinary proceedings, and similarly rejected the argument that there was a right to counsel at such hearings.[134]

Although the complaint in *Wolff* was confined to the issue of remission, Mr Justice White did deal with the question of solitary confinement:

It would be difficult for the purposes of procedural due process to distinguish between the procedures that are required where good time is forfeited and those that must be extended where solitary confinement is at issue. The latter represents a major change in the conditions of confinement and is normally imposed only when it is claimed and proved that there has been a major act of misconduct. Here, as in the case of good time, there should be minimum procedural safeguards as a hedge against arbitrary determination of the factual predicate for imposition of the sanction.[135]

Thus, on the question of loss of remission, the Supreme Court of the United States had come to essentially the same conclusion as the Ontario Court of Appeal in the *Beaver Creek* case: such a decision must be preceded by a hearing in accordance with rules that ensure procedural fairness to the prisoner. The *Beaver Creek* case, however, would seem to lead to a different conclusion from that of *Wolff* and the other American decisions on the issue of solitary confinement. The difference flows from the very narrow approach taken in *Beaver Creek* to the concepts of 'liberty' and 'security of person' and the more expansive view taken by the American courts. The American approach represented an understanding of the realities of the prison experience and the impact of decisions made inside the prison on a prisoner's life. In *McCann*, the plaintiffs submitted that, given the evidence presented to the court, it was open to Mr Justice Heald to find that a decision made under section 2.30(1)(a) did substantially affect a prisoner's civil rights to liberty and security of the person so as to require the decision to be exercised in accordance with the rules of fundamental justice and fairness.

The plaintiffs' argument up to this point was conceived within the traditional jurisprudence of administrative law as exemplified by the *Beaver Creek* case, in which the applicability of the rules of fundamental fairness was determined on the basis of a distinction between judicial and administrative decisions. However, the plaintiffs in *McCann* offered an alternative analytical framework which avoided the somewhat sterile task of labelling proceedings 'judicial' or 'administrative' and which would permit the court to address squarely the central issue of ensuring justice in prison administrative decision-making.

This alternative framework, which has since been received into the mainstream of Canadian administrative law and which has appropriately come to be known as the 'fairness' doctrine, had not received much judicial attention in Canada at the time of *McCann*, although it had been developed in a series of cases decided by the English Court of Appeal. It was on these cases that the plaintiffs relied.

In *In re H.K.*[136] an immigration officer, acting under the Commonwealth Immigrant's Act of 1962, had refused entry to a Commonwealth citizen on the basis that he was over sixteen years of age. An application was made for a writ of habeas corpus and an order of certiorari quashing the immigration officer's decision on the basis that the officer was acting in a judicial or quasi-judicial capacity, and that the rules of natural justice required that the officer should have given the boy full opportunity to remove the officer's impression that the boy was over sixteen years old. Lord Parker CJ, in the course of his judgment, made the following statement:

> I doubt whether it can be said that the immigration authorities are acting in a judicial or quasi-judicial capacity as those terms are generally understood but at the same time, I myself think that even if an immigration officer is not in a judicial or quasi-judicial capacity, he must, at any rate, give the immigrant an opportunity of satisfying him of the matters in the sub-section and for that purpose let the immigrant know what his immediate impression is so that the immigrant can disabuse him. *That is not, as I see it, a question of acting or being required to act judicially, but of being required to act fairly.* Good administration and an honest or bona fide decision must, as it seems to me, require not merely impartiality, not merely bringing one's mind to bear on the problem, but acting fairly [emphasis added].[137]

In *R.* v. *Gaming Board, ex parte Benaim*[138] the plaintiffs applied to the Gaming Board for Great Britain for a certificate of consent which they were required to obtain in order to apply for licensed premises under the Gaming Act of 1968. The plaintiffs were given an interview at which they answered questions based on information already in the board's possession, although its source and detailed content were not disclosed to the applicants. They were then invited to supply further information in writing, after which the board refused to grant the certificate. The plaintiffs sought an order of certiorari to quash the decision on the basis that the board had not observed the rules of natural justice. In considering this, the Court of Appeal refused to classify the decision as administrative or judicial. Citing with approval the judgment of Lord Parker in *In re H.K.*, Lord Denning said that the proper approach was to consider the task of the Gaming Board and the matters on which they had to make determinations. On this basis, he held that the board did have a duty to act fairly. Lord Denning went on to consider the nature of the information that the board would have before it, its source, and its confidentiality, and concluded that the concept of fairness required not that the plaintiffs should be given the source of the information, but they should be given sufficient information so that they would be able to answer any matters of concern to the board. As Lord Denning put it:

> If the Gaming Board were bound to disclose their source of information no one would 'tell' on these clubs for fear of reprisals. But without disclosing every detail, I should have thought that the Board ought in every case to be able to give to the applicant sufficient indication of the objections raised against him such as to enable him to answer them. That is only fair and the Board must at all costs be fair. If they are not, these courts will not hesitate to interfere.[139]

The third of these cases, *In re Pergamon Press Ltd.*,[140] concerned investigation into the affairs of Pergamon under the Companies Act by inspectors appointed by the Board of Trade. During the course of the investigation, the directors of the company refused to answer questions without being given certain assurances. They claimed, in effect, that the inquiry should be conducted as if it were a judicial inquiry in a court of law. The inspectors, while undertaking not to criticize anyone in their report without giving him the opportunity of explanation, had refused to give the assurances. In the course of his judgment Lord Denning stated that while the inspectors were not a judicial or quasi-judicial body, because of the consequences their report might have they were under a duty to act fairly. Lord Denning explained how the result of the discharge of the inspectors' task could have the effect of ruining reputations or careers and that their report could lead to civil or criminal judicial proceedings. Sachs LJ came to a similar conclusion on the duty to act fairly: 'It is ... not necessary to label the proceedings 'judicial,' 'quasi-judicial,' 'administrative,' 'investigatory'; it is the characteristics of the proceedings that matter, not the precise compartment or compartments into which they fall.'[141]

Sachs LJ went on to explain that in deciding, in the words of Lord Reid in *Ridge* v. *Baldwin*, 'what a reasonable man would regard as fair procedure in particular circumstances,'[142] careful regard must be had for the scope of the proceeding, the source of its jurisdiction, the way in which it is normally conducted, and its objectives. He expressed the view that, given the delicate task the inspectors faced in weighing what in many cases would be confidential information and the need to protect the confidentiality of sources, there must be real flexibility in the application of the concept of fair play.

By 1975 the fairness doctrine had already met with some approval in judgments of members of the House of Lords and the Privy Council. In *Pearlberg* v. *Varty*,[143] Lord Pearson commented: 'Where some person or body is entrusted by Parliament with administrative or executive functions there is no presumption that compliance with the principle of natural justice is required although, as Parliament is not presumed to act unfairly, the courts may be able, in suitable cases (perhaps always) to imply an obligation to act with fairness.'[144]

Shortly thereafter, the Privy Council also took up the concept of fairness in a New Zealand appeal.[145] Lord Morris of Borth-Y-Gest, speaking for the majority, said that 'natural justice is but fairness writ large and juridically. It has been described as "fair play in action." Nor is it a leaven to be associated only with judicial or quasi-judicial occasions.'[146]

The plaintiffs in *McCann* submitted that the 'fairness' doctrine had a flexibility that was lacking in the all-or-nothing judicial-versus-administrative approach, and that this flexibility, which emphasized the balancing of the various factors and interests in a particular situation, was peculiarly appropriate to the issues facing the court in the area of prison decision-making. It was that flexibility which had also characterized the American due process decisions where the basic inquiry was whether the individual interest in avoiding grievous loss outweighed the governmental interests in summary adjudication. The plaintiffs argued that by using the 'fairness' doctrine the court could fashion a procedural code for the prison that reflected both the reality of the impact of solitary confinement decisions on a prisoner's life and the reality of prison administrators' need, in some cases, for taking emergency action and for keeping confidential certain kinds of information that may have impelled them to segregate prisoners.

At the time of *McCann*, the fairness test had not yet been embraced by any appellate court in Canada, although it had been the subject of judicial comment in *Re Beauchamp*,[147] a decision of the Ontario High Court. In that case the prisoner argued that suspending his parole without telling him the reason for doing so deprived him of the right to be informed promptly of the reason for his arrest or detention secured by section 2(c) of the Canadian Bill of Rights. Mr Justice Pennell dismissed the application on the authority of the decision of the Supreme Court of Canada in *Ex parte McCaud*.[148] There the court had held that the provisions of section 2(e) of the Canadian Bill of Rights did not apply to the question of the revocation of parole under the Parole Act since revocation was a decision within the absolute discretion of the parole board as an administrative matter and was not in any way a judicial determination. Mr Justice Pennell went on to state:

However that may be, I am of the view that ... the Board must act fairly in accordance with the principles of proper justice. I do not suggest that the National Parole Board is required to invoke the judicial process. But its decisions are of vital importance to the inmate since his whole future may be affected. In my judgment, fairness demands a consideration of the inmate's side of the story before revoking his parole. I appreciate that, in saying that, it may be said that I am going further than is permitted in matters where there is no duty to act judicially or quasi-judicially. When, however, that has been said, the fact remains that the revocation of parole is akin to a punitive measure which carries with it a duty to act fairly.[149]

The fairness test had also been referred to in the majority judgment of the Supreme Court of Canada in *Howarth* v. *National Parole Board.*[150] In that case the Supreme Court of Canada considered for the first time since the enactment of the Federal Court Act whether a decision of the National Parole Board could be reviewed under section 28(1) of the act. That section precludes review by the Federal Court of Appeal of decisions of 'an administrative nature not required by law to be made on a judicial or quasi-judicial basis.' Counsel for Howarth had sought to distinguish the earlier decision of *Ex parte McCaud* on the basis that the Federal Court Act had introduced an expanded form of judicial review, and the court therefore was not bound by the classification set out in *McCaud*. The majority of the Supreme Court rejected that argument, affirmed the *McCaud* decision, and held that revocation of parole was a decision of an administrative nature not susceptible to judicial review under section 28.

Although no Bill of Rights issue was raised in *Howarth*, in the following year in the case of *Mitchell* v. *The Queen*[151] the Supreme Court was faced with a challenge to a parole revocation relying, inter alia, on section 2(e) of the Bill of Rights on the ground that failure to inform a parolee of the reasons for the suspension and revocation of his parole constituted a denial of fundamental justice. The majority of the Supreme Court again dismissed the application on the basis that 'the very nature of the task entrusted to the Parole Board would make it necessary that such a Board would be clothed with as wide a discretion as possible and that its decision should not be open to question on appeal or otherwise be subject to the same procedures as those which accompany the review of decisions of a judicial or quasi-judicial tribunal.'[152]

Howarth and *Mitchell*, not surprisingly, were heavily relied upon by the defendants in *McCann* in their rejection of the plaintiffs' claim to procedural fairness. The defendants argued that the same discretion conferred on the parole board was conferred on the institutional head under section

2.30(1)(a), and that this unfettered discretion was essential to the proper discharge of the prison administrator's responsibilities for the control and management of the penitentiary. Moreover, the defendants argued that the decision to revoke parole was more severe in its consequences than the decision to place a prisoner in solitary confinement. Parole revocation took the parolee from his position of conditional liberty in the free world and returned him to prison; it resulted in the loss of whatever statutory remission had been credited to the prisoner at the time of his parole and in the loss of credit for time served on parole. If these consequences did not give rise to a determination that the decision to revoke parole was required to be made on a judicial basis, then how could it be argued that the decision to place a prisoner into more restrictive confinement within a prison called for that characterization?

From the perspective of the first part of the plaintiffs' argument that section 2.30(1)(a) decisions should be classified as judicial, *Howarth* and *Mitchell* clearly had to be distinguished. The plaintiffs sought to do this by pointing out that under the Parole Act the parole board was given the widest discretion, and the legislation specifically contemplated the granting and revocation of parole without the necessity of a hearing.[153] In contrast, the Penitentiary Act and its regulations had not legislatively excluded the need for a hearing process. In fact, in the commissioner's directives, the Penitentiary Service itself had seen fit to promulgate a procedural code setting out the nature of the hearing required prior to the imposition of certain punishments. The plaintiffs further sought to distinguish *Howarth* on the basis of the evidence they had presented as to the effects of solitary confinement in SCU; although conceptually it might appear to be a lesser deprivation of liberty than that involved in parole revocation, functionally it was more severe.

But if the ruling in *Howarth* was a major link in the defendants' argument that the decision to segregate was an administrative one, there were other elements of the *Howarth* decision that buttressed the plaintiffs' alternative argument that, however classified, the decision to segregate had to be exercised in accordance with the duty to act fairly.

Howarth, it will be recalled, involved an application under section 28 of the Federal Court Act. At the time there was still considerable confusion as to the interrelationship between the jurisdiction of the Trial Division of the Federal Court of Canada under section 18 of the Federal Court Act and that of the Federal Court of Appeal under section 28. Mr Justice Pigeon, in his majority judgment, noted that counsel for the appellant prisoner had relied on cases dealing with the duty to act fairly, tending to show that an argument could be made for some common-law remedy. While these cases were irrelevant to a section 28 application because of the specific wording requiring the decision to be made on a judicial or quasi-judicial basis, Pigeon J recognized that under section 18 there were preserved intact all the common-law remedies for cases not coming within section 28. He expressly left open the issue of whether decisions of the National Parole Board could be questioned (on the basis of fairness) in proceedings before the trial division under section 18.[154]

The plaintiffs in *McCann* contended that the *Howarth* decision specifically acknowledged the possibility that the trial division in an appropriately framed action could impose a duty to act fairly upon a federal decision-maker notwithstanding that the decision in question was administrative rather than judicial in nature. The plaintiffs urged that theirs was a case in which the federal court should find that there was a duty to act fairly; that in a decision to segregate a prisoner such a duty required that the prisoner be given an opportunity to present his case at a hearing and to challenge the facts on which his segregation was sought. The plaintiffs conceded that a hearing could be delayed for a short period to permit the institutional authority to respond to emergency situations, and that the prisoner's right to know the case against him could be tempered in appropriate cases in the interests of preserving the confidentiality of information which, if released, would be detrimental to the safety of other prisoners or the security of the institution.[155]

At the time of the *McCann* trial, I had developed elsewhere[156] a procedural model designed to accommodate the interests both of prisoners and institutional authorities. This model was offered to Mr Justice Heald as an example of what fairness should entail in the context of a decision to segregate. The model had as its centre-piece a hearing presided over by an independent chairperson who could evaluate all of the institution's information, including confidential material, and consider the validity of any claim that the material should be kept from the prisoner. Where the claim to maintain confidentiality was justified, the chairperson could summarize the information for the prisoner, withholding only that material which would prejudice the legitimate interests of the institution or of other prisoners. Such a model would ensure case-by-case scrutiny of the claim to confidentiality, and would guarantee that all information, including that which was withheld from the prisoner, was subjected to evaluation by an independent authority.[157]

It should be pointed out that in suggesting this model to Mr Justice Heald, the plaintiffs were not asking him to rewrite the regulations or draft new commissioner's directives dealing with administrative segregation. Rather, they sought to demonstrate that a judicially imposed requirement of fairness on the prison administration would not nullify the administration's ability to manage the penitentiary.[158]

THE JUDGMENT OF THE COURTS ON-PROCEDURAL FAIRNESS - *McCANN* TO *MARTINEAU*

As I have indicated, the *McCann* plaintiffs' claims to due process were based on alternative arguments: that the decision to segregate was quasi-judicial rather than administrative, or that independent of its classification and even if it were deemed to be an administrative decision, it was required to be made fairly. On either basis a hearing and other procedural safeguards were required. Mr Justice Heald, in the few pages of his judgment devoted to this issue, does not deal at all with the plaintiffs' arguments on the duty to act fairly. Given that the plaintiffs advanced the view that the fairness concept, because of its inherent flexibility, was particularly appropriate to the resolution of the issues before the court, this omission is extraordinary. The judgment of the court was concerned solely with the question of whether the decision to segregate is of a quasi-judicial or an administrative nature. Mr Justice Heald, after citing the trilogy of Supreme Court parole decisions in *McCaud, Howarth*, and *Mitchell* for the proposition that the parole board in the discharge of its functions must have a broad untrammelled discretion not open to question on appeal, then proceeded to consider the nature of the function entrusted to the institutional head of a penitentiary under section 2.30(1)(a). The whole of his analysis of this issue is contained in one paragraph.

When it is considered that the inmate population of the bc Penitentiary was 530 in January of 1974 ... and that most of the other federal penal institutions have populations of several hundreds each, that almost inevitably such an institution will be housing dangerous unpredictable inmates, with a long history of crimes of violence, that many of the inmates had a record of escapes, hostage taking, and a tendency to create disturbances or riots within the institution, it becomes clear that the institutional head must have the power to act decisively and expeditiously to quell disturbances and isolate the offenders, for the protection of other inmates, the staff of the institution, the property of the institution, and the public at large. An example of this kind of situation occurred in October of 1973 at the bc Penitentiary when a serious inmate disturbance, described by some of the inmates as a 'riot' took place. Immediately thereafter it was necessary to incarcerate some 89 inmates in the scu. To say that in these circumstances Regulation 2.30 requires due process before administrative dissociation would render the administration powerless and a chaotic situation would result. The same comment could be made with regard to a mass escape attempt. I am satisfied, from a consideration of the plain words of Regulation 2.30(1)(a), when considered in the context of the scope of the functions of the institutional head, that the decision to dissociate under Regulation 2.30(1) is purely administrative and neither section l(a) nor 2(e) of the Bill of Rights apply so as to entitle the Plaintiffs to the declaration they seek.[159]

Mr Justice Heald's rejection of the plaintiffs' argument that the decision to segregate should be circumscribed by the procedural due process is premised entirely on the assertion that because emergencies (such as riots or mass escape attempts) may give rise to the need to segregate, it would render the penitentiary authorities impotent if they were required to hold hearings in these circumstances. The plaintiffs acknowledged that in an emergency the administration must be able to act summarily and take remedial action which could include segregation of prisoners. But to acknowledge this does not in any way preclude the possibility of a hearing process when the emergency has receded or in the more common situation where the decision to segregate is made in the absence of an emergency. Mr Justice Heald's analysis, which uses mass escapes or riots as the paradigms that necessarily preclude a claim to procedural due process for the prisoner placed in segregation, is far from compelling.

Underlying Mr Justice Heald's decision on the procedural due process arguments in the *McCann* case is a clear judicial reluctance to become involved in the ongoing review of prison decision-making, a reluctance made manifest in subsequent decisions rendered by the Federal Court of Appeal, and particularly through the judgments of Chief Justice Jackett. I intend to conclude this review of the legal arguments surrounding *McCann* with an analysis of the subsequent decisions concerning the reviewability of prison decision-making because, while they make patently clear the Federal Court of Appeal's rationale for maintaining a hands-off approach, they ultimately provide vindication for the plaintiffs' arguments in the *McCann* case.

In the same month that Mr Justice Heald rendered his decision in *McCann*, another judge in the Trial Division of the Federal Court of Canada entered a parallel ruling in the case of *Kosobook and Aeilick* v. *The Solicitor-General of Canada et al.*[160] In that case the plaintiffs had been placed in administrative segregation at Millhaven Institution from January to September 1975; they were confined to segregation cells for twenty-three hours a day with restricted privileges. The initial segregation had followed the stabbing death of another prisoner, and the plaintiffs had been advised that they had been segregated for the good order and discipline of the institution. They were told that this decision was based on an investigation into the stabbing incident in which they were the suspects. They had learned that no charges would be laid but that they would be kept in segregation under section 2.30(1)(a). The Segregation Review Board reviewed their cases monthly, but they were given no prior notice of these hearings and were not allowed to attend. Requests by their counsel for a hearing, the reasons for the decisions, and copies of the material on which the board relied were all denied. The plaintiffs claimed that their segregation under these circumstances was a denial of natural justice; a denial of their right to an unbiased tribunal; a decision made in an arbitrary manner; and an infringement of the Canadian Bill of Rights in that they were not afforded due process of law and were being held in arbitrary detention.

The action was brought by way of statement of claim under section 18 in the trial division. A motion was made to strike the statement of claim on the grounds that it disclosed no cause of action and that the court had no jurisdiction to grant the relief sought. Gibson J granted the motion, holding that under the classification of *Beaver Creek*, the Segregation Review Board did not have any judicial or quasi-judicial functions; the board exercised purely administrative duties and therefore had no duty either to inform the plaintiffs at any time of any factual allegations or to afford them an opportunity to be present or to give evidence in reply. Furthermore, relying upon the Supreme Court decision in *Mitchell*, Gibson J held that any order pursuant to section 2.30, being purely administrative, cannot in any way contravene the Canadian Bill of Rights.

Within one month of the *McCann* judgment, the Federal Court of Appeal handed down its ruling in the case that was destined to replace *Beaver Creek* as the fulcrum of the jurisprudence of judicial review of decisions made behind prison walls. In *Martineau and Butters* v. *Matsqui Institution Inmate Disciplinary Board (No. 1)*[161] two prisoners at Matsqui Institution were charged under Penitentiary Service Regulations 2.29(g) and (h) with the commission of an indecent act and with being two to a cell. As I have indicated earlier, commissioner's directives, made pursuant to the Penitentiary Act and the Penitentiary Service Regulations, establish a detailed procedural code which requires in cases of serious or flagrant offences written notice of charges, a summary of the evidence, a personal hearing, the right to make full answer and defence including cross-examination, a decision based on the evidence, and proof of guilt beyond a reasonable doubt. The charges here were classified as serious or flagrant ones and were referred to the Matsqui Disciplinary Board for a hearing. The prisoners pleaded guilty to the charge of being two to a cell, and not guilty to the charge of committing an indecent act. Both prisoners were found guilty, not of committing an indecent act but of being in an indecent position, and were sentenced to fifteen days' punitive dissociation. The prisoners alleged violations of the requirements of the commissioner's directive, stating in particular that they were not provided with a summary of the evidence against them; that the evidence of each was taken in the absence of the other; that the conviction was for an offence unknown to law; and that Martineau was never given an opportunity to give evidence with respect to the charge. A section 28 application for judicial review was commenced in the Federal Court of Appeal.

In a majority decision the court ruled that it had no jurisdiction to review the decision. Chief Justice Jackett stated:

> In my view, disciplinary decisions in the course of managing organized units of people such as armies or police forces or in the course of managing institutions such as penal institutions are, whether or not such decisions are of a routine or penal nature, an integral part of the management operation. As a matter of sound administration, as such decisions touch in an intimate way the life and dignity of the individuals concerned, they must be, and must appear to be, as fair and just as possible. For that reason, as I conceive it, there has grown up, where such decisions are of a penal nature, a practice of surrounding them with the phraseology and trappings of criminal law procedure. Nevertheless, in my view, disciplinary decisions are essentially different in kind from the class of administrative decisions that are impliedly required, in the absence of express indication to the contrary, to be made on a judicial or quasi-judicial basis in such a way that they can be supervised by judicial process. In my view, that is the principle underlying *Howarth* v. *National Parole Board* ... For that reason, I conclude that the disciplinary decisions here in question, even though of a penal nature, and even though they are required by administrative rules to be made fairly and justly, are not decisions that are required to be made on a judicial or quasi-judicial basis within the meaning of those words in section 28 of the Federal Court Act. In my view, the fact that statutory remission ... is made subject to reduction by such disciplinary decisions does not change the essential nature of such decisions.[162]

In this last sentence Chief Justice Jackett disagreed with the view expressed in the *Beaver Creek* case that where a disciplinary decision affects statutory remission, because it has the effect of extending the period of imprisonment which the prisoner would otherwise serve, it is a decision that affects the civil rights of the prisoner as a person, and is therefore judicial and reviewable.

Chief Justice Jackett concluded his judgment with the statement that clearly signals the policy basis for his judgment and that of Mr Justice Heald in *McCann*:

> I should add that, while I came to the above conclusion on the analysis that I could make of the statute in the light of the best relevant jurisprudence, in my view the result accords with the realities of the situation. Assuming, without

expressing any opinion on the matter. that there should be some improvement in the present arrangements for review of decisions of penitentiary disciplinary tribunals, it does not seem to me that a judicial review by an ordinary court can provide a review of a character that would improve matters.[163]

Mr Justice Ryan dissented.

The Penitentiary Service Regulations, insofar as they relate to inmate discipline, and the Commissioners' Directive No. 213, both infused with legality by their enactment pursuant to section 1.29 of the Penitentiary Act, establish a structure for the administration of inmate discipline imposing a legal requirement that disciplinary decisions, in relation to serious or flagrant offences, must be made on a quasi-judicial basis.[164]

On appeal the Supreme Court of Canada affirmed the majority ruling of the Federal Court of Appeal in a 5-4 decision. The issue before the Supreme Court of Canada was an extremely narrow one and was expressed by Chief Justice Laskin in this way: 'The nub of the matter is ... whether the directives prescribing what I may compendiously call natural justice for the appellants were made pursuant to "law" and were, therefore, to be observed by the penitentiary authorities.'[165] (It will be recalled that section 28 of the Federal Court Act exempts from the Federal Court of Appeal's review jurisdiction cases of 'an administrative nature not required by law to be made on a judicial or quasi-judicial basis.')

Pigeon J, delivering the judgment of four members of the court (Judson J, in a separate judgment, simply concurred with Jackett CJ), held that the commissioner's directives cannot be considered 'law' within the wording of section 28. 'There is no provision for penalty, and while they are authorized by statute, they are clearly of an administrative, not legislative, nature. It is not in any legislative capacity that the Commissioner is authorized to issue directives but in his administrative capacity.'[166] Pigeon J also stated that he was of the view that Jackett CJ correctly disagreed with the *Beaver Creek* decision to the extent that *Beaver Creek* would imply a duty to act judicially from the fact that a decision might result in the loss of statutory remission.[167]

For Chief Justice Laskin and three other members of the court it was clear that the commissioner's directives containing the disciplinary code were clearly 'law' within the wording of section 28. Responding to the view of the majority that the rules of procedure laid out in the commissioner's directives had no external force and that the appellants had no right to the benefit of the procedure because the penitentiary authorities are under no legal duty to follow them, the chief justice stated:

This is much too nihilistic a view of law for me to accept ... The absence of a penal sanction for the rules or directives can be no more compelling on whether law is involved (with a corresponding duty of obedience) than is the absence of a penal sanction in respect of rules of procedure governing the orders of other tribunals which are found by the courts to be quasi-judicial bodies and whose decisions are reviewable under section 28(1) of the Federal Court Act. The reviewing court imposes a sanction by the very fact of review.[168]

The *Martineau* case was soon back before the courts. Because of the uncertainty concerning the interrelationship between sections 18 and 28, proceedings had been commenced concurrently under both sections. The section 18 proceedings had been adjourned sine die pending the disposition of the question whether the court had jurisdiction under section 28. With the resolution of that matter by the Supreme Court of Canada in *Martineau (No. 1)*, the section 18 proceedings were resumed, this time on behalf of Martineau alone. Martineau sought an order in the nature of certiorari for the purpose of quashing the decision of the disciplinary board. The matter came before Mahoney J for a preliminary determination of the issue of whether, in the circumstances, the trial division had jurisdiction to grant the relief sought. Mahoney J, after citing the judgment of Mr Justice Pigeon in *Howarth* (which, it will be recalled, was relied upon by the *McCann* plaintiffs as supporting the jurisdiction of the trial division to review administrative decisions in light of the fairness doctrine), concluded:

I take it that in Canada, in 1975, a public body, such as the respondent, authorized by law to impose a punishment that was more than a mere denial of privileges, had a duty to act fairly in arriving at its decision to impose the punishment. Any other conclusion would be repugnant. The circumstances disclosed in this application would appear to be appropriate to the remedy sought.[169]

In a terse three-page judgment, again written by Chief Justice Jackett and concurred in by Kelly J and Heald J (who had been elevated to the Federal Court of Appeal after the *McCann* case), the Federal Court of Appeal reversed the trial judge's ruling. The court held that the remedy of certiorari was only available for decisions that were required to be made on a judicial or quasi-judicial basis and that, since *Martineau (No. 1)* had determined that disciplinary decisions were not of such a nature, the relief was not available in the trial division.[170]

Chief Justice Jackett's judgment also contained an appendix wherein he stated:

In a probably futile attempt to avoid misunderstanding as to the effect of our decision, we deem it advisable to say that, in our view, it does not mean that there is an area where there is a *legal* grievance for which there is no *legal* remedy ... Fundamentally, what is meant by deciding something on a quasi-judicial basis, is that it be decided on a fair and just basis ... There are, however, Ministers and officials who have purely administrative powers that are not subject to judicial review. Such persons must also exercise their powers on a fair and just basis because they are acting on behalf of the public; but they are answerable, not to the courts, but to their superiors or to the appropriate legislature. They are not required to act on a quasi-judicial basis ... Where a person is aggrieved by a decision that should have been made on a quasi-judicial basis he may attack it by way of a certiorari proceeding or section 28 proceedings; but where he has a grievance in respect of other decisions that are required to be made on a fair or just basis ... his remedy is political [emphasis in original].[171]

Clearly the chief justice was saying that the grievances of federal prisoners flowing from unfair and unjust treatment at disciplinary hearings are not legal grievances but political ones and that the route for their redress is not through judicial review but through the political process. For federal prisoners, who do not have the right to vote in federal elections,[172] the appendix to Chief Justice Jackett's decision in *Martineau (No. 2)*, however well-intentioned, appeared as a mockery of their asserted legal rights.

If the confidence that some prisoners and their lawyers placed in the courts was severely undermined by the Federal Court of Appeal decision, it was, for the time being at least, restored by the decision of the Supreme Court of Canada in *Martineau (No. 2)*.[173] The Supreme Court, reversing the decision of the Federal Court of Appeal, held that there was jurisdiction to grant certiorari under section 18 in the case of a violation of the duty to act fairly in an administrative decision that was not required by law to be made on a judicial or quasi-judicial basis.[174] Two concurring judgments were rendered, one written by Pigeon J (concurred in by five other members of the court), the other by Dickson J (in which four members concurred). The issue facing the Supreme Court, as characterized by Mr Justice Dickson, was 'the question of the supervisory role, if any, of the Trial Division in respect of disciplinary boards within Canadian penitentiaries.'[175] Mr Justice Pigeon, in concluding that there was jurisdiction to review under section 18, cited with approval the judgment of the English Court of Appeal in *R.* v. *Board of Visitors of Hull Prison, ex parte St Germain*,[176] and quoted from the headnote to that decision, summarizing the views of the English Court of Appeal.

The courts were the ultimate custodians of the rights and liberties of the subject whatever this status and however attenuated those rights and liberties were as a result of some punitive or other process, unless Parliament by statute decreed otherwise. There was no rule of law that the courts were to abdicate jurisdiction merely because the proceedings under review were of an internal disciplinary character and, having regard to the fact that under the Prison Act of 1952 the prisoners remained invested with residuary rights regarding the nature and conduct of his incarcerations, despite the deprivation of his general liberty, the Divisional Court had been in error in refusing to accept jurisdiction.[177]

Mr Justice Dickson, referring to the same case, stated:

The court rejected the submission that prisoners have no legally enforceable rights. Megaw lj concluded that the observance of procedural fairness in the prison is properly a subject for review. Shaw lj held that despite deprivation of his general liberty a prisoner remains invested with residuary rights pertaining to the nature and conduct of his incarceration. Waller j accepted the proposition of Lord Reid in *Ridge* v. *Baldwin* that deprivation of rights or privileges are equally important and applied that proposition to the context of prison discipline.[178]

The judgment of Pigeon J, while affirming the existence of a duty to act fairly on the part of a disciplinary board amenable to review by the federal court, indicated that such review was discretionary and should be exercised having regard to 'the requirements of prison discipline.' He added that 'it is specially important that the remedy be granted only in cases of serious injustice and that proper care be taken to prevent such proceedings from being used to delay deserved punishment so long that it is made ineffective, if not altogether avoided.'[179]

The judgment of Dickson J contains a detailed review of the developments in English administrative law characterized by the expanded role of judicial review made possible through the emergence of the duty to act fairly. Of particular importance, Dickson J sees judicial review of an administrative decision as not being dependent upon whether that decision affects the rights of the subject in any narrow sense.

There has been an unfortunate tendency to treat 'rights' in the narrow sense of rights to which correlative legal duties attach. In this sense, 'rights' are frequently contrasted with 'privileges,' in the mistaken belief that only the former can ground judicial review of the decision-maker's actions ... When concerned with individual cases and aggrieved persons, there is the tendency to forget that one is dealing with public law remedies which, when granted by the courts, not only set aright individual injustice, but also ensure that public bodies exercising powers affecting citizens heed the jurisdiction granted them. Certiorari stems from the assumption by the courts of supervisory powers over certain tribunals in order to assure the proper functioning of the machinery of government. To give a narrow or technical interpretation to 'rights' in an individual sense is to misconceive the broader purpose of judicial review of administrative action.[180]

After reviewing the English authorities, Mr Justice Dickson concluded:

The authorities to which I have referred indicate that the application of a duty of fairness with procedural content does not depend upon proof of a judicial or quasi-judicial function. Even though the function is analytically administrative, courts may intervene in a suitable case. In the case at bar, the disciplinary board was not under either an express or implied duty to follow a judicial type of procedure, but the board was obliged to find the facts affecting a subject and exercise a form of discretion in pronouncing judgment and penalty. Moreover, the board's decision had the effect of depriving an individual of his liberty by committing him to a 'prison within a prison.' In these circumstances, elementary justice requires some procedural protection. *The rule of law must run within penitentiary walls.*

In my opinion, certiorari avails as a remedy wherever a public body has power to decide any matter affecting the rights, interests, property, privileges or liberties of any person [emphasis added].[181]

Dickson J also cited with approval Lord Denning's statement in *Selvaragan* v. *Race Relations Board*,[182] in which the master of the rolls sought to formulate the 'fundamental rule' underlying the English fairness cases: 'If a person may be subjected to pains or penalties, or be exposed to prosecution or proceedings, or deprived of remedies or redress, or in some such way adversely affected by the investigation and report, then he should be told the case made against him and be afforded a fair opportunity of answering it.'[183]

Dickson J specifically rejected the existence of the 'disciplinary exception' to certiorari, the notion that judicial review was precluded in cases of members of the armed forces, police, or prisoners when there was a private disciplinary system and a code of rules. The Ontario Court of Appeal in *Beaver Creek* had ten years previously rejected the existence of this exception, but it had re-emerged and had been endorsed by the Federal Court of Appeal in *Martineau (No. 1)*. Mr Justice Dickson's judgment in *Martineau (No. 2)*, coupled with the previous decision of the Supreme Court in *Nicholson*,[184] should have laid this ghost to rest once and for all.

Echoing the views of Mr Justice Pigeon, Dickson J, while concluding that the disciplinary board of a federal penitentiary was under a duty to act fairly, cautioned that this jurisdiction must be exercised carefully.

It should be emphasized that it is not every breach of prison rules or procedure which will bring intervention by the courts. The very nature of a prison institution requires officers to make 'on the spot' disciplinary decisions and the power of judicial review must be exercised with restraint. Interference will not be justified in the case of trivial or merely technical incidents. The question is not whether there has been a breach of the prison rules, but whether there has been a breach of the duty to act fairly in all the circumstances. The rules are of some importance in determining this latter question, as an indication of the views of the prison authorities as to the degree of procedural protection to be extended to inmates.[185]

Dickson J indicated that the duty to act fairly is a flexible one, fully capable of responding to the spectrum of administrative decisions which range from those of a policy-oriented nature to those approaching the judicial. In the case of a decision approaching the latter end of the spectrum, 'substantial procedural safeguards' may be required. These safeguards, however, import 'something less than the full panoply of conventional natural justice rules.'[186]

The Supreme Court decision in *Martineau (No. 2)* does not go beyond this in providing guidance as to what 'fairness' requires in hearings before a prison disciplinary board. This was left to be worked out by the trial judge when considering the application of *Martineau* on the merits. In fact, when that application came to be heard, a consent order was entered that the decision of the disciplinary board be set aside. The federal court was therefore not called upon to deliver reasons for judgment on the merits.[187]

The decision of the Supreme Court of Canada in *Martineau (No. 2)* that penitentiary authorities are under a duty to act fairly in making decisions of a disciplinary nature clearly vindicates the arguments presented by the plaintiffs in *McCann* some four years earlier. It is ironic, however, that recognition of this principle was wrung from the courts in the sterility of a jurisdictional dispute. Had Mr Justice Heald been prepared in 1975 to recognize the role of the courts in ensuring that the rule of law prevailed in the prison, and had he been prepared to consider in an imaginative way the submissions presented by the plaintiffs in *McCann*, he would have had a unique opportunity - having heard evidence which no other judge before or since has heard - of delineating the duty to act fairly in the particular circumstances of the penitentiary's most severe sanction.[188]

5 The Penitentiaries' Response to the *McCann* Case: Canada's New Prisons of Isolation

THE VANTOUR REPORT

A week before Mr Justice Heald handed down his decision in *McCann*, the Study Group on Dissociation presented its report (the Vantour Report) to the commissioner of penitentiaries. The undertaking of a special study of the use of segregation had been recommended by the correctional investigator, Inger Hansen, in her annual report for 1973–4, although there is little doubt that the timing of its establishment was precipitated by the beginning of the *McCann* trial in February 1975. As I have previously indicated, the findings of the study group on the conditions and effects of segregation were fully congruent with the evidence presented at the *McCann* trial.

Prolonged segregation under these conditions lacks any indication of administrative purpose other than to isolate inmates considered to be disruptive to the institutional order. Although we recognize the limitations on social sciences in effecting change in inmates, we must still acknowledge the lack of substantive rehabilitative or therapeutic value in the concept of segregation. It must be recognized that almost all of these inmates would eventually be released from prison. This being the case, segregation as it presently exists is not practical. It further enhances the inmate's antisocial attitude and, in general, constitutes a self-fulfilling prophecy.[1]

The study group also addressed the general issue of the continuing need for segregation and made specific recommendations on facilities for segregated prisoners and the process of segregation. As the starting-point of its analysis, the study group articulated a rationale for segregation within the context of its understanding of the distinctive nature of the prison society.

The Study Group is aware of the growing interest in inmate rights and the concern that inmates are segregated without charges. Many of the persons interviewed expressed the opinion that this preventive aspect of penitentiary administration would not be tolerated should it occur in the community. This argument equates penitentiary life with life in the free community. We do not consider this to be the case ... The etiology of crime and the workings of the legal system operate selectively to the end that a high proportion of prisoners are emotionally and attitudinally maladjusted. A minority is only a step away from active rebellion.

According to Cloward, the series of status degradation ceremonies that occur for offenders throughout the criminal justice system have the following effect: 'Prisoners are less likely to impute legitimacy to the bases of social control in the prison than is typical of persons in other spheres of society. Having been denounced, degraded, segregated, and confined, many renounce the legitimacy of the invidious definitions to which they are subject, and thus further pressure towards deviance is created. This socially induced trait towards deviance, above all else, sets the stage for a major problem of social control in the prison.'

The result is that 'The acute sense of status degradation that prisoners experience generates powerful pressures to evolve means of restoring status. Principal among them are mechanisms that emerge in an inmate culture – a system of social relationships governed by norms that are largely at odds with those espoused by the officials and the conventional society.'

Inmates, then, seek the prestige that was not accorded them in a free society. Cloward argues, however, that since so many inmates are deprived, the prestige is in short supply, and 'consequently, these disenchanted individuals are forced into bitterly competitive relationships ... thus is it hardly surprising to find that the upper echelons of the inmate world come to be occupied by those whose past behaviour best symbolizes that which society rejects and who have most fully repudiated the institutional norms. These are the inmates who refuse or are unable to lower their aspirations and accept their degraded position. Disillusioned and frustrated, they seek means of escaping degradation.'

It is these prisoners who represent major problems for the administration. Generally, the result is a competitive, exploitative and sometimes violent society. Sykes and Messinger note that an additional significant feature of an inmate's social environment is simply 'the presence of other imprisoned criminals ... who are the inmate's constant companions ... crowded into a small area with men who have long records of physical assaults, thievery, and so on (and who may be expected to continue in the path of deviant social behaviour in the future) the inmate is deprived of the sense of security that we more or less take for granted in the free community.[2]

The Vantour Report considered the goals of the penitentiary system in terms of a descending order of priorities, with control as the first priority, dealing with the offender individually and humanely as the second, and providing appropriate correctional opportunities in order to achieve the successful reintegration of the offender into the community as the third. The report concluded:

In order to ensure that the Director can perform this total role, his authority to segregate disruptive or dangerous inmates is very broad and vague and the procedure by which he exercises his authority is simple and swift ... Given the nature of the inmate community and the goals of the penitentiary, segregation of certain inmates is necessary in order to protect both staff and inmates and maximize the rehabilitative potential of the institution ... The Study Group acknowledges the need for this type of preventive administrative act and therefore agrees in principle with Penitentiary Service Regulation 2.30(1)(a).[3]

There is something disarming in the forthrightness of this justification for administrative segregation. The quoted statements identify as the subjects of segregation those prisoners who refuse to accept the degrading and dehumanizing effects of imprisonment. Their resistance, however, is not seen as a challenge for change and reform but as the justification for further oppression. There can surely be no quarrel with a rationale for segregation that focuses on prisoners who are persistently violent toward other prisoners or staff. However, the Vantour rationale for the broad discretionary power of section 2.30 is much more generally cast. It rejects any role of prisoner leadership that is anything other than compliant and submissive. Leadership that calls into question and challenges the legitimacy of penitentiary authority is deemed to demonstrate emotional and attitudinal maladjustment. The Vantour Report is correct indeed in contrasting the prison world with that of free society. But its rationale for segregation reinforces not the legitimization of authority but rather the prisoners' perception of its illegitimacy.

The report sought to identify what it termed 'the principle and goal of segregation.'[4]

Segregation must become a more integral part of the institutional programming. Long-term segregation cases are presently confined in institutions which are not designed for them. These inmates are, as we have pointed out, isolated and forgotten. There appears to be very little administrative intent behind their present situation ...

We have concluded that the most severe hardship for most inmates is the deprivation of association. Therefore, the privilege which has the most meaning for segregated inmates is the privilege of association ... Indeed, the ultimate goal of the criminal justice system is the reintegration of the offender into the community – adjustment to life outside the prison – and the basic fact of that life is association. Similarly, the ultimate goal of a segregation unit ought to be to return the segregated inmate to association, albeit in a maximum security institution, as soon as possible.

This goal can best be achieved through a principle of gradual monitored reintegration of segregated inmates into the population. Such a principle has the following benefits:

- It provides the staff with a means of evaluating the inmate in a manner that is 'measurable' – through observation of his behaviour in the company of staff and other inmates ...
- It provides the inmate with the opportunity to earn his way out of segregation, thus alleviating the atmosphere of hopelessness which characterizes segregation units at present.
- It eliminates the shock that may accompany a sudden reintegration into the population, and thus represents a 'decompression' phase in which the change in his routine is gradual and controlled.

If segregation is recognized as a crucial aspect of institutional life, and the system is serious about the problem of the persistently disruptive and dangerous inmate, then the Penitentiary Service must commit itself to the utilization of physical and human resources for these inmates. Segregation facilities must have appropriate living, working and exercise space. There must be both security and programme staff charged with the sole responsibility of the persistently disruptive inmate. That is, facilities must be designed to accommodate these inmates. Some staff must be there for the express purpose of their custody and treatment.[5]

The study group distinguished between those prisoners who are temporary threats to the good order of the institution and those who represented persistent and serious threats to staff and other prisoners. For those prisoners who could be viewed as temporary threats, the report recommended that all institutions should maintain their own segregation units. For those prisoners who were persistent threats, the study group considered two confinement models: the 'dispersal' model, which would have those prisoners remain in the institution that was responsible for their confinement before they were segregated, and the 'concentration' model, which would place all prisoners requiring long-term segregation in one institution or a few institutions on a regional basis. The study group saw problems with both models. They felt that the dispersal model would not be in the best interests of prisoners requiring long-term segregation. This opinion was based on the view that in the existing penitentiaries the staff must focus their attention on the majority of prisoners and not on the small minority of segregation cases. There was the additional danger that if all maximum-security institutions were responsible for long-term segregation cases they would tend to be organized with a view to providing security for those cases, thus subjecting other prisoners to unnecessary restrictions.[6] They saw the concentration model as problematic because of the dangers involved in confining large numbers of difficult cases in one institution, completely isolated from other prisoners, with no influences on their behaviour from anyone except prisoners with similar attitudes. The study group recommended a compromise between the two models, which it called a 'limited dispersal' model.

A limited dispersal plan means that only certain select maximum security institutions would be responsible for the custody and treatment of potentially long term segregation cases. Such a plan should utilize purpose-built institutions – institutions that are designed, at least in part, to provide programmes for the persistently disruptive inmate. This plan differs from the dispersal model in that all maximum security institutions would not have the responsibility of long term segregation ... Therefore, those institutions which would not have long term segregation facilities would benefit from this plan in that the removal of the persistently disruptive inmates could have a settling or stabilizing effect on the population and would further enhance the development of progressive and meaningful programmes in these institutions ... The limited dispersal model differs from the concentration plan in that those institutions used to confine long-term segregation cases would not be used exclusively for that purpose. Therefore, within the normal population, this plan would provide for programmes designed to reintegrate the segregation cases into the population.[7]

The study group made a series of recommendations on staffing, living conditions, and routine in segregation units. They recommended that there be two phases in segregation: phase one would approximate the type of segregation that already existed and which would be used for as short a period as possible; phase two, limited association, would be an attempt to introduce the prisoner in a controlled manner into the population or at least into association with other segregated prisoners. All prisoners in segregation should be entitled to the same amenities as all other prisoners so far as was reasonable, except for the privilege of association. To the study group this meant that basic cell conditions should not differ from general population cells in size, furnishings, lighting, or temperature; prisoners should have adequate exercise time and should maintain library, correspondence, visiting, canteen, and smoking privileges. The study group recommended that because of the risk that hobbycraft tools might be used for weapons, decisions regarding access to hobby materials should be made on an individual basis.[8]

The study group also addressed the vital matter of the process of segregation. It recommended that the authority to segregate should remain with the director, and that this authority should continue to be exercisable 'on suspicion, even in the absence of hard evidence, that an act had been committed or planned by a particular inmate.'[9] However, the prisoner should be advised in writing of the reason or reasons for his segregation within twenty-four hours of the director's decision. The study group proposed a new review structure for the segregation of prisoners, the overarching feature of which was the establishment of a Segregation Review Board comprising the director as chairman, the assistant director of security or socialization, the classification officer or psychologist, and the security officer in charge of segregation. Under the proposed scheme, the Segregation Review Board must review the case of a prisoner within five working days of the director's decision to segregate and at least every two weeks thereafter if the decision to segregate is upheld. Although the prisoner was to be advised in writing of the board's decision after each review, the study group recommended that he should not be present at the review unless requested to attend by the board. No rationale for this exclusion of the prisoner was offered beyond the statement that 'we do not consider it essential, nor necessarily in the best interests of the inmate, that he be present when his case is being reviewed.'[10]

The study group further recommended that the Segregation Review Board, after assessing the prisoner's situation, develop a plan to reintegrate him into the population as soon as possible; monitor that plan during subsequent reviews; maintain written records on the substance of each review; and forward reports to the Regional Classification Board.[11]

The Vantour Report was greeted with mixed feelings by the plaintiffs in *McCann*. To the extent that it afforded additional confirmation of the conditions and effects of segregation in the British Columbia Penitentiary, it was welcomed as an additional spur to changes in those conditions. Also well received were the recommended reforms in the process of segregation, particularly the requirement of written notice of reasons and an ongoing review process aimed at reintegration of prisoners into the general population. However, in the minds of the plaintiffs the Vantour Report did not go far enough. I have already criticized the report's attempt at a rationale for segregation. Because of the nature of that rationale, the study group was content to leave the authority to segregate untrammelled by any substantive criteria, with the result that their recommendations left the basis for the decision as vague and unprincipled as it had always been.

The second major object of the plaintiffs' criticism was the limited nature of the procedural fairness recommended by the report. The failure to accord the prisoner the right to be present at the deliberations of the Segregation Review Board, either at the initial consideration of the decision to segregate or at subsequent reviews, was regarded as a debilitating flaw in the attempt to establish the legitimacy of the process in the minds of the prisoners affected by it. That flaw was compounded by the failure of the Vantour Report to recommend that the Segregation Review Board be presided over by an independent chairperson. The omission was particularly glaring because the report had recommended that disciplinary hearings be presided over by just such an independent chairperson. The need for an independent presiding officer at disciplinary hearings had been the centre-piece of my own recommendations in a study of the disciplinary process in the penitentiary which was extensively cited by the Vantour Report in its discussion of punitive dissociation.[12] I had also recommended that in light of the severe consequences of administrative dissociation and its potential for use in lieu of disciplinary proceedings, it was vital that the authority to dissociate under section 2.30(1)(a) be made subject to the same independent decision process. The Vantour Report gave no reasons for rejecting this recommendation.

THE WINDS OF CHANGE OR THE WINDOW OF CONTEMPT?

By the end of 1975, the Canadian Penitentiary Service found itself faced with a declaratory judgment of the Federal Court of Canada that the conditions of confinement in the special correctional unit at the British Columbia Penitentiary constituted cruel and unusual punishment or treatment in violation of the Canadian Bill of Rights. In granting this relief, Mr Justice Heald had specifically found that the declaratory judgment was appropriate even though the plaintiffs were no longer in SCU 'because this is a case where the Court can and should give practical guidance to the authorities at the BC Penitentiary and the Canadian Penitentiary Service.'[13] Furthermore, the service had received the report of its own study group condemning the existing practices of administrative segregation and recommending extensive changes. The *McCann* case had generated extensive public commentary in British Columbia and nationally, and, given the admissions of the director of the penitentiary himself that the regime in SCU could not be supported on any rational correctional basis, the time seemed propitious for change.

Within a week of Mr Justice Heald's decision, prisoners being held in SCU under section 2.30(1)(a) were moved out and placed in a range of cells in the B-7 block. These cells were the same as others in the cell block; they had open bars instead of the solid doors of the SCU cells, and they were equipped with standard beds and built-in desk-bookcases. Dragan Cernetic, director of the penitentiary, said that the change was made 'to live up to the spirit of the judgment.'[14] The press were invited in to see the new cells and to tour the special correctional unit. However, by April 1976, after a hostage-taking incident by prisoners in segregation and in the face of increasing hostility of the guards to the move (who demanded that the director resign), the prisoners were moved back to the special correctional unit, the name of which had now been changed to the super-maximum unit (SMU).[15] The only change that had been made to the unit was that the five-inch-square window in the steel doors had been enlarged to eighteen inches by thirty inches. Only two changes were made in the regime of the unit: the light in the cell was turned off from midnight until 6:00 A.M., and prisoners now exercised in the central control area instead of the corridor outside the cells. This move was viewed as constituting 'fresh air' exercise, since the roof of the central control area was, at its extreme ends, open to the outside. There were no other changes.[16] An editorial in the *Vancouver Sun* entitled 'The Window of Contempt'[17] reflected the views of prisoners on the extent to which the penitentiary had responded to the spirit of Mr Justice Heald's decision.

The review process which Dragan Cernetic had introduced when he became director in 1974 continued to be the basis for review after the trial. Mr Justice Heald had held that the decision to segregate was purely administrative and was not subject to procedural safeguards enforceable or reviewable by the courts. The penitentiary authorities were therefore under no legal mandate to change that process. Although no Segregation Review Board was officially established at the British Columbia Penitentiary in 1976, the Classification Board did begin to review cases on the monthly basis set out in the regulations. Prisoners were not involved in any way in this review process. They were given written notification slips at the time of their first segregation and after their review. These notification slips were drafted in very general language, typically doing nothing more than repeating the general provision of section 2.30(1)(a) that a prisoner was being segregated for the good order and discipline of the institution. No evidence was made available to the prisoners that the recommendations of the Vantour Report were being implemented at the British Columbia Penitentiary.

By the end of 1976, other changes had been made to the cells: a metal table-and-stool combination was placed at the back of each cell, and a raised metal bed-frame was bolted to the wall to replace the concrete sleeping platform. However, the new enlarged opening in the door which in May had been obstructed by nothing other than three bars was now covered by a heavy steel-wire grill. Prisoners regarded this 'improvement' as worse than the original small five-by-five-inch opening. Now the little outside light that came in through the window on the other side of the catwalk was glimpsed not only through the wire mesh separating the corridor from the catwalk but also through the steel wire grill over the 'window' in the cell door. It was light as distorted as the existence to which the prisoners were condemned.[18] Beneath the 'window' of the cell, there was a slot which could be closed from the outside and which was used to pass meals to the prisoners. The result of this change was that now even the brief respite from solitude formerly provided by coming out of their cells to pick up their meals at the end of the corridor was gone. Exercise periods were still no more generous; exercise was taken in the central control area, usually under the surveillance of at least three or four guards. In 1977, open-air exercise facilities were constructed at great expense on the roof of the 'penthouse.' These facilities consisted of elaborate cages, the sides of which were made of heavy metal, steel mesh, and wired glass. The combination of steel mesh and wired glass was a mirror image of the view the prisoners had from within their cells. Many prisoners refused to exercise in them rather than endure this distorted view of what the outside offered.

From the prisoners' perspective there were no improvements in the SCU regime. Complaints about hygienic facilities and medical care continued. It was deemed a security risk to provide prisoners with regular toothbrushes, and the ones issued to them were broken off to 1½ inches of handle and one inch of brush. The result was that prisoners could do little more than rub their teeth. As one prisoner pointed out, 'to do this for "security" reasons is ridiculous. There are ten more things in this cell that would make better weapons than a toothbrush - for that matter, the plastic barrel on this pen is six inches long.'[19]

Interviews with the prison doctor and psychiatrist were held in the central control area with guards standing within earshot; there was no privacy. Several prisoners informed me that for this reason they did not bother to see the doctor even though they needed to do so. Several hobbies were for the first time made available for prisoners in solitary: art, petit point, and beadcraft. In a letter Andy Bruce explained why the policy did not result in any change: 'No one does them, because no one is willing to sign the permit that goes along with it. Because of the prevailing attitude and from past experience I think it safe to assume what would happen if I were to put a permit on my wall that says "I agree that all tools, materials and completed hobbycraft are subject to search at any time and that I will have no claim for damages arising from such official action." It presupposes damage, and the effect of that isn't worth the hobby.'[20]

As a member of the Citizen's Advisory Committee at the British Columbia Penitentiary I interviewed prisoners in administrative segregation throughout 1976. I continued to hear prisoners protest at being placed in segregation for investigation of alleged infractions; when these investigations were completed and no charges were laid, these prisoners were still kept in segregation. There continued to be inexplicable inconsistencies in the practice of keeping prisoners in segregation pending disposition of outside criminal charges; prisoners sentenced to punitive dissociation at a disciplinary hearing continued to be kept in administrative dissociation on the expiry of their sentences; and allegations of beatings and harassment by guards who had been named in the *McCann* trial continued.

The extent of any real change in the practice of carceral power at the British Columbia Penitentiary in the year following Mr Justice Heald's declaratory judgment can best be seen from an incident that occurred on Christmas Eve 1976. At the end of September there had been a major disturbance at the British Columbia Penitentiary (and also at Millhaven and Laval) which resulted in extensive destruction of the east wing cell block. After the disturbance prisoners were moved into the prison auditorium, the only space available to hold them while arrangements were made to transfer them to other institutions. In November, as a result of an explosion and fire in the auditorium, some prisoners were moved into the old east wing on the ground floor. The lighting, heating, and plumbing in those cells had been totally destroyed. Plastic sheeting was placed over the shattered windows on the outside walls and temporary heating and lighting was installed. By Christmas Eve only a handful of prisoners remained in the east wing. Jack McCann was one of them. I visited the east wing on Christmas Eve and spoke with as many prisoners as I could, including McCann, about the conditions. The little light that existed outside had difficulty penetrating into the wing because of the heavy plastic on the walls. The naked light bulbs suspended from the ceiling offered little illumination. The cells were in virtual darkness. The attitudes of the prisoners ranged from open hostility to utter despair.

At this point the reader may interject that conditions in the east wing were the result of the prisoners' own destructive activity, and they could hardly complain about having to live temporarily with the implications of this destruction. Apart from the fact that a number of these prisoners, including Jack McCann, had not been living in the east wing at the time of the disturbance, my point is not to equate the conditions under which prisoners were being held there with conditions still prevailing in administrative segregation; rather, I wish to examine the attitude of the keeper toward the kept. On Christmas Eve 1976 Jack McCann informed me that just prior to my visit a prison guard had placed some razor blades on the ledge of one of the cell doors. As he left the range he shouted to the prisoners, 'have a Merry Christmas and a slashing New Year.' I found out later that a number of prisoners had in fact slashed themselves that evening. The parliamentary subcommittee appointed to investigate the penitentiary system in the wake of the riots at the British Columbia Penitentiary and other Canadian maximum-security institutions felt this allegation to be credible enough to include it in its report to Parliament.[21]

A year after Mr Justice Heald's decision, it was clear that the judgment of the court in *McCann* had not changed anything of substance. Behind the thin veneer of physical changes, solitary confinement in maximum security was still characterized by virtually the same inhumanity and gratuitous cruelty that had existed before the trial. Why was this? Why had nothing really changed, despite the declaratory judgment of a federal court judge?

For many prisoners this is a question that is hardly worth asking, because its answer is self-evident. To men who have been systematically dealt with by authority in arbitrary, dignity-depriving ways, asking the courts (who had consigned them to the penitentiary as punishment in the first place) to vindicate principles of fairness and dignity was seen to be as productive as spitting in the wind. The plaintiffs in *McCann* were committed to the court action as a means of demonstrating to the public what was done under the guise of 'correction' within Canada's penitentiaries and as a way to ensure that no more McCaulleys would be driven mad in solitary, that no more Bellemaires would be driven to death, but deep down they had no illusions as to what would really change inside the walls when the lawyers, the judge, and the press went home.

The absence of change in the face of court intervention may in part be explained by the nature of the relationship between the keeper and the kept. Dr Korn, in his evidence in *McCann*, described that relationship as a guerrilla war. The keepers have a deep-seated need to retain their control, to demonstrate the legitimacy of their position, to justify doing to other men that which they know they could or should never do to members of their family or to people who have any meaning to them; the prisoners have a deep-seated need to hold on to that which is most precious to them, their sense of self, their sense of who they are, and to resist becoming the disembodied image of a penitentiary number. Solitary confinement is the ultimate battlefield of that conflict; neither side can afford to let go. This reality is so deep-seated that the declaratory judgment of the federal court is of little consequence. The courtroom simply becomes another battlefield. A judicial decision may be interpreted as a win or a loss by the keeper and by the kept, but not as an improvement in their ongoing relationship. The American experience is instructive in this regard. Judicial intervention in the prisons has proceeded much further in the United States than in Canada. The empirical studies of the effectiveness of this intervention, while in some cases affirming that there has been real improvement in prison conditions, have also described the recalcitrance of prison officials in implementing court decrees.[22]

James Jacobs, in his sociological analysis of Stateville, the maximum-security penitentiary in Illinois, considered the results of the intrusion of the legal system into the prison during the 1970s at the height of the Prisoners' Rights Movement. His observations have a particular relevance to the situation at the British Columbia Penitentiary in the aftermath of the *McCann* decision.

Where the Federal Courts have rebuked administrative practices and established new standards, there has sometimes been little change in the old ways. Court decisions do not enforce themselves ... There are limits to the capacity of the Courts to police decision-making inside the prison ... Where decisions have been implemented, the impact has often been blunted. For example, contrary to the opinion of prison administrators that the Courts have destroyed discipline, there is strong evidence at Stateville and elsewhere that the Court decisions affecting prison discipline have had little effect on the number of inmates serving isolation and segregation time ... [At Stateville] a greater number and percentage of inmates are in special disciplinary confinement today than ever before. This can be explained by the fact that the same individuals continue to make the substantive disciplinary decisions. That the guard who writes the ticket is now barred from the decision-making function is hardly a decisive turn of events when his superior is the decision-maker. The old disciplinary Captain at Stateville became chairman of the new disciplinary committee in 1970. One of his subordinates, a guard officer, was a second member of the committee ... The prison administrators found ways to 'get around' the clear meaning, if not the letter, of the court decisions. Instead of being brought to a hearing within 72 hours of the alleged infraction, an inmate might be brought before the committee and 'continued,' or be placed in 'investigation,' or the 'reclamation gallery' or in some other form of sequestration, not 'segregation' but equivalent to it ... While the Courts might be able to impose a form of decision-making on the prison, they are not in a position to overturn substantive decisions. The Federal Courts are totally unable to sort out who was lying in an old factual dispute or to question whether the substantive judgment of the prison officials, in instituting a lock-up, was correct. By necessity the Courts must assume the good faith of the administration. Therefore, unless the administration itself acts in good faith and assumes a responsibility to supervise the fairness of the process, inmates are essentially little better off than before, without a remedy unless, of course, the administration completely fails to follow the required procedure.[23]

The indirect consequences of the intrusion of juridical norms into the prisons have been more significant than the few substantive holdings which have resulted from the many years of litigation. Seemingly unimportant Court decisions pertaining to Qurans [the holy book of the Black Muslims] and radical newspapers have given legitimacy to inmate protest against authoritarian rule. The 'old' system ultimately depended upon total suppression and total submission. The expression of inmate frustrations in terms of classic constitutional issues provided the ideological basis for a frontal attack upon the entire regime.

[Cases such as *Miller* v. *Twomey* and *Wolff* v. *McDonell* struck at the very heart of the authoritarian system, not because it was impossible to go through the form of a hearing and then throw inmates into segregation, but because they called into question the basis of the authority itself.[24]

The declaration in *McCann* that conditions in solitary confinement in the British Columbia Penitentiary were cruel and unusual punishment or treatment has to be viewed in retrospect as symbolic, in the way Jacobs refers to the 'victories' at Stateville. After the trial, particularly during the negotiations which took place in the midst of the riot in September 1976, prisoners referred to the *McCann* judgment as a demonstration of the illegitimacy of carceral power. In their submission to the parliamentary subcommittee they cited the non-implementation of the decision as the clearest evidence of the lack of commitment to change on the part of correctional officials.

As Jacobs has pointed out in a recent article assessing the impact of the prisoners' rights movement in the United States, an exclusive focus on the extent to which a particular decision has been implemented fails to recognize that prisoners' rights litigation has also had a wider impact on the 'organization of prisoners, citizen and interest group mobilization, legislative and administrative budget-making decisions and law-making, professional standard setting and the redistribution of power inside the prisons.'[25] Using this broad approach, Jacobs concurs in the judgment of the director of the U.S. National Institute of Corrections that 'the role of courts over the past fifteen years in acting as a catalyst for much needed reform in our nation's prisons cannot be overemphasized.'[26]

Given the limited extent of judicial intervention in the prisons in Canada, the potential catalytic effect of the court's role has hardly begun to be realized. Nevertheless, the *McCann* case left more than just an imprint in the law reports. Several community groups sought to mobilize public support for prisoners' rights around the issue of solitary confinement. The issue became the focal point of a play, *Walls*, which had a successful run in Vancouver. The lawyers involved in the case became prime movers in the establishment of a Citizen Advisory Committee to the British Columbia Pentenitiary which included representatives from the three main political parties, the academic and legal communities, and the media. In addition to animating this community support for constructive change, the court case may have played its most important role in influencing the decision to close the British Columbia Penitentiary. For almost fifteen years, successive solicitors-general had paid lip service to the idea of phasing out the penitentiary. (Similar commitments had been given in relation to the other nineteenth-century bastilles. St Vincent de Paul Penitentiary was declared 'unfit for use' several times, but was reopened in 1973 as a result of an unexpected increase in the number of prisoners in Quebec). In 1980 the British Columbia Penitentiary was closed for good. It was the only penitentiary ever to be found by a court to be operating in violation of the Canadian Bill of Rights, and, though other factors were also at work, the *McCann* judgment and the illegitimacy it stamped on the British Columbia Penitentiary should not be readily dismissed as an important determinant in the final decision to close 'The Pen.'

THE PARLIAMENTARY SUBCOMMITTEE AND THE JUSTICE MODEL OF CORRECTIONS

The Heald judgment in *McCann* and the Vantour Report should have provided a major impetus for change in the conditions and regime of segregation. As of the end of 1976 neither of them had had this desired effect. As I have already mentioned, major disturbances broke out in three of Canada's maximum-security penitentiaries in the fall of 1976, leading to a parliamentary investigation. The report of the Parliamentary Subcommittee on the Penitentiary System in Canada was not specifically concerned with segregation, but sought to grapple with what it perceived to be the underlying problems and issues in the penitentiary system. One of those problems was 'the fact that imprisonment - the ultimate product of our system of criminal justice - itself epitomizes injustice.'[27] To correct this fundamental flaw in the system, the subcommittee endorsed two principles:

> *Principle 11*
> The Rule of Law must prevail inside Canadian penitentiaries.
> *Principle 12*
> Justice for inmates is a personal right and also an essential condition of their socialization and personal reformation. It implies both respect for the persons and property of others and fairness in treatment. Arbitrariness traditionally associated with prison life must be replaced by clear rules, fair disciplinary procedures and the providing of reasons for all decisions affecting inmates.[28]

The subcommittee, reporting after the decision in *Martineau (No. 1)* but prior to the decision in *Martineau (No. 2)*, concluded that 'a fundamental problem lies in the general restraint by the courts in exercising their power to ensure that Canadian law applies within as well as outside penitentiaries.'[29] The subcommittee, while critical of the hands-off approach of the Canadian courts, felt that ensuring that the rule of law prevailed behind prison walls was at the outset a task requiring legislative and administrative initiative. The subcommittee recommended that the commissioner's directives be consolidated into a consistent code of regulations having the force of law for both prisoners and staff;[30] that independent chairpersons be appointed immediately in all institutions to preside over disciplinary hearings;[31] that an inmate grievance procedure be established in which prisoners had a substantial role;[32] and, specifically in relation to administrative segregation, which the report called a 'euphemism for solitary confinement,' that, in accordance with the Vantour Report, 'there must be a Segregation Review Board and due notice in writing of the Board's decisions.'[33] The subcommittee noted that it had considered the question of independent chairpersons presiding over segregation review boards, but felt that the proposals of the Vantour Report should be tried and reconsidered after two years of experience.[34]

With these legislative and administrative reforms in place, the parliamentary subcommittee envisaged a vital role for the courts.

> It should then lie with the courts to ensure that those individuals and agencies involved in the management and administration of the revised system adhere to general standards of natural justice and due process of law as they substantially exist elsewhere in the criminal justice system ...
>
> We suggest that it would be both reasonable and appropriate to proceed in such a way as to allow a much greater scope for judicial control over official activity and the conditions of correction in a reformed penitentiary system than is now feasible. Assuming that the system is definitive in its commitment, clear in its intentions, and effective in its prescription, then the nature of the task remaining to be done by the courts in ensuring that the Rule of Law prevails within penitentiaries should not be disproportionate to what they do outside prison walls on an ongoing basis. Abuse of power and denial of justice are always possible under any system, no matter how well conceived or organized it may be. These things are felt no less keenly in prisons than elsewhere, and their consequences in a penitentiary setting are often far more severe.[35]

The parliamentary subcommittee's approach to reform demands (and assumes) a commitment by correctional administrators and staff to what has been called the 'justice model' of corrections. This model has been developed by professionals within the correctional system who seek a 'set of objectives for prisons evolved from a series of propositions concerning [a] view of man and law in the context of justice.'[36] David Fogel has articulated the justice perspective on corrections:

We have to conceive of the period of incarceration and its place in criminal justice in a new way ... We need to conceptualize imprisonment differently and to narrow our rhetorical claims ... The sentence must be seen as a part of the continuum of justice – it must be experienced as just, reasonable, and constitutional. It is in the context of justice that a mission arises for the prison and its staff. The mission is fairness. Discretion must be harnessed by as much voluntary administrative explication of norms as is necessary to produce a sense of fairness for both the keeper and the kept ...

The period of incarceration can be conceptualized as the time in which we try to reorient the prisoner to the lawful use of power. One of the more fruitful ways a person can teach non-law-abiders to be law-abiding is to treat them in a lawful manner. The entire effort of the prison should be seen as an influence attempt based on operationalizing justice. This is called the 'Justice Model.' It begins by recognizing, not by moralizing, what the prison stay is about. Simply stated, it is an enforced deprivation of liberty. It is a taking of some or all of the days of a person's life and his confinement within an area. When men are confined against their will ... the bottom line of the arrangement of life for both the keeper and the kept should be justice-as-fairness. Opportunities for self-improvement should be offered but not made a condition of freedom.

Confinement and compression in a human zoo of large numbers of men, who have in the past resorted to the use of force, fraud and violence, is at best a precarious venture. James Q. Wilson said, 'We have imposed the rehabilitative philosophy in a way that offends simple justice ... when it is possible for one person, by manipulating the system, to go free while another, convicted of the same crime, remains in prison for a long term.' Prison administrators should not now further confuse their staff with a mission either claiming moral or psychological redemption, nor with one which leans on brutality to create orderliness. Justice-as-fairness provides the keeper and the kept with a rationale and morality for their shared fates in a correctional agency ... This model purports to turn a prison experience into one which provides opportunities for men to learn to be agents in their own lives, to use legal processes to change their condition, and to wield lawful power. Men who can negotiate their fates do not have to turn to violence as a method of achieving change ... It takes a great flight of imagination or studied neglect to include the current prison experience as a system of justice. The entire case for a justice model rests upon the need to engage the person in the quest for justice as he moves on the continuum from defendant-to-convict-to-free citizen ...

In the absence of a continuum of justice in the prison, most ends are reached unlawfully. When unlawful behavior is detected, it is itself frequently dealt with in the absence of the very standards of due process which we insist upon outside the prison. The result is a further indication to the convict that lawful behavior has little pay-off. He can be dealt with arbitrarily and usually responds by treating others in the same manner. In the context of prison, justice-as-fairness means having clear rules, ensuring their promulgation, and a procedure for determining and punishing rule infractions rooted in due process safeguards ... Further, it means giving up the foot-dragging, which the litigation so vividly bares ... We should be in the forefront of exposing the indignities of poor medical care ... and inhumane segregative facilities ... Courts should not have to force modern administrators to adopt any of the above procedures – it embarrasses our claim to professionalism ...

In the micro-world of the prison, the justice perspective calls upon the makers of rules to share legitimate power with the enforcers and consumers of the rules. It also urges that all rules and rulings be required to stand the test of being the least onerous way of reaching a lawful end.[37]

Since the parliamentary subcommittee's endorsement of the justice model, the Supreme Court in *Martineau (No. 2)* has, as we have seen, accepted the court's responsibility for ensuring judicial review of prison decisions in light of the fundamental principle of fairness.[38] The solicitor-general of Canada in his official response to the subcommittee's report has accepted principle 11 – that the rule of law must prevail in the penitentiary – and principle 12 – that justice is an essential condition of corrections.[39] There appears, therefore, to be a consensus in the minds of Canadian legislators, the minister responsible for the penitentiary system, and the Supreme Court of Canada that justice-as-fairness should be an essential tenet of life behind prison walls. However, if history teaches us anything in the field of corrections, it is that the rhetoric is often a great deal loftier than the reality. Certainly the rhetoric of the Canadian penitentiary service in the early 1970s did not contemplate the establishment of solitary-confinement units that violated the Canadian Bill of Rights. The British Columbia Penitentiary and its solitary-confinement unit are now closed. Has the closure of the unit also marked the passing of the practices of imprisonment with which it was linked? What has replaced the special correctional unit of the British Columbia Penitentiary? Under what conditions and through what processes are the Jack McCanns, the Donald Oags, and the Andrew Bruces now confined in administrative segregation? Under what circumstances and against what criteria is their segregation reviewed both internally by the penitentiary system and externally by the courts? It is to these questions that the next section of this book will speak.

ADMINISTRATIVE SEGREGATION IN THE 1980s

The Special Handling Units

It will be recalled that the Vantour Report in its recommendations for segregation drew a distinction between prisoners who constituted temporary threats to the good order of the institution and those who represented long-term threats. The report recommended that the first group be retained in segregation units in their own institutions, and that the latter group be sent to special segregation units to be established in the new maximum-security institutions that had been or were being built in each region. Dr Vantour (together with an architect) was subsequently asked to prepare a further report, which sets out an operational model for the physical space and programming requirements of what were to be called 'special handling units.'[40] It is clear that none of the existing segregation facilities in maximum-security institutions came close to meeting the physical requirements set out in the draft Vantour-McReynolds Report; therefore, special handling units, if they were to conform to the Vantour-McReynolds model, would require new construction or at least extensive modifications of the existing facilities.[41]

Although the report was still only in draft form, the Department of the Solicitor-General readily embraced the Vantour-McReynolds concept and proceeded to establish two special handling units (initially referred to as 'federal adjustment centres'), one at the Correctional Development Centre in Laval, Quebec, and the other at Millhaven Institution in Ontario, notwithstanding that neither of the facilities met the physical requirements of the Vantour-McReynolds model. This decision was heavily influenced by the politics surrounding the passage of Bill C-51, the Criminal Law Amendment Act, 1977,[42] which abolished capital punishment. As the trade-off for the legal abolition of the hangman's noose (by virtue of the exercise of the prerogative of mercy, no one had been executed in Canada since 1962) Bill C-51 instituted life sentences with a minimum parole eligibility date of twenty-five years for persons convicted of first-degree murder. The government, to demonstrate to critics of abolition that it was concerned not to undermine the deterrent effect of the law, announced its intention to confine those convicted of first-degree murder in super-maximum security in the new special handling units. This plan was quite contrary to the recommendations in the first Vantour Report, which had stated that no one should be considered a dangerous prisoner within the setting of the maximum-security penitentiary on the basis of his offence in the community 'until it has been established that he represents a threat to institutional staff or other inmates or is an escape risk even in maximum security.'[43] Political considerations, therefore, rather than correctional principles, played a large part in the initial decision to establish Canada's new prisons of isolation.

Although the special handling units at Millhaven and the Correctional Development Centre were not the new facilities envisaged by the Vantour-McReynolds model, that model has played and continues to play a central role in establishing the theoretical framework of operation for these units.

Therefore, before looking at the reality faced by prisoners confined in the new prisons of isolation, it is important to examine carefully this theoretical framework in order to better understand the congruence or dissonance between the rhetoric and that reality.

The Vantour-McReynolds Report sets out the objectives of special handling units:

1 To provide a safe and secure environment for the staff and inmates of the institutions from which dangerous inmates are removed;
2 To provide a safe and secure environment for the staff and inmates in the special handling units;
3 To avoid the physical and mental deterioration that accompany the long periods of dissociation which these inmates have experienced in administrative segregation in the past;
4 To provide inmates with the incentive and opportunity for earning their return to the main inmate population.[44]

Objectives 3 and 4 are clearly of cardinal significance in differentiating the special handling units from solitary confinement in the SCU at the British Columbia Penitentiary, and the report develops in some detail the strategy for achieving these objectives.

Realization ... depends upon the inmates' opportunity for sensory and intellectual stimulation. This can be achieved through the presence of inter-personal contact between staff and inmates, through the provision of appropriate programmes designed to reduce periods of isolation, and through access to activity spaces outside the cell ... The inmate must have the opportunity to demonstrate acceptable behaviour. This requires a process in which the inmate can earn privileges and advance through the shu to eventual return to a less secure environment.

The provision of incentives is the vehicle through which acceptable behaviour is encouraged. All positive actions should lead to increased freedom of movement within the shu.

The above requires a sequence of phases through which all inmates can progress from admission to release.

Phase 1 – Assessment and Orientation

Every inmate admitted into an shu must be assessed and oriented towards the nature of the programme and an individual programme plan (ipp) developed for his stay at the shu. The essence of the ipp is that each inmate can evaluate his own progress whilst staff measure his development. This normally lasts thirty days with the initial evaluation deriving from behaviour displayed during the first two to three weeks. Formal data collection is obtained from interviews. The individual programme plan is developed for each inmate. The length of time for assessment and orientation depends upon the behaviour of the inmate. Inmates refusing to become involved are interviewed regularly at intervals until the ipp is developed and the inmate demonstrates a willingness to participate. Uncooperative inmates remain in isolation with only basic amenities.

Phase 2 – Self-awareness

During this phase, an inmate is expected to operationalize his ipp. He should examine his problems with his classification officer, his case manager, and possibly with other inmates as identified by the case management team. Contact with staff and other inmates is minimal. The inmate may receive increased privileges within this phase. In order to progress from Phase 2 to Phase 3 he should identify his problem areas with the assistance of staff and display a willingness to deal with them.

Phase 3 – Individual Demonstration

Once progressing into Phase 3 the inmate is given an opportunity to deal with his problems through dyads, group settings and individual counselling sessions. Contact with other inmates and staff increases, privileges are considerably extended in response to his cooperation and willingness to reconcile his behaviour. Following extensive and regular evaluation sessions between the staff team and the inmate himself, the inmate's case is presented before the Regional Review Committee for return to his institution. Having achieved this he will enter into Phase 4.

Throughout each programme phase the privileges and means of assessment must be known to both staff and inmate. Regular reviews are carried out every 30 days, providing the Regional Review Committee with data for semi-annual reviews. These enable the inmate to be aware of his progress. Since progress through each phase depends on the management team's perception of inmate behaviour, the inmate must be made aware of their perception and evaluation.[45]

The Vantour-McReynolds model envisaged prisoners being organized in groups of no more than seven people to work with a case-management team comprising a psychologist, a part-time psychiatrist, a case manager (a classification officer), corrections officers, and other ad hoc members as required. Each group of seven would be kept separate from other groups; to accomplish this separation, the physical facility was to be designed around interrelating spaces called 'envelopes,' defined as 'a space surrounded by a secure physical barrier through which total control of access and egress can be exercised.'[46]

The report describes program activities, including one-to-one encounters between the prisoners and staff, group encounters between prisoners and staff, active recreation, passive recreation, visiting, and academic or vocational development, and describes the graduated nature of prisoners' privileges as they move from phase to phase. It is an essential part of the philosophy of the SHU as set out by Vantour and McReynolds that all opportunities to participate in programs are a privilege and not a right. The programs are made available 'to promote the development of acceptable behavioural responses.'[47] Thus such things as cards, chess, and checkers 'are all used for the demonstration of inmate behaviour.'[48] Similarly, 'the provision of any academic or vocational training activities in an SHU is strictly to provide insights into the behaviour of the inmate and to provide an opportunity for the inmate to demonstrate meaningful behavioural change.'[49]

The behavioural-modification theory underlying the special handling units is not unprecedented. A number of such programs were established in the United States and in England in the 1970s. The Special Treatment and Rehabilitative Training (STRT) program initiated by the Federal Bureau of Prisons at its facilities in Springfield, Missouri, was designed for prisoners regarded as hard-core unmanageables: those who had previously spent most of their time in prison in segregation and allegedly had been physically or verbally abusive toward other prisoners and guards. The program was based upon a phase system in which, as in the SHU, prisoners were deprived of regular prison privileges until they modified their behaviour in conformity to official demands. The STRT program was terminated after the initiation of a congressional inquiry and court action.[50]

Also in the early 1970s the Special Program Unit (SPU) was constructed in one of the remodelled cell houses at the old Joliet Prison in Illinois to house the 'hard-core prison troublemakers' from Stateville. The SPU incorporated a three-tiered behaviour-modification plan, the general purpose of which was to 'attempt through intensive therapeutic application, to assist the individuals assigned to acquire the necessary motivation and desire essential for integration into the general prison population.' Personnel assigned to the SPU were responsible for creating 'a therapeutic climate conducive to innovational diagnostic-treatment-program concepts.'[51] This program was challenged by litigation initiated by the American Civil Liberties Union on the basis that confinement in SPU amounted to cruel and unusual punishment and that assignment to the unit was a punitive disposition requiring due process safeguards. The Federal District Court granted the due process relief but refused to find that the unit violated the Eighth Amendment.[52] Prisoners assigned to the unit refused to accept their confinement there and engaged in massive resistance, which took the form of smashing the cells. Notwithstanding the fact that the federal court found the unit not to be in violation of the Eighth Amendment, the Illinois Correction Department quietly abandoned the behaviour-modification experiment, and converted the unit into a regular segregation facility.[53]

The British prison authorities had also preceded Canada in the establishment of special super-maximum units. In 1974 the British home secretary announced that 'control units for intractable prisoners' would be opened. The process was originally described as follows:

If a governor regarded a man as 'intractable,' he made a report to the Prison Department. If the latter agreed, the man was despatched to a control unit. For ninety days, he would remain in isolation. He was not obliged to work but, if he did not, the days on which he refused to do so would not count. At the end of ninety days, he began another ninety days, this time in 'association' with the other members of the unit. If there were no other members, he could, presumably, associate only with the staff. If at any time during the two consecutive phases he misbehaved, he began the whole process again, regardless of any discretion a governor might feel like exercising. The first phase comprised 23 hours in a cell and one hour's exercise. The prisoner was allowed books, photographs, birthday and Christmas cards. There was no hearing and no judicial appeal.[54]

The proposal was greeted with a great deal of criticism from civil-liberties organizations and academics concerned with prisoners' rights.[55] As a result of these criticisms, the home secretary announced in November 1974 that he would introduce some changes in the procedures. A proposal to transfer a prisoner was now to be referred to the board of visitors of the prison in which he was detained and 'transfer would not be authorized against its view unless [the home secretary has] personally considered the proposal and announced that [he believes] it to be right.'[56] The board of visitors in the receiving prison was to be associated with a reviewing procedure, the most important facet of which was a new discretion to be exercised by the board or the governor about 'the extent to which a prisoner should revert if he misbehaves.'[57] These changes did little to abate the criticism directed against control units, criticism which included legal arguments that the establishment of the control units was not authorized by the general segregation power contained in the prison rules.[58] In the face of the criticism the British government in 1975 closed down the one control unit it had established at Wakefield Prison.[59]

The concept of special handling units has proved to be more enduring in Canada. In December 1980 the solicitor-general announced a new 'dangerous-inmate policy' based on the expanded use of special handling units. This new policy has been reflected in significant changes to the divisional instructions and commissioner's directives which provide the administrative framework for the units. Because my own visits to the SHUs and interviews with prisoners being held in them span these changes, I will be referring to both the pre- and post-December 1980 framework.[60]

Divisional instructions and directives describe the SHU as a facility for prisoners who have been identified as 'particularly dangerous.' The pre-December 1980 directive defined such a prisoner as 'one, who, *while under sentence or in custody*, demonstrates aggressive behaviour which poses a threat to staff, inmates or other persons. Such conduct includes the commission of, and attempts to commit, hostage taking or any act resulting in death or the infliction of serious bodily harm [emphasis added].'[61]

The divisional instruction defined such conduct as including abduction, hostage-taking, or forcible confinement; serious incidents of violence; escape or attempted escape involving violence; and conviction for the murder of a peace officer while in custody or at large.[62] The divisional instruction also provided that prisoners shall not be transferred to the SHU on the ground of suspicion alone but 'only as a result of the actual demonstration of aggressiveness or violent behaviour.'[63]

As a result of the introduction of the dangerous-inmate policy, the definition of a 'particularly dangerous inmate' was broadened. The current definition is:

> one whose documented actions or demonstrated intentions while in custody in any jurisdiction, or under surveillance, constitute a persistent and serious threat to staff, inmates or other persons. Such conduct includes but is not limited to, one or more of the following:
> (a) abduction, hostage-taking, forcible confinement or attempts;
> (b) serious incidents of violence;
> (c) escape or attempted or planned escape with violence;
> (d) conviction for the murder of a peace officer, inmate or other person while under sentence;
> (e) the manufacture, possession, introduction or attempted introduction into an institution of firearms, ammunition, high explosives or any offensive weapon, as defined in the Criminal Code.
> (f) incitement or conspiracy to kill or riot; and
> (g) substantiated serious threats against the life of a staff member, inmate or other person.[64]

The new directive reiterates that prisoners shall not be transferred to SHU on suspicion alone; but whereas before December 1980 'the actual demonstration of aggressiveness or violent behaviour' was required for a transfer, the new directive specifies only that 'reasonable and probable grounds for believing an inmate intends or is likely to commit a violent or dangerous act must be supported by documentation.'[65] The purpose of the broader wording as explained by the solicitor-general was 'to include inmates now recognized as posing serious threats so that they will be segregated before not after acts of violence.[66] The new policy was described by the deputy commissioner (security) as 'pro-active' rather than 'reactive.'[67]

The commissioner's directives and divisional instruction together set out a procedure for admission, review, and transfer to and from an SHU and in broad terms identify the nature of the program. Under this framework a prisoner who is viewed by the warden of the institution in which he is confined as meeting the SHU admission criteria must first be placed in administrative segregation under section 2.30(1)(a), now section 40(1). The warden's recommendation for transfer to an SHU must then be reviewed by the Regional Transfer Board and the regional director general before being considered by the National SHU Review Committee. This committee, which is the de facto decision-making body for transfer to and release from SHUs, consists of the deputy commissioner (security), the deputy commissioner (offender programs), the director-general (medical services), and senior regional representatives from the receiving and sending regions. The chairman is the deputy commissioner (security), who is officially the person to whom the authority to transfer prisoners into and out of SHU is delegated.[68] There is nowhere any provision requiring a hearing at which the prisoner can hear the case against him or make any representations on his own behalf. The new divisional instruction provides only that the warden, before forwarding his recommendation for transfer to an SHU, shall notify the prisoner in writing of the proposed action and the prisoner shall be given the opportunity to reply in writing within three days. The prisoner's written response then accompanies the warden's recommendation.[69]

We can assess the nature of the decision-making process leading to the admission of a prisoner to SHU by looking at two cases. The first is currently the subject of litigation and, like the *Martineau* case, will ultimately be decided by the Supreme Court of Canada. The case of Robert Miller arose out of the riot at Matsqui Medium Security Institution in June 1981. As a result of the riot and ensuing fire, the main cell block was extensively damaged. On 5 June Miller, along with a number of other prisoners, was placed in administrative segregation in Matsqui. On 11 July he was transferred to Kent Maximum Security Institution where he was again placed in segregation. *No disciplinary charges were laid against Miller.* On 23 July Miller was transferred to Millhaven and placed overnight in segregation. The next day he was transferred to an induction range and informed that he would be going into the general prison population. On 29 July Miller was escorted from the induction range and taken to the SHU. He was told by the officer in charge of the unit that he could expect to remain there for two years. No written or oral information about the reason for his transfer was given to Miller prior to his confinement in the SHU. Several weeks later, he received a letter from the chairman of the National SHU Review Committee explaining that his confinement in the SHU was authorized by reason of his being 'an active participant in a riot.'

He was not advised of the evidence alleged to exist against him. In October 1981 he appeared before the National SHU Review Committee and was informed of his tentative transfer dates to phases three and four. Again, he was given no details concerning the evidence against him. After this appearance before the review committee the other prisoners who were alleged to have been involved in the Matsqui riot and who were transferred to SHU at the same time as Miller was, were charged with criminal offences arising from the riot. *Miller was not charged with any criminal offence.*

Miller wrote to a lawyer from British Columbia who made enquiries of the RCMP and the crown counsel involved in the investigation and laying of charges in the Matsqui riot cases. It appeared that the investigating police officers were of the opinion that the guards' evidence as to Miller's participation in the riot was so weak that they did not even refer the case to crown counsel to consider what, if any, charges should be laid against him. Yet that same evidence which had failed to meet the police officers' relatively low threshold of proof necessary to justify a referral to crown counsel was regarded by the National SHU Review Committee as sufficient to justify transferring Miller to the SHU. There was nothing in Miller's prior criminal or prison record involving him in any violent incidents in or out of prison; yet without any hearing at which he could challenge the case against him, he found himself designated a 'particularly dangerous' prisoner requiring SHU confinement.[70]

The second case, although it concerns the readmission of a prisoner to SHU, raises further disturbing questions about the fairness of the administrative process. As a case study it is of special importance because it involves Andy Bruce, one of the *McCann* plaintiffs, and provides a basis of comparison between pre- and post-*Martineau* decision-making. Since the *McCann* trial Bruce had been continuously in segregation, first in the British Columbia Penitentiary, then in SHU at Millhaven until his transfer to Edmonton maximum-security institution in May 1982. Since his original criminal conviction in 1970 he has endured over eleven years in segregation, far more than any other prisoner in Canada. Two months after his transfer to Edmonton, on 25 July, he was charged with a disciplinary offence under section 39(k) of the Penitentiary Service Regulations for 'doing an act calculated to prejudice the discipline and good order of the institution' in that he was 'in a condition other than normal.' Two days later, on 27 July he was charged again with the same kind of offence. According to Bruce, on this occasion he had seen a nurse and the head of medical staff before and after being charged, and they could testify that there was nothing wrong with him. On 2 August a third charge for 'being in a condition other than normal' was laid against Bruce, and he was taken to segregation. Bruce alleges that while handcuffed and in segregation he was severely beaten by four guards. He suffered injuries which, in his view, exacerbated an ulcer condition for which he later required an operation. Bruce subsequently swore informations against the guards, alleging assault causing bodily harm. The justice of the peace before whom the informations were laid refused to issue summonses.

On the morning of 6 August Bruce appeared before the segregation review board. He was told that as a result of his outstanding charges for being in a condition other than normal, a recommendation would be made for his return to SHU. At this point Bruce had not been convicted of any charges. Later that day Bruce appeared before a disciplinary board presided over by an independent chairman to answer to the two charges of 25 July and 2 August. Bruce requested an adjournment to enable his lawyer to represent him at the hearing. He argued that given the serious effect conviction would have on him – return to SHU – the duty to act fairly required that he be represented by counsel. The adjournment was refused. In his defence to the charges, Bruce gave evidence that he had had an ear infection and had been receiving medication during the periods covered by the two charges. After taking the medication he became dizzy and unsteady on his feet and it was while in this condition that he had been seen by officers who had wrongly assumed that he was under the influence of non-prescribed drugs. Bruce was convicted of both charges and sentenced on the first to thirty days' punitive segregation, and on the second to a further thirty days suspended for ninety days.

After the hearing Bruce received a written notification from the segregation review board confirming that a recommendation would be made for his return to SHU. That notification of 6 August stated that 'all facts pertinent to [his] case would be included in the recommendation.' On 9 August Bruce received a copy of the warden's recommendation for his return to SHU. The only reason given for the recommendation was Bruce's conviction on the charges of being in a condition other than normal. On that same day a fourth charge was laid against Bruce for possession of contraband. It was alleged that a small amount of cannabis resin had been discovered in a sweater in the cell from which he had been removed seven days previously. It appears that the drug, which had not been discovered in the careful search of his cell conducted immediately after his transfer to segregation, had been found in a subsequent search.

On 12 August Bruce appeared before a disciplinary board to face the remaining 'condition other than normal' charge of 25 July and the contraband charge of 9 August. The hearing was presided over by an independent chairman other than the one who had presided over the first set of charges. Bruce again requested an adjournment to permit legal representation. This time his request was granted and the hearing was adjourned to 26 August. Bruce meanwhile filed grievances concerning what he regarded as the unfair conduct of the previous disciplinary-board hearing. On 26 August Bruce appeared before the disciplinary board with his lawyer. The institution failed to produce the officer who had laid the 'condition other than normal' charge; Bruce requested that the charge not be dismissed for lack of evidence but rather be adjourned further to permit the officer to appear. Bruce was anxious that there be a hearing on the merits at which he could call the nurse and medical officer to give evidence that he was not in a 'condition other than normal.' The independent chairman dismissed the charge with no evidence being heard.

At the hearing on the 'contraband' charge, a prisoner witness testified that it was another prisoner who had placed the sweater and cannabis resin in Bruce's cell *after* Bruce had been taken to segregation on 2 August. This prisoner had assumed that Bruce was going to be transferred back to SHU in Millhaven and that the sweater would be packed without further search as part of his personal effects. It was alleged that the cannabis resin secreted in the pockets of the sweater was destined for another prisoner already in SHU. The independent chairman adjourned the hearing to 17 September to hear evidence from the staff member who had searched Bruce's cell the first time without discovering any drug.

On 27 August Bruce received a second warden's recommendation for transfer to SHU. This supplemented the first by giving as reasons not only the conviction of the two charges of 'being in a condition other than normal' but also gambling, trafficking, enforcement (strong-arming), and threatening violence against other prisoners. It appears that the 'threatening' allegation was based on the information of a protective-custody prisoner who was placed on the same tier as Bruce and who stated that he was in fear of him. (It should be noted that any protective-custody prisoner who found himself on a tier with population prisoners, let alone a prisoner of Andy Bruce's reputation, would be legitimately fearful by virtue of physical proximity to those prisoners, regardless of any overt action on their part.) Pursuant to the new divisional instruction, Bruce was given three days within which to respond to the second recommendation for transfer to SHU. In his response Bruce requested that he be given the facts and evidence upon which the new allegations were based. He pointed out that the allegations referred to his having engaged in these activities during the months of May and June, and asked why they had not therefore been included in the warden's first recommendation of 9 August. In effect, his response was a request for further and better particulars of the allegations so that he could properly meet the case against him. His handwritten response was sent to the warden through the prison mail system on the morning of 30 August. On 31 August the National SHU Review Committee met in Ottawa and authorized Bruce's transfer to the SHU in Millhaven. At 5:00 A.M. on 1 September Bruce was awakened and taken in handcuffs and leg-irons to a waiting plane. By evening he was back in a steel-lined cell in SHU. A deputy commissioner informed the press in an interview concerning Bruce's transfer, 'we didn't want to give him an opportunity to arrange for people to interrupt the transfer by attacking the vehicle taking him to the airplane.'

On 2 September Bruce was notified in writing by the chairman of the National SHU Review Committee of the reasons for the transfer:

> In your case, the warden of your institution recommended you for transfer to the shu as you are considered to have become a serious threat to inmates ... It is not intended to supply you with the name of the inmate referred to as being in fear of you, but there is no doubt in my mind and in the minds of the committee that he did genuinely feel threatened. The discovery of cannabis resin in your cell gives me reasonable grounds for believing you to be involved in drugs, whether or not charges are brought in criminal court, and your convictions on the two charges by the independent chairperson supports my belief, in spite of whatever legal process you may wish to launch. I have noted that the 27 July charge was dismissed in warden's court and have accordingly taken this into consideration. With regard to the notification that you were found gambling and that there are reasonable grounds for believing you were involved in drug trafficking, you have been given the opportunity to comment on or about that allegation in your reply to the notification, but have not done so. Also, transfers to the Special Handling Unit are not ordered by the court as a result of criminal charges but rather are part of the transfer process applied in compliance with Commissioner's Directive 274 and Divisional Instruction 718 ... Finally, I have reasonable grounds also to believe that while in segregation and since you were counselled, your drug activities have not ceased.

As a result of Bruce's transfer to SHU the adjourned hearing on the contraband charge was never resumed. The charge was simply withdrawn.

On the basis of such allegations and suspicions, without any hearing or process through which he could know and challenge the full case against him, Andy Bruce was again designated a 'particularly dangerous' prisoner and returned to the SHU to face his twelfth year of segregation.

Once a prisoner has been transferred to a special handling unit, his case is subject to a review every month by institutional authorities and every six months by the National SHU Review Committee. Prior to December 1980, the commissioner's directives provided that the decision to transfer the prisoner out of an SHU 'shall be based upon the inmate's demonstrated lack of hostility and his adjudged ability to assume responsibility and to associate with staff and other inmates without posing any threat to their safety.'[71] The new directive and divisional instructions have added to these criteria two further requirements:

(a) Normally, completion of two years in the first three phases.
(b) A firm conviction by the National shu Review Committee that the inmate no longer represents a serious danger to staff or other inmates.[72]

The divisional instruction specifically provides that prisoners must be kept aware of their status and are to be informed of the results of the monthly institutional review in writing by the director of the institution.[73] Prisoners are not to be informed of the nature of the recommendations made to the national committee; under the old divisional instruction, the director was required to notify them in writing of that committee's decision.[74] The current directive provides only that the national committee shall notify the prisoner orally of its decision.[75]

The six-month review by the national committee is intended to ensure that SHU admission and release decisions are not based upon the unprincipled exercise of discretion. The deputy commissioner (security) has provided this description of the national-committee review process:

> The review process begins with a detailed study at National Headquarters of the Warden's last monthly review, and relevant files and reports. In Ottawa the Committee is chaired by the Deputy Commissioner of Security and consists also of the Deputy Commissioner of Offender Programmes, Director General, Medical Services, and other officers at the discretion of the Chairman. When it sits in the institution, representatives of receiving regions also attend as do the Warden and Institutional and Regional officers. A representative of the Federal Correctional Investigator also attends throughout.[76]

Although prisoners are not permitted to attend the monthly institutional review, they are permitted and encouraged to appear before the national committee's six-monthly hearings. 'The Committee operates as an administrative board and conducts interviews in a similar manner to a parole hearing. The Committee is brought up to date on the performance of the inmate who is then requested to attend. He is encouraged to make any comments related to his stay in SHU and these are considered by the Committee.'[77]

Although the commissioner's directive and the divisional instruction go into some detail concerning the admission, transfer, and review processes, they are more general in dealing with the SHU phase program. The commissioner's directive provides that the program of a special handling unit 'shall be designed so that each individual inmate shall have the opportunity and responsibility to earn in so far as is practicable his unconditional return to the general inmate population of a maximum security institution.'[78] Prior to December 1980, the divisional instruction provided that 'after initial assessment and orientation at the SHU, the program shall consist of at least three phases: (1) a restricted association phase, (2) a limited association phase, and (3) an increased association phase.'[79] The new commissioner's directive of 1 December 1980 expanded the number of phases along with the criteria for admission to SHU. There are now four phases: initial assessment, limited association, increased association, and conditional transfer to a maximum-security institution.[80] Common to both documents is the statement that 'each inmate shall progress through each phase of the programme at a rate determined by his demonstrated ability.'[81]

The phase program is elaborated upon in internal institutional documents put out by the authorities at the two special handling units. At Millhaven, in phase one, 'an inmate has the following basic amenities, food, bedding, clothing, shower, one hour exercise, closed visits, correspondence, medical, psychiatric and dental care, access to library books and to legal documents.' In phase two, 'inmates will receive all amenities of phase one plus: minimum exercise of one hour, common room (½ range every other night if range count is 15 or more), movies, limited telephone calls to family, television in the cell, bonus pay system, limited access to recreation area.' In phase three, 'inmates will receive all amenities listed above, plus [access to the] recreation area every day. Contact visits (once every other month) if approved by the Inmate Training Board.'[82]

The Correctional Service of Canada perceives the special handling units to be qualitatively different from segregation units such as the SCU at the British Columbia Penitentiary, both in terms of the conditions of confinement and the procedures for admission and review of prisoners. In literature available to the public, the Correctional Service points out that SHU cells provide standard accommodation and are equal in size to those of the regular population, and although the prisoners are in dissociation 'they are not in solitary confinement. On the contrary, the SHU inmate is out of his cell an approximate 7½ hours a day, if he so chooses, for participation in a variety of sports and common room activities.'[83] From statements such as these, and indeed from the commissioner's directive and divisional instruction, the units appear on paper to be real improvements. But how is life within the units perceived by the prisoners confined there? Do they see their imprisonment as differing from their confinement in the old segregation units? To seek answers to these questions I visited the two special handling units in August 1980 and interviewed prisoners and those responsible for the administration of the units – wardens, psychologists, classification officers, and guards. Since that first visit I have communicated further with those prisoners, and have interviewed other prisoners in British Columbia who have served time in an SHU and who are now in the population of Kent Maximum Security Institution. In November 1981 and December 1982 I again visited the SHU in Millhaven, and in May 1982 I returned to the SHU in the Correctional Development Centre. While this data base is not as extensive as that which was available to me in considering the conditions in the special correctional unit at British Columbia Penitentiary, it is in my view sufficient to form a valid judgment about the real differences between the old and new regimes.

The Millhaven special handling unit for English-speaking prisoners is located in E unit, one of the four wings of the main penitentiary. Millhaven, opened in 1971, is one of the new maximum-security institutions. The cells in the SHU are the same size as all others in the penitentiary, six feet by ten feet. The walls of the SHU cells are lined with steel, and the outside windows, which in the normal-population cells are wired glass, are covered with steel slats. These slats restrict the natural light coming into the cell and impede the prisoner's view out of it. Each cell has a solid steel door with a five-inch peephole window. Inside the cell there is a steel bed, a steel desk-chair combination, a sink-toilet combination, and, except for the cells of phase-one prisoners, a television set. There are three ranges of cells in E unit; these are known as F, G, and H. Each range contains two floors. On range 2-F there is a 'recreation area.' Institutional documents subdivide this area into the 'hobbycraft' room, the 'music' room, the 'library,' the 'tutoring' room, and the 'gym.' In fact these areas are cells, some of which have had the connecting walls removed. At the time of my visit in August 1980, the library was a cell furnished with an empty bookcase. The music room was a cell with a shelf on which a single guitar rested. The gym was a double cell equipped with a punching-bag and exerciser. There was also what was called a common room, which contained a television and in which movies were shown. Prisoners were permitted to gather in the common room in small groups. There was an outside exercise yard surrounded by a high wall. Prisoners usually visited with their families and friends in the regular visiting area used by the general population; when other prisoners from the population were there, SHU prisoners were required to go into a cage which provided a physical barrier between them and other prisoners. As with all prisoners, regular visits were conducted through a plexiglass screen by telephone. Interviews with institutional staff, parole officers, and lawyers were held in two special 'interview rooms' inside the SHU. These rooms were really plexiglass cages with steel doors and remote-control locks. The prisoner was separated from the interviewer by a plexiglass barrier in the middle of which was a small opening covered by a thick steel grill. The interview was conducted through this grill. The movement of prisoners within the SHU was strictly controlled. Only one prisoner was allowed out of his cell at a time on any floor, and was always accompanied by at least two guards. These conditions were substantially unchanged when I revisited the SHU in 1981 and 1982.

It will be recalled that two features of the special handling unit model as described in the Vantour-McReynolds Report distinguished the units from the old-style segregation units: activities outside the prisoner's cell which would provide sensory and intellectual stimulation, and opportunities for the prisoner to earn his return to the general population through a phased program. How well does the SHU at Millhaven achieve these objectives? In phase one of the program there is no real difference between the regime in Millhaven and that in the segregation unit in the British Columbia Penitentiary. The prisoners are locked up for twenty-three hours a day, with one hour for exercise. There is no contact with other prisoners. In phases two and three prisoners are permitted to have television sets in their cells, and to have one or two hours of exercise in the yard daily. In phase two they are permitted to spend four hours in the common room every other evening; in phase three the time is increased to four hours every evening. This means that in total a prisoner in phase two spends an average of six hours out of his cell every forty-eight hours, while a phase-three prisoner can be out up to six hours every day. While these figures are less than the seven and one-half hours a day claimed by the Canadian Correctional Service in its official literature, they show that there is much more time for prisoner association than had been available in the segregation unit at the British Columbia Penitentiary.

Nevertheless, all of the prisoners I interviewed at the SHU in Millhaven were of the view that the unit, despite the television sets, common rooms, and exercise yard, was as bad as the old-style segregation units they had all experienced. Clearly this judgment was not based on the physical conditions or amenities made available to prisoners, harsh and limited as they still are. Rather, just as the most important evidence in the *McCann* case dealt with the psychological implications of segregation, so the prisoners at the SHU in Millhaven, in their accounts of their experiences, dealt again and again with the psychological reality they saw lying behind their incarceration.

It may seem paradoxical, given that the phase program was designed to distinguish in positive ways between special handling units and the old-style segregation units, that the program is the focal point for much of the prisoners' protests. The prisoners see the phase program as a cruel parody of reform. They are told about the three phases when they come into the SHU at Millhaven and that there are opportunities for the prisoners to advance through the successive phases and to attain eventual release from the unit. They are told that classification and psychological staff members will be available to assist them and to evaluate their performance. Every prisoner I interviewed denied the reality of this model. Three of the prisoners, including two who were plaintiffs in the *McCann* case, expressed their experience in this way:

This place is Tomb City. They want you to do nothing. There is no program. The jobs are made up – the library without any books.[84]

How do you get out of here – you do nothing. Not get charged. But even that will not guarantee that you get out. If you do nothing they may say they are not sure where you are coming from. One guy has been here three years and he was told at his six month review 'We don't know you.' This place is no different than the bc Pen. I don't know when they will let me out or what I have to do to make them let me out ... The difference between this place and the bc Pen? In the bc Pen they treated me as if I didn't exist. Here, when my father died someone put a note telling me about it under my cell door. It's no different. They treat you as if you weren't a person.[85]

They play psychological head games with you. My Classification Officer told me that he was recommending that I be put into phase 3 because my attitude had changed. That's bullshit – my attitude hasn't changed at all. I'm just the same as when I came in here. I've done enough time. I've been here one of the longest. That's why they want me to go into phase 3.[86]

I asked every prisoner I saw what he understood to be required of him by the administration in order to be promoted into the next phase and ultimately to be released from the SHU. Every prisoner told me that he did not know what he had to do except put in a certain amount of time, which was at least one year but which might be a lot longer, and meanwhile not cause any trouble. None saw any positive actions that he could take, since all that was available was television, the common room, and the yard. There were no real work opportunities in the SHU apart from cleaning. While prisoners are permitted to take correspondence courses, the prisoners I interviewed who had sought to explore this avenue had given it up largely owing to their inability to concentrate in the unit and the impersonality of the feedback they received.[87]

The Vantour-McReynolds model placed much emphasis on the need for ongoing evaluation in the regular review of prisoners in the special handling units. I have already explained how the commissioner's directive and the divisional instruction provide both for a thirty-day review at the institutional level and for a six-month review at the national level. The prisoner is permitted to attend the six-month review. I questioned the prisoners about the review process, since, on paper at least, it is designed to remedy the deficiencies revealed in the *McCann* case. However, as far as the prisoners are concerned, the changes have not rendered the review process in the SHU any more legitimate or fair. Two documents prepared by prisoners explain why.

Inmates in the shu whose cases are brought before the monthly Segregation Review Board should be allowed to appear in front of the Board and present their cases. The way the Board is now being operated is not just. Every month, each inmate gets a slip of paper saying that his case was heard by the Segregation Review Board and that the decision was for the inmate to remain in the shu. They never give any of the facts that were presented at the Board, or what their decisions were based on. Every inmate should have the right to present his case in front of the Segregation Review Board every month so that he knows why the decision that is rendered in his case, is rendered ... Right now nobody knows what goes on at the Boards, or if in fact there is even a Board that sits every month. All we know is that we get a piece of paper every month saying that it has been decided that we remain segregated for the next 30 days. Unless there is something that goes on at the Boards that you want hidden from the inmates, such as a picking of straws, or arbitrary decisions being rendered, without two sides of a case being presented, then there is no reason why every inmate can't be allowed to present his own case at the Segregation Review Board.[88]

Inmates of G-2 Tier feel that without input regarding their cases, the Review Board is once again making arbitrary decisions based on information supplied to them by the penitentiary staff, completely disregarding and relegating inmates' status to that of a number to be dealt with as they see fit. The inmates of G-2 Tier therefore request their presence at the 30-day Segregation Review Board so that they may make full answer and defence against staff allegations and reports.[89]

The prisoners believe that the thirty-day review process at Millhaven is not based on hard evidence measured against clear criteria but, like segregation at the British Columbia Penitentiary, is based on various staff members' feelings and intuition about the prisoners' attitudes. The prisoners rejected the idea that the board was receiving any valuable or reliable information from either the classification or the psychological staff, because prisoner contacts with those staff members were infrequent. Several prisoners told me that they had not seen the classification officer in over three months, and that they had not had a proper interview with a psychologist in that period.[90]

Prisoners showed me copies of the notification slips they had received reporting the outcome of their thirty-day reviews. The slips confirmed their assertions that they revealed nothing of the evidence or the basis of the board's conclusions. Moreover, it appears from some of these notification slips and from the responses made to the prisoners' grievance that they be permitted to attend the thirty-day review that the authorities at Millhaven perceived that review to be subordinate to the six-month review conducted by national headquarters. The authorities' response states that

> authority to transfer inmates in or out of shu ultimately lies with National Headquarters. They review the cases every six months at which time all inmates have a chance to appear before the Board. Time and staff deployment do not allow for the requested procedure which normally takes two to three days. Unless, therefore, there are exceptional circumstances we will continue with the present procedure of interviewing inmates every six months.[91]

The review notification slip received by Prisoner A in November 1979 also suggested that the Millhaven authorities, in their monthly review, did not see themselves as having the authority to change a prisoner's status - even to another phase within the unit - without the approval of the National SHU Review Committee. Prisoner A was informed that he was to be retained in dissociation

> ... for the maintenance of good order and discipline in the institution. The six-month shu Review Committee on October 31 and November 1, 1979, indicated that you remain in phase 2 and that you will be reviewed at the next six-month review.[92]

This is the clearest possible indication that whatever Prisoner A did or did not do during the six months, he would remain in phase two, negating any suggestion that during that six-month period he could, by his behaviour or any other means, improve his situation within the SHU. The new divisional instruction now provides that the warden of the institution in which the SHU is located may authorize the progression of a prisoner through phases one, two, and three, as well as the return of a prisoner to an earlier phase. The power to advance a prisoner through the phases is circumscribed by the provision in the new directive that the National Review Committee 'shall approve an individual program for the inmate's progression and set a tentative date for his advancement to phase 4.'[93]

While the National Review Committee pays close attention to the documentation produced by the institutional monthly reviews, the prisoners' perception that the six-month review process is the effective source of decision-making in relation to the release of prisoners from the special handling unit, and a powerful influence on major changes of status within the unit, is an accurate reflection of reality.[94]

Does the fact that prisoners are permitted to attend the six-month review board hearings remedy the alleged deficiencies in their inability to hear and respond to evidence presented during the monthly reviews? The prisoners are all of the view that the nature of their participation in the six-month review process does not guarantee the fairness of that procedure in terms of their right to make full answer and defence and to comment on the matters brought before the six-month board. In order to provide an empirical basis for my own judgment as to the adequacy of the six-month review process, I requested the opportunity to attend the review board hearings in the fall of 1980. That request was denied on the basis that, because of the highly sensitive nature of the information exchanged, my presence would impede the functioning of the review committee.

Nevertheless, it is still possible to assess whether the six-month review meets minimal standards of fairness. As I have mentioned, Mr J.U. Marcel Sauvé, the deputy commissioner of security, states that the review committee 'conducts its interviews in a similar manner to a parole hearing.'[95] The prisoners I interviewed all felt that their appearance before the National Review Committee was severely hampered by their not knowing what was contained in the monthly reviews or the nature of the assessments prepared by classification and psychological staff. The same criticisms have also been levelled against the way in which parole hearings are conducted. In essence, they aver that the prisoner is given no notice of the case with which he has to contend. However, recent amendments to the parole regulations have sought to deal with these points by requiring that an applicant for parole be provided with all relevant information in the possession of the board.[96] In particular, parole applicants are given a copy of the assessment prepared by their case-management team, which is made up of representatives from the parole and institutional staffs. While there are important exceptions to the information given to parole applicants, there has at least been recognition by the parole authorities that fairness requires some advance disclosure of the information on which the parole board will base its decision. There is no similar awareness of this essential tenet of the doctrine of fairness in the penitentiary authorities' review of SHU cases. Prisoners are given no written or oral information in advance of the hearing. They are not shown the monthly review reports, nor are they present during the part of the hearing in which the vital information about their conduct and behaviour in SHU is discussed. The divisional instruction specifically provides that prisoners are not to be informed of the nature of the recommendations made to the National Review Committee by institutional staff.[97] Prisoners' participation, therefore, is ineffective in that the prisoner cannot challenge or reinterpret the evidence on which the committee will base its decision. Furthermore, proceeding with the parole analogy, the new parole regulations permit the presence of an assistant (who may be a lawyer) at the parole hearing.[98] Prisoners appearing before the National Review Committee are not permitted to have the assistance of anyone.

The failure to disclose the institutional staff's evaluation of the prisoner has serious implications in regard to the underlying model of the special handling unit as set out in the Vantour-McReynolds Report. According to that model, an integral purpose of the review was to 'enable the inmate to be aware of his progress. Since progress for each phase depends upon the management team's perception of inmate behaviour, the inmate must be made aware of their perception and evaluation.'[99] The practice of non-disclosure of the evaluation confounds that model of behavioural change.

The pre-1982 divisional instruction provided that the prisoner was to be informed in writing of the national committee's decision.[100] The new instruction provides that the committee inform the prisoner orally of its decision.[101] Will this provide the prisoner with enough information to make him aware of the basis for the committee's decision and with enough guidance as to what is required of him in the future to bring about a change in his status and eventual release from the SHU? A number of the Millhaven SHU prisoners showed me the notifications they had received from the national committee. Typically, the notifications indicated the nature of the decision but provided no details about the evidentiary basis on which that decision was made. For example, the April 1980 notification to Prisoner A simply stated, 'this is to advise you that your confinement in the SHU was reviewed by the SHU National Review Committee. The decision of that Committee is that you will remain in phase two.'[102] Comparison with other prisoners' notifications showed that this was a standard form of notification. Prisoners' experience with the new procedure of oral transmission of the decision has so far not revealed any significant departure from the conclusionary nature of the communication of the committee's decision.

Therefore, while the review process, particularly the national review process, was designed to be a significant step in responding to the need for fairness in decisions affecting confinement in the special handling unit, the reality falls far short of meeting that standard. It also fails to conform to the behaviour-modification rationale for special handling units laid down by Vantour-McReynolds. The review process is thus doubly flawed when measured against the external standard of fairness and against the internal objective of inducing behavioural change.

The perceived and actual lack of fairness in the review process is enough in itself to undermine the legitimacy of imprisonment in SHU in the minds of the prisoners. That sense of illegitimacy is reinforced in Millhaven by feelings, bordering on outrage, which flow from the perceived hypocrisy of the phase program. As I have described, the prisoners feel that there are no real opportunities for demonstrating in positive ways that they have reformed or changed, apart from simply doing their time and not assaulting anyone in the unit. In my interviews with prisoners and the staff in SHU, I tried to discover the reality behind the phase program. How were judgments made by the institutional staff to recommend progression and ultimate release from the SHU? What criteria were used? I asked these questions of every staff member I interviewed, from the psychologist to the head of classification to the guards on duty in the unit. It was a profoundly disturbing line of inquiry. Initially when asked to differentiate between phases two and three, several of the guards could not think of any real difference in the regimes. Eventually it was conceded that prisoners in phase three were permitted to use the common room every day as opposed to every second day for phase-two prisoners. Yet in the guards' view this difference seemed not to reflect a reward or incentive but rather was based on the fact that the rules permitted no more than fifteen prisoners at a time in the common room. Since there were more than fifteen prisoners in phase two and substantially fewer than that in phase three, the different treatment was thought to be based on numbers rather than on merit. Indeed, I was told that if the number of prisoners in phase three increased to more than fifteen then they would not have common-room privileges every night. Another difference that came to light after some further thought by the guards was that prisoners in phase three had the opportunity for open visits once every two months. These appeared to be the only differences between the phases, apart from the important fact that in phase three the expectation of ultimate release is that much closer.

Because the guards have important input into the monthly review process, I asked them how they judged the prisoners' behaviour. Their answers indicated that their assessments were primarily based on the prisoners' conduct in the common room and in the yard, and that co-operation with the staff was looked for. I pursued the question of criteria for advancement through the phases with the head of classification at Millhaven. He relied upon the statement in the commissioner's directives and divisional instruction that the principal criterion was 'the inmate's demonstrated lack of hostility and his adjudged ability to assume responsibility and to associate with staff and other inmates without posing any threat to their safety.'[103] I was informed that these judgments were based on guards' reports and the assessment of the prisoner's attitude to the phase program and his participation in its various features. When I asked about the specific programs in phases two and three, I was informed that these were essentially the common-room, hobby, and exercise programs, and the 'TV program.' The TV program turned out to be the manner in which prisoners interact in the common room while watching the television set. In my interviews with the psychologist, who has primary responsibility for the SHU, he conceded that the criteria were necessarily open-ended and somewhat subjective, but contended that the review process was designed to ensure that there was no arbitrariness in decisions.

After two days of questioning I left the SHU at Millhaven without having had any clear answers from the staff to the vital question of what I would have to do if I were a prisoner recently admitted to a special handling unit who wanted to get out in the shortest possible time. It appears to me that the prisoners are correct in their assessment that the phase program at Millhaven is the latest example of the correctional emperor without his clothes. In my judgment the phase program at Millhaven is a sham and bears no resemblance to the theory of phases set out in the Vantour-McReynolds report.[104]

Those in charge of shaping SHU policy in Ottawa might be expected to object to this judgment on the basis that I have not sufficiently taken into account the changes introduced since the time of my first visit to the SHU in August 1980. Although I have already referred to many of these changes, it is necessary to meet this objection. The 1982 divisional instruction now specifies what a prisoner must do to progress through the phases. It states that 'the criteria for inmates' advancement between phases shall be: (a) a demonstrated willingness by an inmate to abide by prescribed rules and regulations; and (b) the practice of responsible behaviour.'[105]

The instruction further provides that the case-management team submit to the national committee, within six months of a prisoner's admission to an SHU, an 'individual program plan' which is to include '(a) an outline of what the inmate is required to do to be considered for progression through each phase; and (b) when possible a tentative date for the individual's advancement to phase four.'[106]

The concept of the 'individual program plan' is taken directly from the Vantour-McReynolds model of the SHU. It is intended to be a practical and specific reflection of the general principle (stated elsewhere in the directional instruction) that 'activities for inmates shall be designed so that each inmate shall have the opportunity and responsibility to progress through each phase at *a rate determined by his own demonstrated ability* [emphasis added].'[107]

Because there are still no real programs in Millhaven, because the world of the SHU is still circumscribed by a television set, a common room, and an exercise yard, the prisoner, even though he is now equipped with an individual program plan, is still no more able than he ever was to demonstrate 'responsible behaviour' beyond not breaking the rules. The prisoners are openly contemptuous of the individual program plans. This is not just because there are no programs in the SHU. Coupled with the introduction in December 1980 of the individual program plan was the provision that henceforth the progression through the first three phases of the SHU program would 'normally' take a minimum of two years, with a further one-year period in phase four at a maximum-security institution.[108] For the prisoners this change overshadows all the others. According to the figures compiled by the National Review Committee, the average length of stay in a special handling unit prior to 1980 was only one year.[109] The assertion by senior officials involved with the formulation of SHU policy that the change was intended in part to benefit the prisoners by removing the indeterminate quality of confinement in SHU has a hollow ring to it, given both the twofold increase in the normal stay in the SHU and the statement in the new commissioner's directive that 'the mere progression through phases one, two and three does not in itself justify a conditional transfer to a maximum security institution.'[110] The effect of this change is not just to double the amount of time a man can expect to stay in SHU. It has also totally undermined the reality of individual program plans. If, as the prisoners are now told, the 'normal' SHU program is two years in the SHU with a month in phase one, twelve to fifteen months in phase two, and the balance in phase three, then of what avail is an individual program plan purportedly designed to enable a prisoner 'to progress through each phase at a rate determined by his own demonstrated ability'?[111] It is my judgment that the changes introduced since 1980 have done nothing to meet the criticisms I have levelled at the SHU in Millhaven. In reality the changes have intensified both the punishment and the hypocrisy of the system.

The charge of hyprocrisy which SHU prisoners make when referring to the phase program relates, as I have tried to show, to the distance between rhetoric and reality. Before one of my visits to SHU and after another, I had interviews in Ottawa with the senior officials directly responsible for the planning and implementation of SHU policy. Sitting in their offices among flow charts and reports, listening to their descriptions of SHU, I found it difficult to believe that they were talking about the same places that I had seen. Yet these officials are no strangers to the SHUs. They visit them at least every six months as part of the National Committee Review process. They believe that the SHU program is qualitatively different from the old-style segregation units. It is my judgment that the words of Charles Dickens, written with reference to those who introduced the original regime of solitary confinement in Cherry Hill, are equally applicable to those who devised the SHUs: 'I am persuaded that those who devise the system and ... also carry it into effect do not know what it is that they are doing.'[112]

Perhaps the best example of the underlying reality of the SHU at Millhaven is to be found in an incident that occurred shortly before my visit in August 1980. A staff-member placed a sign reading 'Psychologist' in the window of the control bubble, inside which an officer armed with a shotgun is present at all times. In the words of the prisoners, it was put there 'to ridicule the inmates of G-2 Tier. This form of psychological taunt is but one subtle way life is made difficult and which inmates feel the necessity to reciprocate in kind.'[113] The administration admitted that the sign had in fact been put up by a staff member. In the special handling unit at Millhaven, behavioural change is induced not by opportunities for intellectual and sensory stimulation, not by offering creative opportunities for prisoners to deal with their anger and their violence, but ultimately by forcing them to look down the barrel of a shotgun. In this it is no different from the regime at the British Columbia Penitentiary.

The prisoners in Millhaven, however, face great difficulty in explaining their situation to the outside world. For one thing, they are confronted by the appearance of progress in the phase program and the fact that they are not (except in phase one) locked up for twenty-three hours a day. Their imprisonment therefore cannot be classified in the same way as the traditional form of solitary confinement practised in the special correctional unit at the British Columbia Penitentiary. The official bureaucracy maintains the myth of the phase program and reacts extremely negatively to any prisoner who would belie its existence. The principle of fairness in reviews is reinforced – on paper – in a procedure that assuages the protests of most civil libertarians who previously challenged the procedures in the old-style segregation units. Yet the prisoners in the special handling unit at Millhaven know that despite these paper changes the underlying reality of long-term segregation has not changed. The real agenda of the special handling unit is to ensure that the prisoners become and remain submissive. It will be recalled that the expert evidence of Dr Fox and Dr Korn in the *McCann* case explicitly showed that this was what lay behind the regime in the British Columbia Penitentiary and the other segregation units with which they had had experience. The early part of this book has traced the origins of the ideology of submission back to the first days of the penitentiary. As two Italian scholars have recently stated,

The first stage of the penitentiary ... has a characteristic tendency progressively to reduce the criminal personality (rich in his deviant individuality) to a homogeneous dimension; to being a mere subject ... Uprooted from his universe, the inmate in solitary confinement gradually becomes aware of his weakness, of his fragility, of his absolute dependence upon the administration, that is, on the 'other'; thus he becomes aware of himself as a subject-of-need. This is what can be described as the first stage of reformation: transformation of the 'real subject' (criminal) into an 'ideal subject' (prisoner).[114]

What has changed in the two hundred years since the birth of the penitentiary is the rhetoric of subjection. Melossi and Pavarini have given us this description of the nineteenth-century rhetoric:

Religion (or rather, religious instruction) becomes the favoured instrument in the rhetoric of subjection ... to show tangible signs of repentance (that is, to have made the long journey to spiritual salvation) is tantamount to giving sure proof of reformation (of progress in the re-educative process). In this light, religious practice is essentially administrative practice: the chaplain is a diligent bookkeeper who must render his account to the administration. The following notes in the diary of a certain Lacombe, the Chaplain at Cherry Hill, illustrate this.

'Number 876. John Nugent, barber, understands pretty well what is required in order to obtain salvation, but seems not to feel; June 9, 1839 – professed conversion; have found it insincere as I supposed; pretends he only meant to try me. Incurable ...

Number 920. George Thomas. Does not read the Scriptures; has no wish to repent. Says he is a free man, obviously deranged. Tell[s] me "go talk to the convicts about such damned stuff" (a dangerous fellow).'[115]

In 1983, the rhetoric of subjection is no longer religious. The new administrative priests are the classification officers, the psychologists and the correctional bureaucrats who make up the review committees. What they seek is a change not in spiritual values but in 'attitude.'

The prisoners in the special handling units have no doubt that their imprisonment is the continuation of the regimes that have preceded it in history. Perhaps the most articulate description by a prisoner of the special handling units and their real objectives is contained in a letter written by Edgar Roussel in 1980. The letter was addressed to the Honourable Mark MacGuigan in his former capacity as chairman of the Parliamentary Subcommittee on the Penitentiary System. At the time of writing, Mr Roussel had spent over two years in the special handling unit in the Correctional Development Centre in Quebec. Mr Roussel describes eloquently the rhetoric of reformation in the SHU. It is to bring about the desired metamorphosis from cocoon to butterfly ... by pretending that we, who have been disconnected from life, are reborn.[116]

The reality, however, has more to do with death than life.

The system aims to reduce the criminal to nothing, restrain the slightest initiative, and in one word, assassinate his personality to make him conform to the microcosm in which he is forced to develop. When the prisoner has become sufficiently conniving, hypocritical and lying that he can pretend to acknowledge the assassination to his executioners, then he is eligible for a transfer.[117]

What does prolonged confinement in the special handling unit do to a man? The correctional authorities answer this question positively by pointing to the fact that few people who have been through the special handling units have been returned for further offences involving violence within an institutional setting, a statement that echoes the evaluation of the Prison of Isolation made in the earlier part of this century. The prisoners are not so positive about their experience. Through the medium of the *McCann* case I have already described the effects of long-term solitary confinement in the British Columbia Penitentiary. Many of the prisoners I interviewed have now experienced both that regime and the SHU in Millhaven. They told me that the harassment that is characteristic of 'the penthouse' is also a feature of the special handling unit – the snapping open of the electronically controlled cell doors for no purpose other than to disturb the prisoner's sleep, the shining of flashlights in prisoners' eyes in the middle of the night, the taunting of prisoners who are on the edge of sanity or who have already slipped over to the other side. They described the fifty-watt night-light that requires them to sleep with their eyes away from the light and which they view as unjustified by any security measures; they see the best evidence of its gratuitousness in the fact that in the Quebec SHU (where, as I will describe, the physical conditions are more rigorous than in Millhaven) much lower-wattage night-lights are used. The prisoners insist that in some highly significant ways the special handling unit is worse than the penthouse at the British Columbia Penitentiary. This is how one of them described it:

What gets you about this place is the level of the violence. On the surface people seem to get on in a reasonable fashion but just below the surface is a terrible rage and anger about how they are being treated. This anger and rage can explode at any moment. You never know who will be the next one to blow. So you live in constant paranoia, the fear that the guy next to you will be next to go and that you may be the next to get it. Most of the violence is never reported for fear that it will get onto the guy's record. We mend our own wounds, even set our own broken bones. Sometimes we have to cut ourselves and infect the wound in order to get pennicilin from the doctor to give to the guys who are badly hurt. I have become a paramedic in this hole.[118]

The undercurrent of violence in the SHU poses a terrible dilemma for the prisoners. If they seek to avoid it by staying in their cells or forgoing exercise in the yard or time in the common room, they will be viewed negatively as demonstrating an unwillingness or an inability to associate with others. If they decide to come out of their cells when they are concerned about being attacked, they feel they are forced to carry a knife or other weapon in order to defend themselves. If a weapon is discovered, the authorities' view that they are indeed dangerous and require further confinement in the SHU is reinforced.

A further behavioural dilemma that confronts prisoners in an SHU is very well expressed by a man who spent over two years at Millhaven before being transferred to Kent.

I'm apparently involved as the range librarian, and I am performing other odd jobs on the Tier, and therefore I am involving myself in the only programs available to prisoners in this unit. It occurs to me that ... perhaps someone on the [Review] Board feels that I am nevertheless dangerous ... I am not 'demonstrating a lack of hostility.' The testimony I have heard from eminent psychiatrists and psychologists was to the effect that this kind of incarceration predictably increases hostility. I indicated that if this was the case, then it would be in effect impossible for me to become less hostile in an environment that creates more hostility. This, in turn, would make it impossible for me to secure my release from the Unit if one of the criteria is that I must demonstrate less hostility. As seems to be customary in the Penitentiary Service, I appear to have been placed in a catch-22 type of situation. Inger Hansen and all the psychiatrists who testified at my trial [*R.* v. *Bruce, Lucas, and Wilson*], also psychiatrists who testified before the Penitentiary Sub-Committee, indicated that placing people in solitary confinement over extended periods of time leads to punishment-induced aggression. And yet, the Penitentiary Service, by Directive 174, requires the inmate to secure his release to demonstrate lack of hostility. In other words, they put you in a situation which, according to psychiatrists, will increase your hostility predictably as a matter of psychology of human behaviour, and yet at the same time, they say that the only way we can get out is if we show less hostility.

How are we supposed to reduce hostility in an environment that increases hostility? They seem to look at violence and hostility in isolation without any concern about the causes. While they may be sincere in their objective to achieve release of inmates from the Unit, they do not appear to be looking at the root of the problem, namely the causes of the hostility or violence. They have no program designed to reduce hostility and violence in these units. I suppose they expect the individual to simply release his hostility and violence through some sort of magical process.[119]

From my interviews with prisoners who have served time in the special handling units, it seems clear to me that their hostility to authority has not been abated by their imprisonment, either through 'some sort of magical process' or in any other way. In the privacy of the interviews they expressed quietly the anger and contempt the units had generated or reinforced. The long-term implications of confinement in the special handling units were dramatically described by one of them: 'They expect you to go "tick, tick, tick" and come out of SHU and just keep on ticking. But when you come out you are so angry ... what they've done is light a time bomb.'[120]

So far I have focused on the conditions in the SHU at Millhaven. There is a second unit located in the Correctional Development Centre (CDC) in Laval, Quebec. Like Millhaven, the CDC is a modern facility; it was opened in 1968. The institution was designed to be a super-maximum-security prison to hold 'incorrigibles' and was originally called the special correction unit. In fact, it was only briefly used as such and, in the words of the Parliamentary Subcommittee on the Penitentiary System, became 'the unwanted foster child of the system.'[121] Its original purpose was revived in 1978 when block 5 was designated the special handling unit for the Quebec region.

Block 5 consists of two ranges of cells with twenty cells in each range. There are two common rooms, an interview room, and a central control area for the custody officers. There is also an exercise yard at the end of one of the cell blocks. The cells are the same size as those in the rest of the institution and are considerably smaller than those in the penthouse of the British Columbia Penitentiary. Each cell is equipped with a sink-toilet combination, a bed which is attached to the floor, a shelf for books and clothes, a radio, and a television set. There is a fluorescent light in the ceiling and a very dim night-light. The cells in the CDC have no windows to the outside to admit natural light. The door contains a window approximately eight inches by eight inches looking into the corridor. Heating and ventilation are provided through a duct-and-vent system. One feature of block 5 differentiates it from all other segregation units in Canada: prisoners in the cells are kept under surveillance by officers patrolling on top of the cells. A catwalk runs the length of the cell block, and a window in the ceiling of each cell permits the armed officers to see into the cell below as they patrol. Prisoners look up through the ceiling window at a gun, and are reminded constantly of the pervasive surveillance by the noise of the guard's boots on the roof as he walks back and forth above the range.

Although a vinyl covering has been laid on part of the roof to muffle some of the noise, it is still an intrusive presence inside the cell.

The following paragraph, taken from a letter written by a prisoner in 1980, provides us with images of life in the CDC that recall Ignatieff's description of the solitary-confinement regime of Pentonville 140 years earlier:

> It is going on midnight and I'm wide awake. The nights are like long black caverns through which you slowly grope toward the light of dawn. I have no window, but a skylight in the ceiling. I can see the roof through the skylight which is set with huge white glass bubbles that let the light filter in during the daytime. I sleep a lot but not truly, always awake sensible to the slow ticking away of the night and the myriad sounds of the prison. Night is the kingdom of the ears, which develop enormously, seizing sounds and passing them on greatly amplified to the brain. There are no mice here like in the old Pen [St Vincent de Paul]. I miss the patter of their little feet; instead, the p-tang of the pressure button in the sinks, the shuffling of the guards feet on my ceiling, or the banging of electric doors, all are borne upon me, a long familiar accompaniment to my night's rest.[122]

Until 1981, when prisoners were first received into the special handling unit at the CDC, they were not placed in block 5. Rather, they were put into the segregation unit of the main institution, which is adjacent to block 5, for phase one of the program. Everyone, including the officials, referred to it as 'the hole.' The cells are similar in size to those in block 5, but the overhead ceiling window is smaller and the steel door is solid except for a judas spy-hole. A prisoner usually spent a month in this hole before moving to block 5.

In 1981 a second wing of the CDC, block 7, was designated part of the special handling unit. Under the current regime prisoners are placed on admission in block 7 for phase one for one month. They are then transferred to block 5 for phase two and returned to block 7 for phase three. Block 7 is also used for SHU prisoners requiring protective custody and for punitive dissocation.

How real is the phase program in the CDC? At the time of my first visit in August 1980, despite the fact that the SHU had been opened for three years, the program existed only on paper. Phase one was simply 'the hole'; twenty-three-hour solitary confinement. The regime in block 5 for phase-two and phase-three prisoners provided for two hours' exercise in the yard each day in the morning or afternoon, and permitted all prisoners in both phases to go into one of the two common rooms from 6:30 P.M. to 10:30 P.M. each night. All prisoners were permitted showers every day. Control of prisoners' movements was even more strict than at Millhaven in all phases. Each time a prisoner left his cell he was escorted by three officers, and in phase two and phase three prisoners were required to enter the common room one at a time through an antechamber. Behaviour in the common room, as in the yard, was observed at all times by armed officers. In all phases prisoner interviews, including those with staff, took place in the interview room, where a thick wire grill separated the prisoner from the interviewer.

In my meetings with the staff and the warden of the CDC there was no pretense that the phase system had been implemented in the unit. Mr Pierre Goulem, the warden, told me frankly that given the limited facilities, which consisted of nothing more than forty cells, two common rooms, and a yard, there was no sense in pretending that there were distinctions in the quality of imprisonment. Mr Goulem had refused to allow block 5 to have representatives on the institution's inmate committee because, in his view, doing so would serve no purpose. The limited facilities meant that there was nothing to negotiate on conditions of confinement. I was informed that national headquarters, however, had been putting pressure on the administration to divide the program into phases and, in accordance with the Vantour-McReynolds model, to call the time spent in the hole phase one of the program.

At the CDC, as at Millhaven, I asked the staff assigned to block 5 about the criteria for release from the special handling unit. The psychologist, who sees people at their request, was able to identify one case in which the prisoner actively sought assistance and asked to take English classes in order to be able to transfer to an institution in the west. He had thereby demonstrated a positive desire and a positive attitude toward change. The psychologist conceded that this was an exceptional case, and that most prisoners did not seek his assistance in that way. In that particular case, the prisoner had been involved in an escape attempt with three others. While this prisoner had been released from the SHU, the others remained there. It was explained to me that while this was partly attributable to the prisoner's positive attitude (the others remained defiant), it was also attributable to the fact that he had not been one of the organizers of the escape. The psychologist explained that in recommending release he looked at the 'quality of the violence' that had brought the prisoner to the CDC in the first place. Thus, in the case of a hostage-taking, the distinction was to be drawn between the case where the incident was not planned or had been precipitated by some emotional crisis and where the staff had not been harmed, and the case where there had been premeditation and where physical harm had been done to one or more of the hostages. In the psychologist's view there was an important principle at stake in making 'the punishment fit the crime.' This viewpoint is highly significant because it points to the underlying reality of the SHUs. They are intended to serve as a means of additional punishment for what are perceived to be outrages to institutional order. Whatever increase in his sentence the prisoner may receive, for at least part of that time the sentence will be served in the SHU and heightened in intensity.

I asked the warden about the criteria applied in the thirty-day reviews. I was told that the criteria for release were very vague in his mind. He conceded that the absence of any real programs made it extremely difficult to judge a prisoner's attitude except in the negative sense of not causing trouble. Mr Goulem did not provide prisoners with a thirty-day notification slip because there was nothing to say, except that the prisoner had to serve more time before he could be released. My interviews with the staff at the CDC in August 1980 confirmed the judgment of the prisoners that 'time is basically the only program.'[123]

To prisoners who have served time both in the solitary-confinement unit of the British Columbia Penitentiary and in the CDC special handling unit, imprisonment in the CDC is experienced as more oppressive. This is caused by a combination of the small size of the cells, the lack of an outside window, the inadequacy of the ventilation, and, most of all, the pervasive 'aerial' surveillance. Clare Wilson, who was one of the defendants in the case of *R.* v. *Bruce, Lucas, and Wilson*,[124] explained to me why the CDC was worse than the British Columbia Penitentiary.

It's like being in a doll house with the top off, the constant peering in by the guards. In the bc Pen at least the gun was across the catwalk. Here it's right over your head. In the bc Penitentiary there was no pretense. There were three concrete walls and a steel door and that was it. You and the guards knew exactly what the score was. Here they give you a television in your cell and a common room and then treat you just the same but they pretend that it's a different trip ... The tv set ... that rationalizes the cage. It's really strange but I have this feeling that I could be nailed to my wall with spikes but as long as I have tv the public would focus on that latter point and ignore the spikes driven through my hands and feet.[125]

Another prisoner, who spent almost two years in the CDC, told me,

You can never understand the helplessness of being in that cell. You are robbed of every moment of your day. There is nothing you can hold sacred in there. These places are for breaking the individuals and turning them into robots. Psychologically, the programs are based on submission and unquestioning obedience.[126]

Edgar Roussel, in his letter to Mark MacGuigan, gave this account of the reality of the prisoners' world in the CDC:

Television acts as an aspirin to calm suffering, while at the same time it is a prism through which the outside world reaches us. But after months of this diet one is nauseated, repulsed and turns off the set, only to be introduced to a new phenomenon; noise! searches, guards' rounds; all is subordinate to noise, more pervasive to those in cells than elsewhere, because there is never a lull. When, late in the evening, one succeeds in falling asleep ... the night rounds begin. And every hour, endlessly, the sound of the guard's steps as he makes his rounds, resounds against the cell ceiling ... it would be difficult to discuss ventilation, as it does not exist; no windows, solid doors, and that heavy air clings like an opaque veil. In summer it's a crematorium oven that even total inactivity renders unbearable: we sweat from doing nothing ... I've slept on the floor of my cell for nearly two years, my head leaning on the bottom of the door so that I may benefit from the smallest breeze – incomparable wealth.

A common room is at our disposition every evening from 18:30 to 22:30, the time spent outside the cell ... A few social games, another television and surveillance, lots of surveillance, make this common room virtually a cell, just a little larger than the one in which we are confined most of the time.

For outside activities, we are put in a courtyard 75 feet by 75 feet ... In the summer, the breeze is cut off by the high walls, while the asphalt of the floor makes the overpowering heat rise. There is no greenery, there are no benches, only the asphalt, the cement, and the wire ...

Our greatest comfort and our only contact with the outside world is through visits ... There is to be no physical contact with our parents, wives and children. This is how the administration extolls the blossoming of the individual.[127]

Since my first visit to the CDC there has been an attempt to implement the phase program. As I have already mentioned, in 1981 a second wing of the CDC, block 7, became part of the SHU. In 1982 a separate exercise yard was built for block 7. On my second visit to the CDC in May 1982 I asked staff and prisoners how the regimes in phase two and phase three had changed since my first visit. I was told that phase-two prisoners in block 5 live under the same conditions and with the same absence of any real programs. Phase-three prisoners in block 7 are now permitted to have their midday and evening meals in one of the common rooms; phase-two prisoners eat in their cells. The men in phase three are given a choice in the evening between two common-room programs. According to the *Inmate Handbook*, common room 7A is for 'TV, inside games, reading, study, and hobbies.' Common room 7B is for 'educational and social-cultural purposes.'[128] In phase three, fifteen prisoners at a time are allowed to associate in the common rooms, compared to the limit of ten in phase two. As a result of the newly constructed exercise yard for block 7, phase-three prisoners (along with phase-one prisoners who are also housed in block 7) have a greater expanse of concrete to run and walk around than those in phase two.

While there is now the appearance of greater privileges for phase-three prisoners, my most recent interviews and correspondence with prisoners in the CDC deny the reality of any improvement in the nature of their confinement. Eating in the same room with the same thirteen 'particularly dangerous' men day in and day out, always under the surveillance of an armed guard, is not seen by prisoners as any real release from the regime of total control over their lives. The prisoners ridicule the statement in the handbook that in phase three there are common-room opportunities for 'social-cultural' programs. The only difference they see between the common-room programs in phase two and those in phase three is that in the phase two common rooms the table and chairs are of a single-unit construction and are bolted to the floor, whereas in phase three, presumably because the prisoners have been sufficiently resocialized, the tables and chairs are free-standing!

The hyperbole involved in describing what goes on in the phase three common room as 'social-cultural programs' characterizes the description of the new improved phase one. Prisoners in phase one are now confined in one of the ranges of block 7. The *Inmate Handbook* described this phase as 'one of decompression, of quiet.' The regime remains the same – solitary confinement for twenty-three hours a day. While the language of the handbook accurately reflects the original theory of solitary confinement as expressed by John Howard, its relationship to the reality of a prisoner's first month in the CDC is as artificial as the opaque light that enters the cells in block 7.

Like the prisoners in Millhaven, the prisoners in the CDC see the recent manipulation of the phase program as insignificant compared to the changes introduced in 1980 through the new commissioner's directive which established the normal duration of containment in the SHU at two years. To the prisoners in the CDC this is the clearest possible evidence that time is indeed the only program in the special handling unit. They are not alone in this judgment; their view is now shared by the prison psychologist. In my interview with him in August 1980 he had expressed the opinion that he was able to help the well-motivated prisoner to achieve his early release from SHU. In May 1982 he expressed extreme cynicism about being able to help anyone in SHU. As he saw it, the establishment of a minimum period of two years in SHU undermined any prospect of motivating prisoners to do something positive in order to get out. He was of the view that because of the minimum term, individual program plans were psychological nonsense. Most important, he expressed the view that the six-month national-committee review process was now a review in name only. 'Talking to the review committee now is like talking to robots. They don't listen. They go through the motions of listening to the individual case but they end up deciding when to release a prisoner according to the time periods in the directive.'[129]

On my second visit to the CDC in May 1982, I also interviewed Edgar Roussel. Mr Roussel had spent a total of four years in the special handling unit, relieved only by a few weeks in Laval Penitentiary. He had also experienced the old-style segregation unit of Quebec's nineteenth-century prison, St Vincent de Paul. As the previously quoted extracts from his letters indicate, he is intelligent and articulate. I showed Edgar Roussel a draft of what I had written about the SHUs and their relationship to the old segregation units such as the penthouse of the British Columbia Penitentiary. I asked him how he would summarize the nature of doing time in a special handling unit for those who would never experience it. This is what he told me.

> A man to be a man must be able to exercise initiative. In here they take that away from you. The worst thing about the shu is that you are totally dependent on the guards. You need them for everything. They even control the temperature of your shower. A man must have ideals. In here there is no respect for your ideals. You are nothing to them except a dangerous animal. A man needs to have a sense of territory even if it is only very small. In here there is no respect for that. Even inside your cell, because of the catwalk above you, the guards are stepping on your territory. Outside your cell, particularly in the common room where you are with ten men chosen as your companions by the guards, you are always stepping on someone's territory. A man must have a clear sense of who he is. In here in order to get out you have to borrow a personality that is not your own. This place breeds deceit at the same time as it breeds violence. I could go along with a segregation unit if it served some purpose. This place doesn't. It's like living on another planet.[130]

I spent two hours with Edgar Roussel in the interview room of block 5. We were separated by a wall on top of which was a thick lattice-wire grill. Looking through that grill it was impossible to see both of Edgar Roussel's eyes at once. After about thirty minutes his face no longer appeared as a whole face but rather as disconnected fragments. Before my eyes, Edgar Roussel appeared to disintegrate. The statement in his letter to the Honourable Mark McGuigan that the aim of the SHU is to 'assassinate' the prisoner's personality never seemed more real. As I left the CDC at the end of the interview, I was shown the small cemetery located just outside the perimeter fence. It is the burial ground for men who die in the penitentiary and whose bodies are not claimed by relatives. Inscribed on the headstones in this small windswept plot of earth are not the names of the men, but their penitentiary numbers. Reducing a man to nothing but a number and burying him is a far more accurate reflection of the psychological reality of the special handling unit than is the rhetoric of Dr Vantour's phase program.

Segregation at Kent Maximum Security – The 'Cadillac' of Canadian Penitentiaries

The British Columbia Penitentiary was closed in 1980. Its replacement, Kent Institution, had started to receive prisoners in 1979. Kent is the most modern of Canada's maximum-security prisons. The commemorative issue of the Canadian Correctional Service's official magazine, *Let's Talk*, published on the occasion of the closing of the British Columbia Penitentiary, described Kent.

> Kent Institution epitomizes a new era in correctional philosophy. An atmosphere of punishment and rigid security have been replaced by one of education, work, and rehabilitation opportunities. Cramped cells, placed tier on tier, the overcrowding, the noise, the institutional green paint of the bc Penitentiary, have been replaced by Kent's bright modern colours and living units, where inmates live in groups small enough for them to get to know each other and their living unit officers. They no longer eat alone in their cells as at the bc Pen, but in a cheerful cafeteria near a pleasant lounge. 'It's like comparing the Black Hole of Calcutta with Buckingham Palace,' former Solicitor-General Warren Allmand said two years ago, referring to the opening of Mission Institution. You could say the same today, comparing bc Penitentiary with Kent Institution.[131]

The solicitor-general, the Honourable Robert Kaplan, in his address on the occasion of the closing of the British Columbia Penitentiary, boldly predicted a new future, one that should not ignore the experience of the past.

> We can all look forward with pride and hope to a new era of corrections with greater opportunities for both inmates and staff to work together in harmony ... We move toward an uncharted future with unknown challenges, strengthened by the rich heritage of example and experience of all those who have lived and worked here. It is worthwhile remembering that 'those who cannot remember the past are condemned to repeat it.'[132]

It has been an underlying thesis of this work that an understanding of the past – in particular, of the origins of penitentiary discipline – is vital to an assessment of present carceral practices. It is therefore appropriate that I should conclude this analysis of present practices with a discussion of Kent Institution which, on another occasion, the former solicitor-general called the 'Cadillac' of Canadian penitentiaries. Behind the facade of its 'bright modern colours,' what has changed in the theory and practice of carceral power for those who face administrative segregation?

It will be recalled that the first Vantour Report recommended that segregation units be established in each institution for prisoners requiring short-term segregation. The original design of Kent Institution provided for only four cells for such segregation. However, soon after its opening, one of the eight 'living units' was designated a segregation area, and H unit has since become synonymous with the 'hole' at Kent. H unit consists of twenty-four cells which are the same size as all others in the institution, being ten feet long, eight feet high, and six feet wide; in each cell a solid door contains a small window that looks out on the corridor and a window on the outside wall that lets in natural light. The cells, which originally had no furnishings in them, have each been equipped with the same steel bedframe, sink-toilet combination, and table-chair combination introduced into the penthouse at the British Columbia Penitentiary after the *McCann* case. These furnishings were transferred to Kent when the British Columbia Penitentiary was closed. A prisoner who has spent a substantial amount of time in H unit has provided this description of the regime.

> In this place people are virtually buried alive in concrete tombs for periods of up to 23½ hours daily. The exercise area itself is only about 20 x 30 feet encircled by cement and bars with wire fencing covering the roof. At no time are more than three prisoners allowed to exercise together, and the exercise they do get only consists of a brisk walk back and forth.
>
> Prisoners in H Unit are not allowed open visits with their families. All they receive are brief telephone visits, where the visitor is on one side of a glass partition and the prisoner is on the other side. Even though the prisoners are skinfrisked both before and after the visits, they are still refused human contact with their loved ones. Unlike the main population, the prisoners in H Unit are not allowed to watch any television or see a movie. The availability of a newspaper is restricted. The only library that exists is a small box of books that is made up of spy stories and westerns, which are exchanged weekly by the guards. Treated differently than the main prison population, the prisoners of H Unit do not have easy access to a telephone for outside calls. Where prisoners in the population are allowed to phone both family and lawyers, prisoners in H Unit can only occasionally telephone their lawyers. That is, if their request forms are not lost or misplaced as the case has been. Prisoners placed in H Unit receive little or no funds

to purchase the items they require for basic survival. They are classified as unproductive and receive the lowest scale of pay within the prison. Thus writing paper, envelopes and communication with the outside world is a major concern. People in the H Unit are not allowed a pen. They are supplied a three-inch-long pencil for their written communication which must be returned to the guards after its use. Sanitary arrangements for prisoners in the H Unit are completely inadequate. They are only allowed two showers per week and are restricted to only one set of clothes and bedding that are exchanged weekly. Also, disinfectant is not allowed inside the cells, nor is there even a mirror inside the cell area. Most everything required for appearance and grooming is dependent upon a guard bringing it to you for brief periods of time once a day. The only time a prisoner gets to clear his cell is a ten-minute period, usually each morning. There is no educational programme or instruction for prisoners in the H Unit. Where the general population, as a whole, have access to this type of programme, the prisoners entombed in H Unit do not. Nor are there any hobbies allowed to H Unit prisoners to help with the idleness and boredom. Unlike other segregation areas in Canada that allow prison population committees access to the segregation area to hear fellow prisoner complaints, grievances and concerns, the administration in Kent will not allow this; all they will allow is written censored communication between the dissociation inmates and the prison inmate committee. Contrary to other penitentiaries that have segregation units, Kent Penitentiary houses both prisoners on disciplinary punishment and dissociation inmates not on punishment together in the same unit. The consequences of this [are] that the Kent staff treat all inmates in the H Unit as if they were being punished due to a breach of the rules and regulations ... In the B.C. Penitentiary, that type of confinement was ruled to be cruel and unusual punishment contrary to the Canadian Bill of Rights. It's shocking to see a new prison like Kent carry on the bad practices that made the B.C. Pen the cesspool it was. Does that mean that you can disguise the monster but never change its heart? This certainly appears to be the case here at Kent.

It's not completely fair to say that the Kent administration did not implement some changes within the dissociation area ...

1 Tables and beds have been installed in the cells, prisoners no longer have to sleep on the floor;
2 Prison population is now allowed to send canteen items to the H Unit via the Prison Committee;
3 Inmates in dissociation are now supplied small amounts of toothpaste in place of the powder that was once given out;
4 The Inmate Committee now has access to the keepers of H Unit ... However, they are still not able to see the prisoners;
5 If there is a rumour that a prisoner in H Unit has been beat up by staff, it has started to happen that the administration would produce the prisoner for inspection by the Inmate Committee. This is indeed a very positive step forward;

6 The use of special food trays was recently approved for H Unit and now prisoners no longer have to eat off soggy paper plates.[133]

Since this description was written there have been further changes. A small library has been placed in H unit; some prisoners are now employed as librarians, tier cleaners, and food servers, jobs which allow them extra time out of their cells; prisoners are permitted to shower every night; some prisoners have been permitted open visits; a plastic mirror has been supplied to prisoners for their own use, and they are now allowed to retain their own Bic pens in their cells. A few hobbies are now authorized for H unit, and several pieces of work-out equipment have been placed in the exercise yard. Following the practice in SHU, television sets have recently been provided to prisoners on a selective basis. Prisoners who keep their cells clean and abide by all rules in the unit are permitted a TV in their cells. Prisoners' discontent with the discretionary manner in which the TV privilege is dispensed is reflected in the fact that within two months of the introduction of the 'TV program,' the three prisoners who met the criteria for a TV voluntarily surrendered the sets.

A prisoner who had served time in segregation both in the British Columbia Penitentiary and in Kent made this comparison:

The segregation area itself I found to be worse than the infamous bc Pen Penthouse. Worse in the sense that a modern updated prison allows an archaic backward attitude to exist. They continue to strip people of their dignity and lock us away in a little cement box for periods of 23½ hours a day. The exercise area that does exist is only 30 x 20 completely enclosed with wire bars and cement ... Unlike other segregation areas in Canada that allow prisoners in segregation to have their cell effects with them that they would normally have within the main prison, the Kent segregation area does not. Even the Commissioner's Directives which govern the conditions in segregation units in Canada are ignored by the people who are put in charge of H unit here at Kent. One guard said to me when I asked for my personal effects as per cd209: 'We don't follow the Commissioner's Directives here.' In 1975, the Federal Court of Canada declared solitary confinement to be cruel and unusual punishment. Yet the administrators in charge of the H Unit at Kent continue to run and operate the solitary confinement unit that is similar to, if not worse than, the bc Pen penthouse.

I ask you, the outside free community, to picture yourselves locked up in your washroom for weeks and months on end. This is the dilemma that prisoners in segregation units are confronted with. It slowly drives you insane. It eats away at you until the hate inside you somehow gives you the strength to survive.[134]

Since Kent opened, I have interviewed many of the prisoners who have been in segregation in H unit, and I have been permitted by the administration to inspect the cells and other areas of the unit. I have also had the opportunity to discuss the conditions with officers in charge of the unit. It is highly significant that one of the officers in charge, who had extensive experience of the penthouse at the British Columbia Penitentiary, was of the opinion that H unit was worse than the penthouse, from both the prisoners' and the staff's point of view. As he explained, the unit is smaller than the penthouse and has a much smaller complement of staff. Most staff members have had no previous experience in dealing with the problems of segregated prisoners. He agreed that there were no programs in H unit and that, given the fact that the unit was often filled to capacity, it was extremely difficult even to ensure that each prisoner had his daily exercise. He conceded that the officer in charge of the unit was left with a great deal of discretion as to how strictly he enforced the regulations. For example, the segregation rules require that prisoners 'shall be skin-frisked whenever they move from their cell to the exercise area and back to their cells.'[135] The officer recognized the degrading effects of skin-frisks and did not insist on them when the prisoners went to exercise unless there was a particular reason to believe that a prisoner might be armed. Similarly, this officer had permitted one prisoner, who in the past had had extreme difficulty handling solitary confinement, to spend substantial periods of time out of his cell cleaning the tier. The officer readily recognized that when his tour of duty was over the next person in charge would probably adhere more closely to the letter of the regulations.

Prisoners being held in administrative segregation and prisoners sentenced to punitive segregation are all confined in H unit. There are few significant differences between the two regimes. A prisoner doing punitive time is deprived of his mattress during the day and has no radio, TV, or reading lamp, and has none of the limited canteen and reading privileges extended to prisoners in administrative segregation. However, I have interviewed a number of prisoners who, although in H unit on administrative segregation, were placed in punitive-segregation cells. These men were allowed to keep their mattresses, but had neither radio nor reading lamp and were not permitted canteen privileges or any books that they had in their personal effects for periods of up to one week. The French-Canadian prisoner described earlier, who had taken taped English-language correspondence courses in order to hasten this release from the SHU, was not allowed to have the tapes or the tape-recorder when he was placed in H unit, despite the fact that these had been permitted in the tighter security of the SHU. When the prisoner raised this issue at his review, the security officer in charge of H unit stated that these items were not permitted because H unit was a combination of punitive and administrative segregation, and discriminating between the two was not feasible given the limited staff available. This confusion of administrative and punitive cases was specifically condemned by the Vantour study group. Cases such as this reinforce the conviction of prisoners that notwithstanding the 'administrative' rhetoric, the purpose of their confinement under section 2.30(1)(a) is punitive.

The similarity of the solitary confinement regime at Kent to that at the British Columbia Penitentiary is compelling, despite the architectural changes. The twenty-three-hour lock-up, the absence of any programs or work, the skin-frisks, the sense of the separateness of the unit from the rest of the institution (reinforced by the inability of the members of the Inmate Committee to visit) and the extent to which the unit is seen by the custody officers as their preserve were all features of the British Columbia Penitentiary. For a prisoner in H unit who has previously experienced the penthouse, the presence of exactly the same 'furniture' reinforces the overwhelming conviction that he has been there before.

The Study Group on Dissociation recommended that the segregation review process be restructured to ensure that the decision to place a prisoner in segregation or continue his confinement there was not made arbitrarily. They proposed the establishment of a segregation review board whose function it would be to review the case of a segregated prisoner within five days of the director's decision to segregate and at least every two weeks thereafter. The board would also be charged with developing a plan to reintegrate the prisoner into the population as soon as possible, and would monitor that plan during subsequent reviews. The principal shortcomings of these recommendations are the study group's failure to recommend the adoption of more precise criteria for segregating prisoners, and the fact that the review process they proposed remained an internal administrative matter rather than coming under the jurisdiction of the independent chairperson whom the study group had recommended preside over disciplinary hearings.

Following the study group report, amendments were made to the commissioner's directives affecting segregation. These provided that every prisoner placed in segregation was to be notified in writing of the reason before the end of the next working day. However, despite the study group's recommendation, no change was made to the existing thirty-day review process.[136] Commissioner's directive 174 set out the function of the review board: 'The Board shall be responsible for determining if there is just cause for continued segregation, and may recommend that the inmate be returned to association with other inmates, recommend that segregation be continued in the present facility, or refer the case to the Regional Transfer Authority with a written recommendation for transfer to the SHU.'[137]

Commissioner's directive 274, which came into effect on 1 December 1980, further provided that the case of each prisoner in administrative segregation for sixty days was to be reviewed by a regional review committee, and, where segregation exceeded ninety days, by a national review committee. Most recently, commissioner's directive 277, which came into effect on 1 November 1982, has sought to elaborate further the administrative-segregation process 'in accordance with principles of fair treatment.'[138] Written reasons for segregation must be given within twenty-four hours, and confirmed by the warden on the working day following segregation; a hearing before a segregation review board (chaired by the assistant warden / socialization, with two other staff members) must take place within three days of a prisoner's placement in segregation; there must be a weekly review by the board for the first two months of segregation and a monthly review thereafter. In addition, there must be monthly reviews by regional headquarters for prisoners segregated more than sixty days and by national headquarters for prisoners segregated more than ninety days. The prisoner is given the right to be heard by the review board once every month; and after spending thirty days in segregation he is, subject to his co-operation, to be given a psychological assessment.[139] Although these new internal rules governing segregation provide a hierarchy of review processes, they leave the segregation decision as unlimited in terms of substantive criteria and devoid of independent scrutiny as it was when described in the *McCann* case.

The continuing arbitrariness of the segregation process and the role of the courts in requiring, through the vehicle of procedural fairness, that certain restrictions be placed on the penitentiary's ultimate carceral power are well illustrated in the case of *Oswald and Cardinal* v. *Director of Kent Institution.*[140] This case is particularly relevant because it marked the first occasion since *Martineau (No. 2)* on which a court has given substance to the duty to act fairly in relation to a prison disciplinary matter and because it concerned the segregation process at Kent Institution. In the case, two prisoners at Matsqui Institution were alleged to have taken a guard hostage at knifepoint on 29 July 1980 and to have confined him for five hours. They were charged under the Criminal Code with forcible confinement and transferred the same day to Kent Institution where, on the oral instructions of the director, they were placed in segregation in H unit. The following day the director orally reaffirmed his instructions to segregate the prisoners. In his affidavit the director deposed that the reason for segregation was that the prisoners, 'if returned to normal association at the said Kent Institution before the disposition of the charges resulting from the incident, represent the probable introduction of an unsettling element into the general population of the said institution.'[141]

Cross-examination of the director on his affidavit revealed that within a week of the oral instructions to segregate given on 29 July, he looked into the matter personally to satisfy himself that there was a need to continue the segregation. McEachern CJ summarized the cross-examination: 'It is fair to say that the main basis for placing and keeping these petitioners in segregation is because of allegations yet to be decided in court that they were involved in an incident at Matsqui Institution. [The director] also agreed that it was his intention that these petitioners would remain in segregation until the charges against them were decided one way or another.'[142] The director conceded that he had never spoken to the crown prosecutor or the police about the charges and, apart from speaking to the director at Matsqui, did not conduct a detailed inquiry into the circumstances surrounding the incident. Although he had talked to the two prisoners, he had not visited them in the segregation unit nor had he examined their institutional files.

The two prisoners had first been segregated on 29 July 1980. Their case was reviewed by the Kent Segregation Review Board using the following criteria: 'the suitability of the inmate to be restored to normal association, impact on the inmate population, and a general standard of maintaining good order and discipline in the institution.'[143] In the August and September reviews the board recommended that the prisoners remain in segregation. In the October review, however, it was recommended that they return to the general population. The director declined to accept this recommendation. Referring to both prisoners, he explained his decision by saying, 'This inmate was involved in hostage-taking at Matsqui for which he is now awaiting trial.'[144] The board continued to recommend that the two prisoners be returned to the general population; but in his evidence at trial the director stated that it was his present intention to leave them in segregation at least until the disposition of the charges against them. The director was asked by counsel for the petitioners, 'What do Mr Cardinal and Mr Oswald have to do to satisfy you that they can be returned to normal association?'[145] The director answered:

> I am afraid that at the moment there is nothing that either one of them can really do but to continue their good behaviour and to demonstrate that they should be released. I accept the statements in respect of their continued good behaviour in segregation. This certainly is an important consideration so far as I am concerned, but – again, as far as I am concerned – I have to take into account the seriousness of the incident in which they are alleged to have been involved, and that is the thing that has weighed most heavily in my decision-making process at the moment.[146]

Counsel for the prisoners sought to characterize this decision-making process:

q And so ultimately it comes down to ... your instinct in terms of what might happen if they are released to population.
a I'm not sure that I really like the word 'instinct,' I think it is more my measurement of whether the situation is appropriate in relation to the dynamics of the institution.[147]

Counsel for the prisoners explored with the director the basis for this 'measurement':

q So there [are] no specific facts pertaining to Mr Cardinal and Mr Oswald upon which you say that their release might lead to or introduce an unsettling element into the population?
a No, but that is my judgment.
q But the judgment is not based on any specific factual matters?
a No, that's correct.[148]

Later in his cross-examination, the director agreed that his judgment might have been 'purely a gut reaction.'[149]

At the time of the prisoners' application for habeas corpus they had remained in H unit for some five months. As McEachern CJ pointed out in his reasons for judgment, the director's intention to keep the prisoners in segregation until the resolution of their criminal charges meant that continued segregation could be measured 'not just in months, but rather in years.'[150]

In their affidavits, Oswald and Cardinal alleged that their 'continued dissociation in solitary confinement [was] having an adverse effect upon [their] physical and mental well-being and [their] ability to adequately instruct counsel to prepare full answer and defence to the pending charges.'[151] Although the director disclaimed any interest in attempting to persuade the petitioners to plead guilty to those charges, he admitted that prisoners do not like segregation and will do anything they can to be released.[152] If the prisoners were to be acquitted of the charges, the director said, he would review the cases in light of that reality. If they were convicted he might request that they be transferred to a special handling unit.[153]

The evidence in this case shows a disturbing correspondence to the evidence already set out regarding the rationale for segregation of several of the plaintiffs in the *McCann* case. The phrase 'pending disposition of outstanding charges,' the counterfeit coin in the currency of a rational segregation decision-making process, has survived as a general justification for segregation in H unit just as it had in the penthouse at the British Columbia Penitentiary. At Kent, however, one new element influences decisions to segregate and was no doubt operative in the *Oswald and Cardinal* case. Under the commissioner's directives no prisoner may be transferred to a special handling unit unless that prisoner is already in administrative segregation in a maximum-security institution. If the director had adopted the recommendation of the review board to transfer the two prisoners into the general population, in the event of their conviction on the charges of forcible confinement of a prison officer, he would not have been able to seek their transfer to a special handling unit. This case clearly demonstrates the perversity of this requirement and the extent to which it is calculated to negate individual assessment of the need for segregation.

The prisoners in *Oswald and Cardinal* sought their release from segregation through writs of habeas corpus. This was an unprecedented use of the writ, which, according to the conventional wisdom, had been thought to be restricted to situations where the release of a prisoner was sought from custody; counsel for the crown argued that it was not available except to gain the complete liberty of the applicants. McEachern CJ rejected this argument:

> In the evolution of society, different forms of detention arise from time to time. Actually these forms of detention have always been with us, but they are only now being examined. Habeas corpus (with or without certiorari in aid), as the bulwark of our liberty, may be an appropriate, and possibly the only appropriate means by which the court, in proper circumstances, may scrutinize the different forms of detention to which our citizens may be subjected.
>
> The principle of a prison within a prison has been mentioned in *The Law of Habeas Corpus*, 1976, by R. Sharpe at p. 149 where that learned author said: 'The situation may be seen as a prison within a prison and the applicant is simply released from the inner prison while being kept within the confines of the outer one ...' Dickson J ... supports this principle in *Martineau* v. *Matsqui Institutional Board (No. 2)*.[154]

The prisoners' case was that the director's decision to continue their segregation was not made in accordance with the duty to act fairly and that their continued detention in segregation under the circumstances was unlawful. McEachern CJ, dealing with this central issue, directed himself to the caveat of Pigeon and Dickson J in *Martineau (No. 2)*: courts should only interfere with prison discipline in cases of serious injustice. Although the chief justice found that the initial decision by the director to segregate the petitioners was lawful, he had some harsh words to say for verbally ordered segregation.

> I cannot express my disapproval of verbally directed detentions (except in emergencies) in strong enough terms; even lettres de cachet required two signatures,

and I would hope that the potential mischief inherent in such a procedure, that is, detention on oral instructions, would ensure that it will not continue. Prolonged verbally directed segregation must be severely condemned. I do not say, however, that a decision and written reasons for segregation must in every case be contemporaneous, there may not always be time for that. But a written record of such a decision, with reasons, should never be long delayed.[155]

In fact, the commissioner's directives do provide for written reasons to be given to the prisoner within twenty-four hours of his segregation. However, such notification was not given to Oswald and Cardinal, and the non-compliance with the commissioner's directives seems not to have been exceptional at Kent in 1980.[156]

The chief justice considered next whether the initial lawful segregation had become unlawful, the legal possibility of which he affirmed; otherwise a prisoner 'might be segregated for a particular reason and thereafter remain in segregation for the full term of his imprisonment, however long that may be, without recourse to the courts or any other tribunal after the reason for segregation has disappeared.'[157] McEachern CJ found that the power given a director by the regulations to impose administrative segregation on a prisoner must be subject to some legal limits. As to what those limits were, he concluded:

Ideally, there should be a better review procedure – one with teeth in it – but Parliament has not seen fit to provide such a review. I am persuaded, therefore, to conclude ... that the proper limit to impose upon the apparent absolute power of the Director is a continuing obligation of fairness which, in my view, controls the exercise of this kind of public power.[158]

Applying the law to the circumstances of Oswald and Cardinal, his lordship held that, while the initial decision to segregate was not coloured with unfairness, the process by which the two men were kept in segregation slipped into unfairness at some stage. Citing 7 October 1980, the day the review board recommended release to normal association, as a useful commencement date for when that stage was reached, his lordship held that while the director had jurisdiction to disregard the recommendation of the review board,

To do so with fairness ... the petitioners ought to have been informed of the reasons of the Director for continuing segregation, and they should have been given a fair opportunity to answer the case against them. They should not have had to make out their case to a mind that was closed or almost closed against them. To continue their segregation in the face of the recommendation of the Review

Board in the particular circumstances of this case raises a reasonable apprehension that they should plead guilty which, by itself, is enough to cast a pervasive appearance of unfairness over these cases. In addition, although a decision based upon a policy (such as one for prisoners who are awaiting trial or for prisoners who have taken a hostage) may be perfectly lawful, fairness requires timely reconsideration of the particular circumstances of each prisoner and individual whose residual rights and privileges are adversely being affected.[159]

There were other matters which the chief justice felt were relevant to the issue of fairness.

Additional to this is the continuing physical effect of segregation upon the petitioners whose assertion of impaired ability to instruct counsel is not answered by the Director. This raises further questions of unfairness, particularly when the institutional psychologist has probably – but not necessarily – joined in the recommendation to release into the general population. That fact should have been ascertained with certainty. Lastly, in the face of five months of segregation, the Director had made no real investigation into these matters. He had chosen, understandably in the first instances, to rely upon what he was told by the Director of Matsqui Institution. But the Director may not even know the reasons why these petitioners say they took a hostage. I agree that no circumstances justify the taking of a hostage – especially at knifepoint – but there may be circumstances, unknown to the Director, that motivated these petitioners at the time of the incident which might make it unlikely that they would do it again, or, more importantly, which might affect an open mind in deciding whether the continued segregation of these petitioners is necessary or desirable. Their explanation for the incident should be given consideration.[160]

The chief justice stressed in his judgment that, notwithstanding his conclusion that the continued segregation of the petitioners was unlawful, the director could continue to segregate them on proper grounds if he was satisfied that their administrative segregation was necessary for the maintenance of good order and discipline at Kent Institution. In the words of the chief justice, 'such a determination, however, must be made fairly and not arbitrarily in the circumstances of these petitioners at this time.'[161] The chief justice accordingly issued an order that Oswald and Cardinal be released into the general population at Kent Institution.

Following the McEachern judgment in *Oswald and Cardinal*, Kent Institution issued new internal rules governing the procedures for the Segregation Review Board:

The Segregation Review Board is responsible to ensure that the act of segregating a prisoner for administrative causes will be carried out humanely and properly according to the Regulations and Directives of the Correctional Service of Canada; and particularly to ensure that no prisoner so segregated shall undergo undue hardship as a result of such segregation; and to ensure that no such segregated prisoner shall remain segregated longer than is necessary for the peace and good order of the institution or than is required to serve his own best interests.[162]

Permanent members of the board are the assistant warden / security (or his representative), the living-unit development officer for G and H units (protective-custody cases are kept in G unit), and the psychologist. The instruction provides for informal review of all prisoners held in administrative segregation once a week by the living-unit development officer attached to G and H units. That officer is required to report verbally and in writing to the chairman of the Segregation Review Board on a number of matters: whether the prisoner wishes to appear before the monthly review board, how long the prisoner has been segregated, the reason for his segregation, when his case was last reviewed by the board, his apparent state of health and his needs, his administrative status, and any other matter concerning the prisoner and bearing on the functions of the Segregation Review Board. The living-unit development officer is also required to report to the chairman within twenty-four hours the case of any newly segregated prisoner and to recommend a time and place for an emergency hearing within forty-eight hours whenever it appears that there may not be a substantial reason for such segregation.[163]

The internal rules further provide that the full Segregation Review Board is to meet for at least one formal hearing every four weeks to review the case of every segregated prisoner, to interview any segregated prisoner requesting to appear before it, and, at the discretion of the chairman, any other segregated prisoner. The board is directed 'in each case to reduce any anxiety in the prisoner's mind about reasons for his segregation, its likely duration, and any other relevant matter of consequence to the inmate, such as the date of his transfer, release from segregation, the Board's recommendations, etc.'[164] Furthermore, the board is directed to 'try to assess the needs and psychological state of the prisoner, and take them into consideration when formulating its recommendations.'[165] The board is also to consider the institutional psychologist's report on every prisoner segregated for more than thirty days.[166] Within three days after every board review, the chairperson is to report in writing to the warden on the board's recommendations and rationale for every case that has been reviewed. Where it appears desirable, the chairperson may first report verbally to the warden so as to apprise him of any urgent need for more immediate action concerning a segregated prisoner.[167]

It is already evident that in the world of corrections, drafting new policies on paper does not necessarily bring any change in carceral practices. The conditions under which prisoners are segregated in H unit seem to have changed little from those existing at the British Columbia Penitentiary after the *McCann* decision, despite the new building. Has the new temporary instruction, coming in the wake of *Oswald and Cardinal*, resulted in a fair segregation process?

Since the new instruction was issued I have sat in as an observer on two monthly meetings of the Segregation Review Board at Kent Institution. The board was chaired on the first occasion by the institutional psychologist and on the second occasion by the assistant warden / offender programs, who normally sits as the chairperson. Also in attendance were a representative of the assistant warden / security, the security officer in charge of H unit, the living-unit development officer assigned to the unit and a representative from regional headquarters. This last official's function was to report in accordance with the commissioner's directive to regional headquarters on all cases of prisoners segregated for more than sixty days. The meetings were conducted informally. They began in the absence of the prisoner, with the chairperson giving a resumé of the prisoner's segregation history together with a recital in broad terms of why the prisoner was segregated. The security officer in charge of H unit was asked if there had been any problems with the prisoner while he was in H unit. The prisoner was brought in and asked if he had any questions to raise with the review board. Several of the prisoners asked to be told in specific terms why they were in segregation. The chairperson usually responded to this question in a very general way, even though in most cases the segregation had resulted from specific incidents. In one case where the prisoner was believed to have planned an escape attempt involving the taking of hostages, he was told that he was in segregation 'because of an investigation being carried out in which you are accused of having something to do with the security of the institution.' In no case was there any presentation of any evidence to substantiate the need for segregation and, not surprisingly, the prisoner was never invited to dispute the evidentiary basis for his segregation (assuming that he was even aware of that basis). The prisoner was then asked to leave and discussion ensued among the board members concerning the recommendation to be made. It did not appear from my observations that what the prisoners had to say made any difference to the board's decisions. Indeed, it was clear that neither the prisoner's views nor anyone else's would have influenced some of the board members. For example, the representative of the assistant warden / security informed the chairperson that before coming to the review board he had been instructed by his superior to oppose the release of particular prisoners from segregation. Under these circumstances it is difficult to conceive of any real review of the case.

The failure of the board to give specific answers to prisoners' questions about why they had been segregated confounds the board's duty, as set out in the instruction, 'to reduce any anxiety in the prisoner's mind about reasons for his segregation.' Furthermore, it defeats the obligation to take into consideration 'the needs and psychological state of the prisoner,' since every segregated prisoner I have interviewed has always insisted that the ambiguity of the reasons for his segregation and the consequent uncertainty of its duration are two of the most disturbing psychological aspects of segregation. Most of all, it totally undermines any sense of fairness in the process. As might be expected, prisoners in H unit are openly contemptuous of the review board.

In several of the cases I observed, prisoners had been charged with criminal offences arising from incidents occurring in the prison, and the warden had requested that they be transferred to a special handling unit. The prisoners were awaiting decisions on their transfers from the National Review Committee, and the hearings consisted primarily of the prisoners asking how much longer this was going to take. It was assumed by the board that these prisoners would remain in segregation until the transfer decisions were made. There was no review of the individual circumstances of these cases because of the requirement in the commissioner's directives that only a prisoner already in segregation could be transferred to a special handling unit.

One case in particular made it abundantly clear that, notwithstanding *Oswald and Cardinal*, individual circumstances would not result in a recommendation to release prisoners who were considered candidates for a special handling unit. In case A, the prisoner had been charged with assault of a security officer at the Regional Psychiatric Centre. He had been transferred to Kent and immediately placed in segregation. Charges of wounding and possession of a dangerous weapon were laid against him. His segregation had been reviewed regularly pending the disposition of these charges. The man's experience in segregation had been stormy, and while in H unit he had been convicted of several disciplinary offences and sentenced to serve time in punitive segregation. He had first been segregated in September 1980 and was still there in March 1981 at the time of my observation of the review process. His trial at that point was only several weeks away. I was already aware of his case, having been consulted by his lawyers concerning certain legal aspects of his defence. Through them I was informed that he had spent a considerable time in segregation at other institutions and at Kent and had not been able to cope with the experience; his anxiety had led to several suicide attempts. As a result of one such incident, in which he had repeatedly cut his wrists while in segregation in H unit, he had been sent to the Regional Psychiatric Centre.[168]

He had been at the centre for several months and had made what he thought was a satisfactory adjustment when he was told that he was to be sent back to Kent. He was not told the reason, though the psychiatrist at his preliminary hearing on the wounding charge testified that it was because he was not participating enough in group therapy. When the guards came to take him back to Kent he had resisted, fearing that he would again be placed in H Unit. In the process of this resistance he was alleged to have stabbed a guard. The prisoner's lawyer had sought to make her client's inability to deal with solitary confinement known to the authorities at Kent. While the warden acknowledged the prisoner's problem, the review board continued to recommend that he be kept in H unit. At the hearing I attended, the officer in charge of H unit told the review board that several of the disciplinary charges that had been laid against this prisoner (which had led to punitive segregation) had been provoked by guards who knew that it was easy to get him to react to insulting comments. It was to counteract what the officer regarded as a regrettable attitude on the part of some of his subordinates that he had allowed the prisoner to work as a cleaner on the tier in order to minimize the time spent in solitary. However, despite the prisoner's known difficulties with segregation, despite the particular circumstances of the offence alleged against him, despite his lawyer's concern that prolonged confinement in segregation was affecting her client's fitness to give evidence at his forthcoming trial, he was kept in segregation until that trial. Significantly, the crown agreed to accept a guilty plea on the lesser offence of assault. The court imposed a sentence of only six months, which certainly suggests that it took into consideration the particular circumstances surrounding the offence, circumstances which the Segregation Review Board had failed or refused to consider. Only then, after seven months in H unit, was the prisoner released into the population.

In a second case I observed, case B, the prisoner was alleged to have knifed another prisoner during the riot of 7 June. This case raised other disturbing questions about the practice of detaining prisoners in segregation pending the investigation and hearing of criminal charges. The prisoner was told at his July review hearing that he was being detained while the RCMP completed an investigation of the incident. At his August review he was told that the investigation had been completed and that he was being detained pending a decision of crown counsel as to whether charges were to be laid against him. At his review in September, he was initially informed that he would be detained pending the completion of the RCMP investigation; when he protested that he had been told that this was already completed, the board corrected itself and again informed him that he would have to remain in segregation until crown counsel had made a decision. The prisoner wanted to know how long this might be and the status of the crown counsel's deliberations. No one on the review board had any knowledge of the matter. I was asked by the prisoner to contact crown counsel to try to find out what was happening. At this point the prisoner had been segregated for over three months. He insisted that he had never stabbed anyone during the riot and that there were dozens of prisoners who could testify to that effect on his behalf. I got in touch with crown counsel, who informed me that this prisoner's file was not in their office. I then contacted the RCMP and was told that they were typing up their report and would be submitting it to crown counsel in a few days! This inordinate delay is largely explained by the low priority given to matters affecting prisoners who are already in segregation. This presents a paradox. Segregation, instead of providing an incentive for speedy investigation in order to minimize the likelihood of prisoners being unjustifiably detained, becomes an excuse for delay which extends, rather than minimizes, what may be unjustified detention.

A third case I observed provides an opportunity to consider the extent to which the rationale of segregation pending resolution of charges is applied on a principled basis. In case C, Prisoner X was charged with attempted escape from Kent in January 1981. He and another prisoner had been apprehended as they came out of a cell window, the bars of which had been cut. There was no violence and no threat to any security officers. Both prisoners had been placed in H unit immediately upon their apprehension and were subsequently charged with attempted escape. The second prisoner was released from segregation on 4 February. Prisoner X was still in segregation one month later. He asked the review board why this was so. The board was unable, either in the presence of the prisoner or in deliberations afterward, to discern any distinguishing features between the cases of the two men in the degree of their involvement in the escape or in their behaviour while in H unit. The board recommended that Prisoner X be released from segregation, and this recommendation was acted upon by the warden. The fact remains, however, that a man was segregated without just cause for a month longer than his co-accused. The review board would be hard put to convince Prisoner X that its review mechanisms protect against arbitrary decision-making.

The regime in H unit at Kent has been of central concern to prisoners since the opening of the institution. Successive prisoner committees have tried to raise the issue with the prison administration. In February 1981, H unit was the subject of an extensive letter-writing campaign by prisoners aimed at bringing the situation to the attention of people on the outside. It was hoped that this strategy would open negotiations with the prison administration. I was one of the people who received copies of the letters.

The letters, parts of which I have already quoted, set out the prisoners' descriptions of the regime and their criticisms and proposals for change in H unit, and gave clear warning of the implications of ignoring the lawful effort of prisoners to improve what they regarded as oppressive and unlawful conditions.

Canada over the past few years has seen fit to build several new penitentiaries, but this country has yet to take any progressive steps which would leave the crude and destructive past practices behind. Kent, at one time christened by our Solicitor General as 'the cadillac of prisons' has turned out to be nothing more than a cosmetic correction, and its construction has done little to remedy any of the penitentiaries system's true afflictions ... The fact that the concept of segregation and solitary confinement has not taken a radical turn, is inexcusable, the tomb within a tomb, in essence, has remained as barbaric as ever.[169]

Many horror tales have been told about this Unit, most of them are loathing in nature and border on madness. It's true that the bulk of our information is undocumented in the traditional sense; however, we have listened carefully over the months to what has been said and we do believe that the information is factual. Our ears do not deceive us, nor do our brothers who have personally experienced these tragedies.

We find it extremely ironic that Canadians can condemn others in other countries for inflicting pain and damage to their peoples when these same practices exist within this country in the full view of the government.

We would ask that this Unit be thoroughly investigated immediately before any further damage is done to those who are presently encaged there. We would ask that the investigation be open and that the findings be made public. If this request is granted then we firmly believe that H Unit will become another object of horror dedicated to Canadian history.[170]

In every prison riot in recent years, and in the past as well, inmates have pleaded for the right not to be treated as animals. They have begged to be treated as men and women with reasonable attention to basic human needs. Because these needs have not been met, inmates have in desperation taken their case to the public. They have struck, rioted and burned, and taken hostages (always at great cost to themselves) – all to bring public attention to their situation.

This again is yet another plea – a plea for a complete inquiry into the unfair methods with which prison justice is dispensed; and a tormented cry for help in abolishing some of those practices which are not only cruel but irreversibly mind-destroying as well.[171]

Attached with this statement are some letters in regards to [H unit] written by those prisoners within this institution that are more articulate than others.

Hopefully, by approaching our dilemma in this way, you will take it upon yourself to help us continue meaningful negotiations with the Kent administration. It is important that we are able to talk and work out our problems in this way. For when the talking stops the trouble soon begins. And whether anyone realizes it or not people in here are talking less and less these days.[172]

By letting the public know our problems we hope we will have your support in our cause. The last thing we can do is have a peaceful demonstration in order to help those who can't help themselves in H Unit. The prison population has exhausted every possible peaceful means of communication with this administration to the point of frustration.[173]

If this place blows up [H unit] will be the main reason.[174]

On 7 June 1981, a few hours after two prisoners were 'scooped' and taken to H unit, there was a riot at Kent Institution. I have spoken about the events of that day to a number of prisoners, including the members of the Inmate Committee, who told me that two of the underlying causes of those events were the lawlessness they saw being practised daily in H unit and the intransigence of the administration. Committee meetings, letters to the outside, the intervention of lawyers, the *McCann* case, the judgment of the chief justice of the British Columbia Supreme Court in *Oswald and Cardinal* - all seemed to no avail. What happened on 7 June was, as the letters quoted above show, a predictable and indeed inevitable result of the lawlessness of carceral authority.[175]

6
A Model for Reform

The riot that took place at Kent in June 1981 can be viewed on one level as a resistance to lawlessness.[1] Rioting is not the prisoners' preferred means of protest because it inevitably brings reprisals against those involved. After the riot, the members of the Kent Inmate Committee and others who were seen by the authorities as ringleaders were all placed in H unit. One month later several of them were charged with disciplinary offences, convicted, and given some of the harshest sentences to be handed down in recent penitentiary history. One individual received ninety days' punitive segregation and forfeited 135 days of his remission. After serving over thirty days in the hole, he was transferred to the special handling unit at Millhaven and subsequently charged with criminal offences.

Lawyers, when confronted with lawlessness and abuse of power, are trained to respond with an armoury other than forcible resistance. We look to a panoply of legislation and regulations to circumscribe authority, and to the courts to supervise and hold officials within the boundaries of that authority. So far we have been woefully impotent in confronting abuses of carceral power. The comments of an observer of American correctional law - an area where judicial intervention has been far more extensive than in Canada - are even more relevant to the Canadian situation.

> Most of what has been accomplished has done little more than remove a handful of vines from the jungle in which offenders find themselves entangled. The basic structure of the prison has not changed at all. The basic structure of the criminal justice system has not changed at all. The level of societal concern for those who find themselves behind prison walls has not changed at all. I am not optimistic about the likelihood that much of what we see will be changed at all. But it could. Whether changes are made or ignored will depend in large part on the quality and scope of the attack that is mounted by those who work outside the walls to change what happens on the inside.

> There are many reasons to believe that the legal community could launch such an attack with a reasonable probability of success. If the members of that community fail to do what they are capable of doing, the rest of us – the preachers and the teachers and the trainers and the many species of therapists – will be glad to make them honorary members of the fraternity of failures we have so studiously cultivated for many, many years. They will have earned it.[2]

This is not a comforting prospect, but it is nevertheless a vital challenge. The question remains as to the nature of the changes lawyers can advocate. At the beginning of this book I suggested that the power to place a man in solitary confinement is the ultimate manifestation of the state's carceral power over the individual. The abuse of this power in Canada's maximum-security penitentiaries casts a shadow of illegitimacy over the nature of imprisonment. In advocating a model to control this power – a model which specifies criteria for its exercise, subjects it to standards of procedural fairness, and prescribes the minimum requirements for the regime under which segregated prisoners will serve their time – I hope to illustrate to prisoners, to prison administrators, and to lawyers that imprisonment can be subjected to the rule of law and that the rights of the kept can be protected without undermining the ambiguous and invidious task assigned to the keepers.

A preliminary point which relates to the implications of such a model of reform must be addressed. Some of the people who have read drafts of this book have argued that having documented the history and nature of the state's ultimate carceral power and having sought to demonstrate its illegitimacy, I should lend the weight of this book to the prison-abolition movement. Their argument is that while solitary confinement may be the worst case of the abuse of the keeper's authority and the worst case of the abuse of the human rights of the kept, those abuses characterize the very nature of imprisonment. They argue that it is imprisonment itself, rather than the particular practices upon which I have focused, that is the central evil. They argue further that to fail to draw the abolitionist conclusion and to present a model for reform is likely to confer legitimacy on the prisons, and, in Jessica Mitford's words, 'may strengthen the system in the long run by refurbishing the façade of prison and thus assuaging the public conscience.'[3] The suggestion that I stop my analysis at this point and conclude by condemning not just the practice of solitary confinement but also the prison as an institution has its attractions. It is attractive because in its 'absence of tiresome qualifications, cautious parentheses, and saving clauses [it] seems in itself like a foretaste of the mass liberation proposed.'[4] It is attractive because I agree that the prison, be it the nineteenth-century bastille of the British Columbia Penitentiary or the modern 'correctional institution' of Kent, 'denies autonomy, degrades dignity, impairs or destroys self-reliance, inculcates authoritarian values, minimizes the likelihood of beneficial interaction with one's peers, fractures family ties, destroys the family's economic stability, and prejudices the prisoner's future prospects for any improvement in his economic and social status.'[5] It is attractive because I would like to live in a society whose members had enough respect for each other and for the values of equality and social justice that we would not need the prison.

Yet I have resisted the attractions of the abolitionist stance because it offers little consolation or hope to those now experiencing the most extreme of the pains of imprisonment. I undertook to write this book, as I undertook my involvement in the *McCann* case, to put a stop to practices that no man should impose upon another. This book is grounded in the experiences of Canadian prisoners who have suffered these practices. I have sat with men who have set themselves on fire and slashed their throats, with men who have been driven mad, and with a man who, days later, hanged himself in his solitary-confinement cell. My endorsement of the abolitionist position, however impassioned, is not going to stop the practices that give rise to such experiences. My model for reform is designed to ensure that the practices do cease.

Jessica Mitford has argued that it is possible to distinguish between two types of reform proposals: those which 'will result in strengthening the prison bureaucracy, designed to perpetuate and reinforce the system, and those which to one degree or another challenge the whole premise of prison and move it in the direction of its eventual abolition.'[6] She has suggested that examples of the latter type of reform are proposals aimed at 'returning to prisoners those constitutional rights that will enable them to organize and fight injustice within the system.'[7] This is the thrust of my model of reform. I hope that its presentation will not be interpreted as diminishing the need for Canadian society to give the most serious reconsideration to the future of imprisonment.

THE CRITERIA FOR SEGREGATION

The evidence in *Oswald and Cardinal*, like that in the *McCann* case, demonstrates that administrative segregation can be imposed on prisoners by the warden of the penitentiary on the basis of his intuition or instinct without the need to point to specific factual allegations. Such a state of affairs is anathema to the rule of law. Instinctive decision-making may be acceptable at the blackjack table, but when the stakes involved are the pain of imprisonment in H unit such a system is not to be tolerated. The failure of the 1975 Vantour Study Group Report on Dissociation to bring about any change in an arbitrary process is not in the least surprising in light of the report's refusal to require greater specificity in the criteria for administrative segregation. Without such criteria a review process, however elaborate, will fail to render an unprincipled decision any more principled or fair. So long as the review is of a decision that can be made without reference to principled criteria and without any factual underpinning, the process will remain illegitimate in the minds of those on whom it is imposed.

In the past few years a number of groups in the correctional field have laboured over the task of producing sets of 'standards' which have the avowed purpose of making carceral practices both principled and fair.[8] The most influential of these in the United States and in Canada has been the *Manual of Standards for Adult Correctional Institutions*, prepared by the American Correctional Association's Commission on Accreditation for Corrections.[9] Its influence is attributable in no small measure to the fact that the commission is made up of professional corrections administrators; therefore the code is a 'homegrown' one rather than one imposed by outsiders.[10] The manual is at present the basis upon which Canadian penitentiaries seek accreditation. The manual recommends limited due process protection for segregation in the form of a hearing and a review process, and goes further than the Vantour Report in seeking to place some substantive limitations on the discretion of prison administrators. Under the rubric of 'Special Management Inmates,' standard 2-4214 and its accompanying commentary state:

> Written policy and procedure provide for the operation of segregation units for the supervision of inmates under administrative segregation, protective custody and disciplinary detention.
>
> *Discussion*: The Classification Committee or Warden/superintendent, in an emergency, may place in administrative segregation an inmate whose continued presence in the general population poses a serious threat to life, property, self, staff or other inmates, or to the security or orderly running of the institution. An inmate pending investigation for trial on a criminal act or pending transfer, can be placed in administrative segregation. This segregation may be for relatively extensive periods of time.[11]

Clearly these limitations are not excessively rigorous; in the case of segregation pending resolution of criminal charges they are non-existent.

Another set of standards, prepared by a group of law professors and lawyers active in correctional litigation, contains a much more restrictive code aimed at holding in check the tendency to abuse the administrative-segregation power. The *Model Rules and Regulations on Prisoners' Rights and Responsibilities*[12] would permit administrative segregation in only two circumstances: (1) pending a hearing before a disciplinary board where 'the inmate constitutes an immediate threat to institutional order or the safety of particular inmates' (segregation is limited to three days except where the inmate requests a three-day continuance or in an emergency situation);[13] (2) where 'the [warden] determines, on the basis of reliable evidence that [an inmate] is in immediate physical danger' (segregation is limited to a sixty-day period).[14] Since the second of these situations provides for protective custody, the model rules, in effect, permit administrative segregation only in the limited case of pre-trial detention. In my opinion this code is too narrow to do justice to legitimate institutional interests, just as the *Manual of Standards* is too broad to do justice to the legitimate interests of prisoners.

In an earlier study of the prison disciplinary process, I proposed a set of standards to cover the spectrum of situations in which I thought administrative segregation could be justified, and which sought to do justice to both sets of legitimate interests.[15] Those standards (and the accompanying administrative process) were subsequently revised and incorporated in the first Canadian Prisoners' Rights Code. The code was prepared under the direction of an assistant deputy minister of the solicitor-general's department but has never been adopted as a statement of departmental policy.[16]

In the course of writing this book these revised standards have gone through a further refinement and are set forth here in the form of a segregation code, not as a final draft, but as a responsible proposal which seeks to be fair to prison administrators and to prisoners. The full text of the code will be found in the appendix.

It is clear that prison authorities regard it as imperative that in certain circumstances they be able to segregate prisoners while they conduct investigations of incidents that pose serious threats to the security of the institution or to persons within it. In my view this is a legitimate institutional interest. To permit segregation, however, purely for investigative purposes without either substantive or temporal limitations invites abuse of this power. Therefore, I propose that the warden be authorized to segregate,

1(a) pending the investigation of allegations which, on reasonable and probable grounds, implicate the prisoner in

  (i) attempted escape;
  (ii) possession of dangerous contraband;
  (iii) actual or threatened violence to another person or incitement to violence

of other prisoners;

(iv) wilful destruction of property where there is a substantial likelihood that the destruction will be continued;

(v) refusal to obey the lawful order of an institutional officer where there is a substantial likelihood that the refusal will be continued and will lead to widespread disobedience by other prisoners.

(b) pending the investigation of an alleged disciplinary or criminal offence where there is a substantial likelihood that the prisoner will intimidate potential witnesses to the offence.

In order to prevent subsection 1(a) from becoming a general justification for segregation and to avoid the situation I observed at Kent (where prisoners were kept in segregation for over three months pending an investigation), I propose that no prisoner shall be kept in segregation under this subsection for more than two weeks unless evidence is presented to the hearing officer that all due diligence has been exercised by the authorities in pursuing their investigations and that further time is needed to complete those investigations. If it is demonstrated that there has been due diligence and that further time is needed, the code places an overall one-month limit on segregation pending investigation: given the relatively focused nature of investigations into offences committed in prisons and the accessibility of people to be interviewed, a month is a reasonable length of time for completion of the investigation and the laying of charges. The only exception to this time limit would be in the case where there is a riot or other incident that involves extensive interviewing of many witnesses. The code provides for this exception, and requires a clear demonstration that the nature and extent of the investigation justifies an extended period. The code further provides that if segregation beyond the two-week period is being sought and, a fortiori, investigation beyond the one-month period, it must be justified against the more stringent criteria of section 2. Section 2 is concerned with segregation after charges have been laid but prior to trial. The intent of this provision is to accommodate legitimate institutional interests in permitting segregation while an investigation is underway and to place a prisoner in a no less favourable position than he would have been in if the investigation had been speedily completed.

Where charges have been laid against a prisoner and are pending, either before an internal disciplinary board or in outside criminal court, segregation is authorized where

2(a) the offence, if proved, will lead to an increased security rating of the prisoner, requiring his transfer to another institution;

(b) the offence involves actual or threatened violence to another person or incitement to violence of other prisoners and there is a substantial likelihood that
  (i) the offence will be continued or repeated or
  (ii) there will be violent reprisals by other prisoners;
(c) the offence involves the wilful destruction of property where there is a substantial likelihood that the destruction will be continued;
(d) the offence involves the refusal to obey the lawful order of an institutional officer and there is a substantial likelihood that the refusal will be continued and will lead to widespread disobedience by other prisoners;
(e) the prisoner, at the time of being charged with an offence, reacts in a violent or uncontrolled manner.

A prisoner detained under subsection (e) shall be released from segregation as soon as he has ceased to act violently and has regained control.

We can see how these criteria could influence administrative action by looking at some of the cases studied in Kent Institution. In the case of the two prisoners who were charged with attempted escape, one prisoner was segregated for a month and the other for two months. I have already dealt with the lack of justification for the discrimination in the length of segregation, but a prior question arises as to the need for anything but a temporary segregation in the first place. The escape attempt was not accompanied by any violence, and the prisoners gave themselves up as soon as they were apprehended. There would be justification for an initial period of segregation under subsection 1(a) to determine whether other prisoners were involved in the escape attempt. Subject to one qualification, there would be no justification for segregation solely because of the nature of the offence, because Kent is a maximum-security institution and prisoners confined there are all viewed as potential escapees.[17] The exception would be the case where a prisoner had made repeated escape attempts from maximum security, particularly under circumstances that endangered his own life or the lives of others. One such case occurred at Kent where a seriously disturbed prisoner had tried to go 'over the fence' on a number of occasions, heedless of the security officers and of the danger in which he placed himself.

In case D, one prisoner was charged with the murder of another. The killing had taken place at Kent some ten months previously. The prisoner had been placed in H unit two weeks before formal charges were laid and had remained there pending the disposition of the murder charge. Again, increased risk of escape cannot be regarded as a factor, particularly in this case, where the prisoner was already serving a life sentence with a minimum of twenty-five years before parole eligibility. The investigation of a murder may, under certain circumstances, justify segregation if the prisoner's continued presence in the population would enable him to intimidate potential witnesses. However, the issue of intimidation of witnesses must be viewed in the context of prison life. By far the most potent factor inhibiting a prisoner from giving evidence against other prisoners is the spectre of being labelled a 'rat,' which will inevitably place the prisoner so labelled in acute physical jeopardy, not just from the man he 'fingers' but from other prisoners, particularly associates of the accused man. The 'rat' will almost certainly have to be placed in protective custody before or at the same time as the accused prisoner is segregated for investigative purposes. Therefore, where administrative segregation is invoked under subsection 1(b) and where the offence does not justify segregation under subsection 1(a) there must be evidence that there are witnesses in the population and that the accused prisoner, as opposed to other prisoners, poses a serious threat to their safety. In case D, however, the accused prisoner had remained in the population for almost ten months before charges were laid. Clearly his continued presence in the population had not been used to intimidate witnesses or, if it had, he was singularly unsuccessful. More likely still, the informants were already in protective custody or on the street and therefore out of the sphere of potential intimidation. The accused prisoner's segregation would not be justified on the basis of intimidation of witnesses, nor could it be justified (in this particular case) on the basis that his return to the general population would prompt violent reprisals by the dead man's associates. This fear of reprisals is a legitimate institutional interest and is one which is incorporated in the code. In the absence of any evidence that the accused prisoner was threatening any other person in the institution or that his presence in the population would prompt reprisals there would not be, under the suggested criteria, any justification for continued segregation.

Furthermore, the code requires that an important interest of the prisoner be considered in any segregation decision: the prisoner must be able to prepare for his defence of charges pending against him. When the accused in case D complained at his review board hearing of the prejudice to him in relation to interviewing potential witnesses, he was told his lawyer could conduct the interviews. Given that Kent is a two-hour drive from Vancouver and that the defence counsel was being paid on a legal aid tariff, it seems fanciful to expect defence counsel to interview all of the prisoners who might be able to give evidence on the accused's behalf, since the killing was alleged to have taken place in the washroom of the gymnasium at a time when there were dozens of prisoners in the vicinity. Thus, in case D, section 2 of the Segregation Code would compel a finding that the prisoner be permitted to remain in the population, in contrast to the existing practice of compelling his detention in segregation.

Case E permits us to assess the application of these criteria in relation to internal disciplinary charges. A prisoner was facing charges of robbery and attempted murder arising from incidents that took place while he was on the street. The charges were not regarded as warranting segregation once he was admitted to Kent Institution. The prisoner had always been an active and articulate proponent of prisoners' rights and was soon elected to the Inmate Committee. It was in his capacity as a committee member that he took part in discussions with the general population immediately before the riot of 7 June. After the riot he was placed in segregation along with other members of the committee and other individuals who were viewed by the institution as being ringleaders. He was initially charged with a disciplinary offence relating to the riot, but this was dismissed by the independent chairperson of the disciplinary board. In late July he was charged with other disciplinary offences relating to the riot, but as of the first week of September there had been no hearing of these charges.[18] Neither had the prisoner appeared before the Segregation Review Board in the July and August reviews of his case. He had, however, received written notification from the board: 'This is to advise you that your case has been reviewed by the Segregation Review Board ... and a decision has been made that you will remain in administrative segregation for the good order and discipline of the institution until your case is again reviewed.'

The prisoner's position was particularly invidious because he wished to be actively involved in the preparation of his defence against the outside charges, including researching the relevant case law. His restricted access to law books and case reports and the limited number of telephone calls he was permitted to make to his lawyers while he was in H unit were having a marked effect on him in his court appearances. But this prisoner was prejudiced not only in the preparation and presentation of his defence on the outside charges; he was further prejudiced in relation to the internal disciplinary charges pending against him. The majority of those accused with him of being involved in the riot of 7 June had been charged and convicted in disciplinary court in July and had been given sentences which included punitive segregation. By the beginning of September these sentences had been completed and the prisoners had been released into the population or transferred to other institutions. Yet this prisoner had served three months in administrative segregation and, quite apart from whatever sentence might be imposed if he was convicted at the disciplinary hearing on the internal charges, he had already served more time in segregation than any of his co-accused. The prejudice in this case was intensified because the prisoner, by his own account, was not present at certain locations where the incidents that gave rise to the charges against him were alleged to have taken place. In an interview with me he insisted that he was in a completely different part of the prison when the incidents occurred and that his presence there could be corroborated by other prisoners who were not involved in the riot. However, because he had not had a hearing before a disciplinary board and because the Segregation Review Board did not conduct any examination of its own into the incident, his prima facie defence to the charges had not been taken into account by those reviewing his administrative segregation.

Applying the criteria developed in the Segregation Code, this prisoner's segregation for so lengthy a period would not have been justified. The outstanding charges do not warrant segregation after the riot any more than they did before, particularly in light of the prejudice caused by his segregation to the preparation and presentation of his defence. While segregation would have been justified for a limited period after the riot to permit the investigation of the events of 7 June, the institution should have proceeded to have the disciplinary offences against this prisoner dealt with speedily. When this did not happen, and when the threat of any recurrence of a major disturbance in the institution had receded, the prisoner should have been released into the population. If at a later time the charges against him resulted in a conviction and a sentence of punitive segregation, he would have had to serve that sentence at that time.

One of the realities facing the authorities in maximum-security prisons is that they become aware of situations that pose threats to the security of the institution or to individuals within it which, while justifying preventive action by the authorities, may not be amenable to formal methods of proof. This poses a dilemma for the prison authorities as internal disciplinary charges are increasingly subjected to the requirements of due process. At Kent, as at other maximum-security institutions, the authorities receive much information (typically from prison informers) which, in their view, justifies investigation and action but which does not lead to specific charges being laid against prisoners. However, this informal covert intelligence-gathering regularly leads to transfers to other institutions and to decisions to place prisoners in administrative segregation. The need to be able to take such action is compelling from the institution's perspective of preventive security; but the danger of abuse of segregation on suspicion without formal proof of charges is no less compelling from the prisoner's perspective. The criteria I have proposed acknowledge the need for an institutional authority to be able to segregate without preferring formal charges, but seek to limit that authority to a restricted range of situations. Where a decision is made that no charges will be laid, segregation beyond the investigative stage would be authorized only

3 ... where there are grounds to believe beyond a reasonable doubt that the prisoner has committed, attempted to commit or plans to commit acts which represent a serious and immediate threat to the physical security of the institution or the personal safety of staff or prisoners.

The requirement that the grounds be established beyond a reasonable doubt, like the equivalent standard of proof in a criminal trial, is designed to ensure that the prisoner is not subjected to a serious deprivation of his liberty (albeit institutional liberty) unless there is a clearly established case. Indeed, 'proof beyond reasonable doubt' is the standard required in the commissioner's directive dealing with the hearing of serious disciplinary charges; this is a clear affirmation that such a standard has relevance behind prison walls. However, the incorporation of the criminal standard of proof does not mean that the segregation decision is subjected to the full procedural panoply of a criminal trial. In particular the evidentiary rules are not imported into the code. While the code permits reliance on a wider range of evidence than would be admissible in a criminal court, under section 3 that evidence must meet the same high standards of proof as in a criminal case.

How would such a criterion operate in practice? Case F is illustrative. Information was received from two prisoners that several other prisoners were planning an escape attempt involving the taking of prison guards as hostages. The informants were interviewed initially by the assistant warden (who was also the chairman of the Segregation Review Board). They described the nature of the plan and the location of several caches of weapons, holes in cell walls which had been lightly plastered over, and wire-cutting equipment. This information was corroborated by investigation and discovery of the caches and security breaches. As a result the prisoners who were alleged by the informants to be involved were placed in administrative segregation. No internal disciplinary charges or external criminal charges were laid against them. Having regard to the legal prerequisites for conviction of attempted escape or attempted forcible confinement under the Criminal Code, it is clear that criminal charges could not properly have been laid, since the acts were merely preparatory. Even though a charge could have been laid under the much broader categories set out in the Penitentiary Service Regulations, which include doing 'any act that is calculated to prejudice the discipline or good order of the institution,'[19] the practice of the penitentiary authorities is not to proceed before an internal disciplinary court if the primary evidence is that of a prisoner informant. This practice is based on the desire to protect the identities of informants in order to prevent reprisals against them and to ensure their future availability as sources of information. In addition, the commissioner's directives relating to the hearing of disciplinary offences require that all evidence be given in the presence of the prisoner and that he be given an opportunity to cross-examine all witnesses.[20] Both of these requirements could not be satisfied if the identity of the informant is kept from the prisoner charged with the offence.

The dilemma for both the prison administrator and the accused prisoner is acute. The institutional authorities receive information which after careful scrutiny they view as reliable and which reveals a serious threat - as in case F - to institutional security and the safety of penitentiary staff. However, because of the constraints of the standard of formal proof in criminal prosecutions and because of the desire to maintain prisoner informants' anonymity in an internal disciplinary proceeding, they cannot lay charges against the prisoner involved. For the prisoners, the lack of specific charges and of a forum in which they can confront their accusers, test the reliability of the evidence against them, and present evidence on their own behalf means that they are deemed guilty of the wrongdoing without even the barest rudiments of a trial and that they may be subjected to segregation for a longer period than if formal charges had been laid against them and a conviction duly recorded. The unfairness to the prisoners under these circumstances persists during their segregation. As I have pointed out, the lack of specific allegations means that the prisoner has no notice of what is required of him in order to dissipate the threat he is deemed to pose. The fact that the institutional authorities are not required to articulate the details of the wrongdoing means that the review may be based not on any specific acts but on the generalized threat the prisoner is deemed to present. To hold in check this tendency to rely upon these generalized perceptions, the code requires evidence of a serious and immediate threat to the physical security of the institution or to the personal safety of staff or prisoners.

In case F, initial segregation would be justified under subsection 1(a) because the penitentiary authorities are warranted in conducting a thorough investigation in order to ascertain whether further evidence might be found to justify charges being laid against the prisoners. Once it was ascertained that none could be found, further segregation would be justified under section 3 only if it could be established beyond a reasonable doubt that the prisoners were involved in a violent escape plan and that, notwithstanding the discovery of the escape plan and security breaches, they continued to constitute a serious and immediate threat to security or the safety of others. Relevant considerations would be the extent of the planning, the likelihood of the existence of an alternative plan, the previous involvement of the prisoners in violent escapes or hostage-takings, and their prior behaviour in Kent Institution.

The nature of the change that the standard-of-proof provisions of section 3 would bring about to existing segregation priorities can be seen by examining another case that has recently come before the courts, the *Morin* case. After the killing of a prisoner in LeClair Medium Security Institution Réjean Morin and two other prisoners, Cousineau and Blanchette, were transferred on 22 September 1980 to Laval Maximum Security Institution and were placed in segregation. On 2 October 1980 Cousineau pleaded guilty to the offence of manslaughter and received an eighteen-year sentence. On 5 December 1980 Morin was transferred to the special handling unit of the CDC. He was advised by the director that he was there because of his involvement in the murder. On 30 May 1981 Morin was acquitted of the murder charge after a trial by a superior court judge and jury. He was not released from the SHU, however. The National SHU Review Committee determined that in light of all the facts at their disposal, Morin was a 'particularly dangerous inmate' within the SHU criteria. In making that determination the review committee took into account a statement made by the deceased before he died which implicated Morin, Cousineau, and Blanchette; a statement allegedly made by Cousineau to police officers implicating Morin; and a statement by Blanchette implicating Morin and Cousineau. At Morin's trial, the statement by the deceased prisoner was not admitted into evidence because it did not meet the requirements of a 'dying declaration' (one of the recognized exceptions to the exclusion-of-hearsay rule); Cousineau's statement was not admitted into evidence when Cousineau testified that he had never made any statement implicating Morin and had never signed the document alleged to be his statement. Blanchette gave evidence at the trial consistent with his prior statement implicating Morin.

In his affidavit in response to Morin's application for certiorari to quash the decision to keep him in SHU, Deputy Commissioner Sauvé, the chairman of the SHU Review Committee, recited the evidence he and his committee had relied upon, and stated;

> I am aware of Mr Morin's acquittal, however notwithstanding this acquittal and the fact that some of the documents filed as exhibit I–4 to I–8 of my affidavit (especially I–7) [Cousineau's alleged statement] may not have been admissible in a court of law within its legal process of punishing a crime and accepting evidence through the conditions set forth by the Canada Evidence Act, my decision was an administrative one following an entirely different process and purpose and I do not feel that I have to believe beyond any reasonable doubt that Mr Morin is

guilty of the murder of Mr Payeur which evidently he is not before I consider him a dangerous inmate as per cd 274.[21]

Mr Sauvé described how he viewed the nature of the discretionary power to place a prisoner in SHU; coming from the deputy commissioner of corrections this statement can properly be seen as expressing the official view of the correctional authorities in relation to SHU and to segregation generally.

I do not consider my decisions in the case as being excessive, absurd or arbitrary [as Morin had alleged] but in taking care of security in our institutions I have to take into account my ... experience, instinct, 'gut feeling' with a person and a situation; last, I might add that exercise of discretion in the type of administrative decision is not easy in this case and others, and in case of doubt it is my duty to favor the best interest of the service and quite frankly I prefer being told that I am wrong about a person than not having put him in a shu and learn afterwards that he has been involved in an incident.[22]

How would section 3 of the segregation code change the nature of this process? It would not preclude consideration of the statement of the deceased victim or that of Cousineau. As will be seen in the next section of the proposed hearing process, it would give Morin an early opportunity, with the assistance of counsel, to challenge his segregation; to point to the dangers of relying upon evidence that cannot be tested by cross-examination (the deceased's statement); to argue that limited weight should be given to a statement that has been denied by its alleged maker to be his when that denial has been accepted as credible by a superior court judge (the Cousineau statement); to question the reliability of a statement and testimony implicating him in a deadly assault when that statement and testimony have evidently been rejected as not credible by a jury which has acquitted him of the murder charge (the Blanchette statement and testimony). But over and above this, Réjean Morin would be able to argue that, contrary to Mr Sauvé's view of existing practices, to justify segregation under section 3 of the code the evidence must implicate the accused prisoner in the violent death of another prisoner beyond a reasonable doubt and that, again contrary to Mr Sauvé's view, when the correctional authorities seek to subject him to the most onerous form of imprisonment he, and not the correctional service, should get the benefit of any doubt.

A HEARING AND REVIEW PROCESS FOR SEGREGATION

The segregation criteria I have suggested will not achieve the purposes of reform unless they are implemented within a procedural context perceived by prisoners to be fair. The *Manual of Standards* makes specific provision for the administrative segregation process. The relevant sections provide:

> 2–4215: The warden/superintendent or shift supervisor can order immediate segregation when it is necessary to protect the inmate and others. The action is reviewed within three working days by the appropriate committee.
>
> 2–4217: Written policy and procedure provide that inmates are placed in administrative segregation only after a hearing before the warden/superintendent or shift supervisor, classification committee or their standing committee specifically designated for this purpose.
>
> *Discussion*: Placement in administrative segregation should be preceded by the inmate receiving notice of the intended placement, appearance at the hearing and an opportunity to present his or her case to the hearing officers.
>
> 2–4218: Written policy and procedure provide for a review of the status of inmates in administrative segregation by the classification committee or other authorized staff group every seven days for the first two months and at least every thirty days thereafter.
>
> *Discussion*: The Classification Committee should review the status of every inmate who spends over seven continuous days in administrative segregation. The hearing should determine whether the reasons for initial placement in the unit still exist; if they do not, the inmate should be released from the unit. Provision should be made for the inmate to appear at the hearing, and the results of the review should be communicated to the inmate.[23]

The relative lack of specificity in the due process requirements for the hearing and review process is in stark contrast to the lengthy list of such requirements specified for disciplinary hearings of major rule violations. In such cases the standards provide for written advance notice to the prisoner of the charges, a hearing before an impartial tribunal, the right to appear in person and hear evidence (except confidential information), the right to present evidence, the right to be represented by a staff member, and the right to be advised in writing of a decision based on the evidence.[24]

The adequacy of the *Manual of Standards* in ensuring a fair hearing and review process for 'special management inmates' may be judged in light of the fact that Millhaven Institution with its special handling unit has been accredited.

In 1974, when I first considered the question of procedural fairness in prison disciplinary decision-making, I outlined a proposal which contained a hearing procedure for serious disciplinary offences presided over by an independent chairperson appointed from outside the Penitentiary

Service. I also urged that the administrative-segregation decision was so charged with negative consequences for a prisoner that it too should be subject to the imprimatur of an independent hearing officer. This proposal was suggested by the need for a decision-maker who was free of the biases of institutional personnel,[25] and was designed to reconcile the tension that exists between the institution's need to maintain confidentiality and the prisoner's need to know the case against him. This was how I envisaged the reconciliation of these interests:

A solution to this problem of reconciling the institution's interest in maintaining confidentiality of the sources of certain kinds of information and the inmate's interest in a fair hearing ... arises from the special role of the independent chairman. This official could be presented with all of the institution's information, including confidential material and could make a judgment as to the reliability and, in light of other non-confidential corroboratory evidence, the justification for keeping the information from the inmate. Since it could be expected that the claim to confidentiality would be readily made and since it makes it more difficult for the inmate to answer the charge, directives should clearly establish a presumption in favour of disclosure of all information to the inmate, leaving the institution with the burden of establishing the need to maintain confidentiality in the particular case. Such a procedure, while recognizing a claim to confidentiality, would allow for case by case scrutiny and where the claim is upheld, the inmate access to the information refused, there would at least have been an evaluation by an independent judge.[26]

The Correctional Service, prompted by the recommendations of the Vantour Study Group Report on Dissociation, has implemented the proposals I put forward in 1974 for independent hearing officers for serious disciplinary offences in maximum- and medium-security institutions. The Vantour Report recommended against independent hearing officers dealing with segregation cases and instead put forth its own proposals for the Segregation Review Board. The Parliamentary Subcommittee on the Penitentiary System recommended that the Vantour proposal 'should not be judged and found wanting until it has been tried. The adequacy of protection should be reconsidered after two years of experience.'[27] Based on my observations of the segregation process at Kent Institution, the system must be found wanting, in large measure because of the absence of specific criteria for segregation. This absence means that there is no presentation at the hearing of any of the evidence on which the institution is relying to justify segregation. Consequently, the prisoner is denied any real opportunity to cross-examine or to answer the case against him. He is told that he is to be detained in segregation 'pending an investigation of possible charges' or 'pending disposition of outstanding charges.' This does not constitute an invitation to the prisoner to defend himself against the allegations made against him, nor does it indicate whether those allegations justify continued segregation. What I propose in the Segregation Code is a process which, while permitting the warden to order segregation for up to seventy-two hours without a hearing (providing only that written reasons for the order be given to the prisoner within twenty-four hours), requires that continued segregation be authorized only on the order of an independent hearing officer. At the end of the seventy-two-hour period a full hearing is to be held, at which time the institution's case will be presented to the hearing officer in the presence of the prisoner, unless there is a substantiated claim to maintain confidentiality for particular evidence, in which case the hearing officer would summarize that evidence for the prisoner. The prisoner would have the right to cross-examine witnesses (save those to whom confidentiality was extended) and to present evidence on his own behalf, including the calling of witnesses. The hearing officer would be required to provide detailed written reasons for the decision. The importance of this requirement to the overall process has been ably expressed by Chief Judge Foreman of the US District Court in a case concerning administrative segregation: 'The Court emphasizes that reasons are required in part to facilitate later review, both administrative and judicial. To serve this function, the reasons cannot be merely boilerplate. Detailed reasons facilitate later review, help prevent arbitrary decisions, and provide the affected individual with a rationale for the decision.'[28]

If continued segregation is authorized by the hearing officer, further reviews would be required every week, subject to the same procedural requirements. At these reviews an onus would be placed on the institution to develop a plan to reintegrate the prisoner into the population, and the hearing officer would monitor that plan at any subsequent reviews. Except under very limited circumstances, segregation would be terminated after a ninety-day period.

One further feature of these proposals was part of my original scheme for the hearing of serious disciplinary offences: the prisoner is to be allowed representation by counsel or counsel-substitute. This feature has not been accepted by the Correctional Service in relation to the hearing of serious disciplinary cases. While I maintain that the original reasons for advocating the right to counsel in relation to this kind of case still remain valid,[29] an even stronger case can be made for representation in the administrative-segregation process. Many of the cases that the institution views as justifying segregation (and which under my proposed criteria will still permit segregation), involve a situation where the prisoner has been or may be charged with a criminal offence. Since the circumstances surrounding the alleged offence will be critical in the hearing officer's assessment of whether there is a need for segregation or its continuation, the prisoner needs to be advised of the implications of his giving evidence of the circumstances surrounding the alleged offence and what protection against self-incrimination (such as the provisions of the Canada Evidence Act and section 13 of the Charter of Rights and Freedoms) might be available to him. Furthermore, the thorny issue of confidential information is clearly a matter on which counsel could be expected to make a more informed presentation than a lay person. Counsel's presence on a case-by-case basis is also likely to ensure that real substance is given to the criteria and that they do not degenerate into a semantic substitute for 'the good order and discipline of the institution.' Indeed, based on experience in the United States, this case-by-case participation by counsel is likely to be more effective in bringing the rule of law to bear on the prison than the necessarily intermittent nature of judicial review. Jacobs, in his study of Stateville, commented on the cumulative import of the intrusion of lawyers into the decision-making process in the prison. He concludes:

> It is not victory in great judicial decisions that constitutes Prison Legal Services' [a public-interest group which provides lawyers for inmates] greatest impact on Stateville. It is the pls members' daily presence at the prison, their persistent questioning of the rules, their relentless demands to see files and records, and the fear they invoke in the hearts of many of the prison staff that has the most profound effect on the day to day administration of the prison. Somehow the prison authorities must find a way to accommodate these lawyers and law students who so doggedly camp on the doorstep.[30]

One further consideration argues in favour of representation by counsel. The segregation experience cuts the prisoner off from association with most other prisoners, and is calculated to undermine the prisoner's ability to present any defence to a case involving the evidence of other prisoners. Counsel would be able to interview these potential witnesses and limit the prisoner's impairment in this regard. Of course, to the extent that the conditions in segregation remain unchanged, the effect of confinement is itself likely to impair substantially the prisoner's ability to make a proper presentation of either himself or his case. Here again, representation by counsel is a necessary adjunct to a fair hearing.[31]

The issue of the role of counsel in ensuring a fair hearing has already come before the courts in the context of parole revocation and disciplinary-board hearings. In *Dubeau* v. *National Parole Board*[32] Réné Dubeau's parole was suspended, ostensibly because he had violated a parole condition by obtaining a credit card without his supervisor's permission. In addition, while on parole Dubeau had been arrested on a new criminal charge entirely unrelated to credit cards. Pursuant to the provisions of the parole regulations, Dubeau requested a post-suspension hearing. At that hearing, after being asked some brief questions dealing with credit cards, he was questioned about the new criminal charge. He denied committing the offence and requested that his lawyer be allowed to appear with him at the hearing. The request was refused. At the hearing, he answered some questions about the charge, but he refused to discuss a written statement apparently given by him to the police. Upon the revocation of his parole, Dubeau brought application for certiorari in the Trial Division of the Federal Court of Canada to quash the revocation order on the ground that the board had acted unfairly by denying the applicant's request to have counsel present during questioning about pending criminal charges. Smith DJ, citing the decision of the English Court of Appeal in *Fraser* v. *Mudge*[33] to the effect that fairness did not require that a prisoner appearing on a disciplinary charge before the Board of Visitors have the right to be represented by counsel, distinguished that situation from a parole revocation. He held that, at least where there were issues involving participation in criminal offences which would be highly relevant to a revocation decision by the Parole Board, fairness did require the presence of legal counsel where it was requested. Smith DJ distinguished the two situations on the basis that the rationale for the denial of the right to counsel in prison disciplinary matters in *Fraser* v. *Mudge* was that there was a need for swift and speedy decisions, and legal representation would give rise to considerable delay. In the case of parole revocation, the need for a quick decision is not as great or as important as in a prison disciplinary case.

Allan Manson, in reviewing the *Dubeau* case, identified those factors that justifiably require, in the name of fairness, that counsel be provided at a parole post-suspension hearing:

In order to understand how the right to counsel might relate to fairness in these circumstances, let us try to appreciate Dubeau's situation. His liberty is about to be determined by a decision of the Parole Board. He is asked questions about his new criminal charge, including questions relating to a statement apparently given to the police. If he refuses to answer, can the Board characterize him as uncooperative and recalcitrant and then take these factors into consideration? If he does answer, can his remarks to the Parole Board be used in a subsequent criminal trial against him? Put in the context of the evidentiary rules relating to admissibility of statements by an accused, is the Parole Board a 'person' in authority? Would his response be protected in a confidential communication as discussed in *Slavutych* v. *Baker* [1976] 1 SCR 254 if a Parole Board member was served with a subpoena ... ? The situation is rife with complex legal questions. If fairness is the test, even if it only means providing an adequate opportunity to respond to allegations, surely Dubeau's predicament without the assistance of a lawyer cannot be characterized as a fair opportunity to respond.[34]

The cogency of these comments is reflected in the recent amendment to the parole regulations which permits the participation of an assistant in parole hearings, who may be legal counsel.[35] Manson's comments are equally relevant to the segregation hearing process, and recognition of the right to representation is equally necessary to ensure that fairness is delivered rather than merely ordained.

The penitentiary authorities have specifically addressed the question of representation by counsel in prison disciplinary hearings. Commissioner's directive 213 provides in section 12(a) of annex A: 'Occasions have arisen where an accused has made formal or informal demands that he be represented by counsel. Such demands shall be met with the response that he is not entitled to counsel and that the hearing will proceed without the accused person being represented.'[36]

In the *Minott* case,[37] Mr Justice Nitikman held that the commissioner's directive, not having the force of law, could not legally circumscribe the powers of the independent chairperson to conduct the hearing which were conferred by section 38.1(1) of the Penitentiary Service Regulations. Mr Justice Nitikman held that while there was no right to counsel in prison disciplinary hearings, the independent chairperson had the discretion to permit representation by counsel and must exercise that discretion in light of the principle of fairness and free from the constraints of section (12)(a) of annex A. In the *Davidson* case,[38] Mr Justice Cattanach came to a similar conclusion on the non-binding effect of section 12. As to the circumstances in which fairness would require legal representation, he expressed the view that most disciplinary breaches involved 'simply questions of fact' and not of law, and that in such cases the presence of counsel was not essential to ensure fairness.[39] With great respect to Mr Justice Cattanach, this is an extremely narrow view of the role of counsel in such a hearing. In most hearings outside the prison, the lawyer's role is directed at least as much to the establishing of the relevant facts as it is to the application of the relevant law. Indeed, the process of examination and cross-examination of witnesses by people trained in these skills is regarded in the common-law system as the best means of getting to the truth of disputed facts. The commissioner's directive itself recognizes that cross-examination is an essential component of a fair disciplinary hearing by providing for the cross-examination of all witnesses. According to the views of Mr Justice Cattanach, the prisoner must do this himself without the benefit of counsel in all cases except where points of law are involved. The effect of this view is that the prisoner, a lay person, has to develop a skill which, in the outside world, is regarded as the hallmark of the professional.

The asserted rationale for the decision in *Fraser* v. *Mudge* (a rationale endorsed in the *Davidson* case) – that prison disciplinary matters cannot be taxed with the need for legal representation because to do so would overburden swift decision-making – is not supported by the empirical evidence. In the *Minott* case, Mr Justice Nitikman, relying on the affidavit evidence of legal aid lawyers that where a prisoner pleaded not guilty to a disciplinary charge it was common for the case to be remanded and that there were legal resources available to meet requests for prisoner representation, found that such representation should not entail any appreciable delay in the hearing.[40] In my own experience at Kent Institution, speedy justice is not a conspicuous feature of the disciplinary system. Not until more than five weeks after the riot of 7 June were the first charges heard, and in one instance three months elapsed without the case coming before the disciplinary board. But whatever the reality of the need for urgency in disciplinary cases, I believe that the model procedure I have suggested gives full weight to the fact that at a certain stage the decision to segregate may have to be made speedily without the burden of a hearing with counsel present. At a later stage, when the case is referred to the independent hearing officer, the balance of convenience shifts so that participation of counsel at that point, far from undermining the process, is required to ensure the accuracy of the hearing's fact-finding and its legitimacy in the eyes of the prisoners.

The last two elements of my proposed segregation process are closely related. First, in every case where the institution seeks to continue segregation for more than thirty days the hearing officer shall hear expert evidence as to the effects of such continued segregation on the individual prisoner. Second, there is to be a ninety-day outer limit on the duration of administrative segregation. I have described how segregation practices have given rise to great psychological and physical suffering. The purpose of the first proposal is to ensure that the hearing officer is made aware of the effects of the segregation decision on a case-by-case basis; where the evidence demonstrates that continued segregation will cause substantial psychological or physical harm, the prisoner must be released from segregation. Under the proposed code, the independent hearing officer will hear the evidence of two experts in psychiatry or psychology. One of these is to be appointed by the warden, the other by the prisoner. (If the warden and prisoner agree on the same expert, only one opinion is required.) The requirement of two experts is based on my own experience and that of the prisoners I have interviewed that psychiatrists and psychologists who are employees of the prison authorities have not sufficiently demonstrated the necessary independence of mind to justify exclusive reliance upon their evidence as to the effects of segregation. An expert from outside the prison system who is free from the strong institutional pressures to uphold a common front is more likely to 'tell it like it is.' It may be that the transfer of the decision-making power from the warden to the independent hearing officer will encourage prison psychiatrists and psychologists to be more forthright in their opinions on the effects of segregation. It might just as easily push them into an even closer identification with the prison administration's view of the case. For the time being, therefore, it is likely that prisoners and their counsel would look to experts outside the prison system to participate in the hearing and review process.

The ninety-day limit on the duration of administrative segregation may appear to be the most radical element of my proposed segregation code in light of present practice. In fact, the limitation was an integral part of the original regimes of penitentiary discipline. At Pentonville, nine months soon became the maximum time spent in solitary. The Crofton system in Ireland, long the inspirational source for the Canadian prison inspectorate's ideas on penal reform, had a similar time limit. Underlying the time limits of the nineteenth century was the belief that if solitary confinement was extended beyond a certain point, the reformatory objectives of penitentiary discipline would be undermined rather than enhanced. My resurrection of an outer time limit is designed to serve a number of purposes which have less to do with positive assumptions of rehabilitating men in prison than with the negative, albeit more realistic, conviction that we must not permit the segregation experience to debilitate men in prison. Thus the ninety-day limit is designed to change the open-ended nature of administrative segregation, which every segregated prisoner I have interviewed has regarded as the principal factor in the undermining of prisoners' psychological integrity. Furthermore, because the authorities will no longer be able to lock up prisoners indefinitely, the time limit is designed to provide an incentive to develop and implement responsive programs for segregated prisoners aimed at easing their reintegration into the population within a clearly defined period. The ninety-day limit provides a limited agenda for both the keeper and the kept. The only exception to the ninety-day limitation would be the case where a segregated prisoner commits further acts which under the proposed criteria justify a further period of segregation. That additional period of segregation would also be subject to a ninety-day limit.[41]

I would be less than honest if I did not admit to a further reason for suggesting an outer time limit on segregation. I believe that the adoption of the full reform slate I am advocating will bring about significant changes in the nature of segregation. I may be wrong. I believed that the *McCann* case would bring about change. I have described how subsequent events proved me wrong and why I believe that the lack of change may have much to do with the deeply entrenched adversarial relationship between the keeper and the kept. That relationship is highly resistant to structural change, especially where the agent of change – the judgment of a court – is itself the product of an intensely adversarial process. Most of my proposals accept that in the context of maximum-security institutions, the nature of this relationship is not likely to change. Indeed, most of the proposals can be viewed as attempting to ensure that in the ongoing battle the prisoners have sufficient legal armour to defend themselves adequately against the prison's heaviest assault. It is just possible that, as has already happened with the SHUs, my proposals will make segregation appear more rational and civilized but leave it in fact no less repressive for the men who endure it. If I am wrong again and if despite my elaborate code segregation remains the soul-destroying experience it has always been, then the ninety-day limit will at least render the repression finite. The time limit will reduce the likelihood of prisoners setting themselves on fire like Jack McCann to escape the madness, slashing their throats like Donny Oag to focus their pain, slipping over the edge of insanity like Tommy McCaulley, and ultimately, like Jacques Bellemaire, 'letting the light go out.'

How would this model procedure operate in practice? Let us go back to the facts of case F. Having received the informant's warning about the planned escape and hostage-taking, and having corroborated this through discovery of the weapons cache, the warden will be authorized to segregate the prisoners on the reasonable and probable ground that they represent a serious and immediate threat to the physical security of the prison or the physical safety of staff or prisoners. Within twenty-four hours the warden will be required to advise the prisoners that they are suspected of planning an escape and hostage-taking. At the hearing before the independent officer two days later, they would be entitled to be represented by counsel who would see that the case against the prisoners was substantiated by specific evidence. At that point the warden could raise the issue of the confidentiality of the information and the need to protect the source of that information. In case F, the prisoners involved knew full well who the informants were. Soon after their segregation they had asked to see me, and in the interview they told me that they had been given no reason for their segregation by the warden other than a written notification that they were there 'for the good order and discipline of the institution.' However, they had been told informally by the psychologist that they were being segregated because of their suspected involvement in an escape and hostage-taking plan. In their interview with me they denied any involvement and suggested that the two prisoner informants, who they alleged were homosexual lovers, had concocted a false story in return for the institution's agreement to transfer them together to another institution. The two informants were indeed transferred into protective custody soon after the accused prisoners had been segregated. The accused prisoners suggested that the idea that they were planning an escape and a hostage-taking was fanciful because they had been well-behaved in the institution, had never committed any disciplinary offences, and had been working in the kitchen for months with easy access to knives and other potential weapons, yet had never sought to use these under circumstances where hostage-taking was not difficult. One of the prisoners had set out all these facts in a letter to the chairman of the Segregation Review Board.

At a hearing before the independent hearing officer, the institution's case would be entered into evidence. Only in the most exceptional cases would prison informants be prepared to testify at such a hearing, and therefore reliance would usually be placed on a written statement (which would not identify the source of the information). While the independent chairperson would be told the informant's identity, the administration usually would be able to maintain a claim to confidentiality of the source of information against the segregated prisoner. In case F, however, since the prisoners already knew who the informants were, the non-disclosure of the source of the information in the statements taken from the informants would not be justified. At the hearing the accused prisoners, with the assistance of counsel, could challenge the credibility of the informants' story, and could cite in particular any ulterior motive they might have for fabricating such a story in order to effect a transfer. They could also present their own evidence and call other witnesses (including prison staff) to attest to their prior good behaviour. The independent hearing officer would be required to assess the corroboratory evidence relied on by the institution – discovery of the security breaches and the arms caches. Counsel for the accused prisoners would no doubt argue that these could have been effected and collected by other prisoners, particularly since the holes in the walls were in a cell block other than the one in which the accused prisoners lived; further, the evidence of other security breaches was not necessarily corroborative of the involvement of the accused. Again, a judgment would be made by the independent hearing officer as to the likelihood of the informants telling the truth in certain material elements (the arms and security breaches) but fabricating the names of the prisoners involved. Highly relevant here would be a letter written by one of the informants shortly before he was transferred in which he stated that he was not certain of the degree of involvement of one of the accused prisoners. In this connection also the hearing officer would have to weigh the fact that all of the prisoners involved, both those accused and those providing information, were French Canadians, against the accused's statement that they did not associate with the two informants so that, even if they had been hatching a plot, they would not have made the informants privy to this information. (In Kent, francophone prisoners associate exclusively with other - though not all other - francophones.)

The warden himself released one of the accused prisoners from segregation after three weeks. He told me (but not the prisoner) that the letter from the informant had cast doubt on this accused's involvement and that this accused's prior behaviour in Kent had been impeccable. In light of this, it seems reasonable to expect that a hearing before an independent hearing officer would have resulted in a decision to release that prisoner into the population, thus avoiding a three-week detention. But let us assume that the hearing officer concluded that the evidence of the informants was reliable and sufficiently corroborated and that it did implicate the other accused; what implications would flow from this in terms of continuing segregation? If the authorities were continuing their investigation into security breaches and there were further inquiries to be made, the continued confinement of the accused in segregation until the completion of those investigations might be justified. However, when the investigations were completed would the circumstances justify further segregation? The authorities would have effectively taken preventive action to halt the escape plot and the prisoners would have been alerted to the fact that their plan was discovered and that henceforth they would be very carefully watched. The fact that these men, who by virtue of their maximum-security status are deemed to be escape risks, have demonstrated that they are prepared to act upon their potentiality, while it gives the authorities cause for greater viligance against them, does not require that they be subjected to the rigours of segregation. Only if their previous behaviour in the institution and the particular circumstances of the plot indicated that, despite greater surveillance, there was a substantial enough likelihood that they would again seek to take hostages (thus constituting an immediate threat) would segregation be justified.

Another case that illustrates the hard judgments that are required, and how the criteria and process I am advocating would render these judgments more rational and legitimate, involves prisoners who were locked up in H unit at the same time as the prisoners suspected of the escape plot. In case G the prisoners were suspected of attempting to murder another prisoner who, as a result of the injuries he sustained, was hospitalized for several months with multiple facial fractures and possible brain damage. The institution received information about the identity of the attackers and the motivation for the attack from a variety of prisoner sources. This suggested that although only two prisoners actually perpetrated the attack, it was an organized effort on the part of a larger group. Under the proposed Segregation Code, within seventy-two hours the institutional authorities would present to the hearing officer the information they had gathered to that point about the circumstances of the attack. The authorities would argue that investigations were continuing, that charges of attempted murder might be laid against the two prisoners, and that the release of these prisoners into the population would constitute an immediate threat to their physical safety because of the possibility of violent retaliation from friends of the injured prisoner. Given the presence of organized gangs in Kent Institution, this is both a real and an immediate threat. In a case such as this the role of the independent hearing officer in reviewing weekly the need for continued segregation and monitoring the institution's plan to reintegrate the prisoner into the population assumes primary importance. In case G reintegration would require either a transfer to another institution or an arrangement, necessarily with prisoner involvement, to ensure that there would be no retaliation. The Inmate Committee could play a vital role in working out an informal truce between the factions involved and in submitting their representations to the hearing officer.

Let me complete this field-testing of my proposed Segregation Code by considering its application to what is probably the single event most feared by prison staff – a hostage-taking. There is no doubt that these incidents have become more common in recent years, although they are still infrequent. A hostage-taking is an event that will always bring forth a demand by the staff that the prisoner involved be segregated. This is not an unreasonable demand from the point of view of people who have to live with that prisoner in a face-to-face situation. There is very little in this world which destroys one's confidence in the safety of face-to-face relationships more completely than finding a knife pressed against your throat by someone who gives every indication that he will use it. There is no question that under the proposed criteria such an event would be valid cause for segregation; the act clearly constitutes an immediate threat to the personal safety of an individual. A question remains as to the duration of that segregation, however. Under present arrangements a prisoner involved in a hostage-taking incident would certainly be a candidate for a special handling unit and would spend at least two years there. How would my proposed scheme deal with the continued segregation of a hostage-taker? In most cases criminal charges would be laid without delay and the question for decision by the hearing officer would be whether segregation was required pending the hearing of these charges. This would require a determination under section 2(b) whether there was a 'substantial likelihood that the offence will be continued, or repeated' which, of course, would depend upon the circumstances that gave rise to the hostage-taking and the institutional record of the prisoner. Under the proposed code, the authorities would not be able to continue his segregation beyond ninety days. They would have to develop a plan to reintegrate the prisoner into the population, one which would allay the staffs' concern for safety. Lest this response to hostage-taking be viewed as too lenient in light of the seriousness of the prisoner's conduct, it must be remembered that segregation is not intended to be the appropriate punitive sanction for hostage-taking: that is reserved for the criminal court. Segregation, although at present identified by staff as a means of dealing with the felt need to 'intensify' imprisonment in order to achieve punitive purposes, is not designed for any end except limited preventive detention.

THE CONDITIONS OF SEGREGATION

In the previous two sections I have suggested that the American Correctional Association's *Manual of Standards*, like the recommendations of the Vantour Report, is deficient in not articulating specific criteria to limit the power of administrative segregation and in failing to provide adequate procedural safeguards in the segregation hearing and review process. However, the manual is more explicit in setting out minimum standards for the conditions of segregated confinement. These standards require prisoners in administrative segregation to be clothed like other prisoners; to be provided with basic personal items for use in their cells, unless there is an imminent danger that the prisoner will destroy an item or injure himself;[42] to receive the same meals as the general population;[43] to have the same issue and exchange of bedding, linen, and clothing as the general population;[44] to be provided with the same opportunities for visits, correspondence, and telephone privileges as are available to the general population, unless there are substantial reasons for withholding such privileges;[45] to have the opportunity to shave and shower at least three times per week;[46] to receive a minimum of one hour per day of exercise outside their cells, unless security or safety considerations dictate otherwise;[47] to have access to legal materials and the opportunity to borrow reading materials from the institutional library; to be allowed to participate in institution programs to the same extent as the general population, providing their participation is consistent with the safety and security of the institution;[48] and to receive daily visits from the senior correctional supervisor in charge, a qualified member of the medical department and, by request, members of the program staff.[49]

It is clear that these standards are designed to ensure that the segregated prisoner is afforded the same rights and privileges as the prisoners in the general population, apart from freedom of movement outside the cell. As I have already pointed out, the present penitentiary regulations, in theory, provide that a segregated prisoner shall not be deprived of any of his privileges and amenities; but they subject this provision to an enormous qualification: 'except [those] that cannot reasonably be granted having regard to the limitations of the dissociation area and the necessity for the effective operation thereof.'[50] The depressing reality which existed in 1975 at the British Columbia Penitentiary and which continues to exist at Kent Institution is that this qualification has been used to justify discriminatory and debilitating treatment of segregated prisoners. The recommendation of the Vantour Report that prisoners in segregation be entitled to the same amenities as other prisoners (except for the privilege of association) 'insofar as is reasonable'[51] has proved to be totally inadequate in bringing about any real change in this situation.[52]

The standards in the manual are also subject to qualifications. Standard 2-4222 seeks to prevent abuse of some of those qualifications by requiring that whenever a prisoner is deprived of any usually authorized item or activity, a report of the action is to be made and forwarded to the chief security officer. The commentary to this standard requires that the withholding of any item or activity should be for no longer than is necessary to ensure the safety and well-being of the prisoner, staff, and other prisoners. This is clearly designed to ensure that decisions to withhold privileges are made on an individual basis. However, in my judgment the mere reporting of a withholding is not likely to ensure that it is well founded. The policy of individualizing and justifying restrictions on the rights and privileges of segregated prisoners would be more effectively secured if such decisions were referred for ratification to an independent hearing officer.

Some of the other qualifications in the standards require rather more extensive amendment. Subjecting the entitlement of segregated prisoners to participate in institutional programs to such vague qualifying phrases as 'the safety and security of the institution' is little more than an open invitation to continue the past practices of de facto exclusion. If the purpose of the standard is to ensure that segregated prisoners are not excluded from programs, this purpose would be better achieved by requiring the institution to provide a range of programs suitable for prisoners working by themselves or in small groups, programs which minimize security and safety risks. The concern, in other words, should not be to provide an illusory standard of equality of opportunity to participate in all institutional programs but rather to provide separate but equal opportunities.

Would the adoption of the conditions of segregation set out in the *Manual of Standards* (subject to my amendments) ensure adequate reform of conditions? An appropriate way to answer this question is to look at the proposals that the prisoners at Kent Institution have suggested for H unit. The following is taken from a list of proposals presented to the institutional authorities by the Inmate Committee early in 1981.

Prisoners in H Unit should have more access to law books; a prisoner from H Unit should be elected as a member of the Inmate Committee so he can voice all their unique and special problems; an open visiting program must be worked out so that the prisoners in H Unit can visit with their families and friends other than a screened visit; a longer and better exercise program must be worked out for H Unit prisoners, perhaps using the gymnasium during the day when the main population is not using it; an education program must be set up for the prisoners in H Unit with their own separate area and instructor; prisoners in H Unit [should] be allowed more showers, clothes and bedding changes and more sanitary conditions; prisoners in H Unit [should] be allowed to have their personal effects; prisoners in H Unit [should] be permitted to go to church and to participate in religious programs if they so desire; prisoners in H Unit [should] be allowed to have a tv, either in the tv rooms or in their cells; prisoners in H Unit [should] be allowed limited hobby work that does not present any type of threat to either staff or other prisoners.[53]

With few exceptions the prisoners' proposals are consistent with the minimum requirements of the *Manual of Standards* as amended. The institution's response to the prisoners' proposals was a statement that facilities at H unit did not permit the kind of programs envisaged. Measured against the *Manual of Standards*, this response to the prisoners' proposals would simply not pass muster. It is clear that the prisoners at Kent can bring forth reasonable proposals that do not undermine the legitimate concerns of security, yet which respect those matters that prisoners view as essential to maintain a semblance of legitimacy and dignity in their confinement.

The Canadian experience with special handling units is particularly relevant to the issue of the conditions of segregated confinement. That experience demonstrates that those prisoners who are regarded as the most dangerous in the penitentiary system can be confined under the strictest security regime without being locked up for twenty-three hours a day and without restricting to the point of extinguishment all the ordinary rights and privileges of prisoners in the general population. Let me be quite clear about this. I have had some harsh things to say about the special handling units and I will be making recommendations regarding them shortly. The fact remains that they provide irrefutable evidence that the rigours of segregation regimes such as the one that exists at H unit in Kent Institution are not justified on security grounds.

The Kent prisoners' list of proposals was an abortive attempt on their part to start negotiating the conditions of their confinement. In *Justice Behind the Walls* I suggested that a negotiation model is an alternative to a 'due process' model for resolving certain aspects of the relationship between the keeper and the kept.[54] The due process model sees the prisoner, the prison staff, and the administration as engaged in an ongoing battle in which the interests of the combatants are viewed as irreconcilable. The due process model proceeds on the assumption that the principal way to legitimize state power and prevent its abuse is by pouring specificity into the criteria for decisions and girding the making of those decisions with rules that ensure fairness. The negotiation model proceeds on the assumption that the prisoner, the staff, and the administration are part of a community characterized by often conflicting but still reconcilable interests. In the negotiation model, formal bargaining brings a redistribution of power along mutually accepted lines on the assumption that such redistribution will provide an alternative check against abuse of power. The negotiation model, it has been argued, also gives prisoners a sense of dignity, self-respect, and responsibility for their own lives, values which the prison traditionally has deadened and which the due process model does little to quicken.[55]

In *Justice Behind the Walls* I recommended that in the context of prison disciplinary practices a dual system of prison justice be established, with negotiation predominating where there was a reconcilability of interests and due process where there was not. I further recommended that in cases of serious offences, regardless of reconcilability, where the exercise of power could take the form of lengthening the term of imprisonment (through loss of remission) or severely limiting institutional freedom (through punitive segregation) the due process model should be the principal method of controlling that power. I now propose a dual system for dealing with administrative segregation. Reconcilability of interests will rarely exist when the prison administrator seeks to segregate a prisoner and the prisoner seeks to resist such segregation. Because of this and because administrative segregation is the most serious and the most abused exercise of power in the Canadian penitentiary, I have used the due process model in constructing criteria and procedures in the Segregation Code.

I suggest, however, that the *conditions* of segregated confinement are amenable to a negotiated settlement. Although (as the *McCann* case illustrates) the interaction of prisoners and guards has all the indicia of deep-seated irreconcilability of interests, this is largely a function of existing practices and conditions. But it is clear that the prisoners, the guards, and the prison administration have a common interest in avoiding conditions that result in the constant escalation of force and counter-force. In his evidence in *McCann*, Dr Stephen Fox spoke of the need for a program of negotiation, 'of equal dialogue' between the prisoners, guards, and administration, as the only alternative to the cycle of violence. As the experience at Kent illustrates, such negotiation is not possible at present because there are no minimum standards to provide a reference point for negotiation; nor do the prisoners have recognized standing to negotiate on such matters. I suggest that with the promulgation of a Segregation Code that establishes minimum standards for conditions of confinement along with clear criteria and a fair process, the precise contours of segregated confinement within a given institution could fruitfully be the subject of a properly recognized system of tripartite prisoner-staff-administration negotiation.[56]

A new segregation unit is being built at Kent to replace H unit. My review of segregation practices at Kent demonstrates that new architecture alone is not capable of ensuring the legitimacy of carceral authority. What is more critical is a willingness on the part of the administration and staff to negotiate with the prisoners the regime under which they will live their institutional lives. My proposed model for reform is intended to provide a common agenda for the beginning of that negotiation process.

THE FUTURE OF SPECIAL HANDLING UNITS

The special handling units are seen by the penitentiary authorities as a successful response to the problem of the dangerous prisoner, so much so that recent announcements by the solicitor-general point to more such units being established. In light of my description of the regimes of the SHUs, it will come as no surprise to discover that, in my judgment, an extension of those regimes will further compound the illegitimacy of Canada's ultimate carceral power. I have described how the physical space and program requirements set out in the Vantour-McReynolds Report, which is the theoretical model for the SHUs, have simply not been met. Consequently, the whole idea of the phased return to the general population, while described by the Penitentiary Service as the chief difference between these units and regular segregation, is a correctional fiction.

It would be a significant step forward if all segregation units in maximum-security institutions were made to conform to the requirements of the Vantour-McReynolds Report in their physical and program resources. However, the behaviour-modification assumptions concerning the way SHUs or any other segregation unit should be operated must be abandoned.

It is ironic that at the very time the SHUs were established (on an overtly behaviouralistic model), the federal government's Task Force on the Creation of an Integrated Canadian Corrections Service recommended that 'rehabilitation ... must cease to be a purpose of the prison sentence.' The reasoning behind this was stated as follows:

Since the early 1960s, one of the most widely held beliefs in corrections management has been, and still is to a great extent, that the best way to protect society is to 'rehabilitate' the offender ... It makes the assumption that correctional practitioners are able to change or modify the personality which further assumes that criminal behaviour is somehow an expression of some underlying personality disturbance which requires extensive therapy and treatment before the criminal behaviour ceases. As a correctional goal, these claims have been challenged as being unrealistic, unsubstantiated and unattainable. The concept of rehabilitation has raised unrealistic expectations of altering criminal behaviour ... The approach gives correctional practitioners a strong inducement to employ coercion in the guise of humane treatment, and to enforce participation in treatment programs as a requisite to release ... Resulting distrust among offenders of the institutional treatment program further undermines the possibility of effecting fundamental behavioural change.[57]

The assumption that as a result of such subtle manipulations of the correctional environment as the provision or withholding of a television set, or permitting association every night in a small common room as opposed to every other night, the most dangerous prisoners will become non-dangerous, is as 'unrealistic, unsubstantiated and unattainable' as any that have been made about the rehabilitative ideal.

Nor is the behaviouralist underpinning of the SHU any more attainable when conceived not in terms of rehabilitation but rather in terms of inducing a conditioned response of submission to and compliance with authority. Few prisoners who find themselves in segregation (and particularly not men like Jack McCann, Andy Bruce, and Edgar Roussel) will, without resistance, abandon the struggle for individuality, for the assertion of their distinctive personalities, and concede that they are merely puppets in the latest act in the repertoire of the 'grand theatre' of carceral authority.

It is important to understand the implications of my position that the behavioural-modification basis for segregation units must be abandoned as illegitimate. As I have made clear, this position does not in any way entail the rejection of the various programs which the Vantour-McReynolds Report recommended as part of the segregation regime. It does, however, entail rejection of the Vantour-McReynolds rationale for making these programs available. As I have pointed out, that rationale was to provide opportunities for the prisoners to demonstrate 'meaningful behavioural change' and for authorities to assess the behavioural interaction of prisoners in order to determine the rate of their progression through the phases and their ultimate release. In my view, the principal justification for permitting segregated prisoners the rights and privileges of normal visitation, correspondence, library, work, and educational programs is that they are essential components of a prison regime which, consistent with carrying out the sentence of the court, should reduce the inherently debilitating effects of imprisonment by adopting the least restrictive means of confinement. The segregation regime is not 'beyond the ken' of this correctional mandate. I hope I have demonstrated that present carceral practices relating to segregation are not the least restrictive means we have available to us and that these practices, far from reducing, intensify the most debilitating features of imprisonment.

I have already described how the implementation of the special handling unit concept in 1977 was, together with the introduction of life sentences for murder with minimum terms of up to twenty-five years, part of the political trade-off for the abolition of the death penalty. The federal government has not pursued its original intention of using the units for the incarceration of all these sentenced to twenty-five years for first-degree murder; instead attention has been focused on the dangerous prisoner who poses a serious threat of violence within prison walls. There remains, however, a close relationship between the SHUs and the draconian sentences with which they were linked politically. Professor Normandeau of the School of Criminology at the University of Montreal commented in 1976 that the legislation introducing the mandatory twenty-five year sentences 'is tantamount ... to inventing a new death penalty in disguise which, this time, would threaten the penitentiary personnel as much as the murderers ... Thus we shall probably see a series of blackmailings, riots, hunger strikes, sabotages, hostage-takings, grievous assaults, murders and escapes.'[58]

Professor Normandeau's prediction is already coming to pass. The day before my first visit to the CDC in May 1980 an escape attempt and a hostage-taking occurred in Laval Institution. One prisoner was shot. Eight of the nine prisoners involved were serving twenty-five-year minimum sentences. It should not be surprising that prisoners who are subjected to these sentences are figuring disproportionately in acts of institutional violence. The penitentiary was never conceived as a place for imprisonment for twenty-five years. Prior to 1850, sentences in excess of five years were rare. Lord John Russell expressed the view in 1837 that ten years in prison would be a 'punishment worse than death.'[59] How do Canadian prisoners in 1983 view twenty-five years in prison? Edgar Roussel, who is serving such a sentence, told the solicitor-general in an open letter written from the CDC, 'they have tried to hide the smell of death, though unsuccessfully, by imposing mandatory sentences instead of capital punishment. The rope is longer and the feeling of suffocation isn't quite as apparent, but the results are the same, death!'[60]

Another prisoner I interviewed in the SHU at Millhaven described how he saw his life in the face of a twenty-five year sentence in these chilling terms: 'It is really quite simple. I will escape or I will die trying.' For men whose experience has been characterized by violence to come to see life as time without hope save that of escape is fraught with the prospect of further violence. Under the present policies the institutional response to such violence will be a two-year stint in SHU. But this prospect must fail as a deterrent in the face of a twenty-five year sentence. The prison authorities will then be pressured to escalate the length and rigours of the regime. This will inexorably push the SHU regime backward to (and perhaps beyond) the regime condemned in *McCann*, to the point highlighted by Dr Korn where the effects of the repressive measures taken against the prisoners are such that they can never be let out of their cages.[61] Unless the most serious reconsideration is given to the legitimacy of the two political pillars of abolition, the SHU and the twenty-five-year minimum sentences, I fear the Canadian pententiary system is indeed heading backward toward Jack McCann's 'gates of hell.' The doubling of the length of a prisoner's stay in SHU, introduced in 1980 as part of the 'dangerous inmate policy,' is an ominous road sign in this regression. Others have urged the abandonment of the twenty-five-year minimum sentences;[62] I urge the closing of the SHUs.

There is a further and related reason for closure of these units. Their establishment as repositories for dangerous prisoners is the leading edge of a strategy of segregation characterized by an escalation in the number of prisoners being defined as 'dangerous' and the proliferation of institutions for their control. This has already happened in some jurisdictions in the United States. Sheldon Messinger, in his study of 'the strategies of control' developed in the California prison system, describes how one 'adjustment center' eventually spawned its own segregation unit to deal with the most recalcitrant prisoners.[63] Cohen and Taylor, commenting on the California experience, predicted in 1972 that 'the "complicated Chinese box effect" which resulted "with inmates in the innermost box ideally required to traverse each enclosing one on the way to relative freedom" is, we believe, precisely the way the English penal system is evolving.'[64]

In 1974 the English prison authorities, having established in the 1960s 'maximum-security wings' in three prisons for dangerous prisoners, opened the 'control unit' at Wakefield Prison for the most disruptive prisoners. As I have described earlier, the control unit was short-lived; after only a year in operation and in the midst of public criticism it was closed. However, Cohen and Taylor's prediction of the evolution of the penal system is still an accurate reflection of the situation in Canada.

In 1977 Canada established its two SHUs and defined the dangerous prisoners who would be imprisoned in them. In 1980 that definition was expanded; as a result there has been a dramatic increase in the numbers of such prisoners. In August 1980, when I first visited the SHUs, their combined population was fifty-one. By the time of my third visit in May 1982, in the wake of the expanded definition of 'dangerousness' introduced by CD 274 in December 1980, the number had jumped to 125. In 1981 alone ninety-nine prisoners were approved for transfer to SHU by the National Review Committee.[65] The solicitor-general has recently announced plans for the building of three new SHUs, two of which are said to be replacements for the Millhaven and the CDC units. However, the pressure that is likely to be brought to bear on the system by the growing number of prisoners serving twenty-five years, together with the expanding definition of dangerousness, suggests to me that if these new units are built they will supplement rather than replace the old ones.[66] The way will then be paved for Foucault's 'carceral continuum' to include a hierarchy of SHUs to correspond with a perceived hierarchy of dangerousness, each stage in the hierarchy being characterized by regimes which regressively will, in the words of Professor Norval Morris, 'read like the design of the inner circles of hell.'[67] Canadian prisoners have already experienced such regimes. Jack McCann brought his action in order to put an end to them. As I have tried to demonstrate, they have not ended. Allowing the SHUs to remain on the carceral archipelago will ensure the continuation not only of the dehumanizing regimes that presently exist in Millhaven and the CDC but also of future regimes which, in tightening the web of control over the lives of the men subjected to them, will give new and terrifying meaning to 'cruel and unusual punishment.'

7
The Case for Entrenchment of Prisoners' Rights

In the earlier chapters of this book, I have shown how the prison reformers who introduced the penitentiary into the lexicon of punishment saw the need for rules to check the virtually unfettered discretion of the authorities, which they regarded as lying at the core of the abuses of the old system of imprisonment. The rules were designed as much to bind the keeper as they were to discipline the kept. I have shown how the system of solitary confinement, which, like the system of rules, was integrally associated with a reform movement designed to change the nature of the prison and the men within it for the better, has become the most abused and abusive part of modern corrections. I have shown how its exercise has become devoid of any rules limiting the power of the correctional authorities in its invocation and application. From a historical perspective it is clear that the Parliamentary Subcommittee on the Penitentiary System in Canada, in its 1977 demand that 'justice be recognized as an essential condition of corrections,' was restating a principle that had been propounded as an essential element of penitentiary discipline by the Brown Commission in 1850 and reiterated by Inspector Moylan throughout his long tenure as inspector of prisons. The principle has failed to inform the practices surrounding the penitentiary's ultimate power over prisoners. The parliamentary subcommittee recommended that there be 'clear rules, fair disciplinary procedures and the providing of reasons for all decisions affecting inmates' to replace 'the arbitrariness traditionally associated with prison life.'[1] To ensure the enforceability of the justice principle, they further recommended that the rules and procedures affecting prisoners be consolidated into a consistent code of regulations having the force of law. For this reason I propose that the Segregation Code I have set out should be embodied in regulations and not merely in commissioner's directives. Once this has been done the legal profession and the courts will play a vital role in seeing that the code is enforced as a necessary continuum of the criminal justice system. Under the code the task of ensuring 'that the system is definitive in its commitment, clear in its intentions and effective in its prescription'[2] will fall primarily upon lawyers in their representation of prisoners at hearings before the independent chairperson. That representation will involve the development of arguments on the meaning and application of the code's criteria and procedures, which inevitably will have penumbras of uncertainty at their edges. The role of the courts will be much more focused than it is under the existing law. The code provisions rather than court decisions will identify what fairness requires both in a substantive and in a procedural sense. The role of the courts will be to review rulings by the independent chairperson on issues of interpretation of the code and to consider cases involving allegations that the code provisions have been violated. In the words of the subcommittee, 'the nature of the task ... to be done by the courts in ensuring that the Rule of Law prevails within penitentiaries should not be disproportionate to what they do outside prison walls on an ongoing basis.'[3]

The model of reform I have advocated, while recognizing the important role to be played in certain cases by negotiation between prisoners, prison staff, and prison administration, clearly relies upon legal rules and due process of law to control the exercise of power. Some readers may wonder how, having shown how little effect the *McCann* case has had on subsequent practices of segregation, I can have any confidence that the Segregation Code, attended by its greater intrusion of the law and lawyers, will change what actually happens within the walls. As Richard Ericson has pointed out, 'it is a common feature of bureaucratic organizations that rules intended to influence the actions of agents are routinely absorbed by the agents to conform with their existing practices.'[4] In the exercise of state power outside the walls, in matters such as police powers of arrest and search, the legal and criminological literature has documented that, despite the existence of legal limitations on these powers and the development of rules to ensure respect for individual rights, there exists a great distance between the law in the law books and the practice in the police station. Thus, 'efforts to develop rules relating to the right of the accused to silence while in police custody are absorbed and made useful to the police; efforts to review and control police search practices have no effect but to legitimate what the police wish to do.'[5] Why should it be any different with the Segregation Code? Will the code with its reliance on legalism be nothing more than a veil leading people to 'mistake due process for substantive relief from tyranny?'[6]

These are important questions. To answer them it is necessary to consider how the criminal-justice system outside the prison seeks to reconcile the tension between the exercise of coercive state power and the need to protect the individual against its abuse. Herbert Packer has argued that this reconciliation is sought through the interaction of two competing models of the criminal process,[7] the due process model and the crime-control model. These two models represent separate value systems that compete for priority in the operation of the criminal process. The due process model emphasizes adherence to legal rules and reliance upon formal, adversarial, and reviewable adjudicative processes. It gives a high profile to the role of the lawyer in invoking the rules designed to limit state power and protect the rights of the accused. The crime-control model, by contrast, emphasizes speedy, informal resolution of cases and has its centre of gravity in the early administrative fact-finding stages. Accordingly, it gives a high profile to the role of the police and their ability to investigate crime with minimal interference. One model sees its media mirror image in 'Perry Mason,' the other in 'Hill Street Blues.'

The thrust of much of recent criminological research is that the criminal-justice system in operation in Canada and the United States leans toward the crime-control model, particularly in the lower criminal courts where the great majority of cases are resolved.[8] The typical case is disposed of by a guilty plea negotiated between defence counsel and the prosecutor or the police or both. Defence counsel do not typically see themselves as defenders of liberty and protectors of freedom, but as professionals involved in what Richard Ericson calls the 'ordering of justice.' They usually have 'one-shot' relationships with their clients, and recurring relationships with other professionals in the system – prosecutors, detectives, and probation officers. Because of overburdened court dockets and underfinanced legal aid tariffs, there are strong institutional pressures to process rather than litigate cases and professional pressures to compromise and reach agreement on what is a just and justifable outcome.[9] The accused, who is usually dependent on his lawyer for information about the range of options and possibilities for compromise, may have good reason to agree to a guilty plea rather than go to trial. Doing so may mean spending less time awaiting trial in the appalling conditions that exist in most jails; it may result in a less severe sentence than would otherwise be imposed if he went to trial and was found guilty.

The Segregation Code, in its reliance on specific rules and a hearing process that gives the prisoner the right to counsel and the right to challenge the institution's case, accords with the due process model of criminal justice. Will the right to a hearing become in practice little more than the negotiated acceptance of segregation under the guiding hand of counsel in the service of the crime-control model? I believe there is good reason to think not. While there may be some cases in which prisoners do not contest the factual allegations used by the prison administration to justify segregation (for example, where a prisoner is caught in the act of trying to escape), judging by my experiences with prisoners in the British Columbia Penitentiary and Kent, it seems likely that the institution's allegations will be challenged in a high percentage of cases. But apart from any dispute about the facts, there still remains the issue of whether the facts justify segregation under the criteria set out in the code, and if so how long such segregation should last. Prisoners in maximum security, faced with the severest sanction the prison administration can impose, will not submit to its imposition without protest. There are no compelling reasons for the prisoner to waive his right to protest. He will already be in segregation at the time of his hearing before the independent chairperson. There is nothing to be gained by willingly submitting to further segregation. Prisoners, who are more knowledgeable about the nature of the prison decision-making process than the typical accused in the criminal process, will not easily defer to a lawyer's view of a just and justifiable result.

It will be crucial to the successful implementation of the Segregation Code that lawyers respect their clients' assessments of the severity of the segregation sanction and the legitimacy of their wish to challenge its imposition. Because the code seeks to change the rules under which the prison has traditionally operated, it is vital that the prison administration be compelled to justify its actions within the context of the new rules. The systematic questioning of the administration's authority is fundamental to the operation of the code as a control on the abuse of that authority. Such questioning is most likely to come from the young lawyers and law students upon whom the weight of prison legal work is likely to fall. That is not to say that it should be their burden alone.

In this analysis I have been concerned with a single cluster of issues surrounding the penitentiary's ultimate power. Many other issues require a similar analysis. The Segregation Code is but one part of a prisoners' rights code that is necessary to bring corrections into the mainstream of the criminal-justice system. For this to happen in the area of segregation, or in any other area, it will be necessary for the legal profession as well as the courts to rise to the challenge that is thrown up to them. Let us be quite clear about this. Prison work is neither glamorous nor profitable. To ensure that the role of lawyers becomes entrenched in the administration of prison justice, law schools, law societies, and the legal aid authorities must understand both the history of the challenge and the implications of its rejection. John Howard and his Canadian successors understood clearly that only through rules and the vigilance of outside inspection would penitentiaries fulfil their purpose of legitimizing the pain of imprisonment. The stark record - and the evidence of Jack McCann and his brothers in solitary is as critical to our understanding of present carceral practices as John Howard's writings are to those of the eighteenth century

- leads ineluctably to the conclusion that the rules themselves must have the legitimacy of law, and the inspection process must have the commitment of the legal profession and the courts. Inscribed in stone over the entrance to the law school at which I teach are the words 'Let Justice Be Done Though the Heavens Fall.' Doing time in one of Canada's maximum-security penitentiaries is about as far removed from the heavens as can be conceived. It is, as the parliamentary subcommittee condemned it, 'the most individually destructive, psychologically crippling and socially alienating experience that could conceivably exist within the borders of the country.'[10] If Canadians are prepared to take the motto outside the law school seriously, and if this book has done its job of demonstrating the motto's critical relevance inside the prison walls, we might begin to stop the crippling and destruction of prisoners' lives. The screams in the night might begin to recede from our collective memory.

Appendix
Model Segregation Code*

1 The warden, or in his absence, the officer in charge of the institution, may segregate a prisoner

a pending the investigation of allegations which, on reasonable and probable grounds, implicate the prisoner in
  (i) attempted escape;
  (ii) possession of dangerous contraband;†
  (iii) actual or threatened violence to another person or incitement to violence of other prisoners;
  (iv) wilful destruction of property where there is a substantial likelihood that the destruction will be continued;
  (v) refusal to obey the lawful order of an institutional officer where there is a substantial likelihood that the refusal will be repeated and will lead to widespread disobedience by other prisoners; or

b pending the investigation of an alleged disciplinary or criminal offence where there is a substantial likelihood that the prisoner will intimidate potential witnesses to the offence.

2 Where disciplinary or criminal charges have been laid against a prisoner, the warden may segregate that prisoner where

a the offence if proved will lead to an increased security rating of the prisoner, requiring his transfer to another institution or part of that institution; or

b the offence involves actual or threatened violence to another person or incitement to violence of other prisoners and there is a substantial likelihood that;
  (i) the offence will be continued or repeated; or

* This code does not deal with protective-custody segregation or with punitive segregation imposed as a sanction after conviction of a disciplinary offence.

† Dangerous contraband is contraband which, by its nature, is likely to endanger life or cause serious bodily harm.

(ii) there will be violent reprisals by other prisoners; or

c the offence involves wilful destruction of property and there is a substantial likelihood that the destruction will be continued; or

d the offence involves the refusal to obey the lawful order of an institutional officer and there is a substantial likelihood that the refusal will be continued and will lead to widespread disobedience by other prisoners; or

e the prisoner, at the time of being charged with an offence, reacts in a violent or uncontrolled manner.

A prisoner detained under subsection (e) shall be released from segregation as soon as he has ceased to act violently and has regained control.

3 The warden may segregate a prisoner, notwithstanding that disciplinary or criminal charges have not been laid, where there are grounds to believe beyond a reasonable doubt that the prisoner has committed, attempted to commit, or plans to commit acts which represent a serious and immediate threat to the physical security of the institution or the personal safety of staff or prisoners.

4 Segregation shall in all cases be authorized by written order signed by the warden or officer in charge.

5 Within twenty-four hours of a segregation order the prisoner shall be given a copy of such order which shall set forth

a the relevant subsection(s) of sections 1 to 3 under which segregation has been ordered; and

b a summary of the facts upon which the segregation order has been made.

6 Where the order is made by the officer in charge, the warden, upon his return to the institution, shall review the order and either affirm the order in writing or issue a further order directing that the prisoner be released from segregation. A copy of any such order shall be given to the prisoner forthwith.

7 Where the warden deems it necessary to continue segregation beyond seventy-two hours, he shall refer the case to an independent hearing officer for a hearing. The reference shall include

a particulars of the circumstances of the case which are relied upon to justify continued segregation;

b a statement of whether an application will be made for the presentation of confidential evidence in the absence of the prisoner.

8 A copy of the reference shall be given to the prisoner at least 24 hours prior to the hearing.

9 Where a reference has been made pursuant to section 7, the hearing officer shall convene a hearing not later than seventy-two hours from the time of first segregation to determine whether such segregation shall be continued. The hearing shall be carried out in the following manner:

a Where an application is made by the warden to present confidential evidence, the hearing officer shall determine this issue in the absence of the prisoner. In making this determination there shall be a presumption in favour of disclosure which may be rebutted by substantial evidence that disclosure will endanger another person or the physical security of the institution.

b Where the hearing officer determines that all or part of the confidential evidence may be presented in the absence of the prisoner he shall summarize the evidence for the prisoner.

c Subject to subsections (a) and (b), all evidence shall be given in the presence of the prisoner.

d The prisoner may testify on his own behalf, cross-examine witnesses, introduce relevant documents, and call witnesses who can give relevant evidence on his behalf.

e Every prisoner who testifies at a hearing shall be advised of his rights pursuant to section 5 of the Canada Evidence Act and section 13 of the Charter of Rights and Freedoms.

f A prisoner may have the assistance of a representative of his own choosing at the hearing. The representative may be a lawyer, a law student, member of the staff, or fellow prisoner whom the prisoner selects and who agrees to represent the prisoner at the hearing. The hearing officer may appoint a representative to act on behalf of the prisoner where he deems it appropriate and where the prisoner consents.

g The warden of the institution may appoint a representative to present the institution's case for segregation.

h The hearing officer shall consider any evidence presented on the issue of prejudice to the prisoner caused by being segregated in relation to the preparation and presentation of his defence of outstanding charges.

10 The hearing officer shall determine whether there are grounds for continued segregation in light of the criteria and standard of proof set out in sections 1–3 and shall order either that segregation be continued or that the prisoner be returned to the population. The order shall contain

a a summary of the evidence; and
b reasons for the decision.

A copy of the order shall be given to the prisoner forthwith.

11 Where, under section 10, an order is made that a prisoner be continued in segregation, a review of that decision shall be carried out every seven days before the hearing officer. The review hearing shall be carried out in accordance with the provisions of section 10 and with the following provisions:

- **a** The warden shall present evidence of the plan, if any, which has been proposed for the reintegration of the prisoner into the population.
- **b** The prisoner may make representations as to the proposed plan and any alternative plan for such reintegration.
- **c** Where the Inmate Committee has given written notification to the hearing officer, a representative of the committee may make representations on the proposed plan(s) or on any alternative plan(s).

12 After each review the hearing officer shall determine whether there are grounds for continued segregation and shall order either that segregation be continued or that the prisoner be released into the population. The order shall contain

- **a** a summary of the evidence presented at the review including the plan(s) for reintegration and the steps which have been taken to implement the plan(s); and
- **b** reasons for the decision.

13 **a** Where segregation has been ordered under section 1, the hearing officer shall order the prisoner released into the population after fourteen days unless evidence is presented demonstrating that
  - (i) the investigating authorities have exercised all due diligence in pursuing their investigations; and
  - (ii) further time is necessary to complete these investigations.
- **b** Where the necessary evidence set forth in subsection (a)(i) and (ii) has been provided and subject to subsections (c) and (d) the hearing officer shall order the prisoner released into the population after thirty days.
- **c** Where the investigation arises from an incident involving a large number of prisoners, segregation beyond thirty days may be authorized upon the presentation of evidence demonstrating that owing to the nature and extent of the investigations further time is necessary to complete those investigations.
- **d** In any application for segregation pending investigation of charges beyond fourteen days under subsection (a) or beyond thirty days under subsection (c), the hearing officer shall not authorize further segregation unless the allegations under investigation implicate the prisoner in an offence within subsections 2(a)–(d) of this code.

14 Segregated prisoners shall be afforded the same rights and privileges as general population prisoners in respect to

a visiting and correspondence with and telephone calls to persons or agencies outside of the institution;
b personal effects;
c clothing, bedding, and linen and exchange thereof;
d personal hygiene, including opportunities to shave and shower;
e canteen;
f borrowing from the institutional library and receiving reading material from outside the institution;
g access to legal materials and legal services.

15 a Segregated prisoners shall be afforded access to programs and services that include but are not limited to education, work, counselling, social services, religious services, hobbies, and recreation.
b The programs and services referred to in subsection (a) may be provided on a group or individual basis consistent with the physical security of the institution and the safety of prisoners and staff.

16 Segregated prisoners shall be permitted out of their cells to participate in the programs, services, and activities referred to in subsections 14 and 15 for no less than six hours per day, which shall include not less than one hour of outside exercise.

17 a A prisoner in segregation may be deprived of any usually authorized item or usually authorized activity where there is imminent danger that the prisoner will destroy that item or induce self-injury or injury to another person. In such cases, every effort should be made to supply a substitute for the item or to permit the prisoner to use the item under the supervision of a staff member. No item or activity should be withheld longer than is necessary to ensure the prisoner's safety or the safety of the staff and other prisoners.
b Where the preventive action authorized in subsection (a) has been taken, a report of the action shall be made to the warden forthwith.
c No such preventive action shall be continued for more than seventy-two hours without the written order of an independent hearing officer who shall satisfy himself that further deprivation is necessary, having regard to subsection (a). Before making such an order the hearing officer shall convene a hearing and receive representations from both the prisoner and the institution as to the necessity for the continued deprivation. Where the hearing officer determines that such deprivation shall continue, he may order the provision of a substitute item or give directions for the use of the item under supervision. Any such order shall remain in force for not more than seventy-two hours. Subject to compliance with the hearing provisions

of this subsection, further orders limited in duration to seventy-two hours may be made.

18 a Subject to subsection (c), where application is made to continue segregation beyond thirty days the hearing officer shall hear the evidence of two experts, who shall be psychiatrists or psychologists, on the effects of such continued segregation on the prisoner.

b One of the experts shall be nominated by the warden and the other by the prisoner.

c In any case in which the warden and the prisoner nominate the same expert, the hearing officer need not consider the evidence of a second expert.

d Where, based upon the expert evidence or upon other evidence, the hearing officer determines that continued segregation will cause the prisoner substantial psychological or physical harm, he shall order the prisoner released into the general population.

19 a Where, at a hearing carried out pursuant to the provisions of sections 9 or 11, evidence is presented that there has been a violation of the provisions of sections 14, 15, or 16, the hearing officer, after giving the warden an opportunity to present evidence on the matter, shall make a written determination on whether there has been any violation, and if so its nature and extent.

b Where the hearing officer determines that there has been a violation, he may issue written directions to the warden to remedy the violation.

c Where, at a further hearing carried out under section 11 there is evidence that the directions issued pursuant to subsection (b) have not been complied with, the hearing officer

(i) shall prepare a report detailing the nature and extent of the violation, the directions issued, and the circumstances of non-compliance, a copy of which shall be provided to both the warden and the prisoner and transmitted to the solicitor-general; and

(ii) may order the prisoner released from segregation.

20 No segregation shall be continued for more than ninety days unless during this period the prisoner commits further acts which under sections 1–3 justify further segregation. Any further period of segregation shall also be subject to a ninety day limitation.

Notes

INTRODUCTION

1 Michel Foucault, *Discipline and Punish: The Birth of the Prison* (New York: Pantheon 1977), 256.
2 Michael Jackson, 'Justice behind the Walls – A Study of the Disciplinary Process in a Canadian Penitentiary,' 12 *Osgoode Hall Law Journal* 1 (1974) at 103.
3 Statement of Tommy Smith, 1981.
4 *The Philanthropist* 2 (1812), 2.
5 (1976) 29 CCC (2d) 377.
6 R.R. Price, 'Doing Justice to Corrections, Prisoners, Parolees and the Canadian Courts,' 3 *Queen's Law Journal* 214 (1977) at 279.

1 SOLITARY CONFINEMENT AND THE RISE OF THE PENITENTIARY

1 Michael Ignatieff, *A Just Measure of Pain: The Penitentiary in the Industrial Revolution 1705–1850* (New York: Pantheon 1978), (cited hereafter as 'Ignatieff'). 15
2 The categories of crime, particularly crime subject to summary justice, underwent a rapid expansion in the eighteenth century as a result of what historians have described as an 'attempt to criminalize the customs of the poor in the name of work discipline' and 'the aggrandizement of the property rights of the gentry at the expense of common right and custom' (ibid., chap. 2). Douglas Hay, in an essay reviewing recent historical studies concerned with crime during the English industrial revolution, provides this description of the process: 'The aristocracy, gentry and prosperous middle class ... were bent on a remaking of the English economy and of English society. In the process they enclosed ancient common lands by parliamentary act, destroying a whole corpus of local customary law. They sharpened prosecutions for poaching, although taking game was popularly believed to be a right.

They redefined certain customary parts of the wage as theft, suppressed popular amusements as threats to order and productivity ...' Douglas Hay, 'Crime and Justice in Eighteenth- and Nineteenth-Century England,' in *Crime and Justice: An Annual Review of Research*, vol. 2, ed. Norval Morris and Michael Tonry (Chicago: University of Chicago Press 1980), 46–7. See also E.P. Thompson, *Whigs and Hunters: The Origins of the Black Act* (London, Allen Lane 1975), and Douglas Hay, Peter Linebaugh, John G. Rule, E.P. Thompson, and Cal Winslow, *Albion's Fatal Tree: Crime and Society in Eighteenth-Century England* (London: Allen Lane 1975).

3 Ignatieff, 28.

4 Ibid., 30.

5 Ibid., 30–1.

6 See Torsten Eriksson, *The Reformers, An Historical Survey of Pioneer Experiments in the Treatment of Criminals* (New York: Elsevier 1976), hereafter cited as 'Eriksson'. The idea of an institution that would 'provide a universal pedagogy of work for those who had proved to be resistant to it' (Foucault, *Discipline and Punish*, 121) was further refined in Europe, particularly in the eighteenth century. The Maison de Force at Ghent, conceived by Philippe Vilain, a Flemish politician, became one of the models for reform of the English system (see Eriksson, chap. 4). The relationship between confinement and economics is not a casual one. 'Historians have speculated that confinement had its greatest vogue in times of high unemployment, expanding population, rising prices and falling wages. In such periods confinement had the effect of withdrawing labour from the already overstocked market and putting it to the use of the state': Ignatieff, 12. The most important work in this area is George Rusche and Otto Kirckheimer, *Punishment and Social Structure* (New York: Columbia University Press 1939). This book has stimulated much of the recent scholarship analysing crime and punishment from a Marxist perspective. For an excellent collection of some of this work, including a review of Rusche and Kirckheimer's contribution, see Tony Platt and Paul Takagi, 'Punishment and Penal Discipline,' in *Essays on the Prison and the Prisoners' Movement* (Berkeley: Crime and Social Justice Associates 1980).

7 Ignatieff, 33.

8 Ibid., 34.

9 Ibid., 35.

10 Ibid., 36.

11 See, for example, Gresham Sykes, *The Society of Captives* (Princeton: Princeton University Press 1958); Donald Cressey, *The Prison: Studies in Institutional Organization and Change* (New York: Holt, Rinehart and Winston 1961).

12 Since most poor prisoners had to conduct their own defence and cross-examine witnesses themselves, the 'mock tryals' of the prison subculture were the only form of 'legal aid' they were likely to get: Ignatieff, 40.
13 Ibid., 41.
14 Ibid. 42.
15 Ibid., 45.
16 Henry Fielding, *A Proposal for Making Effectual Provision for the Poor* (1753), 153–4.
17 John Howard, *The State of the Prisons in England and Wales* (London: J.M. Dent 1929; first published in 1777).
18 For further details of the Silenium at San Michele and the Octagon in Ghent see Eriksson, chaps. 4 and 5.
19 Ignatieff, 61.
20 Ibid., 61–2. There was a third component of this moral assault on the poor. Like the hospital and prison reformers, the initiators of the factory system of scientific management rationalized their disciplines of industrial labour as an attempt to reform the morals of their workers. Josiah Wedgwood, the pottery magnate from North Staffordshire, claimed that the drunkenness, sloppy workmanship, idleness, and violence of the potteries had been stamped out in his industrial fiefdom; the punch-clock, the fines, and his own intense and unremitting supervision had transformed the workers and 'made machines of the men as cannot err' (ibid., 63).
21 Ibid., 72.
22 John Howard, *An Account of the Principal Lazarettos of Europe* (London: W. Eyres 1789), 222.
23 Jeremy Bentham, *Rationale of Punishment* (1830), 21.
24 Howard, *State of the Prisons*, 39–40.
25 John Brewster, *On the Prevention of Crimes* (1792), 4.
26 Ignatieff, 77.
27 Jeremy Bentham, *The Panopticon* (1791), reproduced in *The Works of Jeremy Bentham*, vol. 4, ed. John Bowering (Edinburgh: William Tait 1838–43), 37–172.
28 Ignatieff, 78.
29 Jones Hanway, *Solitude in Imprisonment* (1776), 141.
30 Brewster, *Prevention of Crimes*, 27.
31 Ignatieff, 78.
32 (1779) Geo. III, c. 4.
33 William Blackstone, *Commentaries on the Laws of England*, vol. 4 (Oxford: Clarenden Press 1813) 437.
34 Ignatieff, 84.
35 Ibid., 102.

36 Howard, *Lazarettos*, 169.
37 While the Gloucester experiment is often cited as the major step in the implementation of the prison reform process, it is important to note that the construction of the new prisons in Gloucester and in the other counties had a dark underside; they led to the more systematic pursuit of minor offenders. 'Women with illegitimate children, agricultural labourers who stole turnips, weavers who embezzled their masters' yarn, apprentices who absconded – these were the chief objects of the new strategy of summary justice that Gloucestershire's new prison made possible. Whatever reformative purposes Paul had in mind for them, these prisons in fact continued to carry out the old functions of the law, but with a new vigour – penalizing the passage from labour into crime, and enforcing the authority of landlords, masters, and parish officials': Ignatieff, 109.
38 Ibid., 122.
39 Gloucester Record Office, document 2545-1-9, cited in Ignatieff, 124.
40 Gilbert Wakefield, *Memoirs of the Life of Gilbert Wakefield*, vol. 2 (1804), 270–1.
41 London Correspondence Society, *Moral and Political Magazine* 2 (January 1797), 26.
42 *Hansard* 35, 22 July 1800, col. 463–7.
43 Negley K. Teeters, *They Were in Prison* (Philadelphia: Winston 1937), 440 et seq.
44 Negley K. Teeters, *The Cradle of the Penitentiary* (Philadelphia: Temple University 1955), 40.
45 Eriksson, 49.
46 Ibid., chap. 8; Orlando F. Lewis, *The Development of American Prisons and Prison Customs 1776–1845 with Special Reference to Early Institutions in the State of New York* (Montclair, NJ: P. Smith 1967), 77–106.
47 Eriksson, chap. 9; Negley K. Teeters and John D. Shearer, *The Prison at Philadelphia Cherry Hill* (New York: Columbia University Press 1957).
48 Fredrick Demetz and Abel Blouet, *Rapports sur les pénitenciers des États-Unis* (Paris: Imprimerie Royale 1837), 35–7.
49 Charles Dickens, *American Notes for General Circulation* (London, Chapman and Hall 1842), 119–20.
50 M. Coindet, *Mémoire sur l'hygiène des condamnés détenus dans la prison pénitentiaire de Genève* (Paris: Guillaumin 1838); L.A. Gosse, *Examen médical et philosophique du système pénitentiare* (Geneva: Ladoret-Ramboz 1837), cited in Eriksson, 75.
51 Eriksson, 75–6.
52 E.C. Wines and Theodore W. Dwight, *Report on the Prisons and Reformatories in the United States and Canada* (Albany: Van Bethuysen 1867), 56.
53 Michel Foucault, *Discipline and Punish: The Birth of the Prison* (New York:

Pantheon 1977), 239.

54 Ibid. For a discussion of the extensive literature on the European debate see Eriksson, 264.

55 Just as the introduction of the penitentiary in the 1780s was part of a larger vision of bringing the poor into a hierarchical web of social control, the intensification of terror, of which the introduction of the rule of silence was but a part, was directed especially at minor delinquency in work-related offences: Ignatieff, 179.

56 Parliamentary Papers 46 (1834), 19, 39.

57 Parliamentary Papers 30, 3d report, Home District (1837-8), 42.

58 Ignatieff, 195-6. In 1848, the period of solitary was reduced to twelve months and finally in 1852 to nine months: U.R.Q. Henriques, 'The Rise and Decline of the Separate System of Prison Discipline,' *Past and Present* 54 (1972).

59 Ignatieff, 11.

60 Ibid., 3-11; see also Peter Laurie, *Killing No Murder, or the Effects of Separate Confinement on the Bodily and Mental Condition of Prisoners in the Government Prisons* (1846); Henry Mayhew, *Criminal Prisons of London* (1861), 113-99.

2 THE EVOLUTION OF PENITENTIARY DISCIPLINE IN CANADA

1 J.M. Beattie, *Attitudes toward Crime and Punishment in Upper Canada 1830-1850: A Documentary Study* (Toronto: University of Toronto Centre of Criminology 1977), hereafter cited as 'Beattie.'

2 Charge to the grand jury at the 1849 Home District Assizes 1849, *British Colonist*, 30 October 1849.

3 Beattie, 12-13.

4 Ibid., 8.

5 *Journal of the House of Assembly* (1831), appendix at 211-12.

6 In their report, the commissioners cited the directors of the Maryland penitentiary who, in commenting on the discipline at Auburn and Sing Sing, stated 'Experience of those prisons has afforded numerous instances of reformation to prove that their discipline combines all the advantages ever expected from the system and is perhaps as perfect as prison discipline can or need be': *Journal of the House of Assembly* (1832-3), appendix at 26. Paralleling the debate in Upper Canada an intensive debate took place in Quebec on the issue of prison reform. In 1834, the House of Assembly of Lower Canada sent two commissioners to the United States, who recommended that imprisonment in Quebec should follow the basic contours of the Philadelphia separate system. However, a committee of the House rejected the recommendations of the commissioners in favour of the Auburn model. The events of

1838 and 1839 resulting in the Act of Union interrupted any implementation of these plans for the penitentiary for Lower Canada. For an excellent account of the early history of prisons in Quebec and the legislative debates in the 1830s see Ghislaine Julien, *Histoire et Évolution des Prisons de Montréal* (Montreal: University of Montreal School of Criminology 1974), and Luc Noppen, 'La Pied-du-Courant à Montréal,' *RACAR* vol. 3, no. 1, 26.

7 An Act to Provide for the Maintenance by the Government of the Provincial Penitentiary, (1834) 4 Will. IV, c. 37.

8 Ibid.

9 'Rules and Regulations made by the Inspectors of the Provincial Penitentiary Respecting its Discipline and Policy,' reprinted in Beattie, 117 et seq.

10 Beattie, 22. Section IX of the rules and regulations provided that 'the mess tables shall be narrow, and the convicts shall be seated at one side only; so that never being placed face to face, they may have no opportunity of exchanging looks or signs.'

11 *First Report of the Commissioners Appointed to Investigate into the Conduct, Discipline, and Management of the Provincial Penitentiary: Journal of the Legislative Assembly* (1849), appendix B.B.B.B.B. Reprinted in Beattie at 152 et seq. Because this appendix is not paginated, further references to the report will be to the extracts reproduced in Beattie.

12 Ibid., 157.

13 Ibid., 158.

14 Ibid.

15 Ibid., 160.

16 Ibid., 155–6. The introduction of the silent system at Coldbath Fields in England had also led to a dramatic increase in the number of punishments inflicted on prisoners.

17 Beattie, 28 and 156.

18 The commissioners' concern with the institutional failure parallels the contemporary public view of the Commission of Inquiry's mandate. Their concern was not just to report on the individual charges against Warden Smith but also to consider the essential issue of the purpose of a penitentiary. In the 1840s it was felt that what happened in the penitentiary was a matter of great public importance, because the penitentiary was seen as the instrument through which a moral and industrial order would be imposed on the hitherto undisciplined poor. See *Brockville Recorder*, November 1846, reprinted in Beattie at 148.

19 *Second Report of the Commissioners Appointed to Investigate into the Conduct, Discipline, and Management of the Provincial Penitentiary: Journal of the Legislative Assembly* (1849), Appendix B.B.B.B.B., reprinted in Beattie at 161–74.

20 Beattie, 31.

21 Ibid.
22 See chap. 1, n. 60.
23 Beattie, 172.
24 Ibid., 166.
25 Ibid., 171.
26 Supra, n. 19.
27 E. Decazes, 'Rapport au roi sur les prisons,' *Le Moniteur*, 11 April 1919. See Michel Foucault, *Discipline and Punish: The Birth of the Prison* (New York: Pantheon 1977), part 4.
28 Edmund F. DuCane, *The Punishment and Prevention of Crime* (London: Macmillan 1885), 56.
29 Lionel W. Fox, *The English Prison and Borstal Systems* (London: Routledge and Kegan Paul 1952), 47.
30 *Report of the Select Committee of the House of Lords on the Present State of Discipline in Jails and Houses of Correction 1863*, reprinted in Fox, *The English Prison*, appendix C.
31 Anthony Babbington, *The English Bastille* (London: Macdonald, 1971), 220.
32 Albert Krebs, 'John Howard's Influence on the Prison Systems of Europe with Special Reference to Germany,' in *Prisons Past and Future*, ed. John Freeman (London: Heinemann 1978), 45–6.
33 An Act for the Better Management of the Provincial Penitentiary (1851) 14 and 15 Vict. c. 2, s. vi.
34 An Act Relating to the Inspectors of Asylums, Prisons and Public Charities (1859) 22 Vict. c. 110. During the latter half of the nineteenth century the Penitentiary Inspectorate played a leading role in the formulation and administration of Canadian penal policy. The annual reports of the inspectorate provide an invaluable commentary on penal developments. The inspectors sought to keep themselves fully informed of comparative experience in Europe and North America, and the reports contain extensive citations from penal literature of the nineteenth century, including the International Prison Congresses which were initiated in the 1870s. The inspectors saw their annual reports as an important vehicle for upholding John Howard's cautionary principle that public scrutiny of prison administration was an essential element in the control of official discretion. In the 1861 annual report, the Inspectors wrote: 'Publicity is the most effective preventative against abuse, as well for eliciting as for propagating information. The community cannot evince a too deep curiosity in prying into the working of all public institutions ... For these reasons, the Annual Reports should be eagerly sought after, scanned and criticized': Province of Canada *Sessional Papers* vol. 4, (1861), SB 24 at 148.
35 W.A. Calder, 'The Federal Penitentiary in Canada, 1867–1899: A Social and Institutional History, PHD dissertation, University of Toronto, 1975, 41. For a

full description of the Crofton system, also known as the 'Irish Progressive System,' see Mary Carpenter, *Reformatory Prison Discipline as Developed by the Rt. Hon. Sir Walter Crofton in the Irish Convict Prisons* (London: Longman, Longman, Green and Longman 1872); the Patterson Smith reprint series in *Criminology, Law Enforcement and Social Problems* (1967); and Torsten Eriksson, *The Reformers: An Historical Survey of Pioneer Experiments in the Treatment of Criminals* (New York: Elsevier, 1976), 91–7. The Crofton System itself was a development of an experimental disciplinary system initiated in the 1840s by Alexander Maconochie, the commandant of the Australian penal colony of Norfolk Island. See Eriksson, 81–8.

36 *Annual Report of the Inspector of Penitentiaries* (1881), xii.

37 The ticket of leave was a licence introduced in the early nineteenth century in British penal colonies to allow the conditional release of convicts who had been transported. it was a precursor of the modern parole system.

38 Province of Canada *Sessional Papers*, vol. 14 (1862), SB 19, at 60–1.

39 Ibid., 61–2.

40 Province of Canada *Sessional Papers*, vol. 5 (1863) SB 66, 102.

41 Ibid.

42 In the late 1850s and the 1860s considerable criticism was voiced in England about the perceived abuses in the system. See Calder, 'The Federal Penitentiary in Canada,' 51.

43 Calder has commented on the reasons for the inspectors' modification of the original Crofton scheme. Although it was largely a matter of economy, 'public pressure for economy in prison matters was as much the product of social attitudes and values as it was a consequence of Canada's economic circumstances. Penitentiary inmates were drawn in great proportion from the lower class. By definition, too, the prisoner was a member of the 'criminal class,' a pariah group in society. The low social status of the convict made it unlikely at best that any large financial investment would be made in the prison system to further the implementation of a system of reformatory convict discipline untried in the Canadian context. By rejecting the Crofton plan's provision of separate institutions in each of the three disciplinary stages, the Canadian Inspectors eliminated the necessity of immense expenditure in the inauguration of the Irish scheme. This eased the acceptance of the new scheme by central Canadian political authorities. Canadian 19th century social policy as a whole is characterized by a "delicate weave of moralism and economy" that was fully operative with respect to prisons': Calder, 'The Federal Penitentiary in Canada,' 52–3.

44 Penitentiary Act (1868) 39 Vict. c. 75, s. 61.

45 Ibid., s. 62.

46 Ibid., s. 31(6).

47 Calder, 'The Federal Penitentiary in Canada,' chap. 5.

48 Ibid.
49 S. 3.
50 Penitentiary Act (1875) 46 Vict. c. 37, s. 11.
51 *First Annual Report of the Inspector of Penitentiaries* (1875), 8.
52 *Annual Report* (1881), viii.
53 *Annual Report* (1879), 9.
54 Ibid.
55 *Annual Report* (1878), 6.
56 *Annual Report* (1889), xii.
57 St Vincent de Paul (Quebec, 1873); Stoney Mountain (Manitoba, 1877); British Columbia Penitentiary (1878); Dorchester (New Brunswick, 1880).
58 *Annual Report* (1878), 7.
59 *Annual Report* (1888), xiii.
60 Ibid.
61 *Annual Report* (1891), iv.
62 Ibid.
63 Ibid., v.
64 *Annual Report* (1892), x.
65 *Annual Report* (1895), 9.
66 'Rules and Regulations Respecting Prisoners of Isolation and the Punishment and Government of Convicts,' 1893.
67 Ibid., s. 4(a-h).
68 S. 4(j).
69 S. 4(k).
70 S. 4(l).
71 Wines and Dwight, in their exhaustive review of prisons in North America, reported that the original Kingston cells were 'the smallest we met with anywhere ... The prisoner's bed fills up the entire width of the cell and he can have no use of his little abode, till he has hung his mattress on the wall': E.C. Wines and Theodore W. Dwight, *Report on the Prisons and Reformatories of the United States and Canada* (Albany: Van Benthuysen 1867), 103.
72 *Annual Report of the Inspector* (1896), 10.
73 Ibid., 'Schedule of Convicts Received into Prison of Isolation.'
74 See *Annual Reports* 1897–1903.
75 *Annual Report* (1897), xiv.
76 *Annual Report* (1901), 10.
77 *Annual Report* (1900), 10.
78 *Annual Report* (1901), 50.
79 *Annual Report* (1913), 41.
80 *Annual Report of the Superintendent of Penitentiaries* (1934), 22.
81 An Act that Provides for the Maintenance and Government of the Provincial Penitentiary (1834) Will. IV, c. 27, s. 27.

82 'Instructions for the Directors of Penitentiaries' (1870), s. 361. Other punishments authorized by the 1870 rules were a diet of bread and water not exceeding nine consecutive meals; hard bed with or without cover, not exceeding six consecutive nights; ball and chain; flogging with the cats; forfeiture of days of remission; shot or weight drill.

83 By contrast, the English Prison Regulations of 1865 limited the period of time which a prisoner could spend in punishment cells for a violation of rules to one month. Regulations for Government of Prisons, s. 58, schedule 1, the Prison Act (1865) 28 and 29 Vict. c. 126. The 1877 act prohibited the warden from ordering any prisoners to be confined in a punishment cell for any term exceeding twenty-four hours. The sentences imposed by the Visiting Committee of Justices were limited to a term not exceeding fourteen days: Prison Act (1877) 40–41 Vict., c. 21, s. 43.

84 Penitentiary Regulations (1898), s. 179. The 1898 regulations added to the previous repertoire of punishments the Oregon boot; shackling the prisoner to the cell-gate during working hours; and the application of water from the hose. The same regulations substituted flogging with a leather paddle for the previous flogging with the cats.

85 *Annual Report* (1892), ix.

86 Penitentiary Regulations (1933), s. 166. The 1933 regulations also abolished the punishments of shackling the prisoner to the cell-gate, the Oregon boot, the ball and chain, and the application of water from the hose.

87 *Annual Report of the Superintendent of Penitentiaries* (1933), 39. (The office of inspector had been changed to superintendent by the Penitentiaries Act of 1918.)

3 SOLITARY CONFINEMENT IN THE AGE OF CORRECTIONS: CRUEL AND UNUSUAL PUNISHMENT

1 Although rehabilitation in the modern penitentiary has been redefined, the original ideology based on the moral conversion of the poor can still be found, particularly in the philosophy of some of the old-style prison wardens. Joseph Ragen, who from 1936 to 1961 was the warden of Stateville, the maximum-security penitentiary in Illinois, defined the function of the modern penitentiary in this way: 'There is much good in the worst of us ... Rehabilitation takes as its major premise the thesis that ignorance is the root of all evil, that if man is equally familiar with right and wrong, he will in the majority of instances choose the former. Most of the men in prison have a corrupted courage. They dare to rebel against an unsupportable environment, but they were mentally and spiritually untrained to prosecute rebellion morally. It has for years been admitted that slums constitute the most insidious social menace known, and the greatest task of the penologist lies in counteracting

the influence of the slums. Something like 90% of all prison populations in this country are recruited from the marginal and submarginal sections of the large cities. The prison authorities must take this chronically underprivileged mass of humanity and place it on the path of morality.' Joseph Ragen and Charles Finstone, *Inside the World's Toughest Prison*, (Springfield: C.C. Thomas 1962), 695. On 15 May 1980 at the official closing ceremonies of the BC Penitentiary, Tom Hall, who from 1961 to 1964 was the warden of the penitentiary and later the first director for the western region of the Canadian Penitentiary Service, echoed Warden Ragen's sentiments in calling for the moral rearmament of penitentiary discipline which would have at its centre the inculcation in prisoners of 'morality, decent behaviour and proper work habits.'

2 See, for example, American Friends Service Committee, *Struggle for Justice: A Report on Crime and Punishment in America* (New York: Hill and Wang 1971).

3 Michael Jackson, 'Justice Behind the Walls,' 12 *Osgoode Hall Law Journal* 1 (1974).

4 Laval Institution (formerly St Vincent de Paul Penitentiary) in Quebec dates back to 1873; Stoney Mountain Penitentiary in Manitoba to 1877; and Dorchester Penitentiary in New Brunswick to 1880.

5 In this area as in many others there is a history to be written on the language of carceral power. Michael Ignatieff provides some information on changes in the language of discipline in the nineteenth century: 'Around the end of the Napoleonic wars, a language of discipline free from familial or animal taming connotations began to make its appearance. The word "cell" replaced the word "apartment," with its association to a household dwelling. Discipline displaced economy. Prison populations, not families, were referred to in official parlance. The metaphors of command also became increasingly military in derivation': Michael Ignatieff, *A Just Measure of Pain: The Penitentiary in the Industrial Revolution 1750–1850* (New York: Pantheon 1978), 190. It is a curious paradox of history that in the twentieth century we are resurrecting some earlier forms of language. Recent developments in the penitentiary have seen the term 'cell block' replaced by 'living-unit.' In the early 1970s the term 'warden' was replaced by 'director.' Recently, the 'directors' reverted to their former selves and are now known as 'wardens.'

6 Penitentiary Service Regulations SOR/62, s. 2.29. Since the 1962 regulations were in force at the time of the *McCann* case, and the section numbers in use at the time have entered the special language of the penitentiary, I will be referring to those numbers. Although the numbers are changed in the 1978 regulations, no alterations have been made to the wording of those sections with which I will be concerned. Section 2.29 of the 1962 Regulations is now reproduced as s. 38, Penitentiary Service Regulation SOR/79-625.

7 Now s. 40 SOR/79–625.
8 For an analysis of the problems of protective custody see Canadian Penitentiary Service, *Report of the Study Group on Protective Custody* (Ottawa: Solicitor-General of Canada 1972); James Vantour, *Report of the Study Group on Dissociation* (Ottawa: Solicitor-General of Canada 1975), chap. 5 (cited hereafter as 'Vantour Report').
9 Document filed 10 August 1973, no. T-3860–73.
10 The choice of lawyers raised an interesting strategy issue. In 1974 several lawyers in Vancouver had shown interest in the prisoner's rights movement as part of a larger concern to extend legal representation to groups who hitherto had gone unrepresented. The lawyers were young, bright, and enthusiastic, but relatively inexperienced in civil litigation before the superior courts. Also interested were several senior members of the bar whose legal practices were primarily commercial civil litigation but who from time to time had undertaken civil rights cases. The advantages of having counsel drawn from the first group was that there would be a strong commitment to and identification with prisoners' rights issues; counsel drawn from the second group would be more likely to gain the ear of a federal court judge and their involvement would lend the case credibility. After discussing the options with Jack McCann, the decision was made to approach a senior member of the Vancouver bar, Bryan Williams, who with one of his partners, Donald Sorochan, agreed to take the case. Both of them demonstrated as great a comitment to a full and vigourous presentation of the issues as could be asked of any lawyer.
11 Filed in the Federal Court of Canada, Trial Division, 4 June 1974, no. T-2343–74.
12 Jack McCann was serving a sentence of eighteen years for armed robbery and escape; Andrew Bruce and Jake Quiring were serving life sentences for murder; Ralph Cochrane was serving a life sentence for armed robbery; Mel Miller was serving fifteen years for robbery and attempted murder; Donald Oag was serving twelve years for manslaughter; and Pat Dudoward was serving eleven years for burglary.
13 Reasons for judgment, Heald J, 29 CCC (2d) 337 (FCTD) at 366, hereafter cited as 'Heald judgment.')
14 RSC 1960, c. 44.
15 S. 2.07 (now s. 17 SOR/79–625) reads: 'Toilet articles and other articles necessary for personal health and cleanliness shall be issued to every inmate.'
16 S. 2.06 (now s. 16 SOR/79–625) reads: 'Every inmate shall be provided, in accordance with directives, with the essential medical and dental care that he requires.'
17 S. 3.05 (revoked in 1972) read: 'Where an inmate is found to be suffering from mental disease he shall be segregated immediately from other inmates and shall be provided with psychiatric treatment appropriate to his condition.'

18 See *Weldon* v. *Neal* (1885) 15 QBD 471; *Becher* v. *Home Office et al.* [1972] 2 All ER 676 (C.A.); Federal Court Rule 334.

19 [1975] FC 272 (FCA).

20 1960–1, c. 53, s. 26.

21 The issue of a prisoner / plaintiff's right to be present during his trial came up again in the case of *Magrath* v. *The Queen* (1978) 38 CCC (2d) (FCTD) where Magrath sought to appear in order to act as his own counsel. The crown again took the position that the court only had jurisdiction to issue a writ of habeas corpus ad testificandum for his attendance as a witness. Because Magrath was required to attend as a witness to present the plaintiff's case, he remained in the court for that period, and then counsel for the crown renewed the objection. Magrath then successfully argued that he would have to be present to hear the defence evidence in the event that it became necessary for him to give reply evidence. At the conclusion of the defence's case (Magrath having decided not to call evidence in reply), counsel for the crown renewed his objection to Magrath's continuing presence. Magrath was returned to the prison and not until Collier J. severely criticized the crown position did the minister instruct the institutional authorities to provide Magrath with a temporary absence pass to enable him to attend court to make his submission. The minister indicated that as a matter of policy in the future prisoners would be entitled to attend court to argue their own cases: see John W. Conroy, *Canadian Prison Law* (Vancouver: Butterworths, 1980), 54.

22 In his reasons for judgment, Heald J stated: 'Generally speaking, I believe and accept the evidence of the plaintiffs as to the conditions suffered by them in SCU at the BC Penitentiary and I also accept their account of the effect of those conditions on them' (368).'

23 The laxity in classification was the subject of critical comment in the Vantour Report, 14.

24 Evidence of Dr Stephen Fox, 22–3.

25 Heald judgment, 347.

26 Ibid., 348.

27 Oag testified that at the time of the killings he had been standing guard over the custody officers who had been taken hostage during the riot, and therefore would have been able to call these officers as defence witnesses. However, Oag's understanding of the plea bargain negotiated between crown and defence lawyers was that the charges of murder against some of the prisoners would be dropped only if all of the prisoners who were thought to be the ringleaders of the riot pleaded guilty to the manslaughter charge.

28 Oag, commissioned evidence. Although this charge is one which the reader may have difficulty believing, a commission of inquiry into the Kingston riot found that this incident did occur: 'We find that on [Wednesday] 10 to 12 custodial officers had been stationed in the southerly portion of P corridor,

each armed with a riot stick ... The officers positioned in P corridor were directed to stand some five feet east of the westerly corridor wall and approximately eight feet apart. We can only conclude that the objective and the result of such positioning of staff was to ensure that no inmate could pass through the corridor out of range of a riot stick. We find that on Wednesday, when the inmates left the buses and proceeded down P corridor, either singly or in pairs, substantial numbers of them were assaulted by officers standing either on the platform or in the corridor. In short, we find that the inmates in the course of admission to the penitentiary were in this way required to run 'the gauntlet.' Our conclusion is founded on the evidence of relatively senior staff members who were present. Such evidence is substantiated in all material particulars by the evidence of inmates heard by the Commission.' J.W. Swackhamer, *Report on the Commission of Inquiry into Certain Disturbances at Kingston Penitentiary during April 1971* (Ottawa: Information Canada 1973), 34. This example of concerted unlawful violence by prison staff in the wake of a riot unfortunately cannot be dismissed as an aberration. In August 1976 in the aftermath of the worst riot in English prison history prisoners at Hull prison in England were subject to systematic beatings, adulteration of their food, and destruction of their personal property. A number of prison officers were charged and after a three-month trial were convicted of conspiracy to assault prisoners and were given suspended prison terms: see J.E. Thomas and Richard Pooley, *The Exploding Prison: Prison Riots and the Case of Hull* (London: Junction Books 1980).

29 Letter from Donald Oag to the author, May 1974. See also Oag, commissioned evidence.

30 See supra, n. 17.

31 Heald judgment, 362.

32 Interview with Andy Bruce, May 1974.

33 Ibid.

34 Evidence of Dr Stephen Fox, 23–4.

35 Heald judgment, 353. A prisoner in solitary in another Canadian penitentiary told the correctional investigator he felt that the nature of the regime in solitary is designed to 'set the prisoner up': '... Not content with forcing men to live in an environment that is already dehumanizing, a total void is created around the inmate in dissociation in order to better destroy him. One can only believe that the administration is deliberately trying to anger him in order to then be able to punish him.' *Annual Report of the Correctional Investigator 1973–1974* (Ottawa: Information Canada 1976), 54. The study group on dissociation, in its summary of the effects of segregation, concluded that 'segregation enhances the inmate's anti-social attitude, and in general, constitutes a self-fulfilling prophecy.' Vantour Report, 24.

36 Notes of evidence.

37 That relationship was projected into the courtroom in *McCann*. As part of the security precautions, each plaintiff, in addition to wearing leg-irons, was handcuffed to a guard in the courtroom.

38 The important purposes served by 'making things happen' is well explained in the statement of a prisoner confined in the security unit of Durham Prison: '[The prisoner] at least proves that things – any form of "things" – can happen, that life is not solely an authoritarian controlled existence of ennui, that one can break out of this, one can "live" and not just exist, perhaps it entails living dangerously, perhaps leading finally to self-destruction but it does offer choice – the choice of existing the existence of non-events or living the life of events, good or bad, which are at least one's own creation.' Stanley Cohen and Laurie Taylor, *Psychological Survival: The Experience of Long Term Imprisonment* (Harmondsworth: Penguin Books 1972), 125.

39 Dr Richard Korn in the course of his evidence elaborated upon the process of escalation of hostility between prisoner and guard: 'One of the most important things that happens to [guards] is a loss of sensitivity to what the prisoners are feeling, particularly in extreme situations, and this loss of sensitivity is absolutely essential to them to do their job ... You can't do that job if you put yourselves in the shoes of the men who are suffering, so the first thing then is insensitivity ... That process happened to me. Another thing happens, and this happens with the most conscientious guard. Here you are, you are stuck there just the way they are. You are doing everything for them, giving them their food, checking on them, and this is your own perspective – I am talking about well-motivated guards and my assumption is that most of the people who come into this field begin at least with a good motivation – and what you get in return is hostility and provocation. You know, as the guard, you didn't do anything to this man, so you begin to think of them as bad people and you begin to react. You begin to react and they react to your reaction. You see, from the inmate's point of view the inmate can't reach the people that he is really angry at, but there is the guard in blue. I can get at him. So you have a process of escalation. The men, in order to fill the time and depressing boredom ... have to effect something. You are not human unless you can make something happen. Well, the way you make things happen ... is to do something unusual to get the guard's attention ... you see there is nothing you are expected to do for yourself in solitary ... In a good isolation unit you can in effect simply be a well-taken-care-of animal. That doesn't work with a human being, so this process takes place. The guards feel unjustly treated, they begin to retaliate in small ways. The inmates react back, and the hostility begins to build.' (Evidence of Dr Korn, 32–4), cited hereafter as 'Korn.') Perhaps the most dramatic evidence of the inherent nature of the relationship between prisoner and guard in a highly coercive environment is a study conducted by Philip Zimbardo. The

researchers studied normal people who volunteered to play the roles of prisoners and guards in a simulated prison situation. Because of the results the researchers had to stop the two-week experiment after only six days. In a simulated prison environment normally non-sadistic people became cruel and sadistic. They threatened, were physically aggressive, used instruments (nightsticks, fire extinguishers, etc.) to keep the prisoners in line, and referred to them in impersonal, anonymous, deprecating ways to reduce their individuality: Craig Haney, Curtis Banks, and Philip Zimbardo, 'Interpersonal Dynamics in a Simulated Prison,' 1 *International Journal of Criminology and Penology* 69 (1973); Philip Zimbardo, 'The Psychology of Imprisonment: Privation, Power and Pathology,' in *Theory and Research in Abnormal Psychology*, ed. David Rosenhan and Perry London (New York: Holt, Rinehart and Winston 1975), 270.

40 A guard at Millhaven informed a parliamentary subcommittee that this practice was part of the technology of surveillance to ensure that a prisoner was alive at night. 'The first time you go by, you look at the configuration of the blanket, because the normal human being moves 16 times a night. On the next trip ... if that individual has not moved, then it is time to take action. So you make a loud kicking on the door. I do not mean you stand back and break the door, enough to wake every inmate on the range. But you do it loud enough to wake him. Because it is such an abnormal thing to be kicking on the door, they mostly wake right up.' (Cited in Gerard McNeil with Sharon Vance, *Cruel and Unusual: The Shocking Reality of Life Behind Bars in Canada* (Toronto: Deneau and Greenberg 1978), 23.

41 The use of tear gas is controlled by CD 714 and the provisions of the Criminal Code, ss. 27 and 32.

42 This diary, as its name implies, kept a record of exceptional occurrences. Its existence was revealed during the pre-trial discovery process.

43 The annual report of the correctional investigator for 1974–5 contains a detailed account of an incident in another institution where tear gas was used to force a man to come out of his cell so that he could be taken to solitary confinement. Gas was used repeatedly, resulting in burns to the outside and inside of the prisoner's ear. See *Annual Report* (1974–1975), 52–6.

44 Letter from Jack McCann, 14 January 1973.

45 Korn, 17.

46 Ibid., 22. In his sociological analysis of Stateville, James Jacobs discusses the nature of traditional authority in maximum-security institutions. He points out that the traditional system 'ultimately depended upon total suppression and total submission.' Many of the actions and decisions of the security staff 'were grounded in the tradition of overwhelming the inmate with their power and authority.' Such a tradition 'compelled decisions that could not be rationalized': James B. Jacobs, *Stateville: The Penitentiary in Mass Society* (Chicago: University of Chicago Press 1977), 95 and 118.

47 Examination for discovery of Mr Fred Leech, assistant director of security, 142–3.
48 'Running score' of Jack McCann, entered as evidence.
49 This disturbance was precipitated in part by the death of a prisoner in SCU.
50 Notes of evidence.
51 Bruce testified that the hostage-taking followed six suicides in SCU in Prince Albert Penitentiary, and was meant to draw attention to the terrible conditions and plight of the prisoners. The only demands made by Bruce and Quiring for the release of the hostages were the improvement of conditions in SCU and transfer to the BC Penitentiary.
52 The 'disposition of outstanding charges' rationale does not explain why, for the first few months of their confinement in SCU after their return from Prince Albert, Bruce and Quiring were permitted to exercise for half an hour per day only on the condition that they wore handcuffs and leg-irons, notwithstanding that during exercise there was no one else on the range with them and that at all times they were covered by an armed guard on the catwalk.
53 *R.* v. *Berrie et al.* (1976) 24 CCC (2d) 66. (BC Prov. Ct.).
54 In *R.* v. *Berrie et al.* Judge Govan stated in the course of his judgment: 'It is ironic that Collins, the guard who wielded the razor, was wearing a beard, as did Cernetic' (68). He also commented, 'Conditions in this maximum security prison border on the primitive and it is remarkable that such conditions and treatment as described by Brown are allowed to continue in this day and age' (ibid.).
55 George Brown had previously attempted to kill himself after an extended period of solitary confinement in the Stoney Mountain Penitentiary. He had been transferred to the Regional Psychiatric Centre in British Columbia for treatment. I had interviewed him in that institution concerning an appeal he wished to initiate. Because the initiation of this appeal was very important to Brown's state of mind and involved some complicated circumstances, I had been told by the director of the institution that he would not be transferred back to the penitentiary until I had completed my interviews with him. However, because of some 'error in communication,' Brown was transferred back to the BC Penitentiary shortly after my conversation with the director. Brown attempted to tell the officers who came to take him back to the penitentiary that he was supposed to stay at the centre, but to no avail. On his entrance to the penitentiary, because of his protests he was immediately placed in solitary confinement, from which three months earlier he had been taken after his suicide attempt. Brown's introduction to the BC Penitentiary coincided with Mr Cernetic's first day as director; on my insistence that Brown's life was in jeopardy if he was left in SCU, he was very quickly released. This history of Brown's attempted suicide in solitary was well known to the officers in charge of SCU; this magnifies the enormity of their act of forcibly shaving him.

56 CD213, May 1974 (superseded by CD213, May 1979).

57 Jackson, 'Justice behind the Walls.'

58 Interview with Andy Bruce, 1974. The Study Group on Dissociation stated that on the basis of its interviews with prisoners in both punitive and administrative dissociation, 'inmates in punitive dissociation ... exhibited less resentment towards the administration than did segregated inmates. Although an inmate in punitive dissociation may deny guilt, he at least knows the administration's reason for having him dissociated. An inmate deprived of the opportunity to hear the charge or respond to it is likely to demonstrate considerable resentment towards the administration': Vantour Report, 22.

59 The dramatic change in Dudoward's status from dangerous to non-dangerous prisoner by virtue of a change in the jailer is reminiscent of an incident described in the first report of the new warden of Kingston in 1869: 'I found five convicts wearing a chain; one had carried it for six months, three for seven months, and one for nine years! In the last case, it had not been taken off when the man was sick in hospital!! I am happy to say that I have had no reason to regret removing the chains from any of them. Their behaviour has amply justified my treatment of them, and particularly in the case of the convict last referred to.' Annual report of the warden of Kingston in *Annual Report of the Directors of Penitentiaries* (1869).

60 Vantour Report, 9. It should be pointed out that although there are some recent studies on the effects of long-term imprisonment, none of them deals with confinement under the conditions of isolation that characterised SCU. By far the best of these studies and the one that is most relevant to understanding long-term segregation is Cohen and Taylor's *Psychological Survival*, supra, n. 38. For a review of the recent research see H. Bryan McKay, C.H.S. Jayewardene, and Penny B. Reedy, *The Effects of Long-term Incarceration* (Ottawa: Supply and Services, 1979).

61 Vantour Report, 1. The establishment of the study group was recommended by Inger Hansen, the correctional investigator, in her annual report of 1973–4, where she reprinted three accounts of life in solitary sent to her by prisoners: *Annual Report of the Correctional Investigator 1973–74* (Ottawa: Information Canada 1976), 45–55.

62 Ibid., 22, 23.

63 Ibid., 22–4. The report concludes: 'Most inmates interviewed expressed resentment, bitterness, considerable hatred and described deep depression, loneliness, concern about their physical and mental well-being, and a feeling of hopelessness. Reactions such as slashing themselves, self-mutilation, and suicide are not uncommon' (at 24).

64 Korn, 48.

65 Hermann Hesse, *Magister Ludi* (New York: Bantam Books 1970), 365.

66 Heald judgment, 353.

67 Ibid.

68 Ibid.

69 Notes of evidence.

70 Interview with Andy Bruce, May 1974.

71 Heald judgment, 353.

72 Notes of evidence.

73 Ibid.

74 Dudoward's evidence on the effects of solitary was the briefest of all the plaintiffs' evidence. Dr Stephen Fox, one of the experts called by the plaintiffs who interviewed them all prior to the trial, explained to the court: 'Dudoward won't deal with what happened to him. Dudoward won't even talk about what happened to him ... It is the ultimate human experience, to be no one. To come to the place of total extinction for some people is unexpressible, there is no way they can tell you what it felt like and there are others who can, more articulate, more introspective, more close to it ... Dudoward is out. The best thing maybe for him to do is to fight to get rid of all the marks, all the scars': evidence of Dr Stephen Fox (cited hereafter as 'Fox'), 61-2.

75 A Canadian study in sensory and perceptual deprivation reported 'exaggerated emotional reactions and excessive irritation by small things': see Berton, Heron and Scott, 'Effects of Decreased Variation in the Sensory Environment,' 8 *Canadian Journal of Psychiatry* 70, (1954).

76 Notes of evidence.

77 Fox, 62. The day after Miller testified he alleged that he was approached by one of the guards and threatened with physical violence. Although the guard denied in court making the statement to Miller, he did admit that he had expressed the following opinion to the supervisor of recreation at the penitentiary: 'I should have put him [Miller] under the apple tree a long time ago.' 'Under the apple tree' was a reference to the penitentiary burial grounds: see Heald judgment, 352.

78 Notes of evidence.

79 Ibid.

80 Letter from Jack McCann, 20 July 1972.

81 Fox, 55.

82 Ibid., 68.

83 Another poem written by Jack McCann while in solitary confinement is entitled, 'Come Death, Possess Me.'

84 See Anthony M. Marcus and Chris Conway, *Nothing Is My Number: An Exploratory Study with a Group of Dangerous Sexual Offenders* (Toronto: General Publishing 1971).

85 Korn, 30. As assistant warden at the New Jersey State Prison, Dr Korn was involved in creating the special segregation wing for members of the organized-crime syndicates who were sentenced following the Kefauver

hearings. Dr Korn testified that the prisoners included several Mafia dons, and, prior to the establishment of the segregation wing, they virtually controlled the prison.

86 Fox, 30.

87 Ibid., 25, 27.

88 Korn, 17–18. Letter from Jack McCann, 20 July 1972: 'I don't think they believe I'm human, they can't, to them I'm some sort of object yet undefined.' In a 1974 letter, Donald Oag wrote: 'So far as the institution goes, it appears that I no longer even exist ... I don't know what else to say or do now. I appear to be a nonentity and therefore am ignored. What is to become of me?' Dr Frank Rundle, formerly head psychiatrist at Soledad Prison in California, has described the adaptive behaviour of prisoners confined in Soledad's 'adjustment center': 'Some prisoners, after days of such isolation, would become so desperate for relief that they would set their mattresses afire so as to force the staff to open the door and remove them from the torture chamber, even though they knew it would probably be for only a few minutes. Others would burst out in a frenzied rage of aimless destruction, tearing their sinks and toilets from the walls, ripping their clothing and bedding, and destroying their few personal possessions in order to alleviate the numbing sense of deadness or non-being and to escape the torture of their own thoughts and despair. In this absolutely insane world that was the Adjustment Center, "madness" was at least partially functional and adaptive. The crazy ones were those who tried to follow the rules of the world outside.' Frank L. Rundle, 'The Roots of Violence at Soledad,' in *The Politics of Punishment: A Critical Analysis of Prisons in America*, ed. Erik Olin Wright (New York: Harper Colophon Books 1973), 167.

89 Korn, 30–1.

90 Fox, 31–2. Other commentators have pointed out the extent to which the prison regimes surrounding solitary confinement induce violence and are themselves criminogenic. 'Persons [who are] in this emotional stage of rage, or who have a deep inability to feel or care, are persons who are dangerous to others as well as to themselves. On the emotional level, the effect of solitary is comparable to prison personnel teaching the prisoner how to use explosives, or how to sharpen his aim with a gun. If the guards did something like this it would be clear that prisons were promoting violence and criminal behavior. In reality, the prison is doing just this on a motivational level through its use of solitary confinement. It is handing the prisoner a gun to use whenever he gets the opportunity, either in the prison population or later when released into society': Thomas Benjamin and Kenneth Lux, 'Solitary Confinement as Psychological Punishment,' 13 *California Western Law Review* 265 (1977), at 277.

91 Fox, 31.

92 Ibid., 44-5. The equation between the solitary-confinement experience and the approach of death is one which Jack Henry Abbott, an American prisoner who has spent many years in solitary, has explored in his compelling account of life in the hole. 'A man is taken away from his experience of society, taken away from the experience of a living planet of living things, when he is sent to prison. A man is taken away from other prisoners, from his experience of other people, when he is locked away in solitary confinement in the hole. Every step of the way removes him from experience and narrows it down to only the experience of himself. There is a *thing* called death and we have all seen it. It brings to an end a life, an individual living being. When life ends, the living thing ceases to experience. The concept of death is simple: it is when a living thing no longer entertains experience. So when a man is taken farther and farther away from experience, he is being taken to his death': Jack Henry Abbott, *In the Belly of the Beast: Letters from Prison* (New York: Random House 1981), 52-3. The two ultimate responses to solitary confinement - death and madness - exemplified by the cases of Bellemaire and McCaulley, are also examined by Jacobo Timerman, who was held captive in solitary for over two years by the junta in Argentina. Jacobo Timerman, *Prisoner without a Name, Cell without a Number* (New York: Albert A. Knopf 1981), 88-92.

93 Fox, 37.

94 Ibid., 39.

95 Ibid. 37-9.

96 Ibid., 40.

97 Korn, 39-40, 20-1. Jack Henry Abbott has provided this chilling image: 'Time descends in your cell like the lid of a coffin in which you lie and watch it as it slowly closes over you. When you neither move nor think in your cell, you are awash in pure nothingness.' Jack Henry Abott, *In the Belly of the Beast*, 44-5. For an excellent descripton of 'prison time' see Cohen and Taylor, *Psychological Survival*, chap. 4.

98 Korn, 42.

99 Fox, 48.

100 Ibid., 42.

101 Korn, 52.

102 Fox, 48-9.

103 Notes of evidence.

104 Fox, 46. Jack Henry Abbott captures the essence of the ultimate release from the psychological horrors of the hole: 'I do not want to talk any more. There is nothing you can say of interest. I cannot remember ever being happy. No one has ever been kind to me. Everyone betrays me. No one can possibly understand - they are too ignorant. You have not suffered what I have endured. You call me names (homosexual). You do not understand. You mock

me (screwball). This world is nothing. An illusion. Death is the release.' Abbott, *In the Belly of the Beast*, 50.

105 Korn, 43–4. The expert evidence called by the plaintiffs in *McCann* on the effects of solitary confinement is the most extensive evidence on the subject which has been presented to a Canadian court. Much of the evidence of Dr Fox and Dr Korn was also led in the subsequent case of *R.* v. *Bruce, Lucas, and Wilson*, (1977) 36 CCC (2d) 158 a case which I will be discussing later. In that case the additional evidence of Dr Milton Miller, then head of the Department of Psychiatry at the University of British Columbia, summarized the cumulative effects of life in solitary confinement. 'Many aspects of solitary experiences at the British Columbia Penitentiary are damaging to people who are placed there ... The attitude of the guards who guard the setting, the number of locked doors that one walks towards and through in the last 100 steps towards the solitary room, the manner and state of mind of the individual at the time that he goes into such quarters, the sense of justice with which the person feels that he is sentenced to such quarters, the real or believed nature of extra management of life around such things as food or recreation, exercise; these and the past experiences of the individual, the nature of the experiences of other people in that kind of setting since a man in solitary is likely to feel closely identified with the other men who are in solitary. The length of time in solitary is likely to be a very important consideration ... It seems to me that many, many factors pile up. Perhaps the most damaging or most potentially damaging would be the feeling that one is locked off from help from anywhere, that the immediate guards are enemies, and that beyond the immediate guards no one either cares or is able to reach into the life of the people who are there, so that kind of composite of events looms large, they pyramid, they compound each other and, I think, have an effect well beyond even the cramped ... dismal dimensions of the physical space itself.'

106 C.E.J. Ecclestone, P. Gendreau, and C. Knox, 'Solitary Confinement of Prisoners: An Assessment of its Effects on Inmates' Personal Constructs and Adrenocortical Activity,' 6 *Canadian Journal of Behavioural Sciences* 178 (1974), at 179.

107 Ibid., 188.

108 Ibid., 187.

109 In an earlier study conducted by Gendreau, volunteer inmates were kept for seven days in solitary-confinement cells at Kingston Penitentiary and monitored for changes in their EEG frequency. The results demonstrated that one week of solitary confinement caused the EEG frequency to decline in a non-linear manner. Researchers determined that the shift of EEG frequency to lower levels represented a tendency toward increasing theta activity, which occurs with frustration and stress. Seventy-seven per cent of this total decline occurred within the first four days of confinement, suggesting to the

researchers that most inmates adapt to the confinement within that period: P. Gendreau, N.L. Friedman, G.T.S. Wilde, and G.D. Scott: 'Changes in EEG Alpha Frequency and Evoked Response Latency During Solitary Confinement,' 79 *Journal of Abnormal Psychology* 54 (1972).

110 Peter Suedfeld and Chunilal Roy, 'Using Social Isolation to Change the Behaviour of Disruptive Minds,' *International Journal of Offender Therapy and Comparative Criminology* 19 (1975). It should be said that the authors' interpretation of the follow-up data in this study supporting the positive effects of the dissociation experience is open to question. In the case of one of the prisoners (who since the experience had been released from prison only to be reconvicted), the authors conclude that 'his behaviour in [Saskatchewan Penitentiary] is apparently acceptable since the Regional Medical Centre has not been requested to readmit him' (at 95). This does not follow; the Medical Centre is not viewed by the Penitentiary Service as the first resort for problem prisoners. Indeed, in several cases known to me, clearly disturbed prisoners have been returned from the centre because the centre was not prepared to cope with them. Tommy McCaulley was one such prisoner. Therefore, the fact that there has been no request to readmit the prisoner in the study does not demonstrate a positive adjustment. In another paper Dr Suedfeld states (with reference to the Regional Psychiatric Centre study) that 'data collection was rather subjective and some members of the security staff have mentioned that they disagreed with the nurses as to the amount of improvement exhibited by the prisoners.' See Peter Suedfeld, 'Solitary Confinement in the Correctional Setting: Goals, Problems and Suggestions,' 20 *Corrective and Social Psychiatry* 10 (1974). This difference between the therapeutic staff's and security staff's perceptions could well be attributed to the different ways in which the prisoners 'came across' to the staff. Elsewhere I have discussed the extent to which prisoners are prepared to 'play the game' of rehabilitation when dealing with counselling staff: see Jackson, 'Justice Behind the Walls.'

111 Suedfeld and Roy, 'Using Social Isolation,' 94.

112 Ibid., 95. Dr Suedfeld's other research into the potential therapeutic uses of solitude and sensory deprivation also lends support to the plaintiffs' descriptions of the disorganizing effects of solitary. Dr Suedfeld has demonstrated that sensory deprivation (involving the subjects lying on a bed in a dark, silent room) functions as a cognitive disorganizer resulting in decreased belief stability and lower ability to maintain one's attitudes in the face of conflicting information (see Suedfeld and Borrie, 'Sensory Deprivation, Attitude Change, and Defence Against Persuasion,' 10 *Canadian Journal of Behavioural Sciences* 17, 1978). See also Benjamin and Lux, 'Solitary Confinement as Psychological Punishment,' 268 et seq. In Dr Suedfeld's experiments only volunteers are used, and the therapeutic purpose of the sensory-deprivation experience is to change or eliminate some habit or trait viewed

by the volunteer as undesirable (for example, smoking). In these experiments the purpose, as I understand it, is to induce cognitive disorganization, to increase suggestibility, and then, by applying necessary reinforcement measures, to change behavior. In SCU, none of the necessary elements for change is present. The prisoners are not volunteers, there is no agreed and desired agenda for change, and while there does exist a situation which induces cognitive disorganization, the reinforcers are almost exclusively negative, encouraging the generation of greater anger, hostility, and loss of dignity. See also Lucas, 'Solitary Confinement: Isolation as Condition to Confinement,' 9 *Australian and New Zealand Journal of Criminology* 153 (1976), Peter Suedfeld, 'Solitary Confinement as a Rehabilitation Technique: Reply to Lucas,' 11 *Australian and New Zealand Journal of Criminology* 106 (1978).

113 Evidence of Dr Suedfeld, 43.

114 Summary of evidence of Dr Suedfeld, 14.

115 Evidence of Dr Suedfeld, 83. In his reasons for judgment, Heald J stated that he found the evidence of Drs Korn, Fox, and Marcus more persuasive than that of Dr Suedfeld, primarily because they had spent considerable time with the plaintiffs and therefore were able to observe firsthand the effects of solitary on them. However, the learned judge also found nothing in Dr Suedfeld's evidence which contradicted the evidence of the plaintiff's experts in any material particular: Heald judgment, 368.

116 Evidence of Dr Scott, 44–5.

117 Ibid., 48.

4 *McCANN* V. *THE QUEEN*: THE STRUCTURE OF THE LEGAL ARGUMENT

1 *Ruffin* v. *Commonwealth*, 62 Va. 790 (1871).

2 Cited in W.A. Calder, *The Federal Penitentiary in Canada, 1867–1899: A Social and Institutional History* (PHD dissertation, University of Toronto 1975), ch. 8, p. 3.

3 See G.D. Kaiser, 'The Inmate as Citizen: Imprisonment and the Loss of Civil Rights in Canada,' 1 *Queen's Law Journal* 208 (1971).

4 Note, 'Beyond The Ken of the Courts: A Critique of Judicial Refusal to Review the Complaints of Convicts,' 72 *Yale Law Journal* 506 (1963); R.R. Price, 'Doing Justice to Corrections: Prisoners, Parolees and the Courts,' 3 *Queen's Law Journal* 214 (1977).

5 The Parliamentary Subcommittee on the Penitentiary System in Canada commented on the nature of the interrelationship between prison conditions and judicial reluctance to interfere: 'The gross irregularities, lack of standards and arbitrariness that exist in our penitentiaries, by their very quantity, make, and always have made, the possibility of judicial intervention

into prison matters a rather impracticable, time-consuming and dismaying prospect, as the judges themselves have pointed out. To open the courts to redress of these conditions would invite inmates to continue to increase the levels of their confrontation with prison staff and management, using the courts for purposes that, just like the present running battle between the opposing sides, are largely unassociated with any genuine interest in improving the operation of the system. By the same argument, however, the present judicial policy invites the perpetuation by the authorities of a system that is so far removed from normal standards of justice that it remains safely within the class of matters in which the imposition of judicial or quasi-judicial procedures would clearly be, in most instance, inconceivable. Further, this would ensure that the sheer immensity of the task of straightening it out is enough to discourage even the most committed members of the judiciary. The worse things are in the penitentiary system, therefore, the more self-evident it is to the courts that Parliament could not possibly have intended for them to intervene. Injustice, as well as virtue, can be its own reward.' (*Report to Parliament, The Subcommittee on the Penitentiary System in Canada* (Ottawa: Minister of Supply and Services 1977), 86, para. 416.

6 *The Role of Federal Corrections in Canada* (Ottawa: Solicitor-General of Canada 1977), 49.

7 (1975) 24 CCC (2d) 401 (BCCA).

8 92 S. Ct. 2726 (1972).

9 Supra, n. 7, at 480. The Supreme Court of Canada in *R.* v. *Solosky* (1980) 50 CCC (2d) 495 (SCC) has expressly endorsed the proposition that 'a person confined to prison retains all of his civil rights, other than those expressly or impliedly taken away from him by law' (at 510).

10 See Edward Shils, 'The Theory of Mass Society,' *Diogenes* 39 (1962), reprinted in *Centre and Periphery: Essays in Macrosociology* (Chicago: University of Chicago Press 1975).

11 James B. Jacobs, *Stateville: The Penitentiary in Mass Society* (Chicago: University of Chicago Press 1977).

12 487 F. 2d 1280 (1st Cir. 1973), rev'd on other grounds, 425 U.S. 308 (1976).

13 At 1283–4. See also Comment, 'Confronting the Conditions of Confinement: An Expanded Role for Courts in Prison Reform,' 12 *Harvard Civil Rights and Civil Liberties Law Review* 367 (1977), esp. at 385–8.

14 Canadian Bill of Rights, SC 1960 c. 44; RSC 1970, appendix III. The Canadian Charter of Rights and Freedoms has now entrenched section 2(b) in a more positive way by providing in section 12 that 'Everyone has the right not to be subjected to any cruel and unusual treatment or punishment.' (Constitution Act 1982, as enacted by the Canada Act, 1982, c. 11 (U.K.) proclaimed in force 17 April 1982.) For a detailed discussion of judicial interpretation of s. 2(b) of the Canadian Bill of Rights and the effect of entrenchment under the Charter of Rights and Freedoms, which incorporates much of the following text and

notes, see Michael Jackson, 'Cruel and Unusual Treatment or Punishment,' *University of British Columbia Law Review*, Charter Edition 189 (1982).

15 Supra, n. 7, 452–3.

16 Ibid., 461.

17 (1970) SCR 282 (SCC).

18 (1972) SCR 889; (SCC).

19 Supra, n. 7, 461.

20 Ibid., 465. In *R.* v. *Shand* (1976) 29 CCC (2d) 199 (Ont. Co. Ct.) His Honour Judge Borins, in considering the applicaton of s. 2(b) to the minimum seven-year sentence for importation of a narcotic under the Narcotic Control Act, adopted the same approach as Mr Justice McIntyre. In looking at the American authority, he said, 'I wish to make clear that my purpose in doing so is because I am of the opinion that the analytical approach taken in the application of the test developed to determine whether certain punishment is cruel and unusual is worthy of close consideration. Clearly, I am not bound by that approach nor by the result reached by the Supreme Court' (212). Although Judge Borin's decision (that in the circumstances of the particular defendant before him it was cruel and unusual punishment to apply the minimum seven-year sentence) was reversed by the Ontario Court of Appeal. Arnup JA, writing for the court, referred to American cases on minimum sentences for drug convictions, which sentences had been challenged under the Eighth Amendment on the basis that they violated the principle of proportionality of punishment to the offence. He stated: 'We are prepared to accept that the so-called "disproportionality principle" has relevance to what is cruel and unusual punishment ... it is a principle that needs to be developed in the Canadian context of our Constitution, customs and jurisprudence. In this development, great assistance can be obtained from the American precedents, across a rather broad spectrum, and to a lesser extent, from some of the articles in the American periodicals': (1976) 30 CCC (2d) 23 at 37–8 (Ont. C.A.). The issue of the relevance of the American decisions on the Eighth Amendment to the interpretation of s. 2(b) was joined again when *Miller and Cockriell* was argued in the Supreme Court. Chief Justice Laskin, writing for himself and two other members of the court in a concurring judgment, clearly saw the U.S. decisions as being relevant. Counsel for the appellants had argued the case adopting the framework suggested by the U.S. authorities, and the chief justice dealt with and dismissed their arguments within that general framework: (1977) 31 CCC 177.

Ritchie J, writing for the majority, held that the Bill of Rights did not create new rights but confirmed existing ones; that s. 2(b) was to be read subject to s. 1; that the declaration in s. 1(a) of the right of the individual not to be deprived of life was qualified by the words 'except by due process of law; therefore at the time when the Bill of Rights was enacted there did not exist any right to life in the case of a person duly convicted of capital murder.' Using this interpretation Ritchie J concluded that 'punishment' in section 2(b) was not intended by Parliament to include the death penalty. Having so concluded, it was not necessary to undertake any detailed analysis of the U.S. cases. He stated that were this necessary, however, he 'would be disinclined to adopt them as applicable in interpreting s. 2(b): 31 CCC (2d) 198. While acknowledging the common heritage of the Eighth Amendment and s. 2(b), he was 'nevertheless satisfied that these two documents differ so radically in their purpose and content that judgments rendered in interpretation of one are of little value in interpreting the other' (ibid.).

The Canadian Charter of Rights and Freedoms, which entrenches rights in a constitutional document, is a much closer approximation of the U.S. Bill of Rights. This fact and the clear mandate for judicial review envisaged by the entrenchment of rights substantially undermine Ritchie J's rejection of the relevance of U.S. authority and strengthen the argument made by the *McCann* plaintiffs. The elevation of Mr Justice MacIntyre to the Supreme Court, along with other changes in the Supreme Court bench, suggests that in future litigation greater attention will be paid to U.S. authority.

21 92 S. Ct. 2726 (1972) at 2766–7. As Mr Justice Marshall indicates, there is some difference of opinion among scholars as to which punishments were meant to be prohibited. Macaulay's *History of England*, relating the clause to the Bloody Assizes, sees it as prohibiting barbarous methods of punishment: (1964) vol. II, 371. The American legal scholar Anthony Granucci has argued that the clause was primarily a response to the trial of Titus Oates and prohibits, not barbarous methods of punishment, but penalties which were excessive: Anthony Granucci, 'Nor Cruel and Unusual Punishments Inflicted: The Original Meaning,' 57 *California Law Review* 57 (1969), 839. Two Canadian legal scholars have concluded that there is not sufficient evidence to connect the 'cruel and unusual punishments' clause with either the Bloody Assizes or the trial of Titus Oates. Nor is there evidence supporting a distinction between barbarous methods of punishment and penalties that are merely excessive. The only meaning supported by the evidence, in their view, is that the clause prohibits unprecedented punishments, not authorized by statute and beyond the jurisdiction of the sentencing court: B. Welling and C.A. Hipfner, 'Cruel and Unusual Capital Punishment in Canada 26 *University of Toronto Law Journal* 26 (1976), 55. Stan Berger, in the most recent Canadian commentary, interpreting the same evidence as that cited by Welling and Hipfner, concludes that that evidence is sufficient to support Granucci's conclusion that the clause was a reiteration of the English policy against disproportionate penalties: Stan Berger, 'The Application of the Cruel and Unusual Punishment Clause under the Canadian Bill of Rights,' 24 *McGill Law Journal* 161 (1978).

Although the majority of American legal scholars who have sought to grapple with the original meaning of the Eighth Amendment have focused on its English sources, a recent study has suggested that this approach is too restrictive. The study suggests that the European philosophers of the Enlightenment - Voltaire, Montesquieu, and (especially) Beccaria - were also important. They argue that Beccaria's *Treatise on Crimes and Punishments* (1788), together with the works on criminal law reform of these other great thinkers, provided the philosophical basis for the principle of proportionality of punishment. Since these works influenced American colonial leaders, the principle of proportionality must necessarily be reflected in the Eighth Amendment. Comment, 'The Eighth Amendment, Beccaria, and the Enlightenment, and Historical Justification for the *Weems* v. *United States* Excessive Punishment Doctrine,' 24 *Buffalo Law Review* (1975), 783. For a criticism of this referential incorporation of Beccaria's views on proportionality, see Charles Walter Schwartz, 'Eighth Amendment Proportionality Analysis and the Compelling case of William Rummell,' 71 *Journal of Criminal Law and Criminology* 378 (1980).

22 *Trop* v. *Dulles*, 78 S. Ct. 590 (1958) at 598.

23 (1970) 2 CCC 4.

24 Resolution 217A (111) United Nations General Assembly, 10 December 1948. The prohibition of cruel, inhuman, or degrading punishment is also reflected in the United Nations Standard Minimum Rules for the Treatment of Prisoners. Rule 31 provides: 'Corporal punishment, punishment by placing in a dark cell and all cruel, inhuman or degrading punishments shall be completely prohibited as punishments for disciplinary offences' (New York: UN Department of Economic and Social Affairs 1958). The prohibition is also contained in article 7 of the International Convenant on Civil and Political Rights, adopted by the United Nations General Assembly in December 1966, to which Canada acceded in May 1976, with effect from 19 August 1976.

25 Norval Morris and Colin Howard, *Studies in Criminal Law* (Oxford: Clarenden Press 1964), 157-8.

26 In the original draft of the Canadian Bill of Rights, introduced in 1958, the forerunner of s. 2(b) was a reproduction of s. 4(2) of the Universal Declaration of Human Rights. The relationship between the form of wording used in the Universal Declaration and that used in s. 2(b) in the Eighth Amendment was considered by the Privy Council in *Runyowa* v. *The Queen* (1966) 1 All ER 633 (JCPC). This case involved a Southern Rhodesian appeal from a death sentence imposed on two Africans convicted of setting fire or attempting to set fire to a house. The death sentences were mandatory under the relevant legislation creating the offence. Section 60 of the Constitution of Southern Rhodesia provided: 'No person shall be subjected to torture or to inhuman or degrading punishment or other treatment.' In citing decisions of the U.S. Supreme Court interpreting the Eighth Amendment's prohibition against cruel and unusual punishment to include those punishments which are

disproportionate to the offence, counsel advanced the argument that a punishment which was out of proportion to the offence may be an 'inhuman' punishment. The Privy Council held that the ban in s. 60 was on any type or mode of punishment that is inhuman or degrading, but it did not enable the court to declare that a punishment was inappropriate or excessive for the particular offence (642–3). In other words, the Privy Council saw the wording of s. 60 as being narrower than those contained in the Eighth Amendment. The necessary implication of this is that Parliament in adopting the wording of s. 2(b) intended to provide a greater, not a lesser, level of protection than that afforded by the Universal Declaration.

Article 3 of the European Convention of Human Rights is drafted in terms similar to article 4(2) of the Universal Declaration of Human Rights. It provides that 'no one shall be subjected to torture or to inhuman or degrading treatment or punishment.' The European Court of Human Rights in 1978 rendered its judgment in *Ireland* v. *United Kingdom*, a case which involved the application of article 3 to certain sensory-deprivation techniques used by the Royal Ulster Constabulary in their interrogation of suspected IRA terrorists. These techniques consisted of wall-standing (forcing detainees to remain for periods of some hours in a 'stress position'); hooding, subjecting detainees to a continuous loud hissing noise; and depriving detainees of sleep and subjecting them to a reduced diet during their interrogation. The report of the European Commission on Human Rights found that no physical injury resulted from the application of the five techniques, but loss of weight and acute psychiatric symptoms were recorded in some of the cases. The commission, on the material before it, was unable to establish the exact degree of any psychiatric after-effects, but it was satisfied that some psychiatric after-effects in certain of the persons subjected to the techniques could not be excluded. The commission found that these techniques constituted the practice not only of inhuman and degrading treatment, but also of torture. The government of Ireland asked the European Court for confirmation of this opinion. The European Court in its judgment of 18 January 1978 found that 'the five techniques were applied in combination with premeditation, and for hours at a stretch; they caused, if not actual bodily harm, at least intense physical and mental suffering to the person subjected thereto and also led to acute psychiatric disturbances during interrogation. They accordingly fell into the category of inhuman treatment within the meaning of article 3. The techniques were also degrading since they were such as to arouse in their victims feelings of fear, anguish and inferiority capable of humiliating and debasing them and possibly breaking their physical or moral resistance': European Court of Human Rights, judgment in *Ireland* v. *United Kingdom* 18 January 1978, para. 167.

The court found, however, that the techniques did not amount to torture within the European Convention. They saw the term 'torture' as referring to deliberate inhuman treatment causing serious and cruel suffering, citing resolution 3452 adopted by the General Assembly of the United Nations on 9 December 1975, which declared that 'torture constitutes an aggravated and deliberate form of cruel, inhuman or degrading treatment or punishment.' While decisions of the European Court of Human Rights are not in any way binding on Canadian courts, because article 3 is a reaffirmation of article 5 of the Universal Declaration of Human Rights, it is an important contemporary interpretation of a clause designed to protect the same values as those protected by s. 2(b) of the Canadian Bill of Rights and now protected by s. 12 of the Charter of Rights and Freedoms.

27 The preamble reads: 'The Parliament of Canada, affirming that the Canadian Nation is founded upon principles that acknowledge ... the dignity and worth of the human person ...'

28 (1972) 92 S. Ct. at 3726.

29 Supra, n. 22.

30 92 S. Ct. at 2743.

31 Ibid. In *Hutto* v. *Finney*, 98 S. Ct. 2565 (1978), the first case in which the Supreme Court had to consider the Eighth Amendment in relation to administrative segregation, the court stated, 'The Eighth Amendment's ban ... proscribes more than physically barbarous punishments ... It prohibits penalties ... that transgress today's broad and idealistic concepts of dignity, civilized standards, humanity and decency' (2570).

32 Ibid.

33 Ibid.

34 (1976) 24 CCC (2d) at 476.

35 Supra, n. 21, 2746.

36 Ibid.

37 Ibid., 2747.

38 Ibid., 2748.

39 217 U.S. 349 (1910).

40 370 U.S. 660 (1962).

41 92 S. Ct. at 2748. In *Furman* v. *Georgia* the majority (of which Brennan J was a member) concluded that the death-penalty statutes before the court in that case violated the Eighth Amendment. The common denominator in the separate judgments of the majority was that the sentence of death authorized under the statutes before the court, in light of the absence of standards to guide judges or juries and in light of its infrequent imposition, was arbitrarily and capriciously applied and therefore ceased to further any state purpose.

In response to the decision in *Furman*, many of the states whose death penalty statutes were thereby rendered unconstitutional rewrote them, and in 1976 the Supreme Court ruled on a number of these revised statutory schemes. The plurality of the court held that for death-penalty statutes to be valid, specified standards for sentencing authorities, whether judges or juries, were necessary to eliminate arbitrary results; further, it was necessary that sentencers make particularized findings regarding the defendant's character or circumstances of the crime: *Gregg* v. *Georgia*, 96 S. Ct. 2909 (1976): *Jurek* v. *Texas*, 96 S. Ct. 2950 (1976); *Profitt* v. *Florida*, 96 S. Ct. 2960 (1976). Although Brennan J was in the minority in the *Gregg* and associated decisions, maintaining his view that the death penalty was unconstitutional per se, the tests he developed in *Furman* were adopted with some modification by the plurality of the court in *Gregg*. The judgment of the court restates those tests: 'An assessment of contemporary values concerning the infliction of a challenged sanction is relevant to the application of the Eighth Amendment ... This assessment does not call for a subjective judgment. It requires, rather, that we look to objective criteria that reflect the public attitude towards a given sanction. Our cases also make clear that public perceptions of standards of decency with respect to criminal sanctions are not conclusive. The penalty also must accord with the dignity of man, which is the basic concept of the Eighth Amendment. This means, at least, that the punishment not be excessive ... The enquiry into excessiveness has two aspects. First ... although we cannot invalidate a category of penalties because we deem less severe penalties adequate to serve the ends of penology, the sanction imposed cannot be so totally without penological justification that it results in gratuitous infliction of suffering ... Where discretion is afforded ... that discretion must be suitably directed and limited so as to minimize the risk of wholly arbitrary and capricious action': *Gregg* v. *Georgia*, 428 U.S. at 2925, 2929, 2932. For an excellent discussion on the development of the death penalty litigation in the U.S. Supreme Court, see Note, 'Furman to Gregg: The Judicial and Legislative History,' 22 *Howard Law Journal* 53 (1979). For an analysis of events leading up to the Furman decision, see M. Meltsner, *Cruel and Unusual: The Supreme Court and Capital Punishment* (New York: Random House 1974).

42 24 CCC (2d) at 468.

43 Granucci, *Nor Cruel and Unusual Punishments Inflicted*.

44 92 S. Ct. at 2799.

45 78 S. Ct. 590 at 598, n. 32.

46 24 CCC (2d) at 465.

47 As Professor Berger has said, 'The irony is that the absence of a non obstante clause was being used by the Court to render operative a punishment which might otherwise violate s. 2(b), when the opening words of s. 2 state this to be the very purpose of including such a clause': Berger, supra, n. 21, 170. For further commentaries on *Miller and Cockriell* see Walter Tarnopolsky, 'Just Deserts or Cruel and Unusual Punishment? Where Do We Look

for Guidance?' 10 *Ottawa Law Review* 1 (1978); J.S. Leon, 'Cruel and Unusual Punishment: Sociological Jurisprudence and the Canadian Bill of Rights,' 36 *University of Toronto Faculty of Law Review* 222 (1978).

48 24 CCC, 453–4. In the Supreme Court of Canada the chief justice, writing for himself, Spence J, and Dickson J, preferred an interpretation that saw 'cruel' and 'unusual' as 'interacting expressions colouring each other, so to speak, and hence, to be considered together as a compendious expression of a norm.' To the chief justice, such an approach was 'in line with the duty of the Court not to whittle down the protections of the Canadian Bill of Rights by a narrow construction of what is a quasi-Constitutional document': 31 CCC (2d) at 184.

Given Mr Justice Ritchie's view of the case – that the person convicted of murder punishable by death had no right to his life, and therefore the death penalty was not intended to be included within the meaning of the word 'punishment' in s. 2(b) – it was not necessary for him to develop any general criteria for the interpretation of s. 2(b). However, he indicated that he shared the view of the majority of the BC Court of Appeal that 'cruel and unusual' were to be read conjunctively.

The use of the language 'cruel and unusual' in s. 12 of the Charter of Rights cannot be taken as resolving this issue in favour of a conjunctive approach. The narrow conjunctive approach favoured by Ritchie J, like his rejection of the relevance of U.S. authorities, is premised on viewing the Bill of Rights as simply another act of Parliament without any special legal significance. The constitutional entrenchment of s. 12 is an explicit rejection of Ritchie J's premise and opens the way for the broad disjunctive approach to what is now clearly a constitutional right.

The emerging jurisprudence on the interpretation of the charter generally supports a broad approach to s. 12. The Ontario Court of Appeal in a number of cases has endorsed 'a large and liberal construction' of the charter. In upholding the right of freedom of expression as guaranteeing the public and press access to juvenile trials, MacKinnon CJ, writing for a unanimous court, characterized the charter as 'a new, living tree, planted in friendly Canadian soil ... which should not be stultified by narrow technical, literal interpretations without regard to its background and purpose. Capability for growth must be recognized.' *Globe and Mail*, 1 April 1983.

49 Since Mr Justice Ritchie agreed with the majority of the Court of Appeal that the retention of the death penalty after the enactment of the Canadian Bill of Rights was a strong indication of Parliament's intention to exclude punishment by death from the ambit of s. 2(b), the plaintiff's argument here was equally applicable to distinguish the majority decision in the Supreme Court of Canada.

It is suggested that the views of the majority of the BC Court of Appeal and the Supreme Court in *Miller and Cockriell* (that there may be an implied repeal of the Bill of Rights) cannot survive the adoption of the Charter of Rights. The entrenchment of rights and the explicit provisions of the charter, which not only provide for a non obstante clause (as did the Bill of Rights) but also limit the duration of such a clause (s. 33), are not consistent with implied repeal.

50 For detailed commentaries on the application of the Eighth Amendment to prison conditions, see Richard Singer, 'Confining Solitary Confinement: Constitutional Arguments for a New Penology,' 56 *Iowa Law Review* 1251 (1971); William Bennett Turner, 'Establishing the Rule of Law in Prison: A Manual for Prisoners' Rights Litigation,' 23 *Stanford Law Review* 473 (1971); Note, 'Prison Discipline and the Eighth Amendment: A Psychological Perspective,' 43 *University of Cincinnati Law Review* 101 (1974); Comment, 'Cruel but Not So Unusual Punishment: The Role of the Federal Judiciary in State Prison Reform,' 7 *Cumberland Law Review* 31 (1976); Ira P. Robbins and Michael B. Buser, 'Punitive Conditions of Prison Confinement: An Analysis of *Pugh* v. *Locke* and Federal Court Supervision of State Penal Administration under the Eighth Amendment,' 29 *Stanford Law Review* 893 (1977); Comment, 'Confronting the Conditions of Confinement: An Expanded Role for Courts on Prison Reform,' 12 *Harvard Civil Rights and Civil Liberties Law Review* 367 (1977); Benjamin and Lux, 'Solitary Confinement as Psychological Punishment,' 13 *California Western Law Review* 265 (1977); Comment, 'Conditions of Confinement for Administratively Segregated Prisoners,' 55 *North Carolina Law Review* 473 (1977).

For a discussion of the most recent U.S. Supreme Court decisions, which have been characterized by a more restrictive view of the role of the courts in interfering through the vehicle of the Eighth Amendment with prison conditions, see Note, 'Eighth Amendment - A Significant Limit on Federal Court Activism in Ameliorating State Prison Conditions,' 72 *Journal of Criminal Law and Criminology* 1345 (1981).

In *Rhodes* v. *Chapman* 101 S. Ct. 2392 (1981), the Supreme Court's latest decision on the Eighth Amendment, the majority of the court, in shielding from unconstitutional challenge the practice of 'double celling,' confined its inquiry to the question of whether the prison conditions involved the 'wanton and unnecessary infliction of pain' or were 'grossly disproportionate to the severity of the crime[s] warranting imprisonment' (at 2399). Although Mr Justice Brennan in a concurring judgment held that the court should question whether the conditions comport with human dignity, the majority decision did not take up the standards of decency and the dignity-of-man underpinnings of previous Supreme Court jurisprudence. Underlying the majority conclusion that 'the Constitution does not mandate comfortable prisons' (at 2400) is the court's discouragement of what it perceives to be the excessively interventionist role of lower federal courts in the state prison systems. See infra, nn. 158 and 188.

51 257 F. Supp. 674 (1966).
52 Ibid., 679.
53 Ibid., 680.
54 453 F. (2d) 661 (1971).
55 Ibid., 676.
56 442 F. (2d) 178 (1971).
57 Ibid., 208.
58 321 F. Supp. 127 (1967).
59 Ibid., 142.
60 408 F. Supp. 534 (1976). Aff'd in part, rev'd in part 600 F. 2d 189 (9th Cir. 1979).
61 The plaintiffs all had extensive records of violence. Several had been convicted of assault on guards while in prison. One of them, Hugo Pinell, after an initial sentence of three years to life for rape, had been convicted successively of aggravated assault on a guard at San Quentin in 1968, aggravated assault on another prisoner at Folsom Prison in 1969, and manslaughter of a guard at Soledad in 1970. He was regarded by prison authorities as one of the most dangerous prisoners at San Quentin.
62 These indictments grew out of the incident that occurred at San Quentin in August 1971. One of the prisoners killed in this incident was George Jackson, one of the 'Soledad Brothers.' For a harrowing account of life in California's Adjustment Centres, particularly at Soledad and San Quentin, see George Jackson, *Soledad Brother: The Prison Letters of George Jackson* (New York: Bantam 1970); *Maximum Security: Letters from California's Prison*, ed. Eve Pell (New York: E.P. Dutton 1972); Thomas Lopez Meneweather, 'A Chronicle of Three Years in the Hole,' in *The Politics of Punishment*, ed. Erik Olin Wright (New York: Harper Colophon Books 1973), chap. 9.
63 408 F. Supp. at 541.
64 Ibid., 541–4.
65 Dealing with the use of restraints, Judge Zirpoli stated: 'The use of restraints on prisoners not actively posing a threat to the security of the institution imposes a burden on the prisoners not warranted by the interests of the institution. Manacles, shackles, waist belts, leg and neck chains are painful devices which inflict corporal punishment on those wearing them. They engender pain, humiliation, rage, and resentment to the point where the use of such restraints is counterproductive to any legitimate penal purpose and is destructive to the prisoners ... Subjecting plaintiffs to the combined use of manacles, waist belt, leg irons and neck chains during their out-of-cell movements makes it impossible for those restrained to demonstrate that they are capable of handling themselves without them. Nothing can be more

degrading and dehumanizing than to force a prisoner to visit his mother or family members under such restraints' (545, n. 15).

66 Ibid., 547. The 9th Circuit Court of Appeals in affirming the main parts of Judge Zirpoli's findings stated, 'Whatever rights one may lose at the prison gates ... the full protections of the eighth amendment must certainly remain in force. The whole point of the amendment is to protect persons convicted of crimes ... Mechanical deference to the findings of state prison officials in the context of the eighth amendment would reduce that provision to a nullity in precisely the context where it is most necessary.' 600 F. 2d at 193–4.

67 (1977) 31 CCC (2d) at 183.

68 RSC 1892, c. 184 (Criminal Code), s. 34. The legislative prohibition on the judicial imposition of solitary confinement contained in the 1892 code is a restatement of a similar prohibition first contained in legislation passed in 1886: An Act Respecting Punishments, Pardons, and the Computation of Sentences (1886) 49 Vict. c. 181, s. 34.

A word or two may be in order concerning the reasons for the abolition of the judicial power to impose solitary confinement. For offences punishable by imprisonment, nineteenth-century English criminal statutes commonly authorized the judge to direct that the offender be kept in solitary confinement for some portion of the imprisonment not exceeding one month at any one time and not exceeding three months in any one year: Sir William Russell, *A Treatise of Crimes and Misdemeanors*, 6th ed., vol. 1 (London: Stevens 1896), 81-3. See, for example, An Act to Amend the Laws Relating to Burglary and Stealing in a Dwelling House (1837), 7 Gul. IV & I Vict. c. 84, s. III. It seems that this judicial sentencing power fell into disuse following the adoption of the separate system of penitentiary discipline in England. Indeed, the 1839 Prison Act provided that the separate confinement of prisoners shall not be deemed solitary confinement within the meaning of any act forbidding the continuance of solitary confinement for more than a limited time: An Act for the Better Ordering of Prisons (1839) 2 & 3 Vict. c. LVI, s. IV. Thus, the period of time a prisoner spent in solitary in nineteenth-century England was governed by the prison legislation rather than the criminal sentencing legislation. Nineteenth-century Canadian criminal statutes, following the English precedent, authorized a judge to impose a sentence for imprisonment with or without solitary confinement: see, for example, An Act Relating to Procedure in Criminal Cases (1869) 32–33 Vict. c. 29, s. 86. This power to impose solitary was also subject to time constraints similar to those in the equivalent English legislation. See (1869) 32–33 Vict. c. 29, s. 94. Even though the separate system was not adopted as a general disciplinary regime in Canada in the nineteenth century, it does not appear that judges made any greater use of their power to sentence prisoners for a term in solitary confinement than did their English counterparts. Judges then, as now, seem to have been content to rely on those administering penitentiaries and prisons to determine the conditions under which imprisonment was served. The legislative abolition in 1886 of this judicial power reflected a division of carceral power which had already been worked out administratively.

69 *Annual Report of the Inspector of Penitentiaries* (1889).

70 Supra, n. 21, 171.

71 Evidence of Dr Richard Korn, 64. Dr Korn's definition of 'cruelty' parallels almost to the words used the formulation of the excessiveness test, which found favour with the United States Supreme Court in *Gregg* v. *Georgia*. There the court stated, 'the sanction imposed cannot be so totally without penological justification that it results in the gratuitous infliction of suffering': 96 S. Ct. R. 2909 at 2928.

72 Ibid., 68.

73 Heald judgment, 368.

74 Notes of evidence.

75 The evidence of the plaintiffs' witnesses on this point are in accord with the views expressed by staff psychologists at the Maine State Prison, who concluded that 'placing a prisoner in solitary confinement creates management problems far exceeding any problem that existed when the prisoner [was] part of the general population.' In solitary, prisoners lack access to normal reinforcements, eventually begin to 'act crazy,' reinforce each others' 'acting-out' behaviour, and become extremely disruptive. The psychologists argued that solitary confinement cannot be justified even as a punishment device, since it only serves to repress unwanted behaviour. In addition to finding that solitary has no value as a treatment or a punishment tool, the psychologists concluded that some prisoners confined in solitary for long periods revert to irrational and bizarre behaviour, eventually exhibiting one of the following behaviour patterns: angry and disruptive acts; depressive reactions; withdrawn and psychotic behaviour: see D. Hasson and J. Quinsey, 'Function of the Segregation Unit at the Maine State Prison,' cited in Benjamin and Lux, 'Solitary Confinement as Psychological Punishment,' 266.

76 Korn, 54–8.

77 Korn, 58.

78 Ibid., 57.

79 See Jackson, 'Justice behind the Walls,' 83–100.

80 Fox, 77–8.

81 Ibid., 82.

82 Ibid., 79.

83 *Jackson* v. *Bishop*, 404 F. 2d 571 (1968) at 580.

84 Heald judgment at 368.

85 (1977) 36 CCC (2d) 158 (BCSC).

86 Ibid., 165–6.
87 Heald judgment at 368.
88 Ibid.
89 Ibid., at 370.
90 Ibid.
91 Supra, n. 85.
92 Ibid., 165.
93 Ibid., 166.
94 Ibid.
95 Ibid., 167.
96 Ibid.
97 Ibid., 169.
98 Ibid., 170.
99 31 CCC(2d) 186–90.
100 Although there have been no cases in Canada since *McCann* and *Bruce, Lucas and Wilson* dealing with 'cruel and unusual punishment' and solitary confinement, the issue has arisen for the first time in England. In 1980, in *Williams* v. *Home Office (No. 2)* [1981] 1 All ER 1211, a case concerning the regime in the control unit at Wakefield Prison, one of the bases for the prisoner's claim that his detention in the unit was unlawful was that it conflicted with the provisions in the English Bill of Rights of 1689 prohibiting 'cruel and unusual punishments.' His counsel relied on the judgment in *McCann* in arguing that the clause be given a disjunctive interpretation. Mr Justice Tudor Williams, while conceding that there was no authority or academic writing in England favouring the conjunctive approach, nevertheless concluded that the words should be so construed because 'the words are clear in their meaning and show an intention to prohibit punishments which are both cruel and unusual' (at 1244). His Lordship concluded that the regime in the control unit was not unusual when compared with the other segregation regimes in the English penal system. As to whether it was cruel, counsel for the prisoner suggested the following formula for approaching this question. He argued that 'there was an irreducible minimum below which the court, reflecting public standards of morality, will not allow society to sink, whatever the pressures may be to take the relevant steps.' Above that level there may be conduct toward prisoners which is cruel because it is disproportionate. This issue, counsel suggested, involved balancing what was done against the need for doing it. Apart from these standards, counsel submitted, the test for what is cruel was objective. The court should look at the regime and ask whether it was cruel in relation to the sort of person who was in the unit; that is, the inveterate trouble-maker (at 1245). Mr Justice Tudor Williams found that the regime did not fall below the irreducible minimum judged by contemporary standards of public morality. He also concluded that

the regime was not cruel either in disproportionality or objectively in the effect of the regime on those subjected to it. His Lordship compared the regime in Wakefield with that in the BC Penitentiary as described in *McCann* and concluded that the conditions in Wakefield were better (at 1248).

101 The functional interrelationship between the plaintiffs' arguments can be seen not only from their historical juxtaposition in John Howard's writings in the eighteenth century and Inspector Moylan's writings in the nineteenth century, but in the specific context of the legal argument in *McCann* where one of the bases for arguing that confinement in SCU was cruel and unusual was that such confinement was applied arbitrarily. Moreover, the lack of procedural fairness prior to the imposition of such confinement and in any subsequent review of that confinement was part of the psychological pain inflicted by such confinement.

102 Dickson J in *Martineau* v. *Matsqui Institution Disciplinary Board (No. 2)* [1980] 1 SCR 602 at 619.

103 [1968] 2 DLR (3d) 545 (Ont. C.A.).

104 Ibid., 547.

105 Although the court refers to 'inmates,' except where citing directly from the judgment I will continue to use the term 'prisoners' when referring to people imprisoned.

106 Ibid., 550.

107 Ibid., 553.

108 Supra chap. 3, note 106.

109 Michael A. Milleman, 'Prison Disciplinary Hearings and Procedural Due Process,' 31 *Maryland Law Review* 27 (1971) at 40.

110 Korn, 65.

111 A competing theory of due process has emerged in the U.S. Supreme Court since 1975. See infra. n. 188.

112 333 F. Supp. 621 (1971).

113 Ibid. 626–7.

114 Ibid., 652.

115 328 F. Supp. 769 (9th Cir., 1971).

116 Ibid., 776.

117 Ibid., 780.

118 479 F. 2d 701 (7th Cir. 1973), cert. denied 414 U.S. 1146 (1974).

119 Ibid., 712.

120 Ibid., 717.

121 357 F. Supp. 1062 (1973).

122 Ibid., 1074–5.

123 Ibid., 1079.

124 378 F. Supp. 521 (1974).

125 Ibid., 528.

126 Ibid.
127 Ibid., 529.
128 Ibid.
129 Ibid., 533.
130 Ibid.
131 94 S. Ct. 2963 (1974).
132 Ibid., 2975.
133 Ibid., 2978–9.
134 Because *Wolff* expressed a more limited view of due process than some of the earlier lower-court decisions, rehearings were granted in a number of cases. The case of *Clutchette* v. *Procunier* was reheard, and the opinion of the Court of Appeals for the 9th Circuit modified to conform to the views expressed in *Wolff*, particularly in respect of confrontation and cross-examination of witnesses and the right to counsel. See 510 F. 2d 613 (9th Cir. 1975). See also *Baxter* v. *Parlmigiano; Enomoto* v. *Clutchette*, 96 S. Ct. 1551 (1976).
135 At 2982. In 1978, in a case specifically dealing with administrative segregation, the Supreme Court affirmed a three-judge federal district court ruling that within seventy-two hours of being placed in segregation the prisoner must be afforded the due process hearing mandated by *Wolff*: *Enomoto* v. *Wright*, 98 S. Ct. 1223 (1978) affirming *Wright* v. *Enomoto* 462 F. Supp. 297 (1976).
136 [1967] 2 QB 617.
137 Ibid., 630.
138 [1970] 2 QB 4.
139 Ibid., 431.
140 [1971] 1 Ch. 388.
141 Ibid., 402.
142 [1964] AC 40 at 65.
143 [1972] 2 All ER 6 (H. of L.).
144 Ibid., 17.
145 *Furnell* v. *Whangarei High Schools Board* (1973) AC 660 (JCPC).
146 For a discussion of the English cases see D.J. Mullan, 'Fairness: The New Natural Justice,' 25 *University of Toronto Law Journal* 281 (1975); See also the decision of Chief Justice Laskin in *Nicholson* v. *Haldimand-Norfolk Regional Board of Commissioners of Police* (1979) 1 SCR 311 (SCC).
147 [1973] OR 607 (Ont. HC).
148 [1965] 1 CCC 168 (SCC).
149 Supra, n. 147, 611–12.
150 (1974) 50 DLR (3d) 349 (SCC).
151 (1975) 24 CCC (2d) 241 (SCC).
152 Ibid., 257. Parole Act SC 1968–69, s. 21(1)(a). For a discussion of *Howarth* and *Mitchell* see Price, 'Doing Justice to Corrections,' 238 et seq.

153 The relevant sections of the Parole Board in force at the time of *Howarth* and *Mitchell* provided that '6. Subject to this Act ... the Board has exclusive jurisdiction and absolute discretion to grant, refuse to grant, or revoke parole ...11. The Board, in considering whether parole should be granted or revoked, is not required to grant a personal interview to the inmate or to any person on his behalf': SC 1968–69, c. 38. Pursuant to amendments to the Parole Act in 1977 and new parole regulations introduced in 1978 there is now a right to a parole and post-suspension hearing: SC 1976–7, c. 53, s. 11; SOR/78–428, ss. 15, 20.
154 Supra, n. 150, 352.
155 For example, in *Rinehart* v. *Brewer*, 360 F. Supp. 105, aff'd. 491 F. 2d 705 (8th Cir. 1974), the court held that in an emergency where a prisoner's behaviour presents a real danger to himself and others, the state's interest in summary segregation may outweigh the need for a prior hearing. In this event procedural protections must be extended as soon as reasonably practicable. In *Rinehart* the court did not set an inflexible deadline for such safeguards, but indicated that in the absence of compelling circumstances, any delay longer than forty-eight hours would probably be considered prejudicial to the rights of prisoners. Also, the U.S. cases have recognized that the prison authorities have a legitimate interest in protecting the safety of anonymous prison informants. In *Wolff*, the Supreme Court noted that if a prisoner informer were forced to reveal himself, as he would be if the right to confront and cross-examine accusers were upheld, he might be seriously endangered when he returned to prison. The court determined that this danger could support the decision not to make his identity known. Such a limitation on the right to confront or cross-examine accusers should not be permitted to overcome the prisoner's right to know the nature of the evidence against him, as distinguished from merely the identity of the informer, and should only limit his right to know the latter when the danger attending disclosure is grave. See 418 U.S. 539, 568–9 (1974).
156 Jackson, 'Justice behind the Walls.'
157 The viability of accommodating prisoners' and institutional authorities' legitimate interests is further supported by the regulations that prevail in other penitentiary systems. In the maximum-security facility in Massachusetts' Walpole Institution, the regulation in force at the time of the *McCann* trial provided in part that testimony at disciplinary hearings could not be taken outside the accused prisoner's presence unless he voluntarily absented himself or unless the chairman determined that exposure would involve a substantial risk of harm to the informant or to institutional security. If such a threat were found to exist, then the officials were to note a finding to this effect in the record of the hearing, summarize the information for the accused prisoner, and give the board's reason for protecting the informant in writing: see *Fano* v. *Meachum*, 387 F. Supp. 664 at 668. The Court of Appeals

for the First Circuit cited this regulation as a 'persuasive indication' that the provision for a summary of information divulged by an informant is not at odds with 'institutional requirements': 520 F. 2d at 380 (1st Cir. 1975).

158 The plaintiffs' position on this issue was conservative, reflecting the judgment that the Canadian judiciary would be most unwilling to adopt the interventionist role of some of their U.S. brethren. The U.S. federal courts have in many cases embraced an expansive role in the fashioning of remedies and the issuing of decrees touching on many aspects of prison life. For example, in *Morris* v. *Trevisono*, 310 F. Supp. 857 (1970), legal proceedings challenging disciplinary procedures in the Rhode Island Adult Correctional Institution led to extensive negotiations between the parties and ultimately to a consent decree implementing draft 'regulations governing disciplinary classifications procedures.' Prior to entering the decree, the court heard the views of prisoners in court, distributed to all prisoners a copy of the proposed rules, provided adequate opportunity for response, and received commentary from eminent penologists. The court retained jurisdiction over the case for a period of eighteen months to allow the parties to develop a working scheme of enforcement. See Harvard Center for Criminal Justice, 'Judicial Intervention in Prison Discipline,' 63 *Journal of Criminal Law and Criminology* 200 (1972). In the 'totality of conditions' cases some U.S. courts have held that prison conditions and practices which might not be unconstitutional if viewed individually can, when viewed as a whole, make confinement cruel and unusual punishment, and have then given prison officials time to prepare plans for alleviating those conditions; others have set forth detailed standards and ordered their prompt implementation. In *Pugh* v. *Locke*, 406 F. Supp. 318 (1976), the Federal District Court set forth a detailed eleven-point program entitled 'Minimum Constitutional Standards for Inmates of Alabama Penal System.' These standards specified the maximum population of Alabama prisons; the equipment and facilities to be provided in each cell; the procedural protections governing the confinement of inmates to isolation cells; the amount, standard, and variety of medical care to be available to inmates; the standard of sanitation and cleanliness and the overall living conditions in the prisons; the sanitary measures to be taken in preparing and serving of food; and rules governing inmate correspondence and visitations. The court gave the prison officials six months in which to file a report indicating their progress in implimenting the standards. The U.S. Supreme Court, despite a reaction against what it regards as the over-extension of the courts' role in reviewing the 'informed discretion of prison administrators' (see note 188, infra) has approved the 'totality of conditions' approach to prison litigation: see *Hutto* v. *Finney*, 98 S. Ct. 2565 (1978); *Alabama* v. *Pugh*, 98 S. Ct. 3057 (1978). See Comment, 'Confronting the Conditions of Confinement: An Expanded Role for Courts in Prison Reform,' 12 *Harvard Civil*

Rights and Civil Liberties Law Review 367 (1977); Comment, 'Prison Reform in the Federal Courts,' 27 *Buffalo Law Review* 99 (1978). See also Note, 'Complex Enforcement: Unconstitutional Prison Conditions,' 94 *Harvard Law Review* 626 (1981).

159 Heald judgment at 374.

160 [1976] 1 FC 540 (FCTD).

161 [1976] 2 FC 198 (FCA).

162 Ibid., 210–11.

163 Ibid., 212.

164 Ibid., 216.

165 [1978] 1 SCR 118 at 121.

166 Ibid., 129. The English courts have also held that the prison rules are regulatory directions only and breaches thereof do not give rise to a cause of action. See Graham Zellick, 'The Prison Rules and the Courts,' *Criminal Law Review* (1981), 602; 'The Prison Rules and the Courts: A Postscript,' *Criminal Law Review* (1982), 575.

167 Supra, n. 165, 131.

168 Ibid., 123. For further commentary on *Martineau (No. 1)*, particularly the majority's view of the directives as non-law within section 28, see Price, 'Doing Justice to Corrections', supra, n. 4, 272–6; H.N. Janisch, 'What is Law – Directives of the Commissioner of Penitentiaries' and 'Section 28 of the Federal Court Act – The Tip of the Iceberg of "Administrative Quasi-Legislation,"' 55 *Canadian Bar Review* 576 (1977). See also John W. Conroy, *Canadian Prison Law* (Vancouver: Butterworths 1980), 9–13.

169 [1978] 1 FC 312 (FCTD).

170 [1978] 2 FC 637 (FCA).

171 Ibid., 640–1.

172 Canada Elections Act, RSC 1970 (1st Supp.), c. 14, s. 14(4)(e).

173 [1980] 1 SCR 602.

174 This central finding of *Martineau (No. 2)* flowed from the groundwork already laid in the majority decision of the Supreme Court in *Nicholson* v. *Haldimand-Norfolk Regional Police Commissioners* (1979) 1 SCR 311 (SCC). In that judgment, delivered after the decision of the Federal Court of Appeal in *Martineau (No. 2)*, judicial review under the Judicial Review Procedure Act of Ontario was allowed of the decision of a police commission to dispense with the services of a constable. By the relevant regulations the right to a quasi-judicial hearing was not available to the appellant because he was still within his eighteen-month probationary period. Although accepting that determination of master–servant relationships would not, per se, give rise to any legal requirement to observance of any of the principles of natural justice, the majority held that in the case of the holder of a public office such as a constable, there was a common-law duty to act fairly which fell short of a

duty to act quasi-judicially, but nevertheless could be enforced by judicial review. The Ontario Act included precisely the remedies contemplated in section 18 of the Federal Court Act.

175 Supra, n. 173, 606.

176 The *St Germain* case was part of the legal fallout from the Hull Prison riot in 1976, the worst in British penal history. The prisoners involved were charged with prison disciplinary offences and brought before the Board of Visitors, an independent body that deals with serious prison charges and whose membership has been characterized as being 'in the great tradition of the English amateur who interests himself in public affairs.' The board handed down extremely heavy sentences. One prisoner was sentenced to the loss of 720 days remission, equivalent to a three-year sentence (later reduced to 600 days by the home secretary). It was these proceedings before the Hull Board of Visitors that were successfully challenged in the *St Germain* case. For a critical account of the role of the Board of Visitors see J.E. Thomas and Richard Pooley, *The Exploding Prison* (London: Junction Books 1980), chap. 5; Graham Zellick, 'Penalties for Disciplinary Offences in Prison' *Public Law* (1981), 228 at 244–6. See also *R.* v. *Board of Visitors of Hull Prison, ex parte Germain (No. 2)* [1979] 1 WLR 140 C.A.

177 [1979] 1 All ER 701 at 702 (C.A.).

178 Supra, n. 173, 625.

179 Ibid., 637.

180 Ibid., 618–19.

181 Ibid., 622.

182 [1976] 1 All ER 13 (C.A.).

183 [1980] 1 SCR 624.

184 Supra, n. 174.

185 Supra, n. 183, 630.

186 Ibid., 629.

187 Martineau of course had long since served his sentence of fifteen days' dissociation, and the practical implication of the final decision in his case, reflected in the consent order, was that all reference to his conviction of the offences was to be expunged from his penitentiary record.

An important issue (which future litigation will no doubt raise) is the effect of the Charter of Rights and Freedoms on the right to procedural fairness. Section 7 of the new charter consolidates s. 1(a) and s. 2(e) of the Bill of Rights by providing in section 7 that 'Everyone has the right to life, liberty and security of the person and the right not to be deprived thereof except in accordance with the principles of fundamental justice.'

No doubt lawyers for the penitentiary authorities can be expected to argue, in the context of administrative segregation, that no liberty interest is involved. I have described how this was the position accepted by the Ontario

Court of Appeal in *Beaver Creek* and I have examined its weakness in light of the concept of institutional liberty. That concept has now been endorsed in Mr Justice Dickson's judgment in *Martineau (No. 2)* which recognized that detention in 'a prison within a prison' deprives a prisoner of his liberty. Assuming therefore that the courts will accept the relevance of s. 7 of the charter to administrative-segregation decisions, a question remains as to what the principles of fundamental justice require. I have described how Canadian courts have consistently held that s. 1(a) and s. 2(e) of the Bill of Rights did not expand the rights to procedural fairness beyond those which existing administrative law recognized. Lawyers for the penitentiary authorities can be expected to urge the courts to take a similar position under s. 7, particularly since administrative law has now developed the duty to act fairly, which recognizes a limited role for judicial review of prison disciplinary decisions. My previous review of the U.S. courts' inquiry as to what 'due process' entails in the prison context has revealed that the courts have sought to balance the prisoner's interest in institutional liberty against the institutional interest in summary adjudication. The Supreme Court of Canada in *Martineau (No. 2)* has stated that like due process, fairness is a flexible standard which has to be interpreted in the distinctive context of the prison. This suggests that arguments based on fundamental justice may not result in any extended procedural protection for prisoners facing administrative segregation that cannot be gained through arguments based on the duty to act fairly. Essential to either line of argument will be the need to explain to the court the full implications of the segregation decision for the lives of prisoners so that the procedural protections extended, whether under the rubric of fairness or fundamental justice, are commensurate with the gravity of the decision.

Other provisions of the charter have a potential impact on the conduct of prison disciplinary decisions. Section 11, which deals with the rights of a person 'charged with an offence,' may be held to be applicable to a prisoner charged with a serious disciplinary offence. In an appropriate case it could be argued that the institution's allegations in an administrative-segregation context constitute the charging of an 'offence' within the meaning of s. 11. In the one case so far decided on section 11 and prison disciplinary matters, Mr Justice Toy rejected the argument that a 'serious disciplinary offence' under the penitentiary-service regulations was an 'offence' within the purview of s. 11(h). In that case it was argued that s. 11(h) which provides that 'any person charged with an offence has the right ... if found guilty and punished for the offence, not to be tried or punished for it again,' barred the laying of criminal charges against a prisoner who had been found guilty before a disciplinary board of offences arising from the same events as those that formed the basis of the criminal charges. See *R.* v. *Mingo et al.* Reasons for judgment of Mr Justice Toy, 26 October 1982.

188 A further irony is apparent when comparing the arguments in *McCann* and the decision in *Martineau (No. 2)*. In *Martineau (No. 2)* Dickson J cites the decision of the Supreme Court of the United States in *Wolff* v. *McDonnell*, which was also relied upon by the plaintiffs in *McCann*. In fact, since the *Wolff* decision there has been some judicial retreat at the Supreme Court level as to the appropriate scope of judicial review. Thus, in *Meachum* v. *Fano*, 427 U.S.215 (1976), prisoners brought an action charging that their transfer to a maximum-security institution violated their due process rights in that they had not received proper notice of the reasons or a hearing prior to the transfer. The lower courts granted the relief sought, but the Supreme Court reversed. The majority opinion by Mr Justice White, while explicitly reaffirming the *Wolff* view that the prisoner retains a variety of important rights the courts must be alert to protect so that he is not stripped of his liberty just because he is in prison, rejects the idea that any grievous loss sustained by a prisoner is sufficient to attract due process. The court specifically rejected the idea that the due process clause in and of itself protected a prisoner facing transfer to another prison. In the view of the *Meachum* court, 'To hold that substantial deprivation triggers due process would subject to judicial review a wide spectrum of discretionary actions that traditionally have been the business of prison administrators rather than of federal courts' (427 U.S.215). The court distinguished *Wolff* on the basis that the relevant Nebraska statute had provided a statutory right to 'good time' which could be forfeited only for serious behaviour; in contrast, the Massachusetts statute involved in *Meachum* conferred no right on the prisoner to remain in the prison to which he was assigned defeasible only upon proof of specific acts of misconduct. Because Massachusetts law created no such legal right, the court held that there was no basis for invoking the protections of the Fourteenth Amendment. *Meachum* falls within a broader doctrinal development in recent due process analysis in the United States which has been termed the 'entitlement' view of due process. Under this approach the existence of an independently grounded legal right or entitlement is the necessary trigger to procedural safeguards. In the absence of such a right, the entitlement view provides no basis for invoking the Fourteenth Amendment's protection of liberty. It is to be contrasted with the alternative 'impact' view of due process, which dominated until the *Meachum* case. As I have explained earlier, this approach stresses not the existence of a formal legal entitlement but rather the likelihood that disciplinary action will lead to significant adverse impact or grievous loss to the prisoner. This grievous loss or adverse impact itself is sufficient to mandate procedural protection.

See 'Two Views of a Prisoner's Right to Due Process: *Meachum* v. *Fano*,' 12 *Harvard Civil Rights and Civil Liberties Law Review* 405 (1977).

The entitlement view of due process parallels in many ways the view taken by the Ontario Court of Appeal in the *Beaver Creek* case, which required as a condition precedent to judicial review that the decision affect the rights of a prisoner, such rights being limited (for all practical intent) to those created by the Penitentiary Act and Regulations. By contrast, the decision of the Supreme Court in *Martineau (No. 2)*, and in particular the judgment of Dickson J, very much reflects the impact view of due process.

Underlying the U.S. Supreme Court's more limited view of the source of due process protection is a developing antipathy towards prisoners' rights on the part of a majority of the court. In *North Carolina Prisoners Labour Union Inc.* v. *Jones*, 97 S. Ct. 2532 (1977), *Bell* v. *Wolfish*, 99 S. Ct. 1861 (1979), and *Rhodes* v. *Chapman*, 101 S. Ct. 2392 (1981), the Supreme Court has emphasized the need for judicial deference to the 'informed discretion of prison administrators' (97 S. Ct. at 2538), particularly regarding 'policies and practices that in their judgment are needed to preserve internal order' (99 S. Ct. at 1878). In the view of some commentators, the *Wolfish* and *Rhodes* decisions particularly have announced the resurrection of the 'hands-off' doctrine under new guises: see Richard Singer, 'The *Wolfish* case: Has the Bell Tolled for Prison Litigation in the Federal Courts?' in *Legal Rights of Prisoners*, ed. Geoffrey Valpert (Beverly Hills, Sage Publications, 1980), 67; Ira P. Robbins, 'The Cry of Wolfish in the Federal Courts: The Future of Federal Judicial Intervention in Prison Administration,' 71 *Journal of Criminal Law and Criminology* 211 (1980); Note, 'Eighth Amendment: A Significant Limit on Federal Court Activism in Ameliorating State Prison Conditions,' 72 *Journal of Criminal Law and Criminology* 134 (1981).

5 THE PENITENTIARIES' RESPONSE TO THE *McCANN* CASE: CANADA'S NEW PRISONS OF ISOLATION

1 J. Vantour, *Report of the Study Group on Dissociation* (Ottawa, Solicitor-General of Canada 1975), cited hereafter as Vantour Report, 24.
2 Vantour Report, 24–6. The references in the extract are to Richard Cloward, *Theoretical Studies in the Social Organization of the Prison* (New York: Social Science Research Council 1960) and Graham Sykes and Sheldon L. Messinger, 'The Inmate Social System,' in *The Sociology of Punishment and Correction*, 2d ed., ed. Norman Johnston, Leonard Savitz, and Marvin Wolfgang (New York: John Wiley and Sons 1970).
3 Vantour Report, 27.
4 Ibid., 29.
5 Ibid., 29–30.
6 Ibid., 31.

7 Ibid., 32. For a more extended discussion on the relative advantages and disadvantages of the dispersal-versus-concentration models see Advisory Council on the Penal System, *The Regime for Long-term Prisoners in Conditions of Maximum Security*, HMSO 1968. See also J.E. Thomas, Policy and Administration in Penal Establishments, in *Progress in Penal Report*, ed. Louis Blom Cooper (Oxford: Clarenden Press 1974), 62–4.
8 Vantour Report, 36–7.
9 Ibid., 37.
10 Ibid., 39.
11 Ibid., 40.
12 Michael Jackson, 'Justice behind the Walls – A Study of the Disciplinary Process in a Canadian Penitentiary,' 12 *Osgoode Hall Law Journal* 1 (1974) at 64 et seq.
13 29 CCC (2d) at 375. See also *Merricks et al.* v. *Nott Bower et al.* [1964] 1 All ER 717 (C.A.).
14 *Vancouver Province*, 9 January 1976.
15 Evidence of Dragan Cernetic before the Parliamentary Subcommittee on the Penitentiary System in Canada.
16 Letters from Paul Desjarlais, 29 April 1976, and Dwight Lowe, 20 May 1976, to the author.
17 *Vancouver Sun*, 17 May 1976.
18 The description by Oriana Fallaci of the light entering the tomb in which Alexander Panagoulis was imprisoned by the Greek junta accurately describes the situation at the BC Penitentiary after the *McCann* decision: 'It wasn't exactly daylight, however, because beyond the bars there was a grill, then an iron lattice, and the sun filtered through that iron lattice as if through a collander: shedding a dim glow, faint strands of yellow': Oriana Fallaci, *A Man* (New York: Simon and Schuster 1980), 109.
19 Letter from Andy Bruce, 13 December 1976, to the author.
20 Ibid.
21 *Report to Parliament: The Subcommittee on the Penitentiary System in Canada* (Ottawa: Minister of Supply and Services 1977) para. 220.
22 A developing literature in the U.S. documents the prison-related difficulties of enforcement of court decrees. See, for example, 'Project: Judicial Intervention in Corrections: The California Experience – An Empirical Study,' 20 *University of California at Los Angeles Law Review* 452 (1973); and Harvard Center for Criminal Justice, 'Judicial Intervention in Prison Discipline,' 63 *Journal of Criminal Law and Criminology* 200 (1972). There is evidence, however, that the totality-of-conditions litigation has induced significant changes particularly but not exclusively in the prison systems of the deep South. See Comment, 'Confronting the Conditions of Confinement: An Expanded Role for Courts in Prison Reform,' 12 *Harvard Civil Rights and Civil Liberties Law Review* 367 (1977) which contains this assessment: 'While

the evidence on the success of judicial intervention in prison administration has not yet been fully marshalled, the evidence that has been accumulated indicates that totality of conditions cases have achieved remarkable success in improving prison living conditions. For example, in the aftermath of *Pugh* v. *Locke*, the Alabama Corrections officials devised and implemented a new classification system at a total cost of $100,000. This new system resulted in reduced overcrowding, improved facilities, and a greatly reduced level of violence ... Moreover, case studies of four totality of conditions cases conclude that in each case, judicial intervention has resulted in a vastly improved quality of prison life. [American Bar Association, *After Decision: Implementation of Judicial Decrees in Correctional Settings*, 1976.]

Similarly, [these] studies have concluded that judicial intervention in totality of conditions cases, while not producing model prison systems, has greatly improved prison living conditions and has raised inmate morale without undermining the staff authority and control.' See also William Bennett Turner, 'When Prisoners Sue: A Study of Prisoner Section 1983 Suits in the Federal Courts,' 92 *Harvard Law Review* 610 (1979).

23 In the California study of the impact of judicial intervention, 87 per cent of the prison administrators interviewed agreed with the statement that 'correctional administrators, if they so choose, could comply with court orders through changes which meet the letter of the court order, but not its spirit, and thereby frustrate the intent of the court': supra, n. 22, 530.

24 James B. Jacobs, *Stateville: The Penitentiary in Mass Society* (Chicago: University of Chicago Press 1977), 113–18.

25 James B. Jacobs, 'The Prisoners' Rights Movement and its Impacts 1960–80,' in *Crime and Justice: An Annual Review of Research*, vol. 2, ed. Norval Morris and Michael Tonry (Chicago: University of Chicago Press 1980), 434.

26 Ibid., 453. As Jacobs points out, recent U.S. opinion on the impact of prison litigation has been divided into those who think it has been ineffective and those who see it as the crucial influence on prison reform. He suggests that the discrepancy 'may be explained by the absence of a methodology for identifying impacts and the absence of criteria for judging their importance: ibid.

27 *Report to Parliament*, para. 411, p. 84.

28 Ibid., 86–7.

29 Ibid., 85.

30 Ibid., recommendation 29, pp. 87–9.

31 Ibid., recommendation 30, pp. 90–1.

32 Ibid., recommendation 36, pp. 96–8.

33 Ibid., recommendation 31, pp. 91–2.

34 Ibid., para. 437, p. 92.

35 Ibid. para. 417–18, p. 87.

36 David Fogel, 'The Justice Model for Corrections,' in *Prisons, Past and Present*, ed. John C. Freeman (London: Heinemann 1978). This essay is adapted from

Fogel's larger work, *We are the Living Proof: The Justice Model for Corrections* (Cincinnati: Anderson Publishing Co. 1975). Professor Fogel was formerly commissioner of the Minnesota State Department of Corrections and executive director of the Illinois Law Enforcement Commission.

37 Ibid., 162–8.

38 The Supreme Court of Canada has, since *Martineau (No. 2)*, also endorsed another of the justice model's tenets – 'the least restrictive means' – in the case of *Solosky* v. *The Queen* (1980) 50 CCC (2d) 497 (SCC). The issue there was whether the penitentiary authorities could interfere with mail sent to or by a prisoner's lawyer. The prisoner sought a declaration that properly identified correspondence between himself and his solicitor was to be regarded as privileged correspondence and forwarded unopened. The penitentiary service regulation provided for censorship of mail 'to the extent considered necessary and desirable for the reformation and rehabilitation of inmates or the security of the institution.' Commissioner's Directive 219 exempts from censorship 'privileged correspondence,' which includes letters to members of federal and provincial legislatures and to ombudsmen. The Supreme Court rejected the primary ground upon which the prisoner rested his case – the solicitor–client privilege – on the basis that it was not applicable to correspondence not directed to obtaining evidence in any proceedings. However, approaching the case on a broader basis – on the premise that a prisoner retains all his civil rights other than those expressly or impliedly taken away from him by law – the court has expressed the view that where a fundamental civil and legal right is involved which has not been so taken away, the courts have to play a balancing role to ensure that any interference with that right by the institutional authorities for valid correctional goals must be the least restrictive means for achieving those goals. Applying that principle to the case at hand, the court found that the prisoner's fundamental right to communicate in confidence with his lawyer had not been taken away by the regulations and directives; that censorship for the purposes set out in the regulations was in pursuit of legitimate correctional goals; that the court had to balance the public interest in maintaining the security of the institution with the interest represented by insulating the solicitor–client relationship; that while ultimately the scale must come down in favour of the public interest, any interference with the prisoner's fundamental right must be no greater than is essential to the maintenance of security and the rehabilitation of the prisoner.

39 Response of the solicitor-general to the Parliamentary Subcommittee on the Penitentiary System in Canada, 5 August 1977, 1.

40 K. McReynolds and J. Vantour, 'Inmates in Special Handling Units; Physical Criteria' (draft), n.d.

41 Interview with Dr Vantour, August 1980.

42 SC 1976–7, c. 53.

43 Vantour Report, 29. In fact, the special handling units have not been used for the initial incarceration of all first-degree murderers, but only for those who have murdered police or prison officers while in custody or at large. However, in January 1983 the special handling unit policy was amended to provide that the prisoner convicted of first-degree murder who has an extensive record of serious violence may be placed in a special handling unit. CD 800-4-04, January 1983 para. 13.
44 McReynolds and Vantour, 'Inmates in Special Handling Units,' 5.
45 Ibid., 8–10.
46 Ibid., 17. According to the Vantour-McReynolds model, the primary envelope is the prisoner's cell, the second envelope is the unit in which not more than seven prisoners can assemble, and the third envelope is the module containing no more than four units.
47 Ibid., 46.
48 Ibid.
49 Ibid., 49.
50 See *Clonce* v. *Richardson*, 379 F. Supp. 338 (1974). For a discussion of this and other U.S. programs, see generally 'Symposium; Behaviour Modification in Prisons,' 13 *American Criminal Law Review* (1975).
51 *Manual of Operation for Special Programme Unit*, 1971, 7.
52 See David Goldberger, 'Court Challenges to Prison Behaviour Modification Programs: A Case Study,' 13 *American Criminal Law Review* 37 (1975).
53 Ibid., 59. See also Jacobs, *Stateville*, 109–11.
54 J.E. Thomas, 'Special Units in Prisons,' in *The Yearbook of Social Policy*, ed. K. Jones (London: Routledge and Kegan Paul 1974), 89–90.
55 See, for example, letters to the editor of the *London Times* from Ms Patricia Hewitt of the National Council of Civil Liberties, 12 October 1974, and from Professor Graham Zellick, 29 October 1974.
56 Thomas, *Special Units*, 90.
57 Ibid. See *Williams and Home Secretary (No. 2)* [1981] 1 All ER 1211, for a fuller statement of the nature of the regime in a control unit (at 1216) and for a review of the history leading to the introduction of the control-unit policy (at 1215).
58 Rule 43 provides: 'Where it appears desirable, for the maintenance of good order or discipline or in his own interests, that a prisoner should not associate with other prisoners either generally or for particular purposes, the governor may arrange for the prisoner's removal from association accordingly': Prison Rules, 1964 (SI 1964, no. 388 as amended by SI 1974, no. 713.) For a discussion of rule 43 see Graham Zellick, 'Prison Discipline and Preventative Detention,' *Criminal Law Review* (1981), 218.
59 One of the prisoners confined in the control unit after being released on parole brought an action claiming damages for false imprisonment in respect of the 180-day period he spent in the control unit and a declaration that the

Home Office had acted ultra vires and unlawfully in setting up and operating the control unit. He argued, inter alia, that his detention could not be justified under the prison rules; that the nature of the regime offended the provision in the Bill of Rights (1689) prohibiting the infliction of cruel and unusual punishments; that his detention was unlawful because there had been a denial of the rules of natural justice in that he had not been specifically told why he was being transferred to the unit and given an opportunity to make representations as to why he should not be detained there. Both the action for damages and the declaration were dismissed: *Williams* v. *Home Secretary (No. 2)*, supra, n. 57. For the reasons for the decision on 'cruel and unusual punishment,' see chap. 4, n. 100. As to the procedural fairness argument, the court held that natural justice required only that the control-unit committee should act fairly when considering the application to transfer the plaintiff to the control unit, and that it had done so.

60 The pre-December 1980 framework is contained in Commissioner's Directive 174, 1979; Divisional Instruction 718, 22 October 1979; the post December 1980 framework in CD 274, 1 December 1980; reissued with minor amendments as CD 800–4–04, 30 November 1982; further amended 19 January 1983: DI 800-4-04, 30 November 1982.

61 CD 174 para. 4.

62 DI 718, para. 3(c).

63 Ibid., para. 3(d).

64 CD 274, para. 4.

65 CD 274, para 8.

66 Press release, Department of the Solicitor-General, 28 November 1980.

67 Affidavit of J.U.M. Sauvé, in *Morin* v. *Comite National charge de l'examen des cas d'USD et al.* Federal Court T-6035–8. Jan. 12, 1982.

68 DI 800–4–04, paras. 6–21.

69 Ibid., para. 13. The latest revision to CD 274, introduced in January 1983, now contains provision for a prisoner to appear at a hearing when the National Review Committee elects to conduct a transfer meeting at the institution in which the prisoner is confined. So far, no such meetings have been held in western Canada. CD 800–4–04, 19 January 1983, para. 8. Based on a document prepared by the Department of the Solicitor-General entitled 'Implication of the Charter of Rights for the Correctional System' dated March 1982, it is clear that these changes are seen as the 'minimum procedures' necessary to ensure that the transfer process conforms to 'the principles of fundamental justice' mandated by s. 7 of the Charter of Rights and Freedoms as the prerequisite to any deprivation of life, work and security of the person. In the same vein, national headquarters has now established a dissociation policy board with a mandate to ensure 'conformity between the dissociation policy and the duty to act fairly.' CD 800–4–06, 30 November 1982.

70 In his application to the Supreme Court of Ontario for a writ of habeus corpus with certiorari in aid, Miller raises a number of important legal issues. Is confinement in a special handling unit an unlawful form of dissociation? Miller's argument is that the duration and conditions of confinement in SHU involve such a dramatic and extensive form of dissociation that they cannot be justified in the absence of specific statutory authority; May confinement in a special handling unit be lawfully authorized by the Deputy Commissioner / Security? Miller's argument is that the Penitentiary Service Regulations confer the authority to dissociate solely on the warden of a penitentiary. Yet CD274 purports to create a special form of dissociation of an SHU and to confer the power to transfer a prisoner into that form of dissociation upon a person other than the warden. Is the review process established by CD274 an unlawful abrogation of the review process established by the regulations? (I will be referring to the argument on this issue after dealing with the review process in the text.) Apart from the legality of the Commissioner's Directive, was the confinement of Miller in SHU in his particular circumstances, unlawful? Miller's argument on this point is that the decision to place him in the SHU, which is a prison within a prison, for a period of two years is a decision with such serious consequences for him that it must be made in compliance with the duty to act fairly. Fairness requires at the very least that Miller be advised of the allegation against him and be offered an opportunity to respond. On 5 March 1982, Mr Justice Steele dismissed Miller's application on the basis that since there was no question of the validity of the warrants of committal, the Superior Court had no jurisdiction to go behind those warrants and review through certiorari the administrative acts of the penitentiary authorities. That jurisdiction lay only with the Federal Court of Canada. The Ontario Court of Appeal reversed on the issue of jurisdiction (1983) 29 CR (3d) 153. Because the Quebec Court of Appeal has come to a different conclusion on this jurisdictional point (see the *Morin* case, chap. 6, n. 22), the matter remains to be resolved by the Supreme Court of Canada, which has granted leave to appeal in both the *Miller* and *Morin* cases.

71 CD 174, para. 9(d).

72 DI 800-4-04. para. 50; CD 274, paras. 14-15.

73 DI 800-4-04, para. 37.

74 DI 718 para. 7(d).

75 DI 800-4-04, para. 44.

76 Letter to the author from J. Sauvé, deputy commissioner (security), 9 October 1980. As part of my research for this book, I requested permission to visit the special handling units at Millhaven and the CDC, to interview prisoners and staff, and also to observe the proceedings in the six-month review hearings of the National Review Committee. Although permission to visit the units and interview the prisoners and staff was granted (I was given excellent co-operation in this regard by officials at both the national and institutional

levels), it was felt that 'because of the highly sensitive security information which is revealed' at the review hearings and 'because of the impact of Part IV of the Canadian Human Rights Act, it would impede the functioning of the Committee' if I, as a non-official, were permitted to attend: Ibid. Two months after this letter, the new Commissioner's Directive specifically provided that the commissioner of corrections 'shall appoint a person from the private sector to attend each six-month review and shall also invite the Correctional Investigator to attend': CD274, para. 18.

77 Ibid.

78 CD274, para. 11.

79 DI718, para. 6(b).

80 CD274, para. 12.

81 DI718 para. 6(c); DI800–4–04, para. 22.

82 Millhaven Institution, *Special Handling Unit, Inmates' Handbook.*

83 Canadian Correctional Service, 'Special Handling Units,' 8 July 1980.

84 Interview with Prisoner A, 26 August 1980. I have not used prisoners' names where the disclosure might prejudice the review of their cases.

85 Interview with Prisoner B, 26 August 1980.

86 Interview with Prisoner C, 27 August 1980.

87 Although much of the evidence presented in *McCann* focused on the aggression caused by long-term solitary confinement, such confinement can also produce pervasive apathy. The coexistence of these effects has been described by a prisoner at Kent Institution: 'Rest assured that both apathy and aggression can co-exist, in extremes, in prison. Apathy here is not a pervading lack of emotion. It is a lack of motivation, an indifference to present and future wellbeing and personal growth. Perhaps it could be termed 'cognitive narrowing' ... apathy is a political act at times, a show of anger and contempt by a people who are powerless. It is that and more. It is the ceasing of creative activity while the mind fights psychological battles. It is an indication, almost as much as violence, of the turmoil within.' (Letter dated February 1981.)

88 Statement of inmate grievances shown to the author, 26 August 1980.

89 Grievance presented 5 August 1980 by sixteen prisoners in the special handling unit, phase 2.

90 The psychologist in charge of the SHU, both before and during the time of my visits, was charged with the task of coordinating the accreditation Millhaven was seeking from the American Corrections Association, and conceded that this had cut severely into the time he had to conduct personal interviews in the SHU.

91 Response dated 5 August 1980.

92 Segregation notification dated 30 November 1979.

93 CD274, para. 16.

94 The de facto subordination of the thirty-day institutional review to the national six-monthly review raises an important point of law. Under section

2.30(1)(a) (now section 40) of the penitentiary regulations, the only review board authorized by law to review administrative-segregation cases is the institutional board. While the so-called national review process is set out in the commissioner's directive and divisional instruction, these instruments do not have the force of law and thus the national review committee has no legal status to make decisions affecting segregation. A fortiori, the institutional boards' lawful authority in these cases cannot be subsumed in and subordinated to the national committee's role.

95 Supra, n. 76.

96 Parole Regulations, s. 17(1) SOR/78–428.

97 Supra, n. 74.

98 Parole Regulations 20.1(1) SOR/81.

99 Supra, n. 45.

100 Supra, n. 74.

101 Supra, n. 75.

102 Notification dated 14 April 1980.

103 DI718, para. 7a(5)(a).

104 My findings on the lack of specific standards for progression through the phases and for release from the SHU parallel those made by a U.S. federal court in relation to a similar unit in the Georgia prison system, which was the subject of a constitutional challenge on the basis that, inter alia, the lack of standards violated due process of law. Like the SHUs, H-House was organized on a behaviour-modification system involving three phases. The judgment of the federal court contains this assessment of the release process: 'Prisoners are placed [in H-House] indefinitely, but are told that they may get out of H-House if their conduct conforms to certain standards. The problem is that those standards are not published or written down anywhere and confusion exists among the various guards, counsellors, and wardens as to what behaviour on the part of the prisoner will gain him release to the less rigorous phases of H-House and eventually back to the general prison population. The criteria are ... largely subjective in nature and arbitrarily administered ... The method now used by the State to choose which prisoner shall leave H-House is the epitome of arbitrary State action forbidden by the Fourteenth Amendment. The most glaring defect is that H-House prisoners are expected to comport with a certain standard of behaviour, but they are not told or given written explanation of what that standard is.' (*Hardwick v. Ault*, 447 F. Supp. 116 (1978) at 124.) The court found that this lack of standards denied the prisoners in H-House due process: 'Procedural due process requires, as a minimum, that notice be given of the rules ... The State punishes prisoners in H-House, but conditions that punishment upon a continuing failure of the prisoner to comport with the rules of H-House. Under these circumstances, simple fairness requires that the rules be written and that

they create objective criteria by which to gauge the progress of an H-House inmate' (ibid.).

105 DI 800-4-04, para. 26.

106 Ibid., para. 34.

107 Supra, n. 81.

108 CD 274, para. 14.

109 As of 30 June 1979 the average stay of prisoners released from the two SHUs was eleven months. The average stay of prisoners still in the SHU was 12.3 months: *Quarterly SHU Statistics*.

110 The extent to which the SHU program remains indeterminate can be readily discerned from the comment made by James Phelps, a deputy commissioner of corrections, on the occasion of the return of Andy Bruce to Millhaven from Sharp's Farm maximum security where he had been for only four months following a three-year term in the SHU: 'He will be tried again in a general population when it is believed that he is capable of behaving. It could be six months or it could be 10 years': *Vancouver Sun*, 4 September 1982.

111 Supra, n. 81.

112 Charles Dickens, *American Notes for General Circulation* (London: Chapman and Hall 1842), 119–20.

113 Inmate complaint, 3 August 1980.

114 Dario Melossi and Massimo Pavarini, *The Prison and the Factory: Origins of the Penitentiary System* (London: Macmillan 1981), 150.

115 Ibid., 154–5.

116 Edgar Roussel, 'L'Enfer du Centre de Développement Correctionnel' (The Hell of the Correctional Development Centre), *Le Devoir*, 29 August 1980.

117 Ibid.

118 Interview with Prisoner A, 26 August 1980.

119 Letter to the author from Dwight Lucas, February 1981.

120 Interview with Prisoner D.

121 *Report to Parliament*, 22. Paul Rose has provided this description of the regime under which in 1970 he and four other members of the FLQ were held in the CDC: 'In 1970 five special FLQ cases without any disciplinary charges, without any notice (a phantom transfer) were transferred for many months to the Special Correction Unit. They were there placed under the observation by armed guards. They were kept naked in tiny strip cells, without any window. The light was on twenty-four hours a day (during the day from 7:00 A.M. until midnight fluorescent lights; during night time a 60-watt bulb). For months they were subject to the most degrading regime: to receive his meal plate the prisoner was required to move to the back of the cell; he was prohibited from moving until the door was completely closed; no food could be kept in the cell between meals; conversation was prohibited; the prisoner was required to earn his clothes piece by piece by good conduct; the prisoner

was not allowed to sit or lay down on his bed between reveille and "lights out." At night even though the light was harsh, the prisoner's head was required to be always in sight; no personal effects were permitted (no books, papers, pens, magazines); after the prisoner had regained his clothes he was allowed one half hour of a day out of his cell for exercise': Robert Lemieux, Paul Rose and Nicole Daignault, *Dossiers sur les prisonniers politiques au Québec*, 2d ed. (Montreal, 1976), 23. For a further account of the regime in the 'special correction units' see Luc Gosselin, *Prisons in Canada* (Montreal: Black Rose 1982), 139 et seq.

122 Letter to the author from Rory Shayne, 2 October 1980.
123 Interview with Clare Wilson, 25 August 1980.
124 (1977) 36 CCC (2d) 158.
125 Supra, n. 123.
126 Interview with Prisoner E at Kent Institution, August 1981.
127 Roussel, *L'Enfer du CDC*.
128 *Manuel des Détenus de l'Unite spéciale de détention (USD)*, August 1981, as amended, 305.
129 Interview with Malcolm Johnson, 19 May 1982.
130 Interview with Edgar Roussel, 21 May 1982.
131 *Let's Talk*, vol. 5, no. 9, 3 May 1980, 1.
132 Ibid., 3.
133 Letter to the author dated 10 February 1981.
134 Letter to the author from Rick Levesque, 25 February 1981.
135 'Rules and Regulations for Segregation,' Kent Institution, 23 November 1979.
136 CD 174, para. 7.
137 CD 274, para. 19.
138 CD 277, para. 4.
139 Ibid., paras. 7–23.
140 Reasons for judgment of McEachern CJ, 30 December 1980 (BCSC).
141 Affidavit of John Dowsett, dated 26 November 1980, para. 8.
142 Reasons for judgment, 9–10.
143 Ibid., 13.
144 Ibid.
145 Ibid.
146 Ibid., 16.
147 Ibid.
148 Cross-examination on affidavit of John Dowsett, Appeal Book, 73.
149 Ibid.
150 Ibid., 10.
151 Ibid., 6–7.
152 Ibid., 16.
153 Ibid.

154 Reasons for judgment, 17. On appeal, the BC Court of Appeal upheld this part of McEachern CJ's judgment, affirming that habeas corpus is available to obtain the transfer from detention in solitary confinement to detention in the general prison population. Furthermore, a provincial superior court has jurisdiction to order certiorari in aid of habeas corpus against a federal board: (1982) 67 CCC (2d) 252. See also on this jurisdictional issue the *Miller* case, supra, n. 70, and the *Morin* case, chap. 6, n. 22.
155 Reasons for judgment, 7.
156 This non-compliance with commissioner's directives is a continuation of a practice which I observed in my study of disciplinary proceedings at Matsqui Institution in 1972, where prisoners were not given the required written notice of the charges alleged against them. See 'Justice behind the Walls,' 33–4.
157 Reasons for judgment, 20.
158 Ibid., 21.
159 Ibid., 22.
160 Ibid., 23.
161 Ibid., 25. The BC Court of Appeal, while affirming that the director had a general duty to act fairly, disagreed in a 2-1 decision with McEachern CJ that there had been a failure to comply with that duty. Nemetz CJ held that the duty to act fairly must be prescribed by the statutory limits in which the challenged powers are found. The chief justice of the Court of Appeal stated: '[The director] is given broad powers under s. 40 of the Regulations. He is not burdened with any standards or guidelines in the exercise of his powers in order that an inmate be dissociated. Procedural standards have not been imposed or implied. He must have enough latitude to respond to the requirements of prison security as he sees fit. This is especially so in cases of violence such as hostage-taking': 67 CCC (2d) at 259. The chief justice concluded that the director was justified in disregarding the review board's recommendation, having regard to his responsibilities with respect to the security of the institution. In so doing he did not have to allow the prisoners an opportunity of explaining the incident. Moreover, 'any procedural unfairness, if it exists, is not of sufficient substance' (at 261) to justify court intervention. See also the concurring judgment of MacDonald JA. Mr Justice Anderson, in dissent on this issue, held that while the prisoners were 'not entitled to a full hearing or to confront witnesses or to counsel, at the very least [they] ought to have been given an opportunity to make representations as to why [they] should no longer be kept in solitary confinement' (at 281). Leave to appeal to the Supreme Court of Canada has been granted.

The reasoning of the majority judgments of the members of the BC Court of Appeal in *Oswald and Cardinal* goes far to nullify the prospect of the fairness doctrine controlling the exercise of the administrative-segregation power. By looking to the untrammelled discretion given by the regulations as the justification for limiting the content of procedural fairness, the court in effect states that the greater the discretion given a prison official, the less the courts will interfere in its exercise. By contrast, the thrust of the arguments made by the prisoners in *McCann* and *Oswald and Cardinal* is that it is precisely where the greatest discretion is given, and particularly where the exercise of that discretion results in the imposition of the prison's most severe confinement, that the most, not the least, procedural control is required through the fairness doctrine.

Unfortunately, the majority decision in *Oswald and Cardinal* reflects the continued reluctance of Canadian courts to interfere with prison decision-making. In the majority of prison cases since *Martineau (No. 2)* the courts, across a broad spectrum of cases, while conceding that there is a duty to act fairly, have immunized the decisions of prison officials from effective judicial review by either pouring minimal content into what fairness requires or invoking Mr Justice Pigeon's caveat in *Martineau (No. 2)* that no serious injustice has been caused. Often, as in *Oswald and Cardinal*, the two strategies for non-interference are applied in tandem. For other examples of this, see *Re Rowling and the Queen* (1981) 57 CCC (2d) 169 (Ont. H. Ct.); *Culhane* v. *A-G of BC* (1980) 18 BCLR 239 (BCCA). The hands-off policy maintained by the Federal Court of Canada in reviewing prison decisions is reflected in the much-cited statement of Mr Justice Addy in *Cline* v. *Rennett*: 'I would like to add that, except in clear and unequivocal cases of serious injustice coupled with *mala fides* or unfairness, judges, as a general rule, should avoid the temptation of using their *ex officio* wisdom in the solemn, dignified and calm atmosphere of the courtroom and substituting their own judgment for that of experienced prison administrators. The latter are truly in the firing line and are charged by society with the extraordinarily difficult and unenviable task of maintaining order and discipline among hundreds of convicted criminals who, as a class, are not generally reputed to be the most disciplined or emotionally stable members of society and who, by the mere fact of incarceration, are being forcibly deprived of many of their most fundamental freedoms. Similarly, courts should avoid laying down any detailed rules of conduct for these administrators since courts have very little practical knowledge of the problems involved in maintaining prison security generally or of the specific tensions, pressures and dangers existing in any particular prison or in any given situation. Such detailed rules of conduct, if any, should be left to the legislators or better still, to those possessing the required expertise who might be charged by the legislators with the issuing of regulations pertaining to these matters' (reasons for judgment, 18 March 1981). The limited extent to which procedural fairness, in the absence of clearly defined substantive criteria for decision-making, is a protection against abuse of power is vividly illustrated by the case of *Perron* v. *The Commissioner of Corrections and the National Parole Board*. Perron, a prisoner at Collins Bay medium-security institution, was employed as bookkeeper in the inmates' canteen and was one of six prisoners with regular access to it. On 26 July 1982 a quantity of contraband was found in the canteen. Perron and four of the other prisoners with regular access were charged with possession of contraband. On 27 July, Perron was transferred to Millhaven maximum-security institution. Perron was told that the reason for transfer was 'the good order and security of Collins Bay institution. Contributing to the above are internal charges which have not yet been disposed of.' On 24 September Perron and the others charged with him were acquitted. The basis of the acquittal was that, while some one or more of those with regular access to the canteen were guilty of the charge, the identity of the guilty party was not proved. Perron was not returned to Collins Bay after his acquittal of the charges. The refusal to return him was based 'on information of a security nature which indicated that he was involved in the drug and muscling activities at Collins Bay while he was there.' Perron, in an application for certiorari to quash the decision of the commissioner to transfer him from Collins Bay to Millhaven and the refusal to transfer him back, relied not only on his acquittal but also on the fact that the authorities at Collins Bay, just prior to his being charged, were prepared to support his application for day parole provided that he successfully completed one more unescorted temporary-absence pass which had been scheduled for 26 to 28 July. Perron's point was that the allegations of his involvement in drug and muscling activities were quite inconsistent with his keepers' positive attitude toward his conditional release. Mr Justice Mahoney accepted the argument that the decision to transfer someone from medium to maximum security was one which attracted a duty to act fairly. His lordship nevertheless dismissed Perron's application for the following reason: 'The problem I have with this application is that, to the extent that there may be merit in the applicant's allegation of unfairness, it lies in a perceived, and, if the facts are as the applicant says rather than the commissioner has found them, *a real unfairness in the result of the commissioner's decision*. That result is not the subject of appeal to this, or any other, court. There was *no unfairness in the process by which the commissioner arrived at the decisions* he had a right and duty to make [emphasis added].' Reasons for judgment 22 December 1982, FCTD.

162 Kent Temporary Instruction 81 / 01, 25 February 1981, para. 2(a).

163 Ibid., para. 7.

164 Ibid., para. 5(e).

165 Ibid., para. 5(f).

166 Ibid., para. 5(g).

167 Ibid., para. 6(a) and (c). The Kent temporary instruction is in many ways

more specific as to the functions of the segregation review board than the current commissioner's directive 277 which has superseded it: infra, n. 191.

168 The prisoner's account of the events leading up to his transfer to the Regional Psychiatric Centre is as horrific as anything I have been told of the practices in the segregation unit at the BC Penitentiary. The following account is based upon an interview with the prisoner conducted by a paralegal worker from Abbotsford Community Legal Services two days after the event: '[While in H unit] F asked the guard for a shower. The guard refused, stating that he had already asked him and that F said No. F continued to badger the guard for a shower until later in the day the guard threatened to punch him out if he didn't shut up. F refused to throw the first punch so the guard left. About twenty minutes later, when the guard was handing out the blankets, F again demanded his shower. The guard immediately began throwing punches at F. When he started to fight back four other guards entered his cell, grabbed F by the hair and proceeded to kick him in the head. They then dragged him into the neighbouring cell and locked the door. F, in a delirious state, kicked out the window and threatened the guards with a piece of broken glass. The guards then proceeded to put on the riot gear. F then began slashing his arms and eventually passed out. The guards dragged F to the end of the tier and shackled his hands. F then became conscious and asked the guards to wait a minute so that he could get his balance. Instead the guards grabbed him by the hair and by the chains on his wrists and carried him to the hospital. F told the doctor to get him out of the segregation unit and the doctor told him he would try. After bandaging the cuts he took F back to his cell. F again slashed his arms. He was sent to the hospital and again bandaged, then sent back to his cell. He slashed his arms again. This time the guards just laughed at him and let him bleed all night until morning. He was then taken in front of the institutional doctor and psychiatrist who ordered that he be sent to RPC': memo on file with Abbotsford Prison Legal Services.

169 Letter dated February 1981.

170 Letter dated 7 February 1981, signed by members of the Kent Lifers Organization.

171 Letter dated February 1981 from 'a concerned prisoner,' Kent Institution. The great majority of letters were unsigned – the prisoners feared reprisal if they put their names to the letters. The reprisal most often mentioned was being placed in H unit.

172 Letter dated 10 February 1981 from 'prisoners of Kent Penitentiary.'

173 Letter dated February 1981.

174 Letter dated 1 February 1981.

175 In March 1983 H unit was again the focus of prisoners' protests. The population of Kent went on a peaceful three-day work stoppage to protest the

extended segregation of an Indian prisoner, Gary Butler, who had been helping other Indian prisoners develop traditional religious ceremonies within Kent. The reason given by the authorities for Gary Butler's segregation was his alleged assault of another prisoner. The general population saw his stand on Indian rights as being the underlying reason for his continued detention in H unit.

6 A MODEL FOR REFORM

1 It is almost always the case that riots do not have single causes. Just a few days before the events of 7 June there had been a major riot at Matsqui Institution, the worst since the September 1976 riot at the BC Penitentiary. As happened in September 1976, a major disturbance in one institution can have a 'trigger' effect on others; but, that having been said, the critical role of the regime in H unit in precipitating the events of 7 June should not be underestimated.

2 Charles W. Thomas, 'The Impotence of Correctional Law,' in *Legal Rights of Prisoners*, ed. Geoffrey Alpert (Beverly Hills: Sage Publications 1980), 259.

3 Jessica Mitford, *Kind and Usual Punishment: The Prison Business* (New York: Alfred A. Knopf 1973), 291.

4 Gordon Hawkins, *The Prison: Policy and Practice* (Chicago: University of Chicago Press 1976), 5.

5 American Friends Service Committee, *Struggle for Justice: A Report on Crime and Punishment in America* (New York: Hill and Wang 1971), 33.

6 As Gordon Hawkins has pointed out, in most abolitionist literature 'the fulfillment of that aim [abolition] is seen as dependent upon the prior achievement of other changes in social organization, changes so universal in scope and radical in nature that by comparison the abolition of prisons seems a relatively minor adjustment': Hawkins, *The Prison*, 5. Jessica Mitford, in concluding that 'prisons are intrinsically evil and should be abolished,' accepts 'the impossibility of achieving more than a superficial reformation of our criminal justice system without a radical change in our values and a drastic restructuring of our social and economic institutions': Mitford, *Kind and Usual*, 273.

7 Mitford, *Kind and Usual*, 293.

8 In addition to those standards referred to in the text, see also National Advisory Commission on Criminal Justice Standards and Goals, *Report on Corrections* (Washington, 1973); American Bar Association (Criminal Justice Section), *Draft of Standards Relating to the Legal Status of Prisoners* (Washington 1977); National Council on Crime and Delinquency, *Model Act for the Protection of Rights of Prisoners* (Hackensack, NJ 1972); United Nations Department of Economic and Social Affairs, *Standard Minimum Rules for*

the Treatment of Prisoners (New York: 1958), endorsed by Canada at the Fifth UN Congress on the Prevention of Crime and Treatment of Offenders, June 1975. See Alvin Bronstein, 'Relevant Standards in Long-Term Confinement Litigation,' 1 *Prison Law Monitor* 40 (1978).

9 Commission on Accreditation for Corrections, *Manual of Standards for Adult Correctional Institutions*, 2d ed. (Washington 1981).

10 This is only partly true because many of the standards reflect the due process requirements which have been mandated by court decisions.

11 *Manual of Standards*, p. 55.

12 Sheldon Krantz, Robert Bell, Jonathan Brant, and Michael Magruder, *Model Rules and Regulations on Prisoner Rights and Responsibilities* (St Paul: West Publishing 1973).

13 Rule V-2, p. 157.

14 Rule VI-6, p. 181.

15 Michael Jackson, 'Justice behind the Walls–A Study of the Disciplinary Process in a Canadian Penitentiary,' 12 Osgoode Hall Law Journal 1, 70 et seq.

16 *A Working Paper Relating to the Protection of the Rights of Persons Confined in Penal Institutions*, ed. B.C. Hofley, (Ottawa: Solicitor-General of Canada 1977).

17 In *Bono* v. *Saxbe*, 450 F. Supp. 934 (1978), the court struck down the practice of placing in the 'control unit' at Marion Federal Penitentiary prisoners who were viewed as 'escape risks.' The court reasoned that Marion was the most secure federal institution designed specifically to prevent escapes.

18 This was caused by a combination of factors. Initially his remand days in the criminal courts conflicted with the day on which the disciplinary board met in H unit. Subsequently, the officers who were the principal witnesses to the alleged offence were on leave. Eventually the charges were heard in late September and the prisoner was convicted and sentenced to the time he had already spent in segregation.

19 S. 39(k), SOR/79–625.

20 CD 213, 17 May 1979, para. 12(3) and (4).

21 Affidavit of Mr J. Sauvé, *Morin* v. *le Comité Nationale chargé de l'examen des cas d'USD*, Federal Court of Canada, T-6035–81, para. 54.

22 Ibid., para. 66 and 69. The *Morin* litigation has a complex history. Initially, Morin applied for a writ of habeas corpus in the Quebec Superior Court, relying on the precedent of *Oswald and Cardinal*. That application was dismissed on 15 November 1981 on the basis that habeas corpus was not available to release a prisoner from SHU to the general population and that such relief could only be obtained from the federal court. (Interestingly, the judge who heard the application, Mr Justice Bergeron, was the presiding judge in Morin's murder trial.) In the course of his judgment, Mr Justice

Bergeron commented that a summary examination of the trial file would convince the correctional authorities that Morin's presence in the SHU was no longer necessary. Morin then appealed this judgment and also commenced section 18 proceedings in the federal court, seeking certiorari to quash the decision to keep him in SHU. This application was dismissed by Mr Justice Marceau on 1 March 1982. The Quebec Court of Appeal affirmed the Superior Court's dismissal of the application for habeas corpus on 16 June 1980. Morin has now appealed the dismissal of his application for certiorari to the Federal Court of Appeal of Canada. Leave to appeal the decision of the Quebec Court of Appeal has been granted by the Supreme Court of Canada.

23 *Manual of Standards*, 55–6.
24 Ibid., standards 2–4357 and 4360–66.
25 Jackson, 'Justice behind the Walls,' 63–5.
26 Ibid., 81–2.
27 *Report to Parliament*, para. 437.
28 *Bono* v. *Saxbe*, 450 F. Supp. 934 (1978).
29 See Jackson, 'Justice behind the Walls,' 67–8.
30 James B. Jacobs, *Stateville: The Penitentiary in Mass Society* (Chicago: University of Chicago Press 1977), 123.
31 Earlier I suggested that it was fanciful to expect Vancouver counsel defending a prisoner on criminal charges on legal aid to have the time to interview numerous prison witnesses. Under my proposed model I would anticipate that the work of representing prisoners on segregation matters would initially be undertaken by the small core of lawyers, law students, and paralegal workers who have hitherto shown interest in correctional law, a pattern which has emerged in the representation of parolees before the Parole Board. The resources of such services as the Abbotsford Prison Legal Services, the Correctional Law Project of Queen's Law School in Kingston and L'Office des droits des détenus in Montreal would be able to provide the nucleus for effective representation of prisoners in the manner suggested in the text.
32 [1980] 6 WWR 271.
33 [1975] 3 All ER 78 (C.A.).
34 Allan Manson, 'Comment: Parole Revocations and *Dubeau* v. *National Parole Board*,' 1 *Correctional Law Newsletter*, 11 (1980).
35 Parole regulations, supra, chap. 5, n. 96. The regulations seek to place certain time constraints on the participation of the assistant, but the actual practice of the Parole Board suggests that these will not be strictly adhered to where the circumstances require otherwise.
36 CD 213, 17 May 1979.
37 *Minott* v. *The Presiding Officer of the Inmate Disciplinary Court of Stoney*

Mountain Penitentiary, FCTD, 27 April 1981.

38 *Davidson* v. *A Disciplinary Board of the Prison for Women* (1981) 61 CCC(2d) 520 (FCTD).

39 Ibid., 534.

40 Supra, n. 37, reasons for judgment, 18.

41 The necessity for a time constraint on administrative segregation has been countenanced in several U.S. decisions. In *Hardwick* v. *Ault*, 447 F. Supp. 116 (1978), the court, in indicating the nature of the changes it would require to Georgia's maximum-security segregation facility to pass constitutional muster, specifically included the restriction of 'confinement in H-house to predetermined time length which may be lengthened only upon showing of a legitimate institutional reason' (127). In *Hutto* v. *Finney*, 98 S. Ct. 2565 (1978), the Supreme Court upheld the District Court's order limiting the time a prisoner could be confined in segregation (albeit punitive) to thirty days, and specifically noted the interdependence of the conditions at the prison and the prior unheeded district court orders to remedy constitutional violations, and concluded that the district court 'was justified in entering a comprehensive order to ensure against the risk of inadequate compliance' (2572). Measured against the Canadian Penitentiaries' response to the judgments in *McCann* and *Oswald and Cardinal*, I would suggest that the ninety-day limit on administrative segregation is also justified.

42 *Manual of Standards*, 2d ed., no. 4221.

43 No. 2–4223.

44 No. 2–4225.

45 No. 2–4226, 4227, 4229.

46 No. 2–4224.

47 No. 2–4230, 4231.

48 No. 2–4232.

49 No. 2–4235.

50 PSRs. 40(2)(6) SOR/79–625.

51 Ibid.

52 Vantour Report, 36.

53 List of proposals, Inmate Committee, Kent Institution, February 1981.

54 Jackson, 'Justice behind the Walls,' 83–100.

55 For a fuller discussion of the negotiation model, see C.R. Reich, 'Bargaining in Correctional Institutions: Restructuring the Relations between the Inmate and the Prison Authority' 81 *Yale Law Journal* 726 (1972); A.F. Rutherford, 'Formal Bargaining in the Prison: In Search of a New Organizational Model,' 2 *Yale Review of Law and Social Action* 5 (1971).

56 The negotiation model has won broad approval in U.S. correctional systems for resolving prison grievances. See, for example, Stephen Gillers, 'Dispute Resolution in Prison: The California Experience,' in *Roundtable Justice: Case*

Studies in Conflict Resolution, ed. Robert B. Goldmann (Boulder: Westview Press 1980). In Canada the Parliamentary Subcommittee on the Penitentiary System recommended a grievance procedure based on the U.S. negotiation model (*Report to Parliament*, recommendation 36, 96–8). Although a modified version of the Subcommittee's recommended procedure has been incorporated in the commissioner's directives, it has not been implemented at Kent Institution.

57 *The Role of Federal Corrections in Canada: A Report of the Task Force on the Creation of an Integrated Canadian Correction Service* (Ottawa: Department of the Solicitor-General 1977), 29.

58 *La Jour*, 5 April 1976.

59 Michael Ignatieff, *A Just Measure of Pain: The Penitentiary in the Industrial Revolution, 1750–1850* (New York: Pantheon 1978), 201. In 1897, of the 110 men imprisoned in the BC Penitentiary, ninety-four were serving sentences of five years and under. Only ten (9 per cent) were serving terms in excess of ten years. The same year, at St Vincent de Paul, only twenty-four of the 418 prisoners were serving terms in excess of ten years: Annual Report of the Inspector of Penitentiaries (1897). In 1982, of the 177 men imprisoned in Kent Institution, only sixty-five were serving sentences of less than five years and seventy (almost 40 per cent) were serving terms in excess of ten years; letter from P.L. LaMothe, assistant warden, Offender Programs, Kent Institution, 26 October 1982.

60 Letter from Edgar Roussel to the Hon. Robert Kaplan, 20 December 1980.

61 Donald Oag, one of the *McCann* plaintiffs, has recently become the subject of the 'Korn effect.' Oag became eligible for release on mandatory supervision on 6 December 1982. He was to be released from Edmonton Institution, having been transferred there after spending four years in the SHU. The National Parole Board, relying largely on Oag's record of violence within the penitentiary, including the fact that 'while in custody [he] had on many occasions slashed himself with razor blades and other sharp objects,' suspended his mandatory-supervision release as he walked through the prison gates because 'he constituted an undue risk of violence to other members of society': *Oag* v. *The Queen et al*, reasons for decision of Mcdonald J, 30 December 1982 (Alta. SC).

62 See, for example, the resolution passed in 1977 by a distinguished group of sociologists, psychologists, criminologists, lawyers, and prison administrators at an international conference convened by the International Centre for Comparative Criminology at the request of the solicitor-general for the purpose of discussing long-term imprisonment. The resolution 'finds no evidence to support the continuing, increasing and systematic use of long term imprisonment. It therefore condemns the use of this sanction': *Summary of the Final Report of the International Seminar on Long Term Imprisonment* (Montreal, International Centre for Comparative Criminology

1977), 88. See also Stanley Cohen and Laurie Taylor, *Psychological Survival: The Experience of Long-Term Imprisonment* (Harmondsworth: Penguin 1972).

63 Sheldon Messinger, *Strategies of Control* (Berkeley: Center for the Study of Law and Society, University of California 1969).

64 Cohen and Taylor, *Psychological Survival*, 191.

65 SHU Report no. 43, Department of the Solicitor-General.

66 It has been projected that by 2001 there will be 789 prisoners serving twenty-five-year sentences for first-degree murder and about 1185 prisoners serving sentences ranging from ten to twenty-five years for second-degree murder. As of March 1983 there were 595 prisoners serving life sentences with minimum parole eligibility of ten years or more, and 185 were serving the twenty-five year minimum sentence: *Let's Talk*, vol. 8, no. 8, 30 April 1983.

67 Norval Morris, *The Future of Imprisonment* (Chicago: University of Chicago Press 1974), 88.

7 THE CASE FOR ENTRENCHMENT OF PRISONER'S RIGHTS

1 *Report to Parliament*, 87.

2 Ibid.

3 Ibid.

4 Richard V. Ericson and Patricia Baranek, *The Ordering of Justice: A Study of Accused Persons as Dependants in the Criminal Process* (Toronto: University of Toronto Press 1982), 224.

5 Ibid.

6 Ibid., 225.

7 Herbert Packer, *The Limits of the Criminal Sanction* (Stanford: Stanford University Press 1968), chap. 8.

8 Ericson and Baranek, *The Ordering of Justice*, chap. 7.

9 Ibid.

10 *Report to Parliament*, 156.

Index

www.ingramcontent.com/pod-product-compliance
Lightning Source LLC
Chambersburg PA
CBHW021849020426
42334CB00013B/252

* 9 7 8 0 8 0 2 0 6 5 1 4 8 *